# Grammar, Gesture, and Meaning in American Sign Language

In sign languages of the Deaf, now recognized as fully legitimate human languages, some signs can meaningfully point toward things or can be meaningfully placed in the space ahead of the signer. Such spatial uses of signs are an obligatory part of fluent grammatical signing. There is no parallel for this in vocally produced languages. This book focuses on American Sign Language to examine the grammatical and conceptual significance of these signs. It guides the reader through the various types of directional signs, the types of spatial representations signs are directed toward, how such spatial conceptions can be represented in mental space theory, and the conceptual purposes served by these signs. The book explains how the pointing behavior of signs accomplishes functions that must be accomplished by any language, spoken or signed. It demonstrates a remarkable integration of grammar and gesture in the service of constructing meaning. These results also suggest that our concept of "language" has been much too narrow and that a more comprehensive look at vocally produced languages will reveal the same integration of gestural, gradient, and symbolic elements.

SCOTT K. LIDDELL is Professor of Linguistics and Program Coordinator for the Linguistics Program at Gallaudet University, Washington, DC. He is the author of *American Sign Language Syntax* (1980), and since the 1970s has published extensively on sign language grammar and the use of sign language in educating Deaf students.

# Grammar, Gesture, and Meaning in American Sign Language

Scott K. Liddell

*Department of Linguistics and Interpretation*
*Gallaudet University*
*Washington, DC*

CAMBRIDGE
UNIVERSITY PRESS

CAMBRIDGE UNIVERSITY PRESS
Cambridge, New York, Melbourne, Madrid, Cape Town, Singapore, São Paulo

Cambridge University Press
The Edinburgh Building, Cambridge CB2 8RU, UK

Published in the United States of America by Cambridge University Press, New York

www.cambridge.org
Information on this title: www.cambridge.org/9780521816205

First published 2003
Reprinted 2004

*A catalogue record for this publication is available from the British Library*

ISBN 978-0-521-81620-5 hardback
ISBN 978-0-521-01650-6 paperback

Transferred to digital printing 2007

To Elaine and Claude

# Contents

# Preface

The recognition that sign languages are real human languages was a watershed event with potentially profound effects, not only in the daily lives of Deaf people, but on an entire set of disciplines related to language and cognition. When William Stokoe (1960) made the original arguments proposing that American Sign Language (ASL) was a real human language, he based his arguments on finding parallels between the abstract grammatical structures of ASL and the types of abstract grammatical structures found in spoken languages. In the four decades since that discovery, sign languages have been analyzed in countries throughout the world. The analyses of ASL and other sign languages demonstrate that sign languages are an incredibly fertile field for research, with potentially far-reaching implications.

There is, however, one major difference between sign languages and vocally produced languages. ASL and all other sign languages I am aware of include significant numbers of signs that can be meaningfully placed or directed in space. One instance of such a directional sign may differ from the next instance of 'the same' sign depending on how the sign is directed or placed in the space ahead of the signer. For example, the verb TELL begins with the index finger in contact with the chin. If the finger moves outward toward the addressee, the verb expresses the meaning 'tell you'. If it moves outward toward a female (non-addressee) present in the room, it expresses the meaning 'tell her'. No one disputes the meaningfulness of this type of directionality.

In the mid-1980s I attempted to write a book chapter describing directional signs in ASL. At that time there were several treatments of spatial phenomena in ASL and I imagined that it would be possible to draw upon these published resources in describing how signs are directed and placed in space. I was unable to write the chapter because, as it turned out, virtually all analyses of how signs are directed in space were based on faulty representations of the sign language data. Specifically, analyses starting in the seventies until the present assume that signers associate entities with a location in space, called a *spatial index* or a *spatial locus*. They further assume that directional signs are subsequently directed toward that spatial index to make reference to the entity associated with it. The assumption that directional signs are physically directed in this way, however, is demonstrably false (Liddell 1990). But this assumption served, and continues to serve, as the basis for theoretical analyses of ASL grammar and the grammars of other sign languages. As a result, we do not have grammatical explanations for how directional signs are really used in sign languages.

The fact that directional verbs can be directed toward entities, including physically present people, presents an analytical problem not faced in the analysis of a vocally produced language because the tongue does not meaningfully point at things in the environment as it participates in articulating words. But meaningfully placing or directing the hands in space is a normal and expected part of the everyday use of ASL and other sign languages. The problem, therefore, is to attempt to understand this rule-governed integration of grammar and gesture present in, apparently, all sign languages. One could hardly ask for a more interesting challenge. My attempts to understand directional signs have occupied most of the past fifteen years of my work.

Since meaningful pointing by vocal articulators would not be regarded as part of the spoken language signal, linguistic theory has not developed the mechanisms for dealing with the ASL data. In fact, linguistic theory has developed in ways that are antithetical to the presence of a pointing articulator. For example, consider the popular belief among most linguists that all meaning comes from morphemes, defined as the smallest meaningful symbolic parts of a word. Although pointing is clearly meaningful, it does not lend itself to a morphemic analysis because pointing is indexic, not symbolic. Its significance depends on what the pointing is directed toward.

Further, the direction of a pointing sign is not limited to a predetermined set of possible pointing directions. Since the hand can point in an unlimited number of directions, the range of pointing movements is gradient. Gradience is a problem because the field of linguistics generally defines language so as to exclude not only meaningful gestures but also to exclude meaningful gradient aspects of the speech signal. Compare, for example, the two instances of *long* in (1) and (2).

(1)     That was a long speech.
(2)     That was a loooong speech!

Both (1) and (2) contain an instance of the word *long*. The form of *long* in (2) is produced with a lengthened vowel, represented by the repeated *o*'s. This appears to add an emotional meaning: *I experienced the duration of that speech as long.* The articulation of *long* in (1) and the articulation of *loooong* in (2) can be expected to differ not only in vowel length, but also in pitch as well as loudness and potentially other vocal qualities. These aspects of the production of the word *long* are gradient (Okrent 2002). That is, the difference between the two articulations goes beyond lengthened versus not lengthened. There are gradient differences in length and loudness, and different possible vocal contours and vocal qualities that a speaker might employ. A typical analysis of the grammar of the predicate nominal in (2) would observe that *a* functions as a determiner, *long* functions as an adjective, and that *a long speech* constitutes a noun phrase. A typical syntactic analysis of this example would say nothing at all about the intonation.

Intonation can be narrowly defined to refer simply to the rises and falls of the pitch of the voice as a sentence is being produced (Bolinger 1986, Schubiger, n.d., Crystal 1991). It can also be defined more broadly, to include suprasegmental features that include tone, pitch-range and loudness, and possibly rhythmicality and tempo (Crystal 1969, Ladd 1996). Whether intonation should be granted "linguistic" status or not has been the subject of debate for decades. Given its meaningfulness, one might expect that when grammarians analyze English, intonation would play a role in the analysis. However, as a rule, the analysis of grammatical representations in English proceeds without regard to intonation. Intonation is not even transcribed as a normal part of the analysis of the grammatical structure of a sentence. This can be taken as evidence that linguists studying morphology or syntax do not consider intonation to be part of the grammatical structures being analyzed.

Linguists are very concerned with describing the features that distinguish one word from another. In tone languages such as Mandarin or Thai, tone contours distinguish one word from another. In these languages tone is given linguistic status. In such languages, multiple words can be formed from 'the same' sequence of consonants and vowels. Such words are nevertheless distinct words with their own meanings and with distinct pronunciations. The different words can be distinguished from one another based on each word's tone or tones. Similarly, in some languages, the length of vowels can also distinguish one word from another. Thai makes both distinctions. Since vowel length and tone distinguish one word from another in Thai, they are considered to be part of the words themselves. Since tone and vowel length are part of Thai words, the grammar of Thai must include both tone and vowel length, both of which must be considered "linguistic."

In general, linguists are not as concerned with features distinguishing one *utterance* from another. There is a joke about a linguistics professor explaining to his class that in some languages two negatives can make a positive, as in "He is not unhappy." The professor then adds that there are no known languages in which two positives can produce a negative. A voice from the back of the class is then heard to say, "Yeah, right!" The joke works because English speakers can easily imagine producing "Yeah, right!" with an intonation that results in an expression of disagreement with what has just been said. If linguists applied the same strict criteria to distinguishing one utterance from another that they apply to distinguishing one word from another, there would be no debate about whether intonation, meaningful gestures, or other gradient phenomena would have to be incorporated into an analysis of the meaning being expressed. While linguists analyzing vocally produced languages have been able to ignore both gesture and gradient aspects of the language signal, this cannot be done with ASL. This is because obligatory, gradient, and gestural phenomena in ASL play such a prominent, meaningful role that they cannot be ignored.

In analyzing directional signs in ASL, it was necessary to come to grips with the issue of whether pointing should be considered a legitimate part of the language signal. Additional theoretical issues must be confronted in coming to an understanding of space in sign languages. It is not sufficient merely to describe what the hand, arms, face, and eyes do when signers sign. That is, it is not very helpful merely to note that a signer directs the hand producing a verb toward the empty space to her left while simultaneously gazing in that direction. It is also important to be able to address the conceptual structures that provide the framework for such directional signing. Recent advances in cognitive linguistics have been essential to making progress in this area. Mental space theory has emerged and undergone considerable growth and development during the past two decades (Fauconnier 1985, 1997; Fauconnier and Turner 1996; Turner 1991). In particular, developments in the blending of mental spaces has proved essential in making progress in understanding the conceptual underpinnings of the ASL spatial data. Cognitive grammar (Langacker 1987, 1991, 1999b) has also come into existence and developed during the same time period. Although developed to account for vocal language phenomena, mental space theory and cognitive grammar provide the conceptual elements necessary for understanding directional signs in ASL. These two theories developed independently and each treats different aspects of meaning. The sign language data have caused me to conceive of meaning construction as a process involving mental space mappings of the type proposed in mental space theory built around a central core of grammatically encoded meanings of the type found in cognitive grammar.

The analyses in this book treat directional uses of signs as gradient and gestural phenomena driven by grammar and by meaning construction. Attempting to characterize the use of space in ASL involves an integration of grammar, gesture, and gradience in the process of constructing meaning by means of mental space mappings. The resulting interconnected conceptual structures are the means that ASL, and perhaps spoken languages more generally, use to communicate.

My initial intention in writing this book was to begin with a comprehensive review of existing morphemic treatments of spatial phenomena. It seemed important to describe the problems with existing proposals fully before presenting my own work. By the middle of 2000 I had written chapters consisting of more than one hundred and fifty pages reviewing that work. At that time I discussed my plans for the book with Brita Bergman. She convinced me that it would be very tedious for a potential reader to wade through such an extensive review of existing work – especially since the point of the arguments is to demonstrate that the analyses do not successfully account for how signers sign. Based on that conversation I discarded the extensive reviews and restructured the book. As a result, this book presents a new way of looking at ASL and its grammar with only minimal reference to and criticism of previous work. My reviews and criticisms of previous approaches date back to 1988, and readers interested in reading that work can find published reviews of much of it in Liddell (1990, 1994, 1995, 2000a) and Liddell and Metzger (1998). It is my hope that organizing the book in this way will allow the reader to proceed through the new material with relatively few interruptions.

Readers already familiar with American Sign Language and its grammer may skip chapters 1 and 2, and begin reading with chapter 3. Such readers may still find chapter 2 useful as a reference in cases where my treatment of grammatical issues in subsequent chapters differs from currently accepted views. Readers unfamiliar with the grammar of a sign language should not skip chapters 1 and 2. The information in those chapters provides the grammatical background needed to understand subsequent chapters. The treatment of ASL grammar in chapter 2 is purposely extensive since I do not want readers of chapters 3 through 10 to come away with the mistaken view that it is gesture, rather than grammar that is responsible for expressing meaning in ASL. Those chapters attempt to demonstrate that, in ASL, meaning is expressed through the interaction of grammar, gradience, and gesture.

SKL

# Acknowledgments

A number of the figures included in this book have been reproduced by the kind permission of various organizations. I therefore give thanks here to the following in respect of these: The Berkeley Linguistics Society for Figures 2.11, 3.1, 3.10, 4.4, 7.1, and 7.3 (from Wulf and Simpson, in press); Mounton Press for Figures 2.3 and 5.12 (from Liddell 1980); Gallaudet University Press for Figures 3.5 and 3.6 (from Liddell 1990); Cambridge University Press for Figures 5.2 and 5.3 (after Fauconnier 1997); Lawrence Erlbaum Associates for Figures 9.1a, 9.2b, 9.3b, 9.3c, 9.4a, 9.5, 9.7, and 9.12 (from Liddell, in press b). Figure 3.9 has been reprinted from *The Science of Illusions*, Ithaca and London, by Jacques Ninio, copyright 2001, by permission of the publisher, Cornell University Press. Figure 5.5a has been reprinted from Spatial representations in discourse: Comparing spoken and signed language, *Lingua* 98:145–167, by Scott K. Liddell, copyright 1996 with permission from Elsevier Science.

Many ASL signers have contributed to this work by allowing their signing to be videotaped for analysis, by discussing possible semantic interpretations of videotaped data, or by providing native speaker insights about ASL grammar. For their help in this I would like to thank MJ Bienvenu, Melissa Draganac, Paul Dudis, Mike Kemp, Allen Markel, Dan Mathis, Wilton McMillan, Amy Novotny, Randy Shank, Marie Shook, Greg Visco, and Silas Wagner. I have also included video data from a teleconference conducted by Marie Philip, who passed away during the writing of the book.

My thanks go to Paul Dudis, Melissa Draganac, and Kristin Mulrooney for their work as research assistants. Paul Dudis also carried out the production of a large number of videotaped sessions where he served as interlocutor with native signers being videotaped. MJ Bienvenu also graciously made herself available for numerous discussions of thorny grammatical issues. Several people provided helpful and insightful comments on an early draft of this book, including Frank Bechter, MJ Bienvenu, Susan Duncan, Melissa Draganac, Elisabeth Engberg-Pederson, Sonja Erlenkamp, Sabine Grindstein, Randall Hogue, David MacGregor, Kristin Mulrooney, Kari-Anne Selvik, Marit Vogt-Svendsen, Sarah Taub, Arnfinn Vonen and Erin Wilkinson. Susan Duncan was also kind enough to discuss issues related to gesture and speech with me over a period of several months as I was working through those issues. My thanks also go to Gilles Fauconnier for a number of useful discussions of mental space theory over the past few years.

Finally, I give special thanks to Brita Bergman, who not only initially convinced me to restructure the book, but also made other suggestions that helped me reorganize chapters. She also scrutinized every argument and figure and challenged any analysis needing support. Her insights and her clear thinking have had a very large impact on this book.

# 1     American Sign Language as a language

Sign languages have developed spontaneously and independently within communities of Deaf users all over the world.[1] American Sign Language (ASL) is one of those many sign languages. The obvious way that ASL and other sign languages differ from vocally produced languages is the means by which their words are produced and perceived. English words are produced by actions within the vocal tract that result in sounds perceived through audition. Signs – the words of a sign language – are produced by actions of the hands, arms, torso, face, and head that produce signals perceived visually.[2]

There have been, and continue to be, a number of misunderstandings about sign languages. Some people see sign languages as grammarless attempts at communicating through gesture or pantomime. It is not uncommon for a relative or acquaintance to tell a hearing person learning a sign language how wonderful it must be to be able to communicate with people anywhere. Such statements are based on the misconception that sign languages are the same worldwide. The statements also contain a hint of the attitude that sign languages are understandable worldwide because they lack real language properties such as grammar, which would clearly differ from one language to the next.

Another misconception about sign languages is that they are patterned after the vocally produced languages spoken in the same country. Those with this view in the United States see signers using ASL as attempting to use signs to produce signed sentences that are the manual equivalent of spoken English sentences. This view treats signs as manually produced English words. From this perspective, a sign whose semantics differs from an English word would be viewed as deviant. Sequences of signs that do not mirror English sentence structure would be viewed as ungrammatical English. In reality, since ASL and English are two entirely different languages with completely different

---

[1] There are significant cultural differences between a person who is audiologically deaf and part of a community using a sign language as the primary language of face-to-face communication and someone audiologically deaf but not part of a sign language-using community. James Woodward introduced the convention of using "Deaf" to describe the former and "deaf" to describe the latter.

[2] Signers who are Deaf and blind perceive signs through touch.

grammars, it would be highly unusual for an ASL sentence *ever* to have exactly the same grammatical structure as an English sentence.

Naturally, such views and misunderstandings have social consequences. For example, some people might look down upon Deaf people, or even feel sorry for them, because they were limited to communicating through gestures rather than through language. Such views also have educational consequences. Consider an example of a Deaf child with Deaf parents. By the time the child reaches school age, that child will be highly fluent in ASL. Although the child will typically have already begun learning English through instruction at home, ASL will be the child's first language. Such a child will arrive at school cognitively prepared to learn what the teachers are prepared to teach, including a second language (e.g. English). A teacher believing ASL was not a language would view such a child as, tragically, without language. This has an obvious effect on how the teacher will interact with the child, what can reasonably be expected of the child, perceptions of the child's intelligence and readiness to learn, and so on.

In 1955, William C. Stokoe took a position as an assistant professor in the English Department at Gallaudet College.[3] He was immediately immersed in an academic culture that saw ASL signs as an important part of communicating with Deaf students, but did not see ASL signs as part of a distinct language. Like most other hearing faculty at Gallaudet College, he arrived without any knowledge of ASL. At that time there were no classes teaching ASL as a language for the obvious reason that "signing" was not considered to be a language. Knowledge of signs, however, was important and classes were set up to teach new faculty members some sign vocabulary. Stokoe was instructed for three weeks in how to sign. At the end of that period he began teaching. Communication with the students was to take place by speaking English while simultaneously producing some sign vocabulary.

This practice of speaking and simultaneously producing signs is called *simultaneous communication* or *SimCom*. Its practitioners assume that SimCom assists Deaf students in acquiring English. They also assume that the simultaneous messages – the spoken message and the signed message – are equivalent. The brief example of SimCom below, videotaped in a high-school classroom in the United States, illustrates several common features of SimCom.

(1)      If you copy words from an encyclopedia
         IF SOAP WORD FROM ENCYCLOPEDIA
         that means you are copying someone else's words.
         THAT THIS\SHOW SOAP SOME OTHER WORD

The lowercase words in (1) are transcriptions of the teacher's spoken English. The uppercase English glosses appearing underneath the spoken words represent the signs produced by the teacher as she spoke. Although the spoken

---

[3] Gallaudet College became Gallaudet University in 1987.

and signed messages are assumed to be equivalent, they are not. The spoken English is grammatical. If just the English were presented to an English speaker, the message would be clear. In contrast to the spoken words, the signs are not organized according to the grammar of any language. The signing is also marred by ill-formed signs. The teacher has twice mistakenly signed SOAP instead of the formationally similar sign COPY. This is probably not the first time the students have seen the teacher make this error so they probably understood that this was this teacher's way of signing COPY. The teacher also produces a sign that looks like either THIS or SHOW while saying, "means." The sign SHOW is made by placing the index finger in contact with the palm of a B base hand facing outward, while moving both hands outward together. THIS is produced by a contacting movement of the index against the upward-facing palm.[4] It was difficult to tell from the videotape which of these two signs the teacher produced. The sign MEAN is produced by making two contacts of a V handshape against the palm of a B handshape, with an orientation change of the two hands between the two contacts.[5] Although production errors such as this are common when a hearing teacher speaks and produces signs at the same time, the biggest impediment to understanding the message is the lack of grammatical organization of the signs. Rather than being organized by the grammar of ASL, the signs in this example appear in an order that matches the order of the corresponding spoken English words. This does not mean that they are organized according to the grammar of English. To help make this apparent, in (2) I represent each sign produced in (1) as if it were an English word. I have also represented SOAP as "copy" and THIS/SHOW as "mean."

(2)     If copy word from encyclopedia that mean copy some other word.

The written result in (2) could be described as broken English. Whatever meaning can be recovered from (2) is certainly different from the spoken English that accompanied the signs.

One can only imagine what the signing of brand-new faculty members with only three weeks of training in ASL vocabulary looked like in the classrooms at Gallaudet College in 1955. Without a coherent signed message students are forced to rely on decoding the speech they cannot hear. Under such circumstances the signs function as clues in attempting to read the lips of the teacher.[6] This example illustrates the important point that all instances of "signing" are

---

[4] The sign THIS is an invented sign designed to be used as part of a system of signs representing English words.

[5] Throughout this book I will describe the handshape produced by extending the index and middle fingers from a fist as a V handshape. It is sometimes also referred to as a 2 handshape.

[6] Lipreading involves constant guesswork since not all the actions within the vocal tract are visible. For example, for even the clearest of speakers, productions of the consonant sounds [t], [d], [s], and [n] look the same to the lipreader. As a result, the words *Dad, sad, tad, Dan, tan, Nat, sat, sass*, and numerous other non-word syllables all look the same. For speakers who articulate less clearly or have a big mustache or beard lipreading is even more difficult.

not ASL. In addition to SimCom, some students are taught to produce signs as if they were English words. Others are taught using artificial sign systems designed to represent English sentences visually.

By his second year, Stokoe was convinced that the students' signing was different from what he had been taught to do. When the students signed with one another, they were not putting signs together as if they were English words. They were putting signs together according to the grammar of a language other than English. Stokoe (quoted in Maher [1996]) describes this situation as follows: "I just knew that when these deaf people were together and communicating with each other, what they were communicating with was a language, not somebody else's language; since it wasn't English, it must have been their own language. There was nothing 'broken' or 'inadequate' about it; they got on splendidly with it" (p. 55). In 1957 Stokoe began a serious examination of the signing he believed to be a language. Three years later, that research culminated in the publication of *Sign Language Structure: An Outline of the Visual Communication Systems of the American Deaf.* This was the first linguistic analysis of any sign language. In it, Stokoe lays out the broad outline of ASL as a real language.

The response to his work at Gallaudet by students and faculty, both hearing and Deaf, was immediate and powerful: "Stokoe must be crazy!" The concept that the signing done by Deaf people was a real language was too radical a concept given the belief systems at the time. Undeterred, Stokoe continued his research. In 1965, collaborating with Dorothy Casterline and Carl Croneberg, he published the *Dictionary of American Sign Language on Linguistic Principles.* By the early 1970s many other linguists and psychologists began studying the properties of ASL. At that time, their published papers tended to begin with brief justifications explaining that ASL was a language. Such explanations were needed since most people still held the view that ASL was not a language. By perhaps the mid-seventies, and most certainly by the early eighties, the weight of published descriptions of ASL and its grammar was sufficient to turn the tide of opinion about the language status of ASL. Studies of various aspects of the grammar of ASL left no doubt that signers using ASL were using a real human language.

The recognition that sign languages were real human languages set off a flurry of activity in a number of academic arenas beginning in the seventies. What does the grammar of a sign language look like? Do Deaf children in Deaf families acquire a sign language in ways that parallel the acquisition of a vocally produced language by children with normal hearing? Can other primates acquire a sign language? How are various aspects of ASL related to memory? How are sign languages represented in the brain? Questions like these have captivated the imagination of growing numbers of linguists and psychologists. More and more sign languages continue to be identified and investigated as researchers around the globe pursue answers to a wide variety of interesting scientific questions.

This book addresses the issue of how meaning is expressed in ASL. The ASL data will demonstrate that grammar is central to how signers express meaning. Beyond that, it will also demonstrate that the meanings expressed by signers exceed what a grammar is capable of encoding and that the language signal does more than encode symbolic grammatical elements. These characteristics, I will argue, are common to all languages.

# 2    A sketch of the grammar of ASL

This chapter begins with a brief description of the abstract system of parts that compose individual signs followed by an overview of the types of complex signs found in ASL. The chapter concludes with a description of some aspects of ASL sentences, focusing on the ordering of subjects and objects and concepts related to transitivity. Although these descriptions are not comprehensive, they are intended to provide sufficient background to make the examples appearing later in the book understandable.

## Phonological representations

### Signs as simultaneous bundles of features

One of Stokoe's first major accomplishments in his work with ASL was demonstrating that signs, like spoken words, are constructed from a limited number of parts used over and over again in new combinations (Stokoe 1960, Stokoe *et al.* 1965). This is a characteristic found in all spoken languages. English, for example, uses roughly forty-five distinctive sounds in the construction of English words. These sounds combine over and over again in different arrangements to produce all the words of English.

Stokoe divides signs into three *aspects*. These three aspects are *location, what acts*, and *movement*. In this analysis, every sign consists of one location, one handshape (what acts), and one or more movements.[1]

FORGET begins with a B handshape just ahead of the forehead, with the palm facing the signer (Figure 2.1). The hand moves to the side of the forehead

---

[1] Stokoe refers to these three aspects as *tab, dez*, and *sig*. In descriptions of the three aspects of a sign, Stokoe lists nineteen handshapes composing the *dez* category. This list suggests that there are nineteen *dez* elements. Actual transcriptions of signs add orientation symbols to these handshape symbols to produce oriented handshapes. When Stokoe notates *dez* elements, he frequently writes a combination of handshape and orientation symbols. When he lists the *dez* elements, he lists only handshapes. A comprehensive list of *dez* elements (i.e. all the possible handshape-orientation combinations) would produce a very long list. In the early seventies, linguists began calling for a fourth aspect: orientation (Battison 1974, Friedman 1975). These proposals called for treating handshape and orientation separately. For the purposes of discussion here, I will talk about handshapes rather than *dez* elements, and describe the orientation of the hand separately.

Table 2.1 *The three aspects of the sign FORGET in the Stokoe system of representing signs*

| Aspects of the sign FORGET | | |
| --- | --- | --- |
| **location** | **handshape** | **movements** |
| forehead | B | rightward movement, closing movement |

Figure 2.1 FORGET

as the hand changes from a B to an A handshape. Table 2.1 lists the three aspects of this sign.

FORGET is produced at the location *forehead* using the B handshape. There are two simultaneous movements in this sign. The rightward movement corresponds to the path movement of the hand. The closing movement changes the handshape from a B to an A. Using this type of representation, Stokoe was able to provide a structural description for virtually any simple sign.

This way of describing signs was intended to create a description of signs at roughly the level of abstraction of the phoneme in spoken languages. A system at this abstract level ignores non-contrastive articulatory differences. Some of the handshape categories, for example, contain physically distinct handshapes. The A category contains the physically distinct handshapes A, T, and S. These three distinct handshapes were combined into a single category since Stokoe did not have evidence they were contrastive. An English parallel may be useful here. The sound associated with the *t* in the English word *top* is different from the sound associated with the *t* in *stop*. In *top* the *t* is aspirated [tʰ] while in *stop* it is not [t]. Although pronounced differently, they are both considered to be examples of the *t* sound in English. That is, they belong to the same phonemic category /t/. In essence, Stokoe was claiming that the (phonemic) category /A/ contains the (phonetically) distinct handshapes [A], [S], and [T].[2]

---

[2] Stokoe created the term *chereme* as the signed equivalent of the phoneme. The terminology did not catch on. Those following Stokoe used the linguistic terms traditionally employed in the analysis of speech.

Table 2.2 *The twelve location categories in Stokoe's system of representation*

| Location symbol | Stokoe's description |
| --- | --- |
| Ø | Zero, the neutral place where the hands move, in contrast with all places below. |
| ∩̣ | Face or whole head |
| ∩ | Forehead or brow, upper face |
| ⊔ | Mid-face, the eye and nose region |
| ∪ | Chin, lower face |
| } | Cheek, temple, ear, side-face |
| π | Neck |
| [ ] | Trunk, body from shoulders to hips |
| \ | Upper arm |
| ✓ | Elbow, forearm |
| α | Wrist, arm in supinated position (on its back) |
| ⅅ | Wrist, arm in pronated position (face down) |

The intention to group nondistinctive locations into phonemic categories is also apparent in his treatment of location. Stokoe lists twelve distinct locations. I will refer to the set of possible articulatory locations in space or on the body as the *signing space*. Stokoe's analysis of the signing space is shown in Table 2.2.

The significance of this list lies in the claim that (phonetically distinct) differences in the placement of the hand are not distinctive within the individual (phonemic) locations. That is, the forehead location comprises a significant portion of the face. In spite of the size of the forehead, the idea is that for the purpose of identifying which sign is being produced, it makes no difference which part of the forehead the hand contacts. For example, FATHER is normally produced by repeating the contact with the forehead shown in Figure 2.2a. If the hand makes contact on the same side of the forehead as the moving arm, this is called ipsilateral contact. If the hand crosses over the midline of the body and makes contact on the contralateral side of the body, the signer would still be understood to be producing FATHER, though the production (pronunciation) of the sign would be odd. This is similar to what would result from pronouncing *stop* with an aspirated *t* [st$^h$ap]. The word would be recognized as an instance of *stop*, but would sound funny.

In general, if the hand moves outside the forehead area, this is significant and will result in either the production of some other sign or a potential but nonexisting sign.[3] For example, keeping the repeated motion and the handshape of

---

[3]  A subset of signs produced at the forehead can also be produced on the cheek or the side of the chin. The lowering or centralization of this subset of signs can be viewed as a kind of phonological reduction (Robert E. Johnson class notes, Gallaudet University).

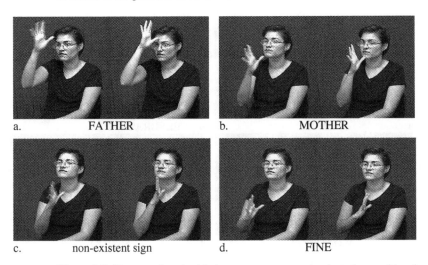

a.          FATHER            b.          MOTHER

c.       non-existent sign      d.          FINE

Figure 2.2 Signs produced with the same movements, orientation, and hand configuration, but differing in location

FATHER constant while changing the location to the chin produces MOTHER (Figure 2.2b). The same motion and handshape at the base of the neck produces a possible, but nonexisting sign (Figure 2.2c).[4] The same motion and handshape at the sternum produces FINE (Figure 2.2d).

Eleven of the twelve locations in Table 2.2 are on the signer's body. The one location not on the signer's body, Ø, is often referred to as *neutral space*, no doubt because Stokoe's original description of the space ahead of the signer described it as, "zero, the neutral place where the hands move [in space], in contrast with all places below" (Stokoe *et al.* 1965:xx). Thus, while Stokoe divided the body into distinctive locations, his analysis leaves the space ahead of the signer undifferentiated. Note that Stokoe's analysis treats the space ahead of the signer as equivalent to a location on the body. The significance of this claim is that when the hand moves to the location Ø (neutral space) as part of the production of a sign, it is simply articulating a sign at a location. Thus, when the hand produces THING it moves to the location Ø. When the hand produces FATHER it moves to the forehead. In this representation system, moving to a spatial place of articulation is treated no differently from moving to a place of articulation on the body. In both cases the hand is merely carrying out articulatory instructions.

---

[4] Producing a sign with thumb contact at the front of the neck would be possible, but unlikely. Signs that make motion toward and contact the neck are generally made on the side of the neck rather than the front. This is likely due to the potential discomfort of contacting the front of the neck too strongly.

Figure 2.3  Signs made in different parts of the space ahead of the signer

When the hands produce different signs in space the hands do not always move to the same physical location. WILL (Figure 2.3a) begins beside the head and moves forward. CELEBRATE (Figure 2.3b) is made on both sides of the body at the same level as WILL, or slightly lower. WONDERFUL (Figure 2.3c) is made at about shoulder level. SCHOOL (Figure 2.3d) is centralized and made at about the level of the chest.

Stokoe did not divide the space ahead of the signer into smaller areas because he had no examples of distinct signs that differed only in their spatial place of articulation. By not dividing space, the analysis claims that differences in spatial placement will not distinguish one sign from another.

Some interesting parallels and differences emerge when we compare how signs and spoken words are articulated. The spoken language analog of the signing space is the vocal tract.[5] Here I will focus on the inside of the mouth where the tongue moves. The movement or placement of the tongue within the oral cavity helps distinguish one articulatory configuration from another. The difference between [t] and [k], for example, is determined by where and how the tongue makes contact inside the oral cavity. Both are voiceless stop consonants. The front of the tongue contacts the alveolar ridge (just behind the upper front teeth) to produce [t] and the body of the tongue contacts the velum (in the back of the mouth) to produce a [k]. In both cases the tongue briefly blocks the flow of air. The productions of these two sounds differ in the location at which the tongue makes contact.

---

[5] Recall that the signing space encompasses all the distinctive locations used in ASL, including 'neutral space', the space in front of the signer.

Just as the hand must be correctly positioned to articulate signs, the tongue must be correctly positioned to produce spoken words. For example, in producing the word *tea*, the tongue must begin by making contact with the alveolar ridge. When the tongue moves away from the alveolar ridge there will be some aspiration followed by the production of the vowel [i:]. The combination of this consonant and vowel, [tʰ] and [i:], produces the word *tea* [tʰi:]. If, instead, the tongue were to begin in contact with the velum, the word *key* [kʰi:] would be produced. This is analogous to the distinction between MOTHER and FATHER described earlier. Keeping the handshape and movements needed to produce FATHER constant, while changing the location to the chin, produces MOTHER. The need to correctly place an articulator demonstrates a clear parallel between spoken and signed languages.

Comparatively speaking, spoken languages are quite limited in the types of articulatory contrasts available to them. The tongue can make only a limited number of such distinctions by contacting different places inside of the mouth. The articulatory placement of the tongue in spoken languages typically distinguishes between interdental (θ, ð), alveolar (t, d, n, s, z), alveopalatal (š, ž, č, ǰ), and velar (g, k, ŋ) consonants. The placement of the tongue also distinguishes between types of vowels (low, mid, and high; front and back). Differences in the front–back placement of the tongue distinguish the high, front vowel in *sheet* from the high, back (lip-rounded) vowel in *tune*. Height differences distinguish the high, front vowel in *sheet* and the low, front vowel in *cat*. In contrast, sign languages have rich potential for articulatory contrasts as a result of the many distinctive shapes that the hand, as articulator, can assume, the potential to use two articulators at once, as well as the large number of distinctive locations.[6]

### Segmenting signs

Systems of representing words or signs are useful to the extent that they help the analyst find solutions to phonological or morphological problems. Although Stokoe's system of representation was widely adopted, it did not appear helpful in understanding either phonological or morphological problems. For example, in describing the formation of ASL compounds, Klima and Bellugi (1979) did not use Stokoe notations. Instead, they described the "shortening," "compression," or "weakening" of signs in addition to loss of repetition. Such terms were used because Stokoe's model did not include the type of structure needed to assist in the description of morphological problems. As long as signs were

---

[6] I have been comparing the most mobile articulators in each articulatory system. Each system also has additional articulators. In producing speech, for example, configurations of the lips and glottis are distinctive. In ASL, the configuration of lips, the positions of the eyebrows, and movements of the head can also be distinctive. In ASL, these articulators tend to be more important in morphological and syntactic constructions than in individual lexical items.

viewed as simultaneous bundles of features, sign notations were rarely seen in solutions to morphological problems in ASL.

Although Stokoe presented signs as unordered, simultaneous bundles of features, he recognized that some signs actually require a sequence of ordered movements for their description. The sign CHICAGO illustrates the point. It is made with a C handshape ahead of the chest with the palm facing outward with the thumb down. To produce the sign the hand first moves right, then moves down. In Stokoe's system the sign would be transcribed as $\emptyset C^{>V}$ [$\emptyset$ represents neutral space; C represents the C handshape; $^{>}$ represents rightward movement; and $^{V}$ represents downward movement].

Without saying so, Stokoe introduces the notion of sequential contrast into the structure of some signs. If the order of the two movements were reversed, it would no longer produce CHICAGO. Instead, it would create a possible, but nonexisting, sign. Thus, the idea that some signs are sequentially structured was an inherent part of the system, even though Stokoe himself presented it as a bundle of three simultaneous aspects.

Liddell (1982) proposes that signs consist of phonological segments divided into movements and holds. Each movement (M) or hold (H) segment contains handshape, location, orientation, and nonmanual features. Thus, a sign like CHICAGO would have the segmental structure: MMH. The initial movement would consist of a complete set of articulatory features (handshape, location, orientation), as would each subsequent segment. Dividing signs into hold and movement segments is roughly equivalent to dividing the speech stream into consonants and vowels. Being able to describe signs in terms of contrasting sequential segments makes it possible to describe morphological processes that could not be adequately described using a simultaneous aspects representation.[7]

There are now a number of proposals concerning the sequential representation of signs (Brentari 1998, Liddell and Johnson 1989, Sandler 1989, and Uyechi 1996). Where there is a need to discuss the sequential, segmental structure of signs, I will represent signs as combinations of movements and holds. For the purposes of this book, however, it will not be necessary to make distinctions between the various proposals concerning sequential phonological representations.

*Nonmanual signals*

A small percentage of simple signs are composed of more than just the activity of the hands. That is, for some signs, it is necessary not only to move the hands

---

[7] Newkirk (1980, 1981) also analyzed sequentiality within ASL signs. In analyzing signs inflected for aspect, Newkirk also describes the importance of movements and holds in the formation of signs. His proposals for segmenting signs came primarily from signs inflected for aspect and he did not extend his proposals for segmentation to the lexicon as a whole.

Figure 2.4  Signs requiring nonmanual signals as part of their production

correctly, but also to correctly configure the face and potentially other parts of the body. The term *nonmanual signals* was introduced in order to be able to describe aspects of signing that go beyond the actions of the hands (Liddell 1977). Figure 2.4 illustrates six simple signs that require specific nonmanual signals in order to be correctly produced.

To properly produce RELIEVED (Figure 2.4a), not only must the hand move as illustrated, but the lips must be rounded and pursed throughout the sign. In addition, the signer blows out a puff of air as the hand moves downward. The form of the nonmanual signal associated with RELIEVED may be related to the common English expression, "phew!" The form of the nonmanual signal, however, differs from what an English speaker does when saying "phew," and more closely resembles what one would do if blowing out a match.

TORMENT (through teasing) is produced with a repeated outward movement of the hands. With each outward movement of the hands, the thumb slides along the fingertips toward the index finger. In addition, the head and lips are configured as shown in Figure 2.4b. If a signer were to produce the correct hand movements perfectly, but omit the nonmanual signals, the result would not be well formed.

TAKE-IT-EASY is also a two-handed sign. Moving together, the two hands first make a downward movement on one side of the body, then the other. Throughout the entire sign, the lips are pushed out as shown in Figure 2.4c. In addition, the signer has her head tilted slightly to the side.

To produce RECENTLY correctly (Figure 2.4d) the signer must slightly turn the head to the side and tense the cheek muscles on that side (or both sides) of the face. GIVE-IN begins with the palm held against the chest. At the same time the lips are tightly pressed together. As the hand moves away from the chest toward a final hold ahead of the chest, the jaw drops and the lips separate (Figure 2.4e). To produce NOT-YET correctly (Figure 2.4f), the tongue protrudes slightly, resting on the lower lip while the head slowly rotates from side to side.

Signs requiring specific nonmanual signals comprise only a small percentage of the ASL lexicon. As we shall see below, however, nonmanual signals are more frequently present as parts of morphologically complex signs as well as in syntactic constructions.

## Morphology

### Introduction

The English word *book* is a morphologically simple word. The word *books*, on the other hand, is morphologically complex. In addition to the meaningful element *book*, it also contains the meaningful plural suffix -*s*. Attempting to divide *book* further into *b* and *ook*, or *boo* and *k*, results in forms which no longer encode the meaning 'book'. That is, *book* cannot be further subdivided without losing its meaning. Meaningful parts of a word which cannot be further subdivided without loss of meaning are called morphemes. Thus, the word *books* consists of two morphemes combined to form a single word. Linguistic morphology is the study of the ways in which languages combine morphemes to form complex words.

ASL has several types of complex signs, including compound signs (Klima and Bellugi 1979, Liddell and Johnson 1986), signs with incorporated numerals (Chinchor 1981, Frishberg and Gough 1973, Liddell 1996b), a small number of prefixes that can attach to signs with numeral values (Liddell 1996b), and a large number of aspectual forms of verbal and adjectival signs (Klima and Bellugi 1979, Liddell 1984b). I will briefly describe these complex signs below.

a.          THINK                  b.              SAME-AS

c.              AGREE

Figure 2.5  The two input signs and the compound AGREE

*Compound signs*

The ASL lexicon contains a large number of compound signs, and a productive means of creating new ones. For example, the compound AGREE (THINK^SAME-AS) was formed by combining THINK and SAME-AS.

The compound formation process typically makes significant changes to the structure of the individual signs that are the original source of the compound. Consequently, the two parts of an ASL compound often differ from the individual signs that enter into the compound formation process. THINK is produced as illustrated in Figure 2.5a. It begins with a movement toward the forehead followed by a hold, where the hand briefly maintains contact with the forehead. The compound THINK^SAME-AS does not begin where THINK begins. It begins with the hand in contact with the forehead. Thus, the compound makes use of only the final hold (the final phonological segment) of THINK. SAME-AS (Figure 2.5b) is produced with a repeated sideways contacting movement of the two hands. Both the repetition and the contact between the two hands are missing in the compound.

Figure 2.6 illustrates the effect of two simple rules (Liddell 1984a, Liddell and Johnson 1986). If the initial sign has a hold segment where the hand contacts the body, the contacting hold rule reduces the initial sign to that single hold segment. The second segment of THINK is just such a hold since the index finger is held in contact with the forehead. The contacting hold rule reduces THINK to that single hold segment. A second rule, the single sequence rule,

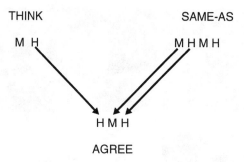

Figure 2.6  Forming AGREE from THINK and SAME-AS

eliminates any repeated MH sequences. This rule reduces SAME-AS from MH MH to a single MH. Thus, AGREE is a typical ASL compound in that there have been significant structural changes to the signs that entered into the compound formation process.

Once created, compounds are subject to the pressures of historical change. The lack of contact between the two hands during the final segment of AGREE probably arose as the result of such a historical change. A typical ASL compound does not consist of two intact morphemes. This is because of the structural changes that take place as a result of compound formation, as well as historical changes subsequent to compound formation. Thus, a typical ASL sign that came into being by means of the compound formation rules is technically not a compound. I will continue to describe them as compounds, however, since the use of that term is widespread and there is no better term.[8]

Similarly, THINK (Figure 2.7a) and OPPOSITE (Figure 2.7b) have combined to form the compound DISAGREE (Figure 2.7c).

THINK is produced with the MH sequence described above. OPPOSITE is produced with an HMH sequence. During OPPOSITE's initial hold the two fingertips are in contact or near one another. They then move apart, followed by a hold in the separated position. Forming DISAGREE from THINK and OPPOSITE is carried out by the same set of compound formation rules.

The same rule that reduces THINK to a single hold in AGREE also reduces THINK to a single hold in DISAGREE. OPPOSITE does not have any repeated MH segments, so there is no repetition to eliminate. The compound formation rules produce the HHMH structure shown in Figure 2.8. Independent phonological rules with wide application in ASL will apply to the output of the compound formation process (Liddell and Johnson 1989).

---

[8] Liddell (1984a) shows similarities between ASL compounds and portmanteau words like the English *smog*. Unlike ASL compounds, words like *smog* are not created by an identifiable set of rules.

a.              THINK                    b.              OPPOSITE

c.                        DISAGREE

Figure 2.7 The two input signs and the compound DISAGREE

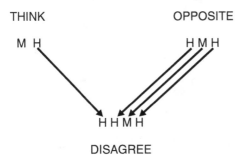

Figure 2.8 Forming DISAGREE from THINK and OPPOSITE

Table 2.3 provides a very brief sample of common ASL compound signs along with their meanings.

Compound signs are lexical units of ASL. That is, the signs in Table 2.3 all exist as words in the language just like the non-compound signs CAT or THEORY. They differ from simple signs in that historically they were created by combining two signs.

### Numeral incorporation

Some complex signs in ASL include numeral morphemes as part of their structure. For example, Figure 2.9 illustrates four signs with an incorporated numeral

Table 2.3 *Some ASL compound signs.*

| Compound sign | Meaning |
|---|---|
| FACE^STRONG | to resemble |
| FACE^SAME | to look like |
| THINK^APPEAR | to get an idea or a thought |
| THINK^DISAPPEAR | to lose an idea or a thought |
| FEEL^SAME | to feel like |
| FEEL^DEFLATE | to feel worthless or have low self-esteem |
| SLEEP^DRESS | pajamas, nightgown |
| TRUE^WORK | seriously, no kidding |
| FORMAL^ROOM | living room |
| BOOK^STORE | bookstore |

a.      {TWO}{O'CLOCK}              b.              {TWO}{WEEK}

c.      {TWO}{DOLLAR}              d.              {TWO}{MONTH}

Figure 2.9  Four signs incorporating the numeral handshape meaning 'two'

encoded by the V handshape. The sign {TWO}{O'CLOCK} 'two o'clock' is produced with a movement that oscillates between the two configurations shown in Figure 2.9a. The sign {TWO}{WEEK} 'two weeks' is produced with a single straight movement of the V handshape across the palm followed by a hold as shown in Figure 2.9b. The sign {TWO}{DOLLAR} 'two dollars' is produced with the single rotational movement illustrated in Figure 2.9c followed by a hold. The sign {TWO}{MONTH} 'two months' is produced with a single downward movement followed by a hold, as shown in Figure 2.9d. While each of these signs expresses a different meaning, they each express the meaning 'two'. In addition, each is produced with a V handshape (index and middle fingers extended from a fist).

Had the signs in Figure 2.9 been produced with a 3 handshape (thumb, index and middle finger extended), the meanings expressed by the signs would be 'three o'clock', 'three weeks', 'three dollars', and 'three months'. Data like this make it possible to associate the V handshape with the meaning 'two' and the 3 handshape with the meaning 'three'. The numeral morphemes found across the set of numeral incorporating signs are expressed by handshapes and encode values from one to nine.[9]

To take a specific example, the V handshape in {TWO}{WEEK} (Figure 2.9b) expresses the meaning 'two'. If one removes the morpheme {TWO} from the sign {TWO}{WEEK}, we are left with less than a full sign – the handshape features are missing. Even though it is less than a full sign, it nevertheless encodes the meaning 'week'. I treat it as a bound root (Liddell 1996b). In order to distinguish these bound morphemes from full signs, I use curly brackets when labeling the bound forms. Thus, {WEEK} labels a bound numeral incorporating root meaning 'week'. This root has no handshape features. Similarly, {TWO} is the bound numeral morpheme expressed by the V handshape. There is also an independent sign TWO produced with a stationary V hand configuration ahead of the shoulder with the palm facing inward. That is, TWO is a sign consisting of movement, handshape, location, and orientation features while {TWO} is a bound root consisting solely of handshape features.

The number of signs that participate in the numeral incorporation process is quite extensive. Table 2.4 contains a partial list of bound roots capable of incorporating numeral morphemes and the typical range of values accepted. The ranges shown should not be taken as absolute since there is some variation from one signer to the next.

The numeral incorporating roots and the numeral morphemes are atypical when compared with morphemes typically found in spoken languages. This is because the morphemes seen in spoken languages typically consist of some number of consonants and vowels. The English suffix -ness, for example, consists of a consonant–vowel–consonant sequence.[10] This morpheme is added to an English adjective as a suffix, thereby creating a noun. Thus, *blueness* is a morphologically complex noun composed from the adjective *blue* and the suffix -*ness*. Morphemes like -*ness* add additional articulatory activity onto the end of the word to which they attach. This is not the case with the examples of numeral incorporation in Figure 2.9, where the numeral morphemes appear simultaneously with the root. For these signs the grammatical complexity is co-extensive with the root, rather than appearing as an addition at the beginning or end of a word.

---

[9] Not all paradigms use the full set of numeral handshapes.

[10] Words with the -*ness* suffix are spelled with a final double *s*. In spite of this spelling convention, the words are pronounced with a single [s] sound.

Table 2.4 *Common numeral incorporation paradigms*

| Numeral incorporating roots | Typical values | Meaning |
|---|---|---|
| {MINUTE} | 1–9 | number of minutes |
| {HOUR} | 1–4 | number of hours |
| {DAY} | 1–4 | number of days |
| {WEEK} | 1–9 | number of weeks |
| {WEEK-FUTURE} | 1–4 | number of weeks from now |
| {WEEK-PAST} | 1–4 | number of weeks ago |
| {MONTH} | 1–9 | number of months |
| {MONTH-FUTURE} | 1–9 | number of months from now |
| {YEAR-FUTURE} | 1–4 | number of years from now |
| {YEAR-PAST} | 1–4 | number of years ago |
| {MORE}$^a$ | 1–4 | number of additional things |
| {TIMES} | 1–4 | number of times (e.g. once, twice, etc.) |
| {DECADE} | 3–9 | 30, 40, etc. |
| {APPROX-DECADE} | 3–9 | approximately 30, approximately 40, etc. |
| {ORDINAL} | 1–9 | first, second, third, etc. |
| {DOLLARS} | 1–9 | number of dollars |
| {HUNDREDS}$_{OSC}$ | 2–5 | 100, 200, etc. |
| {O'CLOCK} | 1–9 | one o'clock, two o'clock, etc. |
| {PLACE-IN-COMPETITION} | 1–9 | first place, second place, etc. |

$^a$ Signs like {ONE}{MORE}, {TWO}{MORE}, and {THREE}{MORE} are distinct from the two-handed non-incorporating sign ONE-MORE. They are one-handed signs produced with the palm toward the signer. The extended fingers oscillate between a straight and hooked configuration.

### ASL pronouns and possessive determiners

Table 2.5 contains a listing of twenty-six distinct pronominal signs. These signs fall into two person categories: first person and not first person (Meier 1990).[11] First person forms are listed in the column on the left and non-first person forms are listed on the right.

In general, ASL pronouns come in first person, non-first person pairs. In two cases, however, there are non-first person pronouns without corresponding first person forms. As far as I can determine, there is no first person characterizing pronoun corresponding to the non-first person pronoun SELF-CHAR; and there is no first person plural pronoun corresponding to the non-first person plural formal pronoun PRO-FORMAL-PL.

---

[11] Meier argues that there is no formal distinction between second and third person pronouns in ASL. I will take up these arguments shortly. He uses INDEX in his glosses for the first person singular and non-first person singular pronouns. Since the term "index" is used in so many different ways in linguistics and in descriptions of sign language, I will use PRO-1 for the first person singular pronoun and PRO for the non-first person singular pronoun.

Table 2.5 *Person and number differences in ASL pronominal signs*

|          | 1st person | non-1st person |
|----------|-----------|----------------|
| **singular** | PRO-1 | PRO |
|          | POSS-1 (MY) | POSS |
|          | SELF-ONLY-1 | SELF-ONLY |
|          | SELF-ONLY-1! | SELF-ONLY! |
|          |           | SELF-CHAR |
|          | PRO-FORMAL-1 | PRO-FORMAL |
| **dual** | PRO-DUAL-1 | PRO-DUAL |
| **multiple** | {PRO-MULT-1}{THREE} | {PRO-MULT}{THREE} |
|          | {PRO-MULT-1}{FOUR} | {PRO-MULT}{FOUR} |
|          | {PRO-MULT-1}{FIVE} | {PRO-MULT}{FIVE} |
| **plural** | PRO-PL-1 (WE) | PRO-PL |
|          | POSS-PL-1 (OUR) | POSS-PL |
|          | SELF-ONLY-PL-1 (OURSELVES) | SELF-ONLY-PL |
|          |           | PRO-FORMAL-PL |

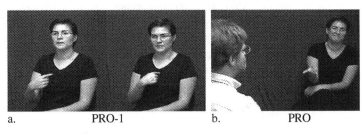

a.          PRO-1                 b.            PRO

Figure 2.10 ASL's singular first person and non-first person personal pronouns

*PRO-1 and PRO*

PRO-1 (Figure 2.10a) makes reference to the current signer. It is produced in citation form with the index finger extended but flexed at the base joint, directed toward the sternum where it makes a single contact.

The non-first person singular pronoun PRO is directed outward and makes reference to the entity it is directed toward. In Figure 2.10b PRO is directed toward the man to the right of the signer and makes reference to that man.

The forms of each of these pronouns do not change depending on whether the pronoun is the subject or object of a verb. This contrasts with the English pronominal system where the grammatical role of the pronoun typically makes a difference in the pronoun's form. In (1a) the English pronoun *I* refers to the speaker. In (1b) reference to the speaker is made by the pronoun *me*.

　　Grammar, Gesture, and Meaning in ASL

Table 2.6 *Case, gender, person, and number differences in English personal pronouns*

| English personal pronouns | | |
| --- | --- | --- |
| | Nominative | Accusative |
| 1st person | I/we | me/us |
| 2nd person | you | you |
| 3rd person | he/she/it/they | him/her/it/them |

(1)　　a. I like chocolate.
　　　　b. The dog likes me.

The difference between the pronouns is in the type of grammatical information encoded. While both *I* and *me* mean 'the current speaker', (i.e. the speaker uttering the token *I* or *me*), they each encode different grammatical roles. In (1a) *I* is the subject of the verb while in (1b) *me* is the object of the verb. Thus *I* not only encodes the meaning 'speaker', it also encodes the pronoun's grammatical role (subject). Similarly, *me* encodes the meaning 'speaker' and a different grammatical role (object). Although English does not generally mark *case*, analyses of English generally treat this as a difference in case, where *I* encodes nominative case and *me* encodes accusative case. The same nominative–accusative difference can be seen in (2), where *he* is the nominative form of the pronoun and *him* is the accusative form.

(2)　　a. He likes chocolate.
　　　　b. The dog likes him.

Table 2.6 illustrates the case differences among the English pronouns. All the pronouns listed, with the exception of *you* and *it*, make a nominative–accusative distinction.

　　English pronouns also make a *person* distinction. The concept of *person* refers to discourse roles. First person describes the role of speaker. Second person describes the role of addressee, and third person is used for everything else. Some of the English third person pronouns also make gender distinctions (*he* vs. *she*, *him* vs. *her*). Thus, the English pronoun *he* encodes a third person discourse role, nominative case, singular number and masculine gender.

　　The ASL pronominal system is quite different from the English pronominal system. ASL pronouns make no case distinctions. That is, as mentioned above, the form of a pronoun does not change to indicate the grammatical role of the pronoun in the sentence. I will illustrate this with the first person singular pronoun PRO-1. In (3) PRO-1 functions as the subject of the predicate SATISFIED. In (4) PRO-1 functions as the object of the verb LOVE. The signs have the same form, regardless of their grammatical role in the sentence. The same is true of all other ASL pronouns. We can conclude, therefore, that ASL pronouns are unmarked for case.[12]

(3)     PRO-1 SATISFIED
        I am satisfied.

(4)     MOTHER LOVE PRO-1
        Mother loves me.

It has long been assumed that ASL uses a three-person pronoun system, and sign glosses reflecting a three-way distinction can be found in publications dating up to the recent past (Stokoe *et al.* 1965, Liddell 1980, Padden 1988, Uyechi 1996). Meier (1990) argues, however, that ASL does not distinguish between second and third person pronominal forms. He presents four arguments supporting his claim. The first depends on the directionality of pronominal signs. In a prototypical conversation the addressee is directly in front of the signer. A singular pronoun referring to the addressee would move directly ahead of the signer toward the addressee. One might think of that direction as signifying second person. A non-addressed participant in the conversation would have to be off to the side somewhere. A singular pronoun referring to the non-addressed participant would move to the side toward that person. If all ASL conversations were physically structured this way, it would be possible to claim that second person pronouns move directly out from the signer and third person pronouns move to the side. However, Meier observes that it is common to find examples where the addressee is not directly in front of the signer. He provides examples where a signer might be signing to two people at once – one on the left and one on the right. Meier argues that a pronoun referring to either of the addressees individually would be directed toward that individual rather than toward the empty space directly ahead of the signer. When addressing the person on the right and using PRO to refer to the person on the left, PRO would be directed toward the person on the left. When addressing the person on the left and using PRO to refer to that same addressee, PRO would also be directed toward the person on the left. The pronoun would have the same handshape, movement, palm orientation, and direction in both cases. Thus, a singular pronoun referring to the addressee and a singular pronoun referring to a non-addressee could have identical forms.[13]

---

[12] There are no standard glosses for ASL pronouns. ASL's first person singular personal pronoun has been glossed variously as I, ME, PRO-1, $IX_1$, and $INDEX_1$, among others. The same types of variation in glossing are also found with the other pronominal forms.

[13] I have modified Meier's argument somewhat. He frames the argument in terms of the "points" that the sign can be directed toward. The assumption behind this argument is that signs are not directed toward real people or things. Instead, signs are directed toward points in the signing space between the signer and the real person or thing. Lillo-Martin and Klima (1990) refer to

The second argument centers on the role of eye gaze. As illustrated in Figure 2.4, some signs include nonmanual signals as part of their lexical structure. That is, the movement of the hand in producing NOT-YET must be accompanied by resting the tongue on the lower lip while producing a side-to-side headshake. The movement of the hand in producing RELIEVED must be accompanied by blowing air out of the signer's pursed lips. Given that some signs include a nonmanual component, it is possible that eye gaze toward the addressee might constitute part of a second person singular pronoun meaning 'you'. If this were so, then eye gaze toward the addressee might be seen as a feature distinguishing second person and third person pronouns. Alternatively, eye gaze might not be part of the pronoun at all. Eye contact with the addressee could be viewed as a feature of conversations rather than a feature of signs. Meier cites data showing that eye gaze at the addressee occurs not only with second person pronominal reference, but also with first person pronominal reference as well as stretches of discourse that make no reference at all to participants in the discourse. He cites data from Baker and Padden (1978) [example (5) below] showing that all instances of second person pronominal reference are not accompanied by eye gaze at the addressee. In (5), Baker and Padden indicate the direction of the eye gaze above the glosses for the signs. During the first instance of the pronoun glossed as YOU, the signer was looking down, and thus not making eye contact with the addressee.

|  | at A up, right down | | at A |
|---|---|---|---|
| (5) | TOMORROW RAIN | YOU GO SWIMMING BEACH YOU | |

If it rains tomorrow, will you go swimming at the beach?

I will now elaborate Meier's argument somewhat. A central question concerns how the participants in a conversation know who the addressee is. For example, in spoken English discourse the word *you* means, 'addressee', but it does not encode the identity of the addressee. In a conversational situation involving a speaker and two other people, if the speaker directs his body, face, and eye gaze toward one of the people, that would appear to be a signal that that person is the intended addressee. In fact, (6) shows that the addressee can even change during a single sentence.

|  | left | right |
|---|---|---|
| (6) | I want you and you to stay. | |

Directing the face and eye gaze to the person on the left during the first instance of *you* identifies the individual on the left as the addressee at that time. Directing

such a point as a referential-locus (R-locus). It is assumed that the R-locus represents the real person or thing. Given such assumptions, directing the sign toward the R-locus makes reference to the real person or thing associated with that R-locus.

one's face and eye gaze to the person on the right during the second instance of *you* identifies that individual as the addressee during the second part of the sentence. It is up to the individuals in the conversation to make the connection between the word *you*, which means 'addressee', and the person who has that conversational role.

ASL discourse can be described in similar terms. The identity of the addressee in an ASL conversation will be apparent based on physical properties of the discourse. In a typical situation involving only two participants, the one not signing will be the addressee. With more participants, the identity of the addressee will be apparent based on characteristics such as the body orientation or the eye gaze of the signer. The non-first person singular pronoun PRO means 'single entity (other than the signer)'. In order to make reference to the addressee the signer would direct PRO toward the addressee. In order to make reference to some other individual or entity present, the signer would direct the PRO toward that individual or entity. It doesn't matter whether the individual or entity being mentioned is the addressee or not.

I am proposing that physical characteristics such as the direction of eye gaze and the orientation of the head and body of the speaker or signer generally make the identity of the addressee clear, regardless of whether the language being used is English or ASL. English has the unique second person pronominal form *you* used to make reference to the addressee. English uses the distinct third person pronominal forms *he, him, she, her,* and *it* if the single entity being talked about is not the speaker or addressee. In ASL discourse the concept of addressee versus other participants is equally important. That is, it is very important to know who is being signed to and who is not being signed to. But that distinction is not reflected in the ASL pronominal system. The non-first person singular pronoun PRO is used regardless of whether the referent is the addressee or not.

Meier's third argument concerns either missing or idiosyncratic first person verb forms. There are some verbs that lack first person object forms. Meier cites PAY-ATTENTION-TO, SEE, RUIN, FINGERSPELL-TO, and PRAISE.[14] There are two variants of the verb CONVINCE that can be directed toward someone with a non-first person role in the discourse. There is a symmetrical two-handed form produced with two active B hands (palm up) making diagonally downward movements that cause the two hands to approach one another. This variant has a symmetrical first person object form in which the two B hands (palm down) move inward, contacting each side of the signer's neck. There is an asymmetrical variant produced by placing an upright index finger toward the relevant person, then contacting the index finger with the

---

[14] There are two distinct signs related to fingerspelling. One is produced with a 5 handshape with wiggling fingers. This sign cannot be directed toward the signer. The other sign begins with an S that opens to a 5. This sign can be directed toward the signer.

ulnar surface of an active B hand making a diagonal downward movement. This variant has no first person object form.

Meier cites a dialectal one-handed first person object form of CONVINCE produced by contacting the side of the neck with the ulnar surface of a single B hand as a demonstration of a first person idiosyncratic form.[15] Given the data I have described, Meier's example is idiosyncratic because it is a one-handed variant of a two-handed first person form. There is no equivalent one-handed variant of the non-first person form. Meier argues that there are no such gaps or idiosyncrasies involving second person and third person participants.

Finally, Meier points out that even if one were to grant a pronominal category that encodes third person, the category is not sufficient to distinguish between all the possible third person forms. That is, there appears to be no limit to the number of third person pronominal forms. How is one to distinguish between a third person form which points left and one which points up and to the right? One could also add that exactly the same can be said of the number of possible directions for proposed second person forms.

Meier's argument is convincing. Directing ASL's singular, non-first person pronoun PRO toward someone's chest identifies that individual as the referent of the pronoun. If that individual happens to be the addressee, then the sign would be translated at *you*. If the fingertip points at someone or something else, then the sign would be translated as *he*, *him*, *she*, *her*, or *it*, depending on the nature of the entity PRO is directed toward and the English pronoun's grammatical role in the translation. The fact that the English translations include second and third person distinctions as well as gender distinctions is merely a translation issue. English forces its speakers to encode gender when using a third person singular pronoun regardless of whether that information is encoded in the language being translated into English.

### Dual personal pronouns

ASL has two dual pronouns: PRO-DUAL-1 'the two of us' and PRO-DUAL 'the two of you/them'. Both are made with a back and forth rocking motion which alternately points at each of the two entities being referred to. These two pronouns are primarily used to talk about humans. PRO-DUAL-1 is used when the signer is one of the two people (Figure 2.11a). When the hand rocks toward the signer, the middle finger points toward the signer. When the hand rocks away from the signer, the index finger points at the other person. If the signer is not one of the two people, PRO-DUAL is used (Figure 2.11b). Both signs are made with a K handshape. PRO-DUAL-1 and PRO-DUAL differ in

---

[15] Meier argues that the one-handed dialectal form that contacts the neck is idiosyncratic because it contrasts with the asymmetrical variant of CONVINCE produced with the raised index finger (in that dialect).

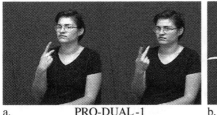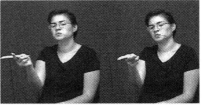

a.        PRO-DUAL-1       b.          PRO-DUAL

the two of us           the two of you/them

Figure 2.11 Distinct first person and non-first person pronouns

their orientation and in their proximity to the signer. PRO-DUAL-1 is produced with the wrist rotated into a supinated (palm up) orientation and is produced near the signer while PRO-DUAL is produced with the wrist rotated so that the palm faces to the side and is located further away from the body.

The K handshape is produced with the index and middle fingers extended, with the thumb in contact with the middle finger. In ASL, the bound numeral {TWO} is produced with the same two fingers extended, but in a V configuration, where the thumb is not in contact with either of the extended fingers. There appears to be a close relationship between the V and the K handshapes. For example, although SEE is generally produced with a K handshape, it is sometimes seen with a V handshape. Similarly, some signers produce WORSE with a V handshape whereas others use a K. Examples such as these suggest that V and K are closely related and that a sign produced with a V handshape can change over time and be produced with a K handshape. The combination of the K handshape and the meaning 'two' associated with these two pronouns suggests that both signs originally contained the bound numeral {TWO}, but as a result of historical change, no longer contain that morpheme.

Just like PRO, the actual production of these two signs depends on the physical location of the entities involved. Although one end of the movement of PRO-DUAL-1 is always directed toward the signer, the other end can be directed wherever the other person happens to be. The sign can be produced toward the far left, the far right, and anywhere in between. It can also be directed toward entities higher or lower than the signer's chest.

*Personal pronouns with incorporated numerals*
The signs in this section are produced with numeral morphemes and can easily be analyzed as having two meaningful parts. These pronouns are all made with a horizontal circular motion. In producing them, the signer does not direct a part of the hand (e.g. the fingertip) toward the intended referent. Instead, the signer produces the sign such that the location and size of the circular motion point to the intended referents.

a. {PRO-MULT-1}{THREE}    b.  {PRO-MULT}{THREE}
   the three of us              the three of you/them

Figure 2.12  Distinct first person and non-first person pronouns

The sign {PRO-MULT-1}{THREE} in Figure 2.12a means 'the three of us' and is produced near the signer. It is produced with a 3 handshape (thumb, index, and middle fingers extended from a fist). In this sign the 3 handshape is a bound numeral morpheme signifying 'three'.[16] The sign is not only produced near the signer, but slightly to the right of center. The rightward placement of the sign indicates that the other two members of the group are located to the right. The sign in Figure 2.12a is composed of the bound morphemes {PRO-MULT-1} and {THREE}. Both {PRO-MULT-1} and {THREE} are bound morphemes since neither contains enough features to constitute a sign. {PRO-MULT-1} has the form of a circular movement made near the signer with an upward palm orientation. I will characterize its meaning as 'group including the signer'. Together, these two bound morphemes constitute a full sign. Equivalent signs with the bound morphemes {FOUR} and {FIVE} also exist. They are produced just like {PRO-MULT-1}{THREE} except that they contain a different numeral morpheme. The bound numeral morpheme {FOUR} is produced with the four fingers extended and {FIVE} is produced with the four fingers and thumb extended.

The non-first person forms are also divisible into two bound morphemes and differ from the first person forms in their placement. As can be seen in Figure 2.12b, the arm is extended away from the body and directed toward the members of the group being referred to. The justification for separating first person and non-first person forms lies in the placement of the signs, and the range of numerals allowed. If these two signs were collapsed into a single category, one would have to say that the sign is produced near the members of the group being referred to. But this description is not specific enough. If the signer is one of the members of the group, the sign is produced near the signer. It is made on a side of the signer which points to the other members of the group, but it is still made near the signer. Distinguishing between first person and non-first person forms allows this fact to be captured in a straightforward way. The second type of evidence for a person distinction comes from informal

[16]  See Liddell (1996b) for a grammatical analysis of signs which incorporate numeral handshapes.

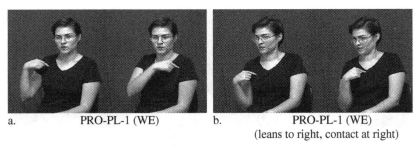

a.                PRO-PL-1 (WE)          b.                PRO-PL-1 (WE)
                                                  (leans to right, contact at right)

Figure 2.13 PRO-PL-1 (WE) without pointing, then pointing by leaning the
body and keeping the hand on one side of the body only

Figure 2.14 PRO-PL

surveys I have taken in my classes during recent years. Some signers in my
classes use the full range of numeral handshapes from three to nine for the
first person forms, but only three through five for the non-first person forms.
Based on these two lines of evidence, it seems reasonable to conclude that the
first person, non-first person distinction is important here, just as it is in the
other pronominal forms we have discussed.

*Plural personal pronouns*
The sign PRO-PL-1, typically glossed as WE, is illustrated in Figure 2.13a. It
begins with the index finger in contact with the ipsilateral side of the chest. The
fingertip then moves in an arc to the opposite side of the chest. A slightly different form of this sign is illustrated in Figure 2.13b. In this form the signer leans
to the right. The movement of the hand also differs from that in Figure 2.13a.
The initial contact on the ipsilateral side of the chest is the same, but the final
contact does not cross to the other side of the chest. This form is used if the
members of the group being talked about are located to the signer's right. It
would be interpreted to mean the group that consists of the signer and those to
the right of the signer.

The corresponding non-first person pronoun, PRO-PL, is also made with an
arc. However, its form differs from PRO-PL-1. As illustrated in Figure 2.14,
the index finger begins pointing across the body. The fingertip then drops

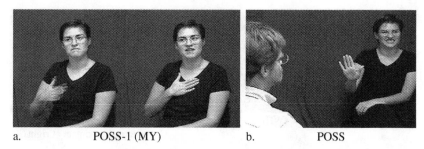

a.                POSS-1 (MY)                b.                POSS

Figure 2.15 ASL's distinct first person and non-first person singular possessive determiners

pendulum-like, followed by an outward arc in which the fingertip points toward the entities being referred to. If a collection of people were located to the right of the signer, PRO-PL would begin its pointing motion at one side of the collection and move the pointing index finger along an arc-shaped path to the other side of the collection.

Had the set of individuals been located elsewhere, the sign would have to be directed differently in order to point toward that set of individuals. The hand has to be directed toward the entities being referred to, regardless of whether the entities are directly in front of the signer, slightly to the right or left, at an elevated level, etc.

### Singular possessive determiners

ASL has a set of two singular possessive determiners, illustrated in Figure 2.15. The first person singular possessive determiner is glossed as POSS-1 or MY (Figure 2.15a). It is produced with a B handshape and the palm makes a single contact with the chest. It typically appears in initial position in a noun phrase, prior to the noun and any other noun modifiers.

Figure 2.15b shows an example of the non-first person possessive determiner, POSS. It is produced like POSS-1, but is directed away from the signer with the palm pointing toward the possessor. As with the nonpossessive pronouns, it makes a difference where the possessor is. In the case of a human possessor, all the signer needs to know is the location of the possessor's chest in order to direct the sign correctly. This sign translates into English as *your*, *his*, *her*, or *its*, depending on the nature of the possessor.

### Plural possessive determiners

ASL has two plural possessive determiners. POSS-PL-1 (OUR), illustrated in Figure 2.16a, is produced by first making a contact at the ipsilateral side of the chest, then making an arc motion across the chest, followed by a contact at the opposite side of the chest by the ulnar side of the hand. Although the hand does

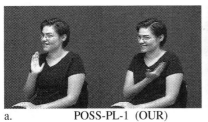

a.         POSS-PL-1  (OUR)        b.              POSS-PL

Figure 2.16  ASL's distinct first person and non-first person plural possessive determiners

not point in the production of this sign, the signer could lean to the right, for example, to indicate that the other members of the group of possessors were located to the right of the signer. Thus, although the signer's hand doesn't point at the other referents, the signer's body can sometimes "point" and accomplish the same purpose.

POSS-PL always points to the possessors. It begins with the palm directed toward one side of the group of possessors then moves in an arc, ending with the palm directed toward the other side of the group.

*SELF-ONLY pronouns*

The signs which I am glossing as SELF-ONLY-1 and SELF-ONLY are both made with an A handshape with the tip of the thumb made prominent by straightening and extending the final joint of the thumb past the fist, as shown in Figure 2.17. SELF-ONLY-1 (Figure 2.17a) means, 'the signer and no one else'. The hand typically makes a double contact at the chest.[17] The non-first person form SELF-ONLY (Figure 2.17b) is made with a double outward movement toward the individual the pronoun refers to. Its meaning is roughly, 'single entity (person) and no one else'. Like PRO, SELF-ONLY is directed toward its physically present referent.

Both pronouns appear to be used exclusively as subjects. Thus, the use of SELF-ONLY in (7) is fine, while the use of SELF-ONLY as an object in (8) is unacceptable.

(7)     SELF-ONLY MAKE PIE
        He made the pie by himself

(8)     * PRO-1 LOVE SELF-ONLY[18]
        I love you – and no one else.

---

[17] Baker and Cokely (1980) report that there is some variation in the form of this sign. Some signers make contact at the chest, as illustrated here, while others produce the sign with the knuckles facing inward.

[18] The symbol * indicates ungrammaticality.

a.                    SELF-ONLY-1

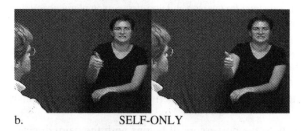

b.                    SELF-ONLY

c.                    SELF-ONLY-PL-1

Figure 2.17  Distinct first person and non-first person pronouns

The pronoun SELF-ONLY-PL-1 'group including the signer, but no others' makes a contact on the ipsilateral side of the chest followed by another contact on the contralateral side of the chest, as illustrated in Figure 2.17c.

The plural form SELF-ONLY-PL means 'group excluding the signer and all others'. It is produced with the same handshape as SELF-ONLY and is directed outward with an arc-shaped movement path that identifies the group being talked about. It typically begins the movement with fist pointing up and the palm oriented out. As the hand moves along the arc the forearm rotates so that at the end of the movement, the thumb is oriented up – the expected orientation for this class of pronouns.

The emphatic form SELF-ONLY-1! is made like SELF-ONLY-1 but with a larger, faster motion, and without repetition. It is used where the referent is obliged to carry out some task without help. Example (9) provides an example of SELF-ONLY-1!, where the signer is ordered to make a pie without help. ORDER-1 is produced with an arc motion from the chin to the chest indicating

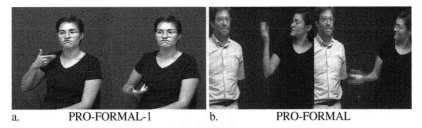

a.           PRO-FORMAL-1           b.           PRO-FORMAL

Figure 2.18  Distinct first person and non-first person formal singular pronouns

that the signer was the recipient of the order. SELF-ONLY-1! would also be
directed toward the signer's chest.

(9)     ORDER-1 SELF-ONLY-1! MAKE PIE
        He/she ordered me to make the pie by myself.

The non-first person form, SELF-ONLY! is made like SELF-ONLY but with
a larger, faster motion, and without repetition. This compound sign THINK^
SELF-ONLY! (make up your own mind), typically glossed as THINK^SELF,
has incorporated SELF-ONLY! as the second element of the compound.

*The SELF-CHAR pronoun*
SELF-CHAR is used when characteristics of the referent are being described.
The non-first person form SELF-CHAR looks like SELF-ONLY, but has a
smaller repeated motion. It refers to some entity whose characteristics are being
described.

(10)    LOOK, GIRL THERE. SELF-CHAR BEAUTIFUL.
        Look at that girl over there. She is beautiful!

Like previous non-first person pronouns examined thus far, this sign must be
directed toward its physically present referent. As far as I can determine there is
no corresponding plural form of this pronoun and no corresponding first person
form.

*Formal pronouns*
There are two singular formal pronouns and one plural formal pronoun in ASL. I
will gloss them as PRO-FORMAL-1, PRO-FORMAL, and PRO-FORMAL-PL.
Examples of the singular forms are illustrated in Figure 2.18. PRO-FORMAL-1
is produced by a single downward brushing movement of the back of the fingers
of a B handshape against the chest (Figure 2.18a).
     PRO-FORMAL (Figure 2.18b) is produced by a single downward movement
of a B handshape with the palm up. As with all the other singular pronouns
described so far, the fingers are directed toward the entity or person being

a.                          TEACHER

b.                          DRIVER

Figure 2.19  Two signs formed with the -ER suffix

referred to. These two signs are most commonly used when introducing an honored guest or when an honored guest introduces himself or herself. The plural form PRO-FORMAL-PL begins much as PRO-FORMAL ends, with a B handshape in a palm-up orientation. The hand then moves along a horizontal path indicating its referents.

*Prefixation and suffixation*

There are a small number of morphologically complex forms in ASL that can be analyzed as resulting from the attachment of a prefix or suffix. Signs such as TEACHER (Figure 2.19a) and DRIVER (Figure 2.19b) can be analyzed as nouns derived by affixing an agent nominalizer onto the verb (Liddell 1977, 1980).[19]

The suffix -ER is produced by two B handshapes with the palms facing one another about shoulder width apart and moving down from (roughly) ahead of the shoulders to ahead of the trunk.[20] The form -ER can be treated as a suffix because it is a bound form, appearing only as part of derived nouns. In general, signers do not use this form as a noun meaning 'person'. In addition, signs produced by the addition of -ER do not show evidence of having been formed from the compound formation rules previously described.

[19] Such signs have also been analyzed as resulting from a compounding process involving a verb and a sign meaning 'person', made with a B handshape (Baker and Cokely 1980).

[20] In the two signs illustrated, the signer's handshapes have some nondistinctive spreading of some of the fingers.

There is one highly significant aspect of signs formed from the -ER suffix. They form a very restricted set. The English *-er* suffix is highly productive. It has combined with an enormous number of English verbs to form nouns. It is also capable of productively forming additional nominals. For example, someone who laughed on cue could easily be described as a *laugher*. This is not the case in ASL.

The number of signs produced from the -ER suffix is quite limited and forming new nouns by adding the -ER suffix to other verbs is also not very productive. A common mistake made by hearing, English-speaking adults learning ASL is to treat -ER as being equivalent to the *-er* suffix in English. Not fully understanding how restricted the -ER suffix is in ASL, they freely add the -ER suffix to verbs, creating signs that would not be produced by native ASL signers.

ASL also has an interesting set of prefixes that attach to numeral signs. For example, there are a large number of signs expressing age that begin with a contact at the chin followed by a numeral sign. The number following the contact at the chin expresses the number of years old. The signs meaning 'four years old', 'in his/her forties', and 'forty-four years old' are illustrated in Figure 2.20.

In each of these examples, the handshape contacting the chin is the same as the handshape of the numeral stem to which the prefix is attached. Although this might give the impression of numeral incorporation, that is not the appropriate analysis for these signs. The initial contact at the chin is best analyzed as a prefix (Liddell 1996b). In contrast to the instances of numeral incorporation described earlier, all instances of the contact at the chin are *followed* by a numeral stem capable of standing on its own without the prefix. The semantic contribution of the contact at the chin is 'age of living thing'.[21] In Figure 2.20a, $\{AGE_0\}$- is prefixed to FOUR, resulting in the meaning 'four years old'. In Figure 2.20b, $\{AGE_0\}$- is prefixed to $\{APPROX\text{-}DECADE\}\{FOUR\}$ producing $\{AGE_0\}$-$\{APPROX\text{-}DECADE\}\{FOUR\}$ 'in his/her forties'. In Figure 2.20c, $\{AGE_0\}$-FORTY-FOUR means 'forty-four years old'.[22]

If the contact at the chin were some kind of numeral incorporating predicate, then when a 4 handshape contacts the chin, the result should mean 'four years old'. While this is the meaning expressed by the sign in Figure 2.20a, such a meaning would conflict with the meanings expressed by the signs in Figure 2.20b and c.

The prefix is unusual in that it has no handshape or orientation features of its own. These features come from the numeral stem to which the prefix attaches. Since all the numeral stems in Figure 2.20 are produced with a 4 handshape,

---

[21] This prefix would never be used, for example, to describe the age of a house or a book.

[22] The subscript in the gloss $\{AGE_0\}$- distinguishes this form from other age prefixes that do have lexically specified handshapes.

a.            {AGE$_0$}-FOUR
              four years old

b.            {AGE$_0$}-{APPROX-DECADE}{FOUR}
              in his/her forties

c.                           {AGE$_0$}-FORTY-FOUR
                             forty-four years old

Figure 2.20  Three signs produced with the {AGE$_0$}- prefix

the prefix is produced with the same 4 handshape. Interestingly, some numeral stems do not contain a numeral handshape. For example, Figure 2.21 illustrates the sign meaning 'fifteen years old'. The sign FIFTEEN is produced with a movement that oscillates between a B handshape with the fingers straight and a B handshape with the fingers bent at the base of the fingers. Neither one of these handshapes are numeral handshapes. When {AGE$_0$}- is prefixed to FIFTEEN, {AGE$_0$}- is produced with the non-numeral B handshape from FIFTEEN, as illustrated in Figure 2.21. The sign {AGE$_0$}-TWENTY-ONE illustrates the same process with a different handshape. TWENTY-ONE is produced with an oscillation between an L handshape with the thumb extended and straight and a similar handshape with the thumb bent at the distal joint. {AGE$_0$}-TWENTY-ONE begins with the fingertip of an L handshape with the thumb slightly bent in contact with the chin.

{AGE$_0$}-FIFTEEN
15 years old

Figure 2.21  The prefix {AGE$_0$}- produced with a non-numeral handshape

Signs such as these provide the final piece of evidence against a numeral incorporation analysis since the contact at the chin for {AGE$_0$}-FIFTEEN takes place with a B handshape and the contact at the chin for {AGE$_0$}-TWENTY-ONE takes place with the fingertip of an L handshape. These are not numeral handshapes and their presence would be difficult to explain in a numeral incorporation analysis.[23]

These are the only prefixes and suffixes reported in the ASL literature. This makes it evident that affixation is not the predominant means of adding morphological complexity to a sign. Internal modifications to the form of a sign and reduplication are much more common, as will become apparent in the following description of aspect in ASL.

### Aspect

Many simple signs in ASL have corresponding morphologically complex forms that express aspectual meanings. These complex forms are not produced through the addition of prefixes or suffixes. Instead, they are typically created through changes in the form of the sign itself. Such changes may result from a *reduplication* process (Fischer 1973), an internal change in the form of a sign, accomplished by the application of a *frame* process (Liddell 1984b), or some combination of these. I will begin with an aspectual form brought about solely by the insertion of features into a frame.

The citation form of TELL is produced as shown in Figure 2.22a. The sign begins with the index finger in contact with the chin then moves outward along a straight path toward the recipient of the telling. The sign TELL[UI] in Figure 2.22b expresses the meaning 'just about to tell'. This is an example of the unrealized inceptive aspect (Liddell 1984b). The hand begins its movement just ahead of the trunk, follows an arc path, and ends with the index finger in contact with the chin.

[23] Liddell (1996b) discusses other age prefixes produced with lexically specified handshapes and a similar set of prefixes for expressing time of day.

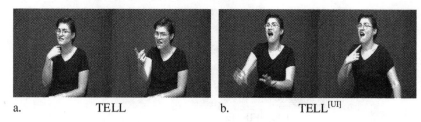

a.          TELL                  b.          TELL[UI]

Figure 2.22  The citation form and the unrealized inceptive form of TELL

The significant fact to observe about TELL[UI] is that the sign *ends* with the fingertip in contact with the chin. This is where the hand *begins* in the citation form of TELL.

By comparing TELL[UI] with the unrealized inceptive forms of signs such as INFORM, LOOK-AT, ASK, GIVE-IN, WASH-DISHES, YELL, FLIRT, TELL-STORY, and ANALYZE it is possible to discover a common process responsible for the changes in form each undergoes. For each of the signs above, the hand(s) begin ahead of the trunk, then move in an arc-shaped path to the initial configuration of the citation form of the sign.

In addition, the signer rotates her trunk in producing TELL[UI]. She has also dropped her jaw, inhaled, and at the end of the sign, is holding her breath by means of closing the glottis.[24] Finally, if there is a significant entity or location associated with the meaning of the sign (e.g. the person being told), the signer will direct her gaze toward that person or location. This set of nonmanual features is common to the unrealized inceptive form of signs.

The number and type of movement and hold segments in the citation form of the sign are not important in determining the segmental structure of the unrealized inceptive form. Regardless of the segmental structure of the citation form, the unrealized inceptive form will be produced with an arc movement followed by a hold. Putting these facts together, we can make the following generalization about the unrealized inceptive forms of the signs in this data set.[25]

a. Regardless of the patterns of movements and holds in the citation form of the sign, the unrealized inceptive form will be produced with an arc movement followed by a hold.

b. The unrealized inceptive form will begin with the hands located ahead of the trunk.

c. The unrealized inceptive form will be produced with a predictable set of nonmanual features including rotating the trunk, dropping the jaw, inhaling during the arc movement and holding one's breath by means of closing the

---

[24] While the use of the glottis could be thought of as unusual for a sign language, its function here appears to be to produce a non-moving configuration. Closing the glottis and thereby stopping the breathing of the signer produces such a static configuration.

[25] There are other unrealized inceptive data sets that behave somewhat differently (Liddell 1984b).

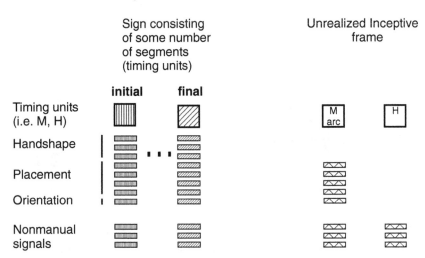

Figure 2.23  An input sign and an unrealized inceptive frame prior to inserting features from the input sign into the frame

glottis during the final hold. If applicable, the signer will also direct her gaze toward a significant person or location associated with the meaning of the sign.

d. The only part of the original sign that appears in the unrealized inceptive form is the set of features producing the *initial* configuration of the hand in the citation form. This set of features will appear inside the *final* segment of the unrealized inceptive form.

Although this is a highly unusual grammatical mechanism, the set of characteristics described in (a)–(d) above do allow for a solution. The key is in understanding that the sequence of segments within the unrealized inceptive form is independent of the sequence of segments in the original sign. The unrealized inceptive form will always begin with an arc movement followed by a final hold. The other constants of the unrealized inceptive form of signs are the nonmanual features and the starting location of the hands ahead of the trunk. All these invariant features together constitute a frame into which a restricted set of features from the original sign is inserted.

The two columns of features on the left of Figure 2.23 separated by the ellipsis represent any given sign stem with any number of segments. Even a sign normally produced with only a single segment can participate in this process. The initial set of features is represented with vertical lines and the final set of features is represented with diagonal lines. Individual features describe handshape, placement of the hands, orientation of the hands, and any nonmanual signals associated with the sign.

The right side of Figure 2.23 contains the frame for creating the unrealized inceptive form of the input sign. It is important to note here that the features in the

40     Grammar, Gesture, and Meaning in ASL

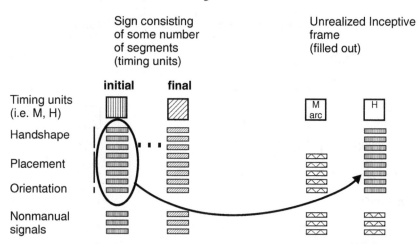

Figure 2.24  How features are inserted into the unrealized inceptive frame

frame are entirely different from the features of the input sign. Those features are
represented by the zigzag lines in the boxes. The (segmental) timing features
at the top of the frame specify an arc movement followed by a hold. In the
unrealized inceptive form of the signs we are considering here, the hands begin
ahead of the trunk. The features that place and orient the hands ahead of the trunk
are represented on the left (the initial segment of the frame). The nonmanual
features associated with the unrealized inceptive aspect include rotating the
trunk and head, dropping the jaw and inhaling during the arc movement, holding
one's breath during the final hold, and gazing at a significant location associated
with the production of the sign. These are the nonmanual signal features at the
bottom of both columns in the frame. In addition, the frame contains no features
placing or orienting the hands during the final hold of the UI form.

Extracting the needed features from the initial segment of the stem and inserting those features into the final segment of the unrealized inceptive frame
will produce the unrealized inceptive form of a sign, as shown in Figure 2.24.

In the phonological framework assumed in this analysis, if there is only a
single set of features of a certain type specified in a sign, then that set of features
will be present throughout the sign. In this case, there is only a single set of
handshape features inserted into the unrealized inceptive frame. The result will
be a sign with a single handshape throughout. That is, through phonological
"spreading" these handshape features will become the handshape features of
both the arc movement and the final hold.[26]

[26] In 1984 I proposed three distinct UI frames, with the appropriate UI frame to use in any given
situation dependent on the verb root. I put no handshape features in any of the three UI frames.
The idea was that handshape from the stem would spread throughout the UI frame and be the
handshape for the entire sign. For the particular frame being considered in the text, there are

a.   MONDAY                              b.              MONDAY[WEEKLY]

c.           NOON                        d.              NOON[DAILY]

Figure 2.25  Additional signs utilizing frames

This grammatical process may be unique to sign languages. It is a grammatical process in which much of the input sign is missing from the complex grammatical form. That is, only some of the features of the input sign are present in the more complex unrealized inceptive form. Most of the features – including the number and nature of the segments – come from the frame rather than from the input sign.

Figure 2.25 illustrates two additional patterns that could also be understood by means of a frame analysis. MONDAY (Figure 2.25a) is produced with repeated, small, horizontal circling movements ahead of the shoulder. MONDAY[WEEKLY] (Figure 2.25b) is made with a single downward movement. There is no circling movement and no repetition in this sign. The frame analysis would work like this. The [WEEKLY] frame for the sign in Figure 2.25b would consist of a downward movement followed by a hold. The initial location would be ahead of the shoulder and the final location would be at the trunk level. The handshape and orientation features from MONDAY would be inserted into the [WEEKLY] frame. The result would be a sign produced with the handshape and orientation of MONDAY, but with the locations and segmental structure of the [WEEKLY] frame. Since the frame does not include a circling movement, and since the circling movement of MONDAY is not copied into the frame, MONDAY[WEEKLY] has no circling movement.

times when the UI form begins with a lax 5 handshape. Such a handshape is not part of the frame and also not part of the verb root. How best to handle this will depend on the degree to which UI forms are lexicalized. If they are lexical forms, they could have acquired unique phonological characteristics.

Table 2.7 *Tense marking through reduplication in Tagalog*

|         | Root  | Future form |
|---------|-------|-------------|
| 'write' | sulat | susulat     |
| 'read'  | basa  | babasa      |
| 'teach' | ʔaral | ʔaʔaral     |

Equivalent signs for other days of the week also exist (e.g. TUES-DAY[WEEKLY], WEDNESDAY[WEEKLY], etc.). These signs would be structured by the [WEEKLY] frame in the same way.[27]

The signs NOON and NOON[DAILY] are illustrated in Figure 2.25c and d. The difference between NOON[DAILY] and MONDAY[WEEKLY] lies in the direction of the movement specified in the frame. MONDAY[WEEKLY] moves down while NOON[DAILY] moves horizontally. Other signs that are structured like NOON[DAILY] include MORNING[DAILY], AFTERNOON[DAILY], and NIGHT[DAILY].

The motivation for the left-to-right versus up-and-down differences between these signs can be seen in the way we construct calendars. Individual days of the week are written horizontally while successive weeks are written beneath one another. As a result, moving from one noon to the next within a given week on the calendar involves a horizontal displacement. Moving from one Monday to the next involves a vertical displacement.

### Reduplication

Adding meaning to a word through a specific type of repetition is called reduplication and is found in many languages throughout the world. For example, in the Philippine language Tagalog, future tense is marked by reduplication, as shown in Table 2.7.

A comparison of *sulat* ('write') and *susulat* ('will write') reveals that the initial consonant and vowel have been repeated at the beginning of the future form. Exactly the same can be said of the other future forms in Table 2.7. Repeating the initial consonant and vowel of *basa* at the beginning of the verb creates the future form *babasa*. Likewise, repeating the initial consonant and vowel of *ʔaral* at the beginning of the verb creates the future form *ʔaʔaral*.

To speakers of languages like English, which do not make systematic use of reduplication rules, the Tagalog future forms above might appear odd. In

---

[27] Some signers produce THURSDAY[WEEKLY] with an initial T handshape during the initial hold followed by an H handshape at the end of the sign. Others use an H throughout. This detail and the fact that SUNDAY[WEEKLY] is two-handed would also need to be accounted for as part of the frame analysis of these two signs.

fact, reduplication rules are a perfectly ordinary way to make complex words and they have grammatical effects equivalent to a prefix or suffix in a language like English. Just as English makes use of a large number of different prefixes and suffixes, a language with reduplication can make use of a large number of *different* reduplication rules. That is, there is more than one way to repeat things, and in a language with reduplication rules, there may be many distinct reduplication rules, each adding its specific meaning by its unique type of repetition.

Reduplication rules can go beyond simple repetitions of parts of the word undergoing the reduplication process. Spoken Thai presents a powerful illustration of the ability of a reduplication rule to produce novel forms. Thai is a tone language and each syllable in a Thai word has either a high, falling, mid, low, or rising tone associated with it. Thai has a number of reduplication rules, including one that produces a highly emphatic form of adjectives. Remarkably, this particular reduplication rule produces a sixth tone. This sixth extra-high tone appears in the emphatic, reduplicated, predicate adjectives, and nowhere else in the language (Haas 1945). This is a striking example of both the power of reduplication rules and the fact that grammatical forms can be marked by phonological features that are highly restricted. The sixth tone in Thai, for example, is restricted to words produced by this specific reduplication rule.

Certain ASL adverbial time signs can be reduplicated in a way that adds the meaning, 'every x', where *x* is a unit of time. Figure 2.26a illustrates the morphologically complex sign meaning 'two months'. It is composed of the bound root {MONTH} and the incorporated numeral morpheme {TWO}.

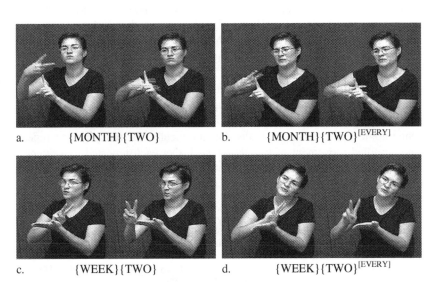

a.          {MONTH}{TWO}              b.          {MONTH}{TWO}[EVERY]

c.          {WEEK}{TWO}               d.          {WEEK}{TWO}[EVERY]

Figure 2.26 Unreduplicated signs and corresponding reduplicated forms

The sign {MONTH}{TWO}[EVERY] 'every two months' (Figure 2.26b) differs from the sign {MONTH}{TWO} 'two months', in that it is produced with shortened, repeated movements and the addition of nonmanual features. This reduplication pattern contributes the additional meaning to the sign.

The signs {WEEK}{TWO} 'two weeks' (Figure 2.26c) and {WEEK}{TWO}[EVERY] 'every two weeks' (Figure 2.26d) correspond in the same way. The sign meaning 'every two weeks' contains a movement like that in the sign meaning 'two weeks', but the movement is shortened and repeated. In addition, the pictures also illustrate the nonmanual differences between the non-reduplicated and the reduplicated forms. This reduplication paradigm includes signs expressing the meanings, 'everyday', 'every x weeks', 'every x months', and 'every x years'. The reduplicated forms involving weeks and months generally incorporate numeral morphemes ranging in value from one to nine, while the 'every x years' paradigm is generally limited to the values one and two.[28]

ASL has a large number of verbs and adjectives with reduplicated forms marking aspect (Fischer 1973, Klima and Bellugi 1979). Verbs marked to express a temporal contour (e.g. duration, frequency, manner, repetitiveness) are said to express aspectual information in addition to the lexical meaning of the verb or adjective. The verb LOOK-AT, for example, is normally produced as shown in Figure 2.27a. The aspectually related verb LOOK-AT[INCESSANT] in Figure 2.27b has short repeated movements and expresses the meaning 'look incessantly' (Klima and Bellugi 1979). Note that it is not preceded by a prefix, nor followed by a suffix. Instead, it is easily recognizable as resulting from a reduplication rule. Although it might appear to be multiple instances of LOOK-AT, this is also not the case. The individual movements are shorter and more tense than the single movement producing LOOK-AT. As a result, each individual movement is different from the movement in LOOK-AT. That the individual movements are not producing LOOK-AT is even more apparent in its durational and iterative forms (Figure 2.27c, d), where the hand's movements are no longer straight. Thus, although the reduplication rules discussed here produce multiple movements, the reduplicated forms are single signs.

In sum, the reduplication rule that produces the incessant form has both phonological and semantic effects. Phonologically, the reduplication repeats the modified movement of LOOK-AT such that each repeated movement is shorter and more tense than the original movement. This rule adds the meaning

---

[28] I treat all four of the reduplicated forms as derived lexical units (Liddell 1996b). Evidence for this comes from the signs meaning 'everyday' and 'every x years'. The former appears to have been derived from a reduplicated form of TOMORROW, but has undergone historical changes that blur its connection to that sign. The reduplicated forms meaning 'every x years', where *x* can be either one or two, are derived from the signs {YEAR-FUTURE}{ONE} and {YEAR-FUTURE}{TWO}. Although the base forms mean 'next year' and 'two years from now', the meanings of the derived, reduplicated forms, however, do not include any future meaning.

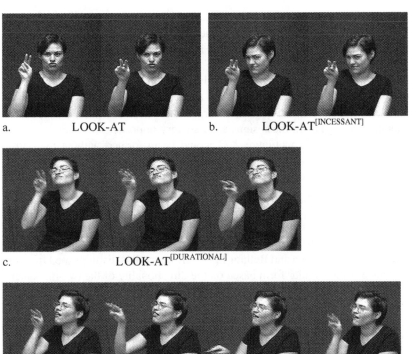

a.              LOOK-AT              b.              LOOK-AT[INCESSANT]

c.                    LOOK-AT[DURATIONAL]

d.                    LOOK-AT[ITERATIVE]

Figure 2.27 Reduplication used as a part of aspect marking on ASL verbs

'incessantly'. Note that these reduplicated forms also tend to appear with specific nonmanual signals, including specific facial expressions as well as head
positions and movements.

Some rules that add aspectual meanings in ASL involve both internal changes
to the form of signs as well as reduplication. That is, the repeated movements
of the hand in a reduplicated form may differ significantly from the movement
of the hand in producing the citation form of the sign. LOOK-AT[DURATIONAL]
(Figure 2.27c) is produced by small repeated circular movements, with the hand
higher on the outward movements and lower on the return.

The individual repeated movements differ from the single straight movement
found in the citation form. Producing these aspectual forms requires changing
the nature of the individual movements and also repeating the changed forms
in specific ways. Thus, for analytical purposes, it is useful to think of the
grammatical process that adds durational meaning as involving two distinct

steps. The first step involves a frame analysis similar to that described for the unrealized inceptive aspect. The frame will produce the required movements of the correct shape. The second step is reduplication in order to produce the proper movement sequences.

The iterative form (Figure 2.27d) differs from the durational form (Figure 2.27c) in both the size and shape of the repeated movements. The outward movement of the iterative form is larger and the return path is deeper. The nonmanual signals in these signs are also very important. It is fair to say that the aspectual forms in Figure 2.27 would be ill-formed without the correct nonmanual signals.

### Numerosity

### Dual and trial verb forms

The dual verb form is similar to two executions of the singular form (Supalla and Newport 1978, Klima and Bellugi 1979). However, it is distinguished from two instances of a singular form based on the directionality of the two movements and the lack of repetition of each directional movement in the dual form. That is, Supalla and Newport (1978) report that even if the non-dual form of the sign has inherent repetition, each of the two movements of the dual form will not have that repetition.

<pre>
                        t
</pre>
(11)    SISTER, BROTHER ASK-QUESTION[DUAL]
        I asked my sister and brother. (Padden 1988:32, example 15)

In ASL, a nonmanual signal consisting of a slight backward tilt of the head together with raised brows is used to mark topics in ASL (Liddell 1977, 1980). In (11) the first two signs, SISTER and BROTHER, are marked as a topic by that nonmanual signal, indicated by *t*. Since the line extends over both SISTER and BROTHER, the signer has indicated that the topic consists of both signs. The topic is followed by ASK-QUESTION[DUAL]. In this context, the sister and brother would be understood to be the ones asked. Figure 2.28 illustrates how

Figure 2.28 ASK-QUESTION[DUAL]

Figure 2.29  A simultaneous two-handed dual form of ASK-QUESTION

ASK-QUESTION[DUAL] could be produced in this case. The initial outward movement is directed toward a location slightly to the right of center. The hand then returns part way back and slightly to the right, then makes a second, shorter outward movement to the right of the initial location. The second movement of this sign is smaller than the first.

Padden (1988) describes another type of dual form produced by the simultaneous movement of both hands. An example of this form is illustrated in Figure 2.29. Here the activity of each hand could constitute a complete independent sign. Note that such a form is only possible in a modality where there are two independent articulators.

Klima and Bellugi (1979) report that some signers also use a trial form in which the movement of the verb is carried out three times in three different directions.

### Multiple and exhaustive verb forms

In addition to verb forms expressing dual number, ASL also has verb forms expressing actions toward larger numbers of entities. I will focus here on the multiple and exhaustive forms.[29]

The citation form of ASK-QUESTION is produced with a single, straight outward movement, illustrated in Figure 2.30a. ASK-QUESTION[MULTIPLE] in Figure 2.30b is a morphologically complex sign that signifies asking many people and treats the asking as a single event (Klima and Bellugi 1979:283).

Klima and Bellugi describe the motion of this sign as a "sweep along an arc" (p. 283). It is useful for analytical purposes, however, to divide the movement of the multiple verb form into an outward movement and a sideward movement. In ASL there is a general lack of sharp angles in the production of signs or sequences of signs. That is, it appears that potential sharp angles are generally smoothed out by the phonology. As a result, the outward and sideward movements have an arc-shaped transition, giving the impression of a single arc rather than two separate movements.

---

[29]  Klima and Bellugi (1979) treat these forms as inflections for grammatical number.

a.      ASK-QUESTION

b.                  ASK-QUESTION[MULTIPLE]

Figure 2.30 The singular form of ASK-QUESTION and the corresponding multiple form

Figure 2.31 GIVE[EXHAUSTIVE]

GIVE[EXHAUSTIVE] is illustrated in Figure 2.31. Note that it also begins with an outward movement. Instead of being followed by a smooth sideward horizontal movement, it contains multiple reduced outward movements as the hand moves along the sideward path.

As with the multiple form, the exhaustive form is also first directed outward, followed by a sideward component. Klima and Bellugi describe the exhaustive

a. the multiple path     b. the exhaustive path

Figure 2.32 The paths and shapes of multiple and exhaustive verb forms

form as "multiple iterations – numerous articulations of the verb – along an arc in the indexic plane, with successive articulations displaced laterally" (p. 284). Fridman (1994) makes a convincing case that during the sideward component of GIVE[EXHAUSTIVE] the hand performs an oscillating (in-and-out) movement, rather than repeated articulations of the verb. The oscillating movement is easiest to see with a verb like ASK-QUESTION[EXHAUSTIVE], where the oscillation is limited to the bending of the index finger, rather than the movement of the whole hand. When the configuration of the finger (e.g. straight versus bent) serves as the basis for the oscillating movement, the path of the hand is smooth. When the configuration of the wrist (e.g. contracted versus straight) serves as the basis for the oscillating movement, the path of the hand appears to move along repeated arcs. It is the repeated oscillating movement of the wrist that gives the impression of in-and-out movements as the hand moves along its sideward path.

Both the exhaustive and the multiple verb forms express plural non-first person arguments. Klima and Bellugi describe the difference in meaning between these two forms as related to the degree to which the verb focuses on individual acts expressed by the verb, with the exhaustive form putting more focus on individual acts.

Formationally, exhaustive verb forms are similar to multiple verb forms in that both begin with a single outward directional movement followed by a sideward movement. They differ in the nature of the sideward movements. The multiple verb forms make a smooth sideward movement without oscillation. For the exhaustive verb forms, the sideward movement is carried out with repeated small oscillating movements. The differences and similarities between these two forms can be seen in Figure 2.32.

Both verb forms express plurality (e.g. plural recipients of questions, plural recipients of things given, etc.). The sideward path created by these two forms may be directed in an apparently unlimited number of ways, depending on the location of the entities it is directed toward.

### Inflection versus derivation

Linguists typically divide grammatical processes producing complex words into two distinct categories: inflection and derivation. The distinction between the two is generally said to revolve around the degree to which grammatical relationships are being encoded by the process.[30] Inflection tends to signal grammatical relationships and does so without changing the grammatical category of the inflected word. In English, for example, the differences between the uninflected *walk* in (12), and *walks* and *walking* in (13)–(14) are considered to be due to inflection.

(12)     I walk.

(13)     He walks.

(14)     He is walking.

In (13), *walks* is considered to be an inflected form of *walk*, with the suffix signifying agreement with the third person singular subject. It is not considered a new word requiring an additional dictionary entry. The same is said of *walking* in (14).

(15)     Ever since the accident, Sue can only get around using a walker.

The word *walker* in (15), however, is distinct from the word *walk*. It is a noun rather than a verb. Whenever a morphological process creates a word of a different category (i.e. noun, verb, adjective, etc.) the grammatical process responsible for creating the new word is said to be derivational. The distinction between inflection and derivation, however, is not always this clear. All prefixes in English, for example, are said to be derivational. Thus, the difference between *happy* and *unhappy* is said to be a derivational difference. Even though both words are adjectives, they are treated as separate words, each with its own meaning. This makes sense when you consider the meaning of *unhappy*. If the prefix *un-* were simply a negating prefix, then *unhappy* and *not happy* ought to mean essentially the same thing. However, *unhappy* and *not happy* have different meanings. The meaning of *unhappy* is more closely aligned with sadness. The phrase *not happy* could be used to describe a larger set of emotional states than merely sadness.

With the exception of compounds, which clearly form new words, the ASL literature generally assumes that morphological changes in ASL are inflectional. I will briefly consider an argument in favor of inflection put forward by Klima and Bellugi (1979). In describing what appears to be SICK[DURATIONAL], they consider whether or not its circular movement is an optional expressive change or a morphological change (1979:252). They argue that the SICK[DURATIONAL] rather than SICK is required under certain specifiable linguistic contexts. For example, SICK[DURATIONAL] makes sense in (16) and the result is judged as

---

[30] Bybee (1985) suggests that rather than the two separate categories *inflection* and *derivation*, there is a continuum with clear cases on both ends and fuzzy cases in the middle.

grammatical. If SICK[DURATIONAL] is replaced by SICK, the result is not acceptable, as shown in (17).[31]

(16)    BOY TEND-(POSS) UP-TO-NOW SICK[DURATIONAL]
        That boy has tended to be sickly all his life.

(17)    * BOY TEND-(POSS) UP-TO-NOW SICK
        That boy has tended to be sick all his life.

Klima and Bellugi suggest that, "Perhaps failing to modulate the sign is analogous to omitting the past tense marker in the sentence *Yesterday the boy jump*, which is of course perfectly understandable, yet not grammatical in English" (p. 253). They conclude that SICK[DURATIONAL] is not simply an "emotive expression," but is rather an inflection. Using similar criteria, they also treat the multiple verb form as inflectional.

If there were only two choices (emotive expression and inflection), then the fact that certain contexts require the multiple form would certainly argue in favor of inflection and against emotive expression. Let us accept Klima and Bellugi's demonstration that a grammatical process lies behind the durative and multiple verb forms, thus eliminating emotive expression as an option. This still leaves at least three possibilities: inflection, derivation, or indeterminate (somewhere in between inflection and derivation).

The evidence for the inflectional status of the multiple verb form provided by Klima and Bellugi is merely suggestive. They note that "The uninflected form of the verb cannot be used in ASL when the object of a verb is multiple in number (unless it is a collective noun in ASL, such as GROUP, or CLASS)." They provide the following examples of grammatical use of the multiple verb form.

(18)    HOMEWORK, TEACHER GIVE[MULTIPLE]
        The teacher gave out homework to them.

(19)    MAN, (ME) ASK[MULTIPLE]
        I asked the men.

These examples, however, do not provide evidence for inflection as opposed to derivation. If the intention is to show number agreement between a plural object and the plural (multiple) verb form, then these examples fall short. In (18), there is no overt object to agree with, and in (19) the topic MAN is unmarked for number.

The fact that the multiple form is required in a specific grammatical context does not distinguish between inflection and derivation. That is, it is not

---

[31] Klima and Bellugi present this as a predispositional inflection on SICK. I am treating it here as a durational form of SICK.

difficult to find a grammatical context in English requiring a derivational form. In (20), for example, the derivation suffix *-ly* is attached to *friend*, producing the adjective *friendly*. Without the derivational suffix, the sentence would be ungrammatical (* *He is a very friend person*).

(20)    He is a very friendly person.

Thus, the case for inflection is not convincing. In analyzing similar forms in Swedish Sign Language, Bergman and Dahl (1994) question the appropriateness of describing such forms as inflectional. They base their hesitance to look at number marking such as the multiple form of ASL verbs as inflection on several different criteria (p. 409). First, they note that the way plurality is marked in sign languages is lexically dependent. That is, the means of marking plurality differs from one verb to the next. Second, the marking of plurality is not simply plural or not. There are a number of different plural distinctions. Finally, cases like the English, *The scissors are on the table*, show that the plural form *are* agrees with its grammatically plural subject. This occurs in spite of the fact that a pair of scissors is one thing rather than two things. Bergman and Dahl note that there are no such cases in the sign language literature. They also note that, from a semantic perspective, the kind of information encoded by number marking in sign languages does "not fit well with aspect as an inflectional category in other languages" (p. 409). They conclude that these forms are not inflectional. In fact, Bergman and Dahl go on to conclude that Swedish Sign Language is "basically an inflection-less language with a very well-developed ideophonic morphology" (p. 418).[32]

Much of this book is devoted to issues surrounding the directional use of signs in ASL. Directing verbs toward physically present referents as well as to abstract locations in space has been claimed to be a type of grammatical inflection called *verb agreement* (Padden 1988). I will be arguing that directing verbs in space has nothing to do with an agreement process and is not inflectional. If correct, this eliminates the strongest candidate for an inflectional process in ASL and raises Bergman and Dahl's question for ASL as well. Are there any bona fide inflectional processes in the grammar of ASL?

## Syntax

### Nonmanual signals

In the early to mid-1970s, many linguists argued that ASL had a very flexible ordering of its signs in the production of sentences. Friedman (1976), for

---

[32] Addressing the issues surrounding ideophonic morphology would take us well outside the scope of this introductory chapter.

example, argued that word order had no grammatical significance and that the order of constituents such as subject and object was essentially random. Fischer (1975) claimed that ASL was basically an SVO language. However, she also claimed that there was considerable flexibility in the ordering of subjects and objects. The flexibility existed if the grammatical relationships could be determined based on the meaning of the verb and the participants in the situation. Thus in (21) where either the mother or the father could love the other, word order had to be SVO. In (22), we understand that houses cannot buy people, and thus, according to Fischer's analysis, the ordering of subjects, verbs, and objects is freer.

(21)     MOTHER LOVE FATHER
         Mother loves father.

(22)     RECENTLY MOTHER BUY HOUSE
         My mother just bought a house.

There were at least two reasons for the controversy surrounding word order. First, the earliest attempts at understanding ASL syntax followed techniques used with the analysis of vocally produced languages. Researchers recorded the signs produced and the orders in which they were produced. At that time it was not yet known that specific facial expressions, head positions, and head movements also make up part of ASL sentences. The incomplete data that linguists were dealing with gave the impression that signs could appear in almost any order in sentences. Secondly, many signs can be directed in space. The information added by the directionality was believed to make a fixed word order unnecessary (Friedman 1976).

Signers' faces are generally quite animated while they sign. In the early 1970s, such facial expressions were largely believed to be expressions of affect. At that time I heard statements that Deaf people were simply more expressive than a typical hearing non-signer. This misperception of the significance of facial expressions, however, meant that facial expressions had been ignored in the analysis of sentence structure.[33] This is precisely how I began my research into ASL syntax in 1974. I transcribed each sign in videotaped utterances then looked for syntactic patterns. I found subjects appearing before and after the verb. I also found objects appearing before and after the verb. Initially it seemed that, indeed, ASL sentence structure was quite flexible. Below I have placed a few examples of what the incomplete data looked like at the time.

---

[33] Without being explicit about the nature of the facial expressions themselves, Stokoe *et al.* (1965:275–276) observe the importance of facial expression and juncture in correctly producing yes–no questions. They observe that hearing adults who omit such signals get no responses from Deaf addressees because they have not produced an utterance recognizable as a yes–no question.

(23)      DOG CHASE CAT (subject verb object)

(24)      CAT DOG CHASE (object subject verb)

(25)      CHASE CAT PRO (verb object subject)

In (23) the subject is in initial position. In (24) the subject is in the middle after the object, and in (25) the subject (a pronoun referring to the dog) is in final position. The verb CHASE appears in the middle, end, and beginning in (23)–(25). The object CAT appears in the end, beginning, and middle in (23)–(25). Strings of signs like these gave the clear impression of extreme flexibility of word ordering in ASL.

While I was looking at word order issues, I also began looking to see how relative clauses were formed in ASL. Restrictive relative clauses are syntactic structures used to provide information that helps identify whatever entity or entities are being talked about. In (26), the English relative clause *who left early* identifies the man I am talking about by the fact that he left early.

(26)      The man *who left early* had to catch a plane.

I devised a story involving several unnamed characters and asked signers to read the story, remember it, then retell it later in ASL. By not naming the characters, I was hoping that signers would produce ASL relative clauses (if they existed). The signers did in fact produce relative clauses, but it was not obvious that they had done so at the time. It seemed to me that facial expression was playing some kind of significant role in the signing I was seeing, but looking at moving video images made it too difficult to see what was going on. In order to get a better idea of what signers were doing, I "froze" the video as each sign was produced and took photographs of the television monitor. Laying those photographs out side by side revealed a very important fact about ASL syntax. It turns out that a specific combination of facial features and head position constitute a grammatical marker for relative clauses (Liddell 1978).

The marking for a restrictive relative clause in ASL consists of raised eyebrows, a backward tilt of the head, and contraction of the muscles that raise both the cheeks and the upper lip. It is significant that all these nonmanual features can be found in each of the first four photographs in Figure 2.33. The nonmanual

|  |  |  |  | r |  |
| --- | --- | --- | --- | --- | --- |
| RECENTLY | DOG | CHASE | CAT | COME | HOME |

Figure 2.33 A relative clause followed by the verb phrase COME HOME

signal begins with RECENTLY and continues through the next three signs, ending with CAT. Not only does the nonmanual signal mark the grammatical function (e.g. relative clause), it also is co-present with all the signs in the relative clause. Thus, it also identifies which specific words make up the relative clause.

### Topics and main clauses

Once I was able to identify the nonmanual signal marking relative clauses, I was able to identify others quickly. One of the most important nonmanual signals for solving the word order issue in ASL was the identification of the nonmanual signal marking topics (Liddell 1977). This nonmanual signal can be found in (27).

$$\overline{\qquad\qquad}^{t}$$

(27)     MY CAT DOG CHASE
         My cat, the dog chased it.

The phrase MY CAT serves as the topic, marked by the nonmanual signal $\underline{t}$. DOG identifies the animal doing the chasing. An ASL topic is structurally separate from the clause that follows it. The separation can be demonstrated by observing where other syntactic nonmanual signals can appear. For example, a side-to-side headshake with a negative facial expression forms a nonmanual signal that can negate a clause (Liddell 1977). Just as the nonmanual signal marking topics accompanies all the signs in the topic, the negating nonmanual signal accompanies all the signs in the clause being negated. Example (28) is well-formed since the nonmanual signal includes all the signs in the clause.[34] But (29) is ill-formed since the nonmanual signal ends too soon.

$$\overline{\qquad\qquad\qquad\qquad}^{n}$$

(29)     WOMAN FORGET PURSE
         It is not the case that the woman forgot the purse.

$$\overline{\qquad\qquad\quad}^{n}$$

(29)     * WOMAN FORGET PURSE
         It is not the case that the woman forgot the purse.

The negating headshake will not co-occur with a topic. Attempting to produce both at the same time results in ungrammaticality, as in (30). This type of evidence demonstrates that the topic is not part of the main clause (Liddell 1980).

---

[34] Aarons et al. (1992) also describe a type of nonmanual negation beginning with the verb and continuing to the end of the clause. Neither type of marking permits the negating nonmanual signal to end prior to the end of the sentence.

<pre>                                    n
        _____
               t
        _____</pre>

(30)    * WOMAN FORGET PURSE
        It is not the case that the woman forgot the purse.

In generative treatments of topics in ASL, it is assumed that the constituent that
will become the topic first appears in its normal syntactic position as subject or
object. A rule then moves the topic out of the main clause to its sentence-initial
topic position (Fischer 1975, Liddell 1980, Aarons 1994). But ASL sentences
can have topics that are neither subjects nor objects (Coulter 1979).

<pre>             t
        _____</pre>

(31)    MEAT PRO-1 LIKE LAMB                     (Coulter 1979:28)
        As for meat, I prefer lamb.

<pre>                   t
        _____</pre>

(32)    VEGETABLE JOHN PREFER CORN    (Aarons 1994:147)
        As for vegetables, John prefers corn.

Topics like MEAT in (31) and VEGETABLE in (32) cannot have been moved
from an underlying object position, since these positions are filled by LAMB
and CORN. There are no other positions available in the syntactic structure. As
a result, even in generative treatments, some topics must begin as topics in the
underlying structure. The generative conclusion is that there are two types of
topics (Aarons 1994). Some are "base generated," meaning that they are topics
at all possible levels of representation. Others are "derived topics," meaning that
at the "deepest" level they are not topics, but at the "surface" level, they have
become topics. Thus, (27) [repeated here] would be analyzed as O (topicalized)
SV. For topics that do not have a subject or object relation with the verb, they
are (and always were) topics.

<pre>             t
        _____</pre>

(27)    MY CAT DOG CHASE
        My cat, the dog chased it.

In cognitive grammar there are no movement rules. Within this theoretical
perspective there are no derived topics. All topics are simply topics. To see how
this analysis works in the case of the ASL data, it is first necessary to look
at the ability to leave out overt arguments (i.e. subject and object) under the
right discourse conditions. Suppose, for example, we consider parallel situations
involving three different languages. In each case, a person receives a compliment
on a new hat. Examples (33)–(35) illustrate possible responses from an English
speaker, a Thai speaker, and an ASL signer.

(33)       Thanks, my mother just bought it.

(34)    khopkhun, mɛ̂ɛ súʉhâi mʉ̂akíi níi ɛɛŋ
        thank you mother buy for recently this only
        Thank you, my mother just bought it for me.

(35)    THANK-YOU, MOTHER RECENTLY BUY
        Thank you, mother recently bought it.

The English response in (33) uses the pronoun *it* to refer to the hat. The Thai response in (34) does not mention the hat and also does not mention who the hat was bought for (i.e. there is no overt object of the preposition *hâi*). The ASL response in (35) also does not mention the hat. Since the speaker does not mention the hat in both the Thai and ASL examples, it is up to the addressee to determine what the mother bought. It turns out to be a pretty simple task. The hat was already mentioned in the compliment that prompted the response. This makes the hat very prominent in the discourse. If we assume that the Thai speaker and the signer are both responding to a compliment about the hat, it follows that they are still talking about a hat. Since the hat is the only entity mentioned in the discourse capable of being bought, then the hat must have been the thing the mother bought.

Examples like (33)–(35) demonstrate a difference between languages like English that expect subjects and objects to be mentioned and languages like Thai and ASL that freely omit subjects and objects if the things being talked about are already prominent in the discourse.

We can now return to example (27), repeated below.

                 _____t
(27)    MY CAT DOG CHASE
        My cat, the dog chased it.

I propose that the function of the topic marking on MY CAT is to make the cat prominent in the discourse. I am not talking about the signs MY CAT being prominent in the discourse. Rather, I am talking about the entity being described by the signs being prominent in the discourse. If that entity, the cat, was not yet a part of the discourse, then mentioning MY CAT as a topic would make it prominent. If the cat was already part of the discourse, then mentioning the cat again as the topic in (27) would certainly make the cat prominent. In either case, the topic phrase MY CAT would make the cat as prominent in the discourse as the hat in the previous examples. That is, when someone makes a compliment about a nice hat, the hat is very prominent in the discourse at that time. As a result, a signer is able to create a sentence without mentioning the hat, as in (35). In that example the verb BUY is used without mentioning the object [THANK-YOU, MOTHER RECENTLY BUY]. I am proposing that (27) works in exactly the same way. I compare these two utterances in Table 2.8.

Table 2.8 *Events making entities prominent in the discourse and the subsequent lack of need to make overt mention of those entities*

| Event | Following clause with an unmentioned object |
|---|---|
| Receive a compliment about a hat | THANK-YOU, MOTHER RECENTLY BUY ___ |
| Produce the topic MY CAT | DOG CHASE ___ |

The two events listed in Table 2.8 make the things mentioned (the hat and the cat) prominent in the discourse. Since they are both prominent, sentences about them will not need to mention them. Thus, given that the hat is prominent, the statement MOTHER RECENTLY BUY is easy to understand. MOTHER is mentioned prior to the verb. This is where subjects appear. Nothing is mentioned after the transitive verb BUY. The addressee must therefore select some entity from the discourse context as the thing bought. It is clearly the hat – the most recently mentioned thing in the discourse. We can look at DOG CHASE in exactly the same way. This time the signer introduces the cat into the discourse by means of the phrase MY CAT, marked as a topic. Having done so, there is no need to mention the cat in the following clause. Suppose instead, the signer had produced a different order of signs, as in (36).

<pre>
           t
</pre>
(36)    MY CAT CHASE DOG
        My cat, it chased the dog.

Like (27) this utterance begins with the topic MY CAT. This topic is followed by a clause that also contains the signs DOG and CHASE. This time, however, DOG *follows* CHASE. This order difference has significance. As in the earlier example, the topic prominently introduces that cat into the discourse, followed by the clause CHASE DOG. We know that subjects precede the verb and objects follow the verb. Since DOG follows CHASE, it must be the object. There is no subject preceding CHASE. The addressee must therefore select some entity from the discourse context as the thing that did the chasing. The cat was the most recently introduced entity in the discourse. This makes selecting the cat as the animal that did the chasing quite simple.

In 1977, I proposed that the topic was structurally separate from the following clause, but that the topic still bore a grammatical relationship to the verb in that following clause. The analysis I have just proposed still maintains the structural separation of the topic, but it no longer maintains that the topic bears a grammatical relationship (subject or object) in the following clause. That is, a topic is just a topic. It mentions some entity that is going to be important in what follows. Exactly how it is going to be important has to be worked out by the addressee.

sketch of the grammar of ASL

*Subject pronoun tags*[35]

There is one final grammatical construction that must be described in order to complete the summary of the ordering of subjects, objects, and topics. ASL has a construction in which a clause is followed by a pronoun coreferential with the verb's subject (Liddell 1977, 1980). In (37), for example, the two signs BOY FALL produce a simple statement about a boy. Note that the subject BOY precedes the verb FALL. Example (38) is like (37) except that it includes a subject pronoun tag with an accompanying head nod (*hn*), making (38) more emphatic than (37). Note that the subject pronoun tag is not serving as the subject of the verb. It is a pronoun coreferential with the subject, placed at the end of the sentence to make the statement more emphatic.

(37)    BOY FALL
        The boy fell down.

                                  _hn_
(38)    BOY FALL PRO
        The boy fell down, he did.

Recall that subjects or objects can be omitted if the entities named by the subject or object are already prominent in the discourse. For example, if someone mentions that particular boy is limping and asks for an explanation, (39) could serve as a brief reply. Since the question is about the boy, there is no need to produce BOY as the subject of FALL. One could make (39) more emphatic by adding a subject pronoun tag at the end.

(39)    FALL
        He fell down.

                                  _hn_
(40)    FALL PRO
        He fell down, he did.

Before the subject pronoun tag was distinguished from the subject of a verb in ASL, examples like (40) made it appear that subjects could be ordered after verbs. However, as (41) and (42) demonstrate, sentences with a non-pronominal subject after the verb are ungrammatical.

(41)    * SWIM BOY
        The boy is swimming.

(42)    * FALL BOY
        The boy fell.

[35] When I introduced this analysis in 1977, I talked about pronouns coreferential with the subject appearing after a clause. Aarons (1994) describes these and similar constructions as tags. I am adopting Aaron's use of the term "tag" in referring to these pronouns as subject pronoun tags.

Table 2.9 *Understanding constituent ordering by distinguishing topics, main clauses, and subject pronoun tags*

|  | Main clause | | | |
|---|---|---|---|---|
| Topic | subject | verb | object | Subject pronoun tag |
|  | MOTHER | RECENTLY | BUY | |
| MY CAT (t) | | CHASE | DOG | |
| MY CAT (t) | DOG | CHASE | | |
| | BOY | FALL | | PRO (hn) |
| | BOY | FALL | | |
| | | FALL | | PRO (hn) |

Table 2.9 includes most of the examples discussed above. Each of the examples is divided into topic, main clause, and subject pronoun tag. An examination of those examples demonstrates that the ordering of subjects and objects within the main clause in ASL is very strict. When subjects are present they precede the verb. When objects are present they follow the verb. It is very difficult to find exceptions to this generalization. Subjects and objects may be omitted if the entities that would be described by the subject or object are already prominent in the discourse. The entity might be prominent because it was just mentioned by someone else, or it could be prominent because the signer has been discussing it or has just mentioned it as a topic.

In Table 2.9, topics precede the main clause and subject pronoun tags follow the main clause. Within the main clause, either a subject precedes the verb or it is omitted. Similarly, either an object follows the verb or it is omitted. The ordering of grammatical elements within the main clause is extremely strict. By now it should be clear that it would be next to impossible to make sense of the ordering of constituents in ASL without attending to nonmanual signals.

### Transitivity

Verbs that can accept a direct object are transitive. Verbs that cannot are intransitive. In English, direct objects normally appear directly after the verb. In (43) the English verbs *tell*, *hate*, and *want*, all accept direct objects (italicized), and are therefore, transitive.

(43)    a. I told *a lie.*
        b. I hate *sad movies.*
        c. I want *a piece of pie.*

Some English verbs, such as those in (44a) and (45a), will not accept a direct object. Attempting to place a direct object after the verb, as in (44b) and (45b) results in ungrammaticality. Thus, the English verbs *fall* and *meditate* are intransitive.

(44)  a.  The apple fell.
      b.  * The apple fell the ground.

(45)  a.  The man meditated.
      b.  * The man meditated his worries.

In (46) and (47) prepositional phrases follow the verbs *fall* and *meditate* and the results are grammatical. However, these verbs are still intransitive. In (46) *the ground* is the object of the preposition *to*, not the object of the verb *fall*. Similarly, in (47) *his worries* is the object of the preposition *about*.

(46)  The apple fell to the ground.

(47)  The man meditated about his worries.

Decisions about transitivity are similar in ASL.

(48)  PRO-1 WANT CANDY.
      I want some candy.

(49)  * PRO-1 STARE CANDY.
      I stared at the candy.

In (48) WANT takes CANDY as its direct object. The verb STARE in (49), however, will not accept CANDY as a direct object.[36] This syntactic difference demonstrates that WANT is transitive and STARE is intransitive.

Some ASL verbs present a puzzle with respect to transitivity. These are verbs that are semantically transitive but syntactically intransitive. A good example of this type of verb is ENJOY. The meaning of ENJOY in (50) and (51) is clearly transitive. Both statements mean to say that the signer enjoyed the movie.

                _____t
(50)  THAT MOVIE PRO-1 ENJOY
      That movie, I enjoyed it. (* I enjoyed myself.)

                _____t
(51)  THAT MOVIE GOOD. PRO-1 ENJOY.
      That movie, it was good. I enjoyed it. (* I enjoyed myself.)

In spite of this semantic transitivity, it is difficult to find an acceptable sentence with an overt object following ENJOY. Given a choice between (52),

[36] In (49), the gloss STARE is used for a sign similar to LOOK-AT, but with no path movement.

where MOVIE follows ENJOY, and (53) with no overt object, signers strongly prefer (53).

(52)      ?? LAST-NIGHT PRO-1 ENJOY MOVIE
          Last night I enjoyed a movie.

(53)      LAST-NIGHT PRO-1 SEE MOVIE. ENJOY.
          Last night I saw a movie. I enjoyed it.

Verbs marked for aspect behave the same way. Example (54) demonstrates that EAT is a transitive verb. The object TOMATO appears after the verb resulting in a fully acceptable sentence. However, the durational form of EAT does not permit an overt object after the verb, as (55) illustrates (Liddell 1980). With TOMATO as a topic, however, the sentence is fully acceptable. This data is parallel to the examples above with the sign ENJOY.

(54)      GIRL EAT TOMATO
          The girl ate a tomato.

(55)      * GIRL EAT$^{[DURATIONAL]}$ TOMATO
          The girl was eating tomatoes for a long time.

$$\overline{\phantom{xxxxxxxx}t}$$
(56)      TOMATO GIRL EAT$^{[DURATIONAL]}$
          The tomatoes, the girl was eating them for a long time.

For some theories of grammar, the concept of a transitive verb that will not allow an object is contradictory. That is, in generative theories, the semantic component of the grammar interprets a syntactic representation. If there is no object in the syntactic representation, the semantic component has no object to interpret. This is not true within cognitive grammar (Langacker 1991). In cognitive grammar there are no syntactic representations. Grammatical representations, regardless of the size and complexity of the representation, are composed of a pairing of form and meaning, which Langacker refers to as the *phonological pole* and the *semantic pole*. Transitive verbs include a semantic subject that Langacker calls the *trajector*, and a semantic object called the *landmark*. For a verb like EAT, the trajector and landmark will be highly schematic and unelaborated. They represent the entity doing the eating and the thing being eaten. The noun GIRL could become the overt subject provided that two things happen. First, the phonological pole of GIRL would need to combine with the phonological pole of EAT. This would occur by placing the phonological pole of GIRL ahead of the phonological pole of EAT, as a separate sign. Secondly, the semantic pole of GIRL would have to combine with the semantic pole of EAT. This takes place by linking the semantic pole of GIRL with the trajector of EAT. In Langacker's terms, the semantic pole of GIRL *elaborates* the trajector. As a result, the combination GIRL EAT produces an ordered phonological sequence and a semantic representation in which a girl (rather than some schematic thing) eats something.

A similar process combines TOMATO with the complex unit GIRL EAT to produce GIRL EAT TOMATO. This would add the phonological pole of TOMATO after the phonological unit GIRL EAT.[37] The semantic pole of TOMATO elaborates the landmark. In the resulting semantic structure, the girl (the elaborated trajector) eats the tomato (the elaborated landmark).

For signs such as ENJOY and aspectually marked forms of transitive verbs, the verbs would still contain a landmark as part of their semantic representations, but would be unable to elaborate them by means of an overt object following the verb. They would need to be elaborated by associating some entity in the discourse context with the landmark.

Let me first illustrate the elaboration of a landmark with the transitive verb SELL. This verb accepts an overt object, as shown in (57). In this case the landmark of SELL would be elaborated by the semantic pole of its object, POSS-1 CAR 'my car'.

(57)    PRO-1 SELL POSS-1 CAR
        I sold my car.

$$\overline{\qquad\qquad t}$$
(58)    POSS-1 CAR PRO-1 SELL
        My car, I sold it.

In (58), the signer makes the car prominent in the discourse context by overtly marking it as a topic. This is followed by the clause, PRO-1 SELL, which contains no overt object. It becomes the addressee's task to elaborate the landmark of SELL by linking it with a conceptual entity already in the discourse context. Since the topic POSS-1 CAR introduces an abstract entity with the characteristic 'my car', as a topic, selecting that entity to elaborate the landmark of SELL is straightforward. Although accomplished by selecting the meaning from the context, the semantic result is the same as that in (57), where the landmark of SELL was elaborated by the semantic pole of POSS-1 CAR.

(59)    PRO-1 SELL
        I sold it.

The statement in (59) would make a good response to the question, $\overline{\text{POSSCARWHERE}}^{\text{wh-q}}$ 'Where is your car?'. The only difference between (58) and (59)

---

[37] In cognitive grammar there is no significance to the order in which symbolic units are assembled. The example in the text could also be conceived of as being assembled by first combining EAT and TOMATO, then later combining GIRL and EAT TOMATO.

is how the car came to be prominent in the discourse. In (58) the signer makes it prominent by overtly mentioning it as a topic. In (59) someone else makes it prominent by asking a question about it. In either case, the addressee is faced with interpreting the meaning of PRO-1 SELL. In both cases, this is done by elaborating the landmark of SELL with the conceptual representation of the particular car being talked about.

I have just described three options for elaborating the landmark of a transitive verb:

a. an overt direct object following the verb
b. a topic
c. some entity already introduced into the discourse (by the signer or someone else)

ENJOY and aspectually marked transitive verbs only have two of the three options available to them. Although *a* is not possible for these verbs, their landmarks can still be elaborated by *b* and *c*.

The general inability of aspectual verb forms to occur with an overt object poses a problem. The problem is that in order to be able to use an aspectual verb form meaningfully, the entity to elaborate the landmark must already be prominent in the discourse. That is, if one wanted to express that someone was typing a term paper all night long, and the term paper was not already prominent in the discourse, (60) would not be a possible way to express that information.

(60)    * POSS-1 FRIEND TYPE[DURATIONAL] T-E-R-M PAPER
        ALL-NIGHT.
        My friend was (intensively) typing her term paper all night.

The problem is that TYPE[DURATIONAL] cannot be followed by an overt object. Given this restriction, signers need a way to make the thing typed prominent. A typical means of doing so is shown in (61).

(61)    POSS-1 FRIEND TYPE T-E-R-M PAPER. TYPE[DURATIONAL]
        ALL-NIGHT.
        My friend typed her term paper. She was typing it all night.[38]

The solution in (61) appears to involve two clauses. In the first, the simple verb TYPE is followed by a direct object. This introduces the term paper into the discourse. The next clause TYPE[DURATIONAL] ALL-NIGHT elaborates the description of the typing by including the aspectual information and the adverb ALL-NIGHT.

---

[38] Fischer and Janis (1990) discuss this example and many others like it. They propose that it illustrates a syntactic structure they describe as a "verb sandwich" because there are two verbs, the first uninflected and the second with "lots of inflection," with something between them. In the text I treat (61) as a sequence of clauses rather than as a single syntactic structure.

## Summary and prologue

The remainder of this book focuses on a single question. How are meanings expressed and understood in ASL? Grammatical structure – understood to mean "structured arrangements of conventional linguistic units" (Langacker 1991:548) – plays a central role in answering this question. In this chapter I have tried to present a treatment of aspects of the grammar of ASL that need to be understood in order to make sense of the following chapters. But grammatical structure alone is insufficient. In addition to grammatical structure, understanding ASL involves conceptual mappings between semantic representations and numerous types of both spatial and non-spatial conceptualizations. The remainder of this book is devoted to exploring how this takes place.

# 3 Pronouns and real space

One of the key articulatory differences between spoken and signed languages lies in the mobility and visibility of the hands. While vocal articulators such as the tongue, the glottis, and the velum are limited to largely unseen movements within the vocal tract, the hands are capable of making intricate, visible, spatial distinctions. Sign languages exploit this capability by allowing signs to be directed and placed in space meaningfully.

Directing pronouns toward physically present entities is a common feature of ASL discourse. Pronouns can be directed toward the signer, the addressee, others present, or toward other things in the signer's environment. I begin with physically present entities because their visibility makes it possible to observe with a fair degree of precision what signers do when directing pronouns.

Beginning here I will use a straight superscript arrow ($\rightarrow$) to indicate that a sign is directed toward a single entity. I will also identify the entity the sign is directed toward immediately after the arrow. Thus, PRO$^{\rightarrow a}$ symbolizes the non-first person singular pronoun directed toward entity $a$. In order to talk about general characteristics of the sign, letters toward the end of the alphabet such as $x$ and $y$ will be used as variables while $a$, $b$, and $c$ will be used to symbolize specific entities. Thus, PRO$^{\rightarrow x}$ symbolizes the pronoun as an abstract grammatical unit and PRO$^{\rightarrow a}$ symbolizes its use in a specific instance where it is directed toward some entity $a$. The superscript arrow $^{\circ}$ will indicate pointing by means of moving along a path, where the extent of the path helps identify the plural entities being talked about. Thus, PRO-PL$^{\circ x}$ is the non-first person plural pronoun meaning 'all of you/all of them'. In producing PRO-PL$^{\circ x}$ the index finger moves along a sideward path that points toward the group of entities being referred to.

PRO$^{\rightarrow x}$ is produced with a short outward movement of the index finger, with the palm oriented to the side. If PRO$^{\rightarrow x}$ is intended to refer to the addressee it will be directed toward the addressee. In Figure 3.1a, PRO$^{\rightarrow \text{man with beard}}$ is directed straight ahead toward the man with a beard, who happens to be the addressee. In Figure 3.1b, PRO$^{\rightarrow \text{man with beard}}$ is directed upward and slightly to the right, but still toward the man's chest. Clearly, the addressee or any other

a. PRO$^{\rightarrow}$ man with beard          b. PRO$^{\rightarrow}$ man with beard

Figure 3.1 Two instances of the singular non-first person pronoun PRO$^{\rightarrow x}$

referent could be located just about anywhere with respect to the signer. If the referent is located somewhere in the immediate environment, the signer will direct PRO$^{\rightarrow x}$ toward that referent. Thus, the directionality of PRO$^{\rightarrow x}$ is not fixed, but varies depending on the physical location of the entity it is directed toward.

Pronouns in any language point *conceptually* to their referents. Consider, for example, the use of the English pronoun *he* in (1), where the speaker is responding to the claim that a nearby man is a doctor.

(1)      I am pretty sure he is a dentist.

In (1), the pronoun *he* is used with the expectation that the addressee will be able to make a connection between the meaning of the pronoun and its referent. Thus, the person uttering (1) assumes that the addressee will successfully link the meaning of *he* with the nearby man claimed to be a doctor. The pronoun *he* describes a single male being other than the speaker or addressee. This semantic information considerably narrows the possible numbers and types of entities the speaker might be talking about. That is, an addressee need not consider whether the speaker is talking about a rock, a woman, two boys, or a river. The search can be narrowed to a single male being. Since the speaker is responding to a statement that a nearby single male is a doctor, an addressee would naturally assume that the speaker is still talking about the same man and would associate the meaning of *he* with that man. That association is typically described by saying that *he* refers to the nearby man.

ASL pronouns also encode meanings that help in the process of understanding which entities are being talked about. PRO$^{\rightarrow x}$, for example, is used to talk about a single entity other than the signer. In (1) an English speaker uses *he* to point conceptually to a physically present nearby man. An ASL signer present in the same room could also use PRO$^{\rightarrow x}$ to point conceptually to the same man. In this case, however, the pronoun would not only point conceptually toward that man, the hand producing the pronoun would also point physically toward him. Thus, the significant difference between the English pronoun *he* and the

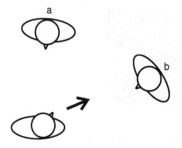

Figure 3.2 Directing PRO$^{\rightarrow x}$ toward *b* indicates that *b* is its referent

ASL pronoun PRO$^{\rightarrow x}$ does not lie in their ability to point conceptually toward their referents – both do that. The significant difference is that during the production of the ASL pronoun the hand also physically points toward the present referent.

PRO$^{\rightarrow x}$ is directed toward a specific part of an entity. If the entity is inanimate, PRO$^{\rightarrow x}$ is directed roughly toward the center of the object (Lacy 1974:35). If the entity is a person, PRO$^{\rightarrow x}$ is directed toward the person's chest. Figure 3.2 represents a situation where PRO$^{\rightarrow x}$ is used in a physical setting with two people present in addition to the signer. The meaning of PRO$^{\rightarrow x}$ is compatible with reference to either person *a* or person *b*. The reference of PRO$^{\rightarrow x}$ is decided based on its directionality.[1] By directing PRO$^{\rightarrow x}$ toward *b*'s chest, the signer clearly indicates that *b* is its referent.

The plural pronoun {PRO-MULT}{THREE}$^{\supset x}$ 'the three of you/them' is also directed toward its referents at chest level.[2] Here the variable *x* stands for a group of three people. This pronoun is able to point despite the fact that it does not have a pointing handshape and its movement is circular.

The sign is produced in a location away from the signer's body, but between the signer and the three individuals being talked about. The arc on the side of the circle away from the signer points toward the entities that make up the group *x*. In Figure 3.3a, {PRO-MULT}{THREE}$^{\supset b,c,d}$ points to *b*, *c*, and *d*, but not *a*. In Figure 3.3b {PRO-MULT}{THREE}$^{\supset a,b,c}$ points to *a*, *b*, and *c*, but not *d*. The size of the circular movement is not fixed, but can vary depending on whether the group is compact or spread out.

There is an important distinction between encoding and pointing. Each instance of {PRO-MULT}{THREE}$^{\supset x}$ encodes the information 'three (human)

---

[1] In addition to directing the sign toward *b*, a signer would also typically glance toward *b* near the beginning of the production of the sign.

[2] Plural pronouns such as {PRO-MULT}{THREE}$^{\supset x}$ (the three of you/them) are used primarily with human referents. When signing about pets such as dogs or cats such signs can also be used. They would not be used with other animals such as tropical fish or inanimate objects such as books (MJ Bienvenu, personal communication).

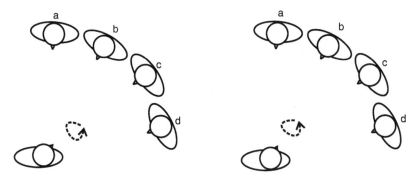

a. {PRO-MULT}{THREE}$^{ɔb,c,d}$   b. {PRO-MULT}{THREE}$^{ɔa,b,c}$
   the three of you/them               the three of you/them

Figure 3.3 Two examples of directing {PRO-MULT}{THREE}$^{ɔx}$ toward its referents

beings other than the signer'. The directionality, however, does not *encode* anything. Its significance can only be determined by following the directionality to see what it leads to. Charles S. Peirce divides meaningful signs (in the semiotic sense of the term *sign*) into icons, indices, symbols, and combinations of these. The sign {PRO-MULT}{THREE}$^{ɔa,b,c}$ is symbolic since it encodes 'three (human) beings other than the signer'. It is also indexic since the hand moves along an arc that points toward *a*, *b*, and *c*.

The signs already discussed illustrate different ways the hands can point. In producing PRO$^{→x}$ the hand moves along a path toward *x*. At the conclusion of the sign the index finger is also oriented so that it points at *x*. In producing {PRO-MULT}{THREE}$^{ɔx}$ the hand is placed between the signer and the group of three individuals being referred to. The placement itself indicates a direction toward the group. In addition, the size of the circular movement also corresponds to how close or far apart the individuals are. If the individuals were close to one another the circular movement would be smaller than if the three were spread out.

## Attempts at discrete morphemic solutions

### Gradience

It should be apparent that the directionality of ASL pronouns depends on the physical location of the entities being pointed at. One only has to imagine the signer standing on a stage in an auditorium with hundreds of seats – some lower than the stage, others at the level of the stage, and several rows of balconies

to visualize the problem. In order to be properly produced, $PRO^{\rightarrow x}$ has to be directed at its referent – and that referent could be any of those seats. In spite of the many possible directions, there are still commonalities across all the different instances of $PRO^{\rightarrow x}$. It is produced with a 1 handshape, a movement-hold segmental structure, a straight movement path, and with the forearm rotated so that the radial side (thumb side) of the hand is up. While all these aspects of the production remain constant, the direction of the pointing changes from one instance of $PRO^{\rightarrow x}$ to the next.

### Operating assumptions in the 1970s

The analyses of ASL by larger numbers of linguists did not begin until the 1970s. At that point in the history of linguistics, there were several unquestioned assumptions and operating principles that influenced the analysis of the pointing behavior of signs. First, the ultimate source of meaning was generally assumed to be the morpheme. Morphemes combine to produce complex words, words combine to produce phrases, clauses, etc. But ultimately, meaning was thought to be reducible to morphemes.

Iconic words had a lower status than non-iconic words. Bolinger (1975) states that "Language has become an almost purely conventional code, with a few exceptions listed as curiosities" (p. 217). The implication here is that words exhibiting onomatopoeia do not participate in this purely conventional code. The following from Westcott (1971) implies that the presence of iconicity has implications for the ability to precisely encode meaning:

linguistic icons, though less precise than linguistic symbols, are more easily understood by those with imperfect mastery of the language in which they occur. Just as threat-signals, despite their imprecision, are understood across species boundaries in a way in which courtship-signals are not, so also are onomatopoeic forms appreciated, if only vaguely, by foreigners in a way in which other forms are not. (Westcott 1971:426)

Gradient behavior was eliminated from linguistic analyses. Gestures of the hands and body were placed outside the scope of the linguistic signal because language was assumed to be purely vocal. Even intonation was generally treated as paralinguistic – outside the scope of linguistics proper. Given the power of such underlying assumptions, how would a linguist specializing in the study of intonation demonstrate that it was truly "linguistic"? The answer appears to be that in order to demonstrate that something is linguistic, one must show its categorical nature. Consider the following from Ladd (1996), who makes a distinction between linguistic intonation and paralinguistic intonation.

The central difference between paralinguistic and linguistic messages resides in the *quantal* or *categorical* structure of linguistic signaling and the *scalar* or *gradient* nature of paralanguage. In linguistic signaling, physical continua are partitioned into categories, so that close similarity of phonetic form is generally of no relevance for meaning: . . . In paralinguistic signaling, by contrast, semantic continua are matched by phonetic ones. (Ladd 1996:36)

In other words, some intonational phenomena are categorical and some are gradient. Those that are categorical are linguistic and those that are gradient are paralinguistic. The distinction above between linguistic and paralinguistic signaling reflects a widely shared assumption about the types of phenomena that linguists will consider in analyzing language. In his analysis of ASL, Supalla (1982) is also explicit about this guiding assumption:

But ASL, being in the important senses an instance of a humanly possible language, has universal design features in common with all human languages. Most importantly: Human linguistic systems are digital, not analogue, a fact independent of the peripheral resources (mouth and ear, or hand and eye) that are used to create the forms. (Supalla 1982:9)

Many linguists today still maintain the correctness of some or all of these assumptions. In the mid-seventies there was an eagerness among those studying ASL to demonstrate that ASL was a legitimate human language. Indeed, without such a demonstration, those studying ASL would not be viewed as doing real linguistics. This was the environment into which the widespread study of ASL was launched. In order to convince others of the status of ASL as a language, it would be necessary to demonstrate strong parallels between ASL and the way spoken languages were thought to be structured.

### Early attempts at a discrete solution to pointing

Generative semantics was a prominent grammatical theory being debated when the initial attempts to deal with directional signs were being developed in the early 1970s. Part of the theory included the idea that grammatical representations contained abstract indices serving referential purposes. Suppose, for example, we are talking about an underlying generative semantics proposition, $X_1$ asked $X_2$, where $X_1$ corresponds to a boy on my right and $X_2$ corresponds to a girl on my left. In English, that underlying proposition might result in the sentence, *He asked her*. Each index has referential value, and corresponds to a unique individual. Lacy (1974) proposes that for ASL, each logical index within a semantic representation (e.g. $X_1$ or $X_2$ ) corresponds to a unique spatial locus (i.e. location) in the space ahead of the signer.[3] Lacy did not attribute any independent meaning to these spatial loci. Their contextual meanings come from their associations with semantic indices. He also made it clear that he expected

---

[3] Many analysts use the term *spatial index* to talk about a spatial location or locus. Some also gloss ASL pronouns using the term INDEX. Since different people mean different things when they use these terms, I avoid terminology such as *index* or *INDEX*.

phonological features to guide the hands toward the correct spatial locus in the production of directional signs.

To sum up, Lacy proposed that directional signs move toward spatial loci associated with semantic indices. By directing a sign toward a spatial locus associated with the addressee, one makes reference to the addressee. Although it is obvious to anyone that directional pronouns point at physically present referents, pointing would not have been considered a legitimate part of a linguistic analysis since pointing is not morphemic. Instead, a spatial locus having referential significance serves as the place of articulation for the pronoun. Given this, the hand is not pointing, but rather, is simply moving to its place of articulation. Thus, by invoking spatial loci, it was not necessary to make the fact that a pronoun actually points at its referent a part of the analysis.

Fischer (1975) also proposes that signs are directed toward spatial loci in order to identify referents. The significance of the spatial loci and the grammatical mechanisms involved in her analysis, however, are very different from those proposed by Lacy. Fischer's proposal attributes the direction of verbs either to incorporating the location of pronouns or to the cliticization of pronouns.[4] In this analysis, at some abstract level, the subject and object of a verb such as ASK-QUESTION would be represented as pronouns. The loci these pronouns are associated with would become part of the verb, providing it with its directional features.

Friedman (1975) makes a third proposal, which also depends on directing signs toward meaningful loci in space: "the signer establishes a reference point in space for referring to a person, object, or location in the actual environment of the signer and the addressee" (p. 946). As can be seen below, Friedman places a different semantic value on these loci. She appears to be claiming that the loci themselves are pronouns or "pro-forms": "in surface constructions which contain multidirectional verbs, index to the spatial 'pronouns' is unnecessary, since the movement of the verb sign starts and ends at or near the space designated for the referents, thus incorporating the pro-forms in the sign for the verb" (p. 956). Friedman (1977) suggests that directing signs toward spatial locations may not depend on traditional phonological features at all, or may depend on some kind of scalar phonological features. Her proposal, however, does not provide examples of such features. Table 3.1 compares key points of the proposals just discussed. It is interesting to observe that these proposals appear to have been developed independently from one another since no paper cites any of the others. In spite of the fact that the significance of the spatial loci differs from one proposal to the next, each proposal

---

[4] Clitics are commonly reduced forms of corresponding non-clitic forms. That is, in the clause *He's nice*, the clitic form of *is* consists of only the consonant sound [z]. Presumably, in the analysis proposed by Fischer, either a pronoun reduces to its location, or the spatial loci are themselves to be regarded as pronouns. Her claim cannot be interpreted to mean that a full pronominal sign cliticizes to the verb, since this never happens.

Table 3.1 *The initial proposals for directing signs toward present entities*

|  | What is a spatial index? | What kind of features guide a pronoun or verb? | Type of grammatical process |
|---|---|---|---|
| Lacy 1974 | a spatial location corresponding to an index of logical structure | phonological features (none proposed) | verbs: deixis pronouns: deixis |
| Fischer 1975 | a location | location features (none proposed) | verbs: cliticization of a pronoun or its location features onto the verb pronouns: not discussed |
| Friedman 1975 | a spatial 'pronoun' | possibly some kind of "scalar" phonological features (none proposed) | verbs: "indexing" pronouns: "indexing" |

shares the idea that a sign is directed toward a meaningful locus in the signing space.

It is not an accident that these and subsequent proposals depend on the concept of a meaningful spatial locus. Linguists studying ASL at that time were operating within the shared set of assumptions described earlier and were bound to describing ASL signs in structural terms. If one were to consider ASL to be a legitimate language, the meaning of ASL sentences must come from morphemes. Since the directionality of pronouns and verbs is meaningful, that meaning must also come from morphemes. Since location was one of the three aspects of a sign's structure proposed by Stokoe, this was the obvious aspect of structure to single out as carrying that meaning.

These three analyses suggest a direction for a possible solution to the problem of directional signs. At the time they were made there were no phonological features capable of describing contrastive uses of spatial locations. Recall that Stokoe had proposed only a single spatial location that made no distinctions between one location in space and another. At this stage in the history of the analysis of ASL, however, the lack of phonological (spatial) features capable of implementing these proposals was not viewed as a problem. It was assumed that at some point such features would be developed. No satisfactory set of features has appeared in the decades following these initial proposals.[5]

[5] Liddell and Johnson (1989) provide a set of spatial features capable of distinguishing a large number of spatial loci. The proposal is based on the concept that there is a large but listable number of possible spatial loci. I have subsequently abandoned this set of features since all the evidence I have gathered since then suggests that the assumption on which the analysis is based is incorrect.

a. The locus *a* between signer and addressee    b. PRO$^{\to x}$ incorporating the spatial affix *a*.

Figure 3.4 The spatial locus between the signer and addressee and how it could be conceived of as becoming part of a pronominal sign

### Subsequent analyses

The concept that directional signs move toward meaningful, linguistically speci-fiable points of articulation in the space ahead of the signer has been adopted by virtually all subsequent analyses of directional signs (*inter alia* Edge and Herrmann 1977, Klima and Bellugi 1979, Gee and Kegl 1982, Shepard-Kegl 1985, Wilbur 1987, Padden 1988, Liddell and Johnson 1989, Sandler 1989, Meier 1990, Engberg-Pedersen 1993, Janis 1995, Neidle *et al.* 1995, Bahan 1996, Meir 1998, Brentari 1998). It is still widely accepted that any directional sign would be composed of at least two morphemes. In addition to the sign root, the sign would also contain a spatial morpheme.

Figure 3.4a illustrates a common situation where an addressee is located opposite the signer. The symbol *a* represents the locus between the signer and the addressee. There are two significant things to mention about the locus *a*. First, it is believed to represent the addressee. Second, it becomes part of the pronoun by becoming the hand's destination as it produces the pronoun. Given the assumptions described above, we can now examine how the structure of PRO$^{\to x}$ could be analyzed given common morphemic assumptions about space.

When the early proposals were being made, signs were thought to be com-posed of three simultaneous aspects: a location, a handshape, and one or more movements (Stokoe 1960). Since location was one of three aspects of a sign, it seemed natural to isolate location as a morpheme, signified by the upper box in Figure 3.4b.[6] The remaining two aspects of a sign – handshape and

---

[6] The analysis presented here makes explicit what was generally implicit in previous analyses. It follows from the assumption that the spatial location is a morpheme.

movement – would constitute the pronoun root, signified by the lower two boxes in Figure 3.4b. Phonologically, these two morphemes fit together to form a complete sign. Treating location as a morpheme made directional signs conform to the phonological structure expected of all signs. That is, just like any other sign, the hand simply moves to its place of articulation. The only difference between the directed form of PRO$^{\rightarrow x}$ and a morphemically simple sign produced in the space ahead of the signer (e.g. CHILD) is that the location PRO$^{\rightarrow x}$ is directed toward happens to be an independent morpheme.

### *The inadequacy of morphemic accounts*

Many additional proposals concerning spatial loci and directional signs have appeared during the subsequent quarter century. It is difficult to say exactly how many different proposals there have been, however, since such proposals are rarely explicit about the similarities and differences between what is being proposed and what has been previously proposed. I estimate that there are somewhere between ten and fifteen distinct proposals concerning how directional signs in ASL make use of spatial loci. In spite of their differences, however, in virtually all the analyses, a spatial locus ahead of the signer becomes associated with a referent. Subsequent reference to that entity is made by directing signs toward that spatial locus. The signs are directed toward the spatial locus because it becomes the place of articulation for the sign.

I will be using facts about directional verbs in this part of the argument since such verbs provide the clearest evidence that there is no single locus representing the entity signs are directed toward. To be consistent with notations in chapter 4, I include the notations $^{\rightarrow y}$, $-1^{\rightarrow y}$, and $^{x \rightarrow y}$ as part of the glosses for verbs. These notations will be fully explained in chapter 4 and can be ignored for the present. The three forms of ASK-QUESTION$^{\rightarrow y}$ illustrated in Figure 3.5 illustrate an important property of verbs capable of being directed toward an entity. In each one of these forms the signer is producing a form of ASK-QUESTION$^{\rightarrow y}$ intended to express the meaning, 'ask y a question'. In Figure 3.5a, the signer and addressee are the same height and the sign moves horizontally at roughly the chin/neck level between the signer and addressee. Assuming that the sign is

a.                              b.                              c.

Figure 3.5 Three instances of ASK-QUESTION$^{\rightarrow y}$

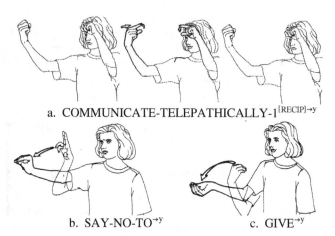

a. COMMUNICATE-TELEPATHICALLY-1[RECIP]→y

b. SAY-NO-TO→y                c. GIVE→y

Figure 3.6  Height differences among indicating verbs. (Drawings by Paul M. Setzer)

directed toward a spatial locus, the locus would be at the signer's chin/neck level. However, if the addressee is significantly taller than the signer, the sign moves upward as shown in Figure 3.5b. This would place the locus significantly above the signer's chin/neck level. If the signer directs the sign ASK-QUESTION→y horizontally between her chin and the taller addressee's chest (Figure 3.5c), the result is unacceptable, in spite of the fact that the signer is directing the sign along essentially the same path as that shown in Figure 3.5a (which is appropriate in that situation).

The toe-to-head height of the addressee is not an issue here. What is important is the location of the addressee's chin/neck. For each of the acceptable instances of ASK-QUESTION→y above, the target of the directional movement is the chin/neck of the *addressee*. If a tall addressee were seated, or even lying down, ASK-QUESTION→y would be directed downward toward the addressee's chin/neck, even though the addressee was tall.

Just as ASK-QUESTION→y is directed toward the chin/neck area, other directional verbs also have specific parts of the body toward which they are directed (Liddell 1990). The sign COMMUNICATE-TELEPATHICALLY-1[RECIP]→y (Figure 3.6a) is directed toward the forehead; SAY-NO-TO→y (Figure 3.6b) is lower, moving toward the addressee's nose/chin; GIVE→y (Figure 3.6c) is lower still, moving toward the addressee's chest.

These facts about how signs are produced are inconsistent with the claim that there is a locus associated with the addressee toward which signs are directed. If there were such a locus, all directional signs referring to the same entity (e.g. the addressee) would be directed toward that single locus. If one were to suppose that such a locus were ahead of the signer at the chin level (or between the

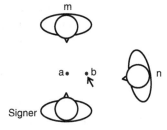

Figure 3.7  Why location *a* does not represent person *m*

signer and the addressee's chin), then although ASK-QUESTION$^{\rightarrow y}$ would be directed toward that locus, GIVE$^{\rightarrow y}$, which is directed at chest level, would not. Pronominal reference to the addressee would also not be directed at that locus. It, too, is directed at chest height. COMMUNICATE-TELEPATHICALLY-1$^{[RECIP]\rightarrow y}$ is directed at the forehead level, well above the locus at chin height. No matter which level one were to select as the level for such a locus, many signs would not be directed toward it.

All the examples discussed so far involve directing a sign toward a locus between the signer and the addressee. If the sign is directed between someone else and the addressee it becomes even clearer that there is no locus ahead of the signer corresponding to the addressee. Consider, for example, the physical arrangement in Figure 3.7. Person *m* is directly ahead of the signer and person *n* is to the signer's right. If the signer were to use PRO$^{\rightarrow x}$ to refer to *m*, the signer would produce PRO$^{\rightarrow m}$. The signer's hand would move toward *m* and stop between the signer and *m* at the spatial locus I have labeled *a*. Since the pronoun is directed toward *m*, it would refer to *m*. However, a verb such as ASK-QUESTION$^{x \rightarrow y}$ has the ability to begin its movement path directed toward the one associated with asking the question and end directed toward the recipient of the question. If the signer commanded *n* to ask *m*, ASK-QUESTION$^{n \rightarrow m}$ would not move toward *a*. It would begin between the signer and *n* on the right then follow a path toward *m*. The hand would follow a path similar to that indicated by the arrow in Figure 3.7 and end its movement at the locus I have labeled *b*. If there were really a locus *a* directly ahead of the signer associated with *m*, ASK-QUESTION$^{n \rightarrow m}$ would have been directed toward it. Conversely, if the signer were to direct PRO$^{\rightarrow x}$ toward locus *b*, it would not refer to *m*. Yet directing ASK-QUESTION$^{x \rightarrow y}$ toward locus *b* does refer to *m*. It should be apparent that the concept of a locus associated with a referent is inconsistent with the ways signs are actually directed.

The most basic requirement of any linguistic analysis is that it be consistent with the data. In linguistics this is called descriptive adequacy. Analyses of directional signs that depend on those signs being directed toward spatial loci do not meet this minimum level of descriptive adequacy. In fact, claims that signs are directed toward spatial loci have been asserted more than they have been demonstrated. It simply became common knowledge that signs are directed toward such spatial loci. Once it becomes apparent that signs are not directed toward such spatial loci, the foundation for such analyses disappears.

Being able to identify and describe proposed spatial morphemes is also an integral part of the descriptive adequacy issue. It is one thing to claim that a particular sign contains a spatial locus, but quite another to identify the particular spatial locus and distinguish it from other possible spatial loci. A descriptively adequate morphemic account should be able to list the possible spatial loci and describe the meanings of each. With such a description it would then be possible to identify which locus was being used in any particular sign. This has never been done. Some other means of accounting for directionality is needed.

## Mental spaces

We use language to talk about things. Typically the things we talk about are separate and distinct from the meanings encoded by the words and morphemes that make up an utterance. For example, if I hold up a blue pen while saying (2), observers of that event will conclude that the blue pen I am holding can write underwater. If I say (2) while holding up a red pen, observers will conclude that the red pen can write underwater.

(2)    This pen can write underwater.

Even though I use exactly the same words in both cases, observers would come to different conclusions about what I was intending to convey in spite of the fact that the meanings encoded by the individual words and phrases do not change.

The phrase *this pen* refers to the blue pen the first time (2) is uttered and refers to the red pen the second time. Suppose that I were to hold up a toy car and direct my gaze at it while uttering (2). This set of behaviors leaves the addressee little choice but to conclude that I mean for there to be a connection between the phrase *this pen* and the toy car being held. An addressee might conclude that what appeared to be a toy car was actually a type of pen. If the addressee were already familiar with the toy car, and knew that it was not a pen, the addressee might conclude that I was confused, joking, or had lost touch with reality.

Finally, suppose I was describing a collection of pens. Having described each one in turn, I then turn and look at the addressee and say (2) with no accompanying gesture of any kind. The addressee would be puzzled because making a connection with the intended entity is a normal expectation of using the phrase *this pen*. The addressee's puzzlement would result from the fact that I had used the phrase *this pen* without providing appropriate clues as to how to connect its meaning to one specific pen within the collection of pens.

Given the proper discourse context, the phrase *this pen* could be uttered without the physical presence of a pen. Suppose I were explaining to a potential manufacturer that I had conceived of a way to make a pen write underwater. After explaining how it would be possible to manufacture such a pen, I could then use the phrase *this pen* as in (3).

(3)     This pen could also write on wax paper.

The word *this* encodes the meaning 'entity proximal to speaker' and *pen* encodes the meaning 'writing instrument that uses ink'. The addressee will therefore seek to identify a proximal writing instrument that uses ink. Assuming that the speaker does not point to a picture or diagram of the pen, the addressee must find the appropriate entity to connect with the meaning of *this pen* without gestural assistance. Recent discourse provides the entity since that discourse has been about a pen that can write underwater. Since it has not yet been manufactured, it does not exist as a physical entity. It does exist, however, as a temporally proximal conceptual entity. In fact, in this context it is the only entity of the type 'pen' available. Thus, the addressee would make a connection between *this pen* and that temporally proximal conceptual writing instrument already discussed.

Exactly the same thing can be said of pronouns. Pronouns such as *I*, *me*, *you*, and *he* are used successfully when their encoded meanings lead the addressee to the intended referents. Suppose, for example, a lawyer asks a witness to identify the person who committed a crime. The witness could respond by uttering (4) while pointing at the guilty person. The pronoun *he* is used to mention a single male being other than the speaker or addressee. Without the pointing, the person to be connected with the pronoun's meaning would not be clear. In order to know which person the speaker has in mind, it is only necessary to follow the direction of the pointing.

(4)     He did it.

Suppose the witness had pointed to someone with long hair, lipstick, and women's clothes while uttering (4). This would lead to the same type of potential conflict described earlier when uttering *this pen* while holding up a toy car. It is possible that the witness knows that a male being lies underneath the clothes and make-up. If so, the seeming inconsistency between the semantically encoded information and the person identified by the pointing gesture could be cleared up by unmasking the man.

An addressee expects to be able to make connections between the meanings encoded by definite noun phrases (e.g. the man, this book) and either physically present entities or conceptual entities in the discourse. The same expectations apply with definite pronouns (e.g. he, you). If the entity being talked about is physically present, a pointing gesture toward the entity clearly identifies it as

## Constructed meaning

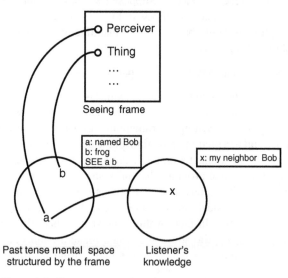

Figure 3.8  Current assumption about meaning construction

the entity to connect with the encoded meaning. Just as the appropriate entity to associate with the phrase *this pen* can be picked from recent discourse, the appropriate entity to connect with the pronoun *he* can also be selected from entities talked about in recent discourse. Suppose that I ask Sue whether Bill bought the car he had been thinking about buying. She could also answer with (4). Since Bill is the only male entity previously mentioned in the discourse, there appears to be no choice but to make an association between Bill and the meaning encoded by *he*. In mental space theory, the entities people talk about as they speak are all conceptual entities within conceptual structures called *mental spaces* (Fauconnier 1985, 1997). The speaker encodes meanings intended to be associated with mental space elements, thereby making crucial use of them in meaning construction.

The following example helps illustrate how mappings between mental spaces are represented in mental space theory (Fauconnier 1997). A sentence like *Bob saw a frog* would invoke a 'seeing' frame such as the one in Figure 3.8. A frame is a type of idealized cognitive model (Fillmore 1982, 1985). Our understanding of seeing includes a perceiver and a perceived entity. The invoked seeing frame, in turn, helps to structure another mental space.

The mental space receiving its structure from the seeing frame contains two elements, *a* and *b*, which correspond to the perceiver and the thing perceived in the seeing frame. Known information about the mental space elements is represented in a rectangle above the mental space. In this case, $a$ has the property 'named Bob' and $b$ has the property 'frog'. The fact that $a$ saw $b$ is represented in the rectangle as *SEE a b*. Elements $a$ and $b$ are not representations of any particular frog or any particular Bob. They are simply two conceptual elements $a$ and $b$ that have acquired the semantic properties 'named Bob' and 'frog'.

In the sentence *Bob saw a frog*, *Bob* is definite and *a frog* is indefinite. That is, a speaker would use the sentence *Bob saw a frog* in a context where the particular person named Bob is identifiable by those participating in the conversation. The use of the indefinite article in the phrase *a frog* introduces a new element into the conversation – an element that is not yet identifiable by those participating in the conversation.

Let us suppose that a particular Bob has already been introduced into the conversation and that it turns out that the Bob being talked about is the listener's neighbor. The listener's representation of this particular Bob is represented as element $x$ in the mental space labeled 'Listener's knowledge'. The connection between $a$ and $x$ represents the mental connection the listener makes in determining which Bob is being talked about. The resulting mental space network in Figure 3.8 represents the meaning of *Bob saw a frog* in this context. Fauconnier (1985, 1997) refers to this as *constructed meaning*.

Note that Figure 3.8 contains no semantic structures. Currently, mental space theory treats linguistic forms as "(partial and underdetermined) instructions for constructing interconnected domains with internal structure" (Fauconnier 1997:35). In this view, then, the semantic structure of an utterance is not an expression of the meaning of the utterance, but rather prompts the construction of a separate set of interconnected domains such as the one illustrated in Figure 3.8. Language structures prompt the construction of these interconnected domains, but are not themselves a part of them.

In this example a connection is made between a mental space element with the property 'named Bob' and the listener's mental representation of a neighbor named Bob. This is consistent with the assumptions of mental space theory in that all the mental space connections link conceptual entities. Suppose, however, that the particular Bob being talked about was physically present. In this situation it appears to be necessary to make a connection between a mental space entity with the property 'named Bob' and the physically present Bob. But the physically present Bob appears to be a physical rather than a conceptual entity.

### Real space

In a normally functioning eye, light of various wavelengths and intensities travels through the lens and stimulates receptors in the retina that send signals to the brain. These signals are interpreted by the brain in forming a visual representation of the types of things being seen. This includes the ability to conceptualize things as discrete entities, to judge their height, distance, size, color, texture, and so on. Based on the light currently stimulating my retinas, I see several things ahead of me, including a keyboard. Because of the mental image of the keyboard I am able to construct based on the stimulation of my retinas, I believe that there is a physical keyboard of a particular size and shape at a location external to me and ahead of me.

I use the term *real space* to label a person's current conceptualization of the immediate environment based on sensory input (Liddell 1995). All instances of real space discussed in this book are constructed from visual input. Other senses also help inform me of my immediate surroundings. My computer's cooling fan produces sounds that I can localize as nearby, low, and to the left. My sense of touch tells me that my back is currently pressing against the back of a chair. I cannot currently see or hear the back of the chair, but I believe it is there because I can feel it.

As one instance of a human conceptualizer, I believe that the elements of real space are real things around me and that they exist where I have conceptualized them. The phrase *where I have conceptualized them* does not refer to the location of the neurological activity in the brain. I am talking about the significance a viewer gives to the neurological activity. When I talk about the locations of elements of real space I mean the locations outside the brain where those entities are conceptualized to exist. That is, real space is *grounded* in that its elements are conceptualized as existing in the immediate environment (Liddell 1995). Thus, when I talk about a real space keyboard ahead of me, I am talking about a keyboard conceptualized as existing in the here and now ahead of me.

I treat the real-space keyboard as if it were the physical entity responsible for the visual stimuli that caused me to conceptualize the keyboard there. That is, for the purposes of everyday interaction with the world we do not distinguish the conceptual entities in real-space from the physical things responsible for our perceptions. We treat real space as if it were our physical environment and we treat real-space elements as if they were the real, physical things around us. One of the consequences of not distinguishing the two is that a real-space *conceptual* entity is treated as a real *physical* entity, having all the physical properties of the physical entity, including being located at a particular place in the immediate environment.

Real space, however, is distinct from the physical entities assumed to be responsible for our perceptions. If I see a book ahead of me, that means that I have received and processed visual stimuli resulting in the conceptualization of a real-space book of a certain size, shape, color, and distance from me. If I believe the book to be within my reach, I may reach out and grasp it. But why should I extend my hand toward the book rather than in some other direction? That is, there is no intrinsic connection between me and the book that would lead me to extend my hand toward it. The only knowledge I have of the book is what I have constructed based on sensory input. I reach for the location of the book *as conceptualized in real space*. When I reach out and grasp the physical book, I receive additional tactile sensory evidence of the correctness of my real space representation.

The physical book is not part of real space since real space only contains conceptual entities. The real-space book is an internal representation of the book conceptualized as being external to me. Fortunately, the locations of physical entities and the corresponding conceptualized locations of real-space entities generally overlap. That is, I reach toward the book as conceptualized in real space. Years of experience give me confidence that I will encounter a physical object there.

These days we are told about developments in "virtual surgery," where a surgeon can operate on a patient at a remote location by manipulating virtual instruments through a visual computer interface. But this is what the brain does all the time as it deals with things external to it by means of its "virtual" real-space interface with reality. Just as the virtual surgeon does not have immediate access to the actual patient being operated on, the brain does not have immediate access to the world the body encasing the brain lives in. The brain uses real space as a means of interacting with its external environment. The difference between the surgeon performing virtual surgery and a normal human operating in the world is that the normal human brain is not aware that real space is its interface with reality. The human brain believes that real space is reality.

At another time or place I may recall having seen the keyboard. That recollection also involves a conceptual keyboard, but I recognize it as a memory rather than as a keyboard existing ahead of me. This conceptualization is non-grounded. When I am sitting in front of a keyboard and attempt to press a key, I expect to encounter something physical (i.e. the key). If my finger were to pass through the key, the shock to my system would be profound. No such expectations are present in recollections of events.

Our perceptions of the environment around us begin as sensory information that is distinct from real space. The sensory input is processed and understood on the basis of actual experience and cultural expectations. Consider the following from Locke (1975), originally published in 1690: "We are farther to consider concerning Perception, that the *Ideas we receive by sensation, are often* in grown People *alter'd by the Judgment*, without our taking notice of it" (p. 145). Locke describes, for example, how our visual system receives signals from a globe as a flat circle "variously shadow'd, with several degrees of Light and Brightness coming to our eyes" (p. 145). From this visual input we perceive a three-dimensional globe.

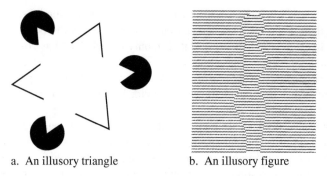

a. An illusory triangle                b. An illusory figure

Figure 3.9  Evidence that cognitive processes operate on visual input

Ninio (2001) provides a different type of support for the fact that perception involves the application of mental processes by examining illusions. For example, consider the image in Figure 3.9a, which Ninio describes as the Kanizsa triangle. Figure 3.9a contains six regions of black ink against a uniform white background. In spite of the physical characteristics of the paper and ink, we perceive a white triangle with clearly defined borders. The white triangle is a cognitive construct that does not exist on the paper. It provides additional evidence that the mind constructs reality by interpreting physiological responses to sensory input.

Figure 3.9b, which Ninio credits to Ehrenstein, consists solely of horizontal lines against a uniformly light background. Even though there is no outlined figure in the stimulus, we nevertheless perceive a clearly outlined figure. The perceived outline is also a mental construct that does not exist on the paper.

When it is possible to demonstrate a difference between real space and the real things we assume to be responsible for our perceptions, real space is called an illusion. But this does not mean that the mind is doing something different in the case of an illusion. Rather, the mind is continually constructing real space using the cognitive mechanisms at its disposal. In general, real space lines up well with physical things in the world. When it doesn't, we are often surprised or amused and use the term *illusion* to label the event.

A fish swimming in a river, as perceived by people standing on the shore, is an example of an illusion in that the perceived location of the fish does not match the actual location of the fish. The refraction of light places the conceptualized location of the real-space fish in a different place from the actual location of the physical fish. A spear perfectly aimed toward the conceptualized location of the real-space fish will not strike the physical fish. This effect is also easily seen in an aquarium. If viewed from the right angle through two different panes of glass at a corner, a single fish may appear to be two different fish. For example,

Figure 3.10 Seeing four fish in a tank containing three

Figure 3.10 shows a single image of an aquarium. The dark vertical bar in the center of the image is the corner of this aquarium. There appear to be four fish in the aquarium: one to the left of the bar and three to the right. In fact, there are only three fish. The two fish labeled fish #1 are the same fish. The first instance of fish #1 on the far left is swimming past a rock. The tip of the same rock appears just to the right of the vertical bar. The second instance of fish #1 is also swimming past the tip of the same rock. In this case, real space contains the four perceived fish, even though the aquarium contains only three physical fish. In this example, real space and reality do not overlap well. Fortunately, real space and reality generally overlap quite nicely. If they did not, we would have a very difficult time functioning.

When the full moon appears in the sky, we do not perceive a globe. We perceive a circular shape in the sky. We also do not perceive the moon and sun at different distances from the earth. Both are described as being "in the sky." Consider, for example, the language in (5).

(5)      Look at that sunset! See how big and orange the sun gets when it is
         close to the horizon.

This language reflects a real space in which the sun is a circular entity in the sky. As that entity in the sky moves to a position where it is "close to the horizon," it can change in both color and size. Scientific theory tells us that the sun is not round, but spherical. It is not in the sky, but rather, at the center of our solar system. While the sun does move as an entity within our galaxy, it does not move across the sky. Instead the earth rotates, giving the illusion of the sun moving across the sky. In addition, the sun never moves toward the horizon. The earth rotates so that from the viewer's point of view the horizon is between the viewer and the sun. From the perspective of a scientific analysis of the solar system, the description in (5) is completely wrong. The sun does not get close to the horizon and does not change its color or size as a result of being near the horizon. But the speaker of (5) is not describing the solar system. The speaker is not even describing the star at the center of our solar system. The speaker is clearly and accurately describing real space.

Discourse about real space differs in an interesting way from discourse about a non-grounded mental space. Suppose, for example, that a speaker and addressee are seated at a table with a red and a blue pen resting between the two on the surface of the table. The speaker's real space will contain red and blue pens corresponding to the physical entities resting on the table. The same can be said of the addressee. The pens in the speaker's and addressee's real-space representations will not be identical since the actual pens on the table are being viewed from opposite directions. However, each of the participants can be confident that the real space of the other contains the two pens. This means that the speaker is in a position to be of assistance in terms of providing clues that will help identify the real space entities being discussed. In (6), for example, the speaker uses the phrase *that one* twice to talk about two elements of real space. It is obvious that the speaker is talking about two different things – but which things? Since they are in the immediate environment of the speaker, the speaker can point to the conceptualized location of each real-space entity as each instance of the phrase *that one* is being produced.

(6)    I don't want that one, I want that one.

While producing the first clause in (6), the speaker could point toward the conceptualized location of the red pen in his real space while saying *that one*. During the second clause, the speaker could point toward the conceptualized location of the blue pen in his real space. The pointing makes the speaker's intentions clear. The first instance of *that one* corresponds to the red pen in the speaker's real space and the second corresponds to the blue pen in the speaker's real space. What the speaker has done is quite natural. Knowing that the addressee has to make the appropriate set of connections in order to understand the speaker's wishes, the speaker provides gestural assistance in making those connections. This works because the speaker can reasonably assume that the addressee's real space contains entities corresponding to those in the speaker's real space.

Knowing where something is located with respect to self entails knowing where the self is with respect to the thing. Thus, I also treat a person's conception of physical self, whether visible to that person or not, as part of real space. However, a person's representation of self differs dramatically from another person's representation because of what is visible to each participant. If the signer and addressee are facing one another, the signer's real space will include a mental representation of the front of the addressee, including the addressee's face. Likewise, the addressee's real space will contain a mental representation of the front of the signer. Almost all the representations of real space in this book are representations of the real space from the point of view of a potential addressee. I do this because it provides a clear view of the signer's hands, the signer's face, and the space ahead of the signer.

Because we perceive a woman smiling when we look at the Mona Lisa, it is normal to talk about the woman in the painting, and wonder about her smile. In fact, there is no woman *in the painting*. There is not even an image of a woman in the painting. Physically, the Mona Lisa is just paint on a canvas. The smiling woman in the Mona Lisa only exists in real space. More specifically, the perceiver conceptualizes the real-space image of the woman to be in the real-space picture. But since the real-space image of the woman is perceived as being in the real-space painting, it is normal to talk about the woman in the painting. Beginning here, I will describe elements of real space using terms consistent with the way elements of real space are conceptualized. Thus, talking about the Mona Lisa in this simplified way, I would describe the location of the real-space image of the woman as being in the painting ahead of the perceiver. Similarly, when I will talk about a pen in real space ahead of a signer, that should be understood to mean that there is a pen in the signer's real space conceptualized ahead of him at that place.

### Meaning and semantic space

During the 1980s and 1990s cognitive grammar emerged as a linguistic theory with very different organizing assumptions from formalist, generative, compartmentalized views of language.[7] In cognitive grammar, meaning is equated with conceptualization. Instead of being compartmentalized, semantics depends upon a speaker's encyclopedic knowledge, with no sharp line between linguistic knowledge and non-linguistic knowledge. Within cognitive grammar there are three types of grammatical elements: phonological, semantic, and symbolic. A symbolic linguistic unit consists of a paired phonological and semantic structure, referred to as its phonological and semantic poles.

When a speaker utters a noun (a symbolic grammatical element), the listener perceives the sounds produced as an instance of the phonological pole of the noun and is able to activate the noun's semantic pole. In other words, perceiving the noun's phonological pole leads to the meaning paired with it. The idea that the phonological structure of a simple word corresponds directly to its semantic structure, with no structure or rules in between, is uncontroversial in all linguistic theories. Cognitive grammar applies this concept to all instances of language use. That is, a sentence differs from a simple word only in the complexity of the symbolization. Regardless of whether an utterance consists

---

[7] See especially Langacker (1987, 1991, 1999b) for extensive discussions of the foundations of cognitive grammar.

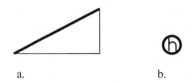

a.                              b.

Figure 3.11 Langacker's representation of the semantic representation of *hypotenuse* (a) and an abbreviated representation (b)

of only a single word or a complex sentence, there are no intermediate rules between phonological structure and semantic structure.

In cognitive grammar, the semantic structure of a noun *profiles* a thing. Langacker uses the example *hypotenuse* to help illustrate profiling. A hypotenuse is one of three sides of a right triangle. If the other two sides are removed, what remains is simply a line – not a hypotenuse. In other words, a hypotenuse is only a hypotenuse in the domain of a right triangle. The entire triangle (the domain) is needed in order to define a hypotenuse (a region in that domain). The heavy line in Figure 3.11a represents the profiled region of the triangle.

Following Langacker (1999a), I will use abbreviated semantic representations. Thus, the circle with the 'h' inside in Figure 3.11b is an abbreviation for the more elaborate diagrammatic representation of the semantic pole of *hypotenuse* in Figure 3.11a. The circle represents a thing while the 'h' is an abbreviation for the type of thing (i.e. a hypotenuse).

Suppose that an English speaker is asked, "How did you find out?" The speaker could respond with (7).

(7)    He told me.
       (The speaker points toward a man on his right while saying *he*.)

The speaker utilizes the pronoun *he* to encode the fact that a single male told him. But the pronoun *he* is not specific about the identity of the individual being talked about. It merely encodes that the individual is male. The left side of Figure 3.12 attempts to represent some of the speaker's mental representations at the time (7) is uttered. The mental representations are drawn inside the outline of the speaker's head in order to emphasize that they are conceptualizations unique to that individual.

In Figure 3.12 real space is represented inside the circle underneath the encoded semantic representation of (7). Since we are focusing here on the pronoun *he*, it is the only overtly labeled semantic element in the semantic representation. As the speaker looks directly ahead he sees the female addressee directly ahead and a man to his right. Clearly the speaker knows which person he is talking about when uttering *he*. In this case, the semantic pole of the pronoun *he* is meant to be mapped onto the man to the speaker's right in real space. This knowledge is represented in Figure 3.12 by the connector

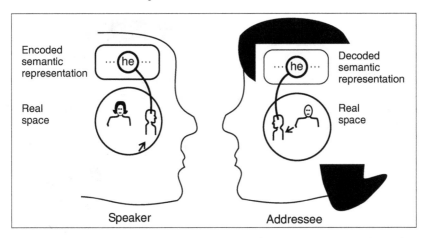

Figure 3.12 Mapping the semantic pole of *he* onto the person being pointed at

between the semantic pole of *he* and the man in real space to the right of the
speaker.

The addressee's mental representations appear on the right in Figure 3.12.
The addressee, being a speaker of English, will have no difficulty decoding the
phonetic signal. The decoded phonetic signal should be virtually identical to
the semantic representation encoded by the speaker. The addressee's real space,
however, differs from the speaker's. As the addressee looks at the speaker, she
sees the male speaker directly ahead and a man to her left.

As a result of successfully decoding the phonetic signal the addressee knows
that a single male individual told the speaker. The decoded phonetic signal,
however, does not identify which male individual did the telling. It is up to the
addressee to make the appropriate connection between the semantic pole of *he*
and the particular male the speaker is talking about.

Addressees make such connections in a number of ways. Suppose the signer
had answered with (8) rather than (7). The first part of the answer introduces a
single male individual into the discourse. The second part of the answer uses the
pronoun *he* to refer to that individual. It is a simple matter in this case to make
an association between the conceptual entity encoded by *he* and the addressee's
brother.

(8)      I saw your brother yesterday and he told me.

Suppose the question had been, "Did Bob tell you?" By answering "he told
me," the semantic entity encoded by *he* would correspond to Bob. In the original example, however, the question ("*How did you find out?*") provides no
contextual help in identifying the referent. The answer contains only minimal

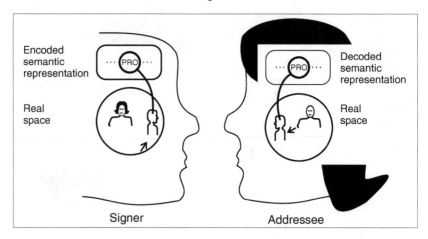

Figure 3.13 Mapping the semantic representation of PRO$^{\rightarrow x}$ onto the person it is being directed toward

semantic help in identifying the individual being talked about. That help comes in the form of the meaning encoded by the pronoun *he*.

Based on the spoken words, the addressee knows that a male individual provided the information and that the identity of that individual is deducible from the discourse. The mere physical presence of a single male individual other than the speaker or addressee is insufficient for making the connection between the semantic pole of *he* and that individual. That is, (7) would be ill-formed without a gesture of some type toward the referent of *he*. If the speaker means for there to be a connection between the semantic pole of *he* and that individual, it is up to the speaker to provide a reason for making that connection. In (7) the speaker provides that justification by pointing at the man while saying "he." The combination of *he* and the pointing gesture leaves no doubt as to the identity of the person to associate with the semantic pole of *he*.

This example demonstrates that, in ordinary face-to-face communication through language, the addressee understands the intent of the speaker as a result of decoding the phonetic signal, then making mental space connections between semantic entities in the decoded signal and mental space entities external to the semantic representation. Addressees in sign language discourse are faced with exactly the same decoding and mapping problem. Once the signal is decoded it is still necessary to make the appropriate set of mental space connections.

In the next example the signer directs PRO$^{\rightarrow x}$ toward a male to his right. From the perspective of the female addressee, PRO$^{\rightarrow x}$ is being directed toward a male to her left. The left side of Figure 3.13 represents the speaker's encoded semantic representation and the speaker's real space. It is apparent that the signer is directing PRO$^{\rightarrow x}$ toward the man to his right. The addressee will recognize the sign as PRO$^{\rightarrow x}$ based on its form. Identifying the phonetic form as an example of PRO$^{\rightarrow x}$ leads to the activation of the semantic pole of PRO$^{\rightarrow x}$, represented on the right in Figure 3.13 by the circle (signifying a thing) with PRO inside it. The semantic structure is not sufficient to understand the intent of the signer. One must also map the semantic pole of PRO$^{\rightarrow x}$ onto the intended referent. The direction of PRO$^{\rightarrow x}$ provides the information needed to accomplish this mapping. The signer has directed PRO$^{\rightarrow x}$ toward the man on his right. This is an instruction to map the semantic pole of PRO$^{\rightarrow x}$ onto that man. This mapping is symbolized by the connector between the semantic pole of PRO$^{\rightarrow x}$ and the man in real space.

The result is identical in all important respects to what an English speaker must do in order to understand the pronoun *he* in Figure 3.12. The only difference in the two examples is the means used to make those mappings. In the English example the vocal tract produces the symbolic element *he* while the hand gestures toward the man to map onto its semantic representation. In the ASL example, a single movement of the hand and arm accomplishes both of these distinct functions. The handshape, straight movement path, and radial-side-up hand rotation encode PRO$^{\rightarrow x}$. The sign's direction points at the real-space entity to map onto its semantic structure.

ASL signers are required to direct pronouns toward the mental space entities their semantic structures are to be mapped onto. The explanation for the requirement to direct pronouns is straightforward. The directionality is an explicit, gestural instruction telling the addressee how to map the pronoun's semantic pole. The addressee needs only to follow the directionality of the pronoun, which will lead to the appropriate entity. The decoding and mapping described above is not unique to pronouns. It is constantly occurring in the everyday use of language. Regardless of whether the language is spoken or signed, the addressee is continually faced with the issue of activating a semantic representation by decoding the phonetic signal and mapping entities within the semantic representation onto conceptual entities external to it.

PRO$^{\rightarrow x}$ may be directed toward the addressee or toward any other person or entity in the immediate environment of the signer. If directed toward the addressee, PRO$^{\rightarrow x}$ would be translated as *you*. If directed toward a male, non-addressee, PRO$^{\rightarrow x}$ would be translated as *he* or *him*. Similarly, if directed toward a female who was not the addressee it would be translated as *she* or *her*. Regardless of the entity PRO$^{\rightarrow x}$ is directed toward, it encodes the meaning 'single entity other than self'. Its significance *in context* comes from not only its semantically encoded meaning but also the mapping between its semantic pole and a mental space entity external to that semantic structure. It is the combination of decoding and mapping that provides the basis for the various English translations.

The directionality of plural signs such as {PRO-MULT}{THREE}$^{\supset x}$ 'the three of you/them' works in exactly the same way. In both Figure 3.3a and Figure 3.3b the meaning encoded by the sign is the same. The placement of the sign serves to show the addressee which three mental space entities to associate with that meaning. In Figure 3.3a the sign is directed toward *b*, *c*, and *d*, while in Figure 3.3b the sign is directed toward *a*, *b*, and *c*.

Had the sign been {PRO-MULT}{FOUR}$^{\supset x}$ rather than {PRO-MULT} {THREE}$^{\supset x}$ then either of the placements in Figure 3.3 would suffice to indicate *a*, *b*, *c*, and *d*. This is because the sign encodes the meaning 'four people other than self' and the sign is directed toward the group of four people in either case.

### Theoretical issues

By mapping semantic structure directly onto an element of real space, as I did in Figure 3.13, I am departing from current practice within both cognitive grammar and mental space theory. Figure 3.14 diagrams how constructed meaning gets from a speaker to a listener given current assumptions within mental space theory.

Mental space theory is typically explained from the point of view of the listener. This begins with a phonetic representation '4' perceived by the listener. The phonetic representation leads to a semantic representation '5', which evokes a frame '6', which in turn structures a mental space '7', the elements of which are potentially mapped onto elements of other mental spaces. Conceptual elements '6' and '7' both participate in the constructed meaning. For the purposes of this figure, I have also represented the speaker's fully mapped set of mental spaces '1', including the frame '2', the encoded semantic structure '3' and its corresponding phonetic representation '4'.

Earlier I described how meaning is constructed from the sentence *Bob saw a frog* using current assumptions about mental space construction and mappings. This invokes a seeing frame such as the one in Figure 3.15, which is like Figure 3.8, except that it also includes an abbreviated cognitive grammar semantic representation.

The seeing frame structures a mental space containing a perceiver and an entity perceived. Information about those mental space elements (taken from

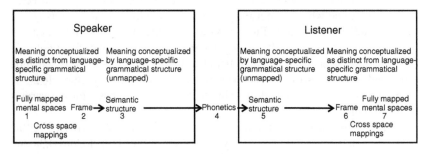

Figure 3.14  Meaning construction given current assumptions

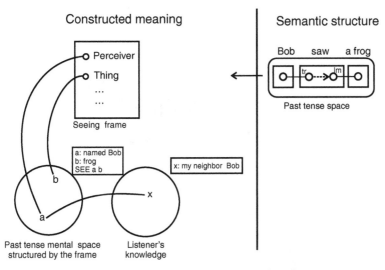

Figure 3.15  An example of meaning construction given current assumptions

the semantic representation) is recorded in the rectangle above the mental space. One has the characteristic 'named Bob' and the other has the characteristic 'frog'. Of particular interest here is the fact that the mental space structured by the seeing frame is a conceptual entity completely separate from the semantic structure.

A pronoun's directionality in ASL provides an instruction for making a mapping between *its individual semantic pole* and the mental space entity or entities it is directed toward. In chapter 4 we will see that the directionality of some verbs also provides similar mapping instructions. There is no obvious way to fit such multiple mapping instructions into the current mental space mapping model. It seems apparent that the directionality is simultaneous with the production of the individual pronoun in order to clearly identify the entity to map onto *its* structure. As a result, in the mental space mappings throughout the remainder of this book, I map semantic representations directly onto entities in other mental spaces.

This results in a different conceptualization of constructed meaning. If applied to the English sentence *Bob saw a frog* it will produce the constructed meaning illustrated in Figure 3.16.

The constructed meaning in Figure 3.16 is built from the semantic structure of *Bob saw a frog*. This semantic structure constitutes a mental space (Langacker 1999a). The past tense of the verb makes it a past tense space. The semantic pole of *Bob* is a mental space entity with the characteristic 'named Bob'. This element of the semantic structure is mapped onto an element known to the listener – the mental representation of a neighbor named Bob.

## Constructed Meaning

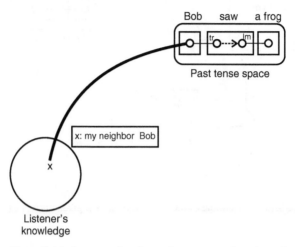

Figure 3.16  An example of meaning construction given the assumptions in this book

I now make some comparisons between the constructed meanings in Figures 3.15 and 3.16. Both include a mental space containing a conceptual element with the property 'named Bob' and a conceptual element with the property 'frog'. In Figure 3.15 these elements came to be as a result of a frame prompted by the semantic structure. In Figure 3.16, these two elements already exist within the semantic pole of *Bob saw a frog*. The semantic pole of *Bob* is a conceptual entity with the property 'named Bob'. The semantic pole of *frog* is a conceptual entity with the property 'frog'. This means that the mental space structured by the frame in Figure 3.15 recreates the two mental space entities already existing in the semantic structure. A comparison of the constructed meanings in Figures 3.15 and 3.16 shows that both ultimately have a conceptual element with the property 'named Bob' mapped onto the conceptual representation of the neighbor with that name. The significant difference between these two ways of constructing meaning is that in Figure 3.16, semantic structure plays a central role since it becomes a part of the constructed meaning. Indeed, from the perspective of the listener, constructed meaning is built around semantic structure. In comparison, current practice in mental space theory sees semantic structure as distinct from constructed meaning.

Assuming that a direct mapping between semantic structure and entities in other mental spaces is capable of producing the full range of constructed

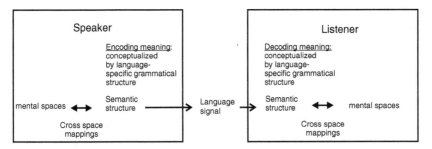

Figure 3.17  Meaning construction given the assumptions in this book

meaning types expected in mental space theory, this produces a model of meaning construction like that shown in Figure 3.17.

In this conception of meaning construction, the speaker begins with a constructed meaning, which includes a fully mapped semantic structure. Not all of this meaning can be expressed phonetically. The part that can is the semantic structure itself. The speaker produces a phonetic representation perceived by the listener as well as gestural elements perceived by the listener. Assuming that the listener is a speaker of the same language, the listener will have no difficulty decoding the phonetic signal. The result of that decoding is a semantic structure (essentially) identical to that produced by the speaker. In cases where gestural elements assist in the mapping process, the addressee will make use of those gestural elements. Otherwise, the addressee must make the mappings without the gestural assist.

This approach to meaning construction includes two conceptually distinct but integrated processes for the listener: decoding and mapping. Decoding produces a semantic structure from a phonetic signal. Mapping makes cross-space connections between that semantic structure and entities in other mental space representations. To the degree that the listener's mapped semantic structure corresponds to the speaker's mapped semantic structure, the speaker has successfully communicated the intended message (Fauconnier 1985).

Although the means of constructing meaning justified by the directional signs of ASL involves the machinery of cognitive grammar and mental space theory, it nevertheless represents a simplification of the process of constructing meaning. In the mappings used here, the only thing separating the speaker's mapped conceptual structure and the listener's mapped conceptual structure is the language signal.

## Summary

Addressees are confronted with the ongoing task of decoding the phonetic signal to activate a semantic structure, then mapping elements of the semantic structure onto other mental space elements. This is true regardless of whether the language in question is spoken or signed. Contextual clues assist addressees in making appropriate mappings. When elements of the semantic representation are meant to be mapped onto the physically present entities, the speaker or signer provides directional clues leading to the appropriate entities. In spoken language discourse the clues take the form of pointing gestures produced outside the vocal tract. This makes it easy to separate pointing gestures from the phonetic signal. In the case of sign language discourse, the symbolization and the pointing both occur through movements of the hands and body. This makes it more difficult to distinguish between symbolization and pointing. Indeed, the history of the analysis of directional signs has been guided by the assumption that the directional aspect of signing is symbolic.

ASL pronouns all encode grammatically defined meanings. They have this characteristic in common with pronouns in any vocally produced language. What distinguishes them from pronouns in a vocally produced language is what they are able to do *in addition to expressing their grammatically encoded meanings*. If ASL pronouns were unable to be directed in space, they would still be fully equivalent to pronouns in a vocally produced language.

I have argued that the *directional* aspect of pronouns is not symbolic, but rather, is an example of pointing. This does not imply that the pronoun itself is not symbolic. I am arguing that the symbolic pronoun can be directed in space in order to point at things. The symbolic pronoun encodes a meaning – just like a pronoun in any other language. The overlaid directionality points to a mental space entity to be associated with its semantic pole. An ASL pronoun's directionality is performing a crucial task in meaning construction by showing the addressee which entity or set of entities to map onto its semantic pole.

# 4   Indicating verbs and real space

Chapter 3 treats an ASL pronoun's directionality toward its physically present referent as a mental space mapping instruction. The resulting mapping connects an element of semantic space with an element of real space. More specifically, it connects the conceptual entity profiled in the pronoun's semantic pole with the entity in real space the pronoun is directed toward. Singular pronouns are directed toward single entities while plural pronouns are directed toward groups of entities.

The directionality of an indicating verb toward an element of real space serves the same function as the directionality of a pronoun toward an element of real space. It provides a mapping instruction between an element of the verb's semantic pole and an element of real space. In traditional terms, a pronoun's directionality leads to its referent or referents. Although the directionality of indicating verbs serves the same function, we do not normally talk about a verb's referents.

The semantic structure of verbs is considerably more variable than the semantic structure of pronouns. Verbs, for example, can be transitive or intransitive. A transitive verb typically involves one entity acting upon another. The directionality of some ASL verbs can indicate one of those entities while the directionality of others can indicate both. In addition, the semantic poles of some verbs contain locative or directional meanings while the semantic poles of others do not. Given the possible variation from one verb to the next, it should not be surprising that indicating verbs vary in the ways they can be directed.

This chapter generally restricts the data to situations in which indicating verbs are directed toward visible entities in real space. This restriction greatly simplifies the task of understanding the directionality since one can see the physical relationship between the verb and any real-space entities it is directed toward.

### Citation forms

ASL has a large number of verbs capable of being meaningfully directed in space toward entities, directions, or places. I will collectively refer to such

Figure 4.1  ASK-QUESTION (citation form)

verbs as *indicating verbs*. If requested to produce an instance of an indicating verb, signers will often produce a form that is not meaningfully directed at anything. This makes sense since the verb is being produced out of any discourse context – other than the request to produce a verb. Signs produced in response to such requests are called citation forms.

The citation form ASK-QUESTION is illustrated in Figure 4.1. It begins its movement just ahead of the shoulder and moves directly outward a short distance. This form merely expresses the verb's meaning, but does not, in addition, point toward any entity associated with its meaning.

The citation forms of one-handed indicating verbs that do not begin with body contact typically move outward a short distance from a starting location close to the body, on the same side of the trunk as the moving arm. ASK-QUESTION, DO-BETTER-THAN, PUT-QUESTION, GIVE, GIVE-OWNERSHIP, and SEND are examples of this type.[1]

If a sign begins with an initial body contact, its citation form will typically begin with that contact followed by a short outward movement of the hands. TELL, INFORM, ANSWER, IGNORE, and ORDER all fit this pattern.

If a two-handed indicating verb is produced with a non-moving *weak hand*, its citation form will typically be produced by placing the weak hand directly ahead of the trunk. The strong hand then carries out its movement with respect to the weak hand. The strong hand typically moves outward toward, contacts, or moves past the weak hand.[2] The verbs ADVISE, ARREST, BOTHER, CONVINCE, FLATTER, FORCE, MAKE-POINT-IN-ARGUMENT, and PICK-ON all fit

---

[1] There are two distinct indicating verbs with meanings related to asking questions. ASK-QUESTION begins with a vertical 1 handshape that changes to an X handshape at the end of the movement. As the hand moves toward the recipient of the question, the index finger bends over. I gloss this sign as ASK-QUESTION. PUT-QUESTION seems to convey either more seriousness of purpose or more authority on the part of the person asking the question. It begins with a closed 1 handshape (index finger restrained by the thumb) which opens to a 1 handshape at the end of the movement.

[2] The signs OWE and one form of STUDY are both exceptions to this statement in that the movement of the strong hand is neither outward nor inward. OWE moves from above the palm to contact with it. The form of STUDY with wiggling fingers is produced with the stationary wiggling fingers directed toward the palm of the weak hand. There is no path movement in this form of the verb STUDY.

this pattern. In addition, some two-handed signs with both hands active, like ENCOURAGE, ABANDON, and FLIRT, are also made in citation form ahead of the trunk.

A small number of citation form verbs move inward toward a location ahead of the trunk. In MOOCH, for example, the weak H hand (index and middle fingers extended and together) begins located ahead of, and slightly to the side of the signer. The strong H hand, with the thumb opposed to the fingers, grasps the ends of the fingers of the weak H handshape and the two hands move together toward a central location ahead of the trunk. INVITE also moves from the side inward toward a central location.

### Semantic representations

The central claim of this chapter is that directing a verb toward elements of real space is best understood as an instruction (or set of instructions) for map-pings between the verb's semantic pole and the mental space element(s) it is directed toward. In cognitive grammar, the semantic pole of a typical transi-tive verb is represented as a temporal relation between two entities. This is quite unlike previous theoretical positions. The semantic pole of a verb such as INFORM, for example, contains abstract conceptual elements corresponding to the person providing the information and the recipient of the information. Figure 4.2a is a diagrammatic representation of the semantic pole of the verb INFORM.

The diagram represents a temporal relationship between the entity providing the information and the recipient of the information. The leftmost side of the diagram shows two circles, connected by a vertical dashed line. The uppermost circle represents the person providing the information. In cognitive grammar, the *trajector* is "the (primary) figure within a profiled relation" (Langacker 1991:555). In an active, transitive verb the trajector is typically the conceptual entity in the verb's semantic pole seen as carrying out the activity of the verb. The trajector of the verb INFORM is the abstract entity providing the information and is labeled *tr*. The circle on the bottom represents the other entity in this

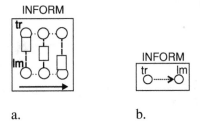

a.                          b.

Figure 4.2  Alternate representations of the semantic pole of INFORM

relationship, called the *landmark* and labeled *lm*. The information conceived of as moving from the provider to the recipient is represented in the diagram as a rectangle. In the diagram, time proceeds from left to right. As time progresses, the diagram represents the information as moving from the trajector to the landmark. It begins at the trajector, moves toward the landmark, and then arrives at the landmark. The three instances of the trajector at the top are connected by dotted lines. This is Langacker's diagrammatic way of showing that the three circles all represent the same entity at different times. Similarly, the three instances of the landmark at the bottom of the diagram are also connected by a dotted line, signifying that there is a single recipient of the information. For ease of exposition, the diagram of the semantic pole of a verb can be simplified. Thus, Figure 4.2b is meant to signify the same semantic information, but in a diagrammatically simpler way.

### Transitive verbs with $^{\rightarrow y}$ forms

The variable $x$ has been used as a variable to indicate that a pronoun such as PRO$^{\rightarrow x}$ is directed toward some entity $x$. In describing verbs, the variable $x$ will represent the entity to map onto the trajector and the variable $y$ will represent the entity to map onto the landmark. Thus, the notation TELL$^{\rightarrow y}$ identifies a verb that is directed toward an entity to map onto its landmark.

#### *Singular objects*

The verb ANALYZE$^{\rightarrow y}$ is produced as shown in Figure 4.3. Two V handshapes begin near one another then separate and move slightly downward. This is then repeated, with each repetition at a lower level than the previous one. Figure 4.3 illustrates two such repetitions. The first and second repetitions are almost identical, with the second repetition slightly lower than the first.

In Figure 4.4a ANALYZE$^{\rightarrow y}$ is directed toward the man opposite the signer. Since ANALYZE$^{\rightarrow y}$ does not move on an outward path away from the signer,

Figure 4.3  ANALYZE$^{\rightarrow y}$

ANALYZE$^{\rightarrow y}$

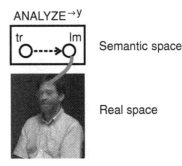

Semantic space

Real space

a.        ANALYZE$^{\rightarrow y}$

b. Mapping the landmark onto the man
ANALYZE$^{\rightarrow y}$ is directed toward

Figure 4.4 How directionality assists in meaning construction

its motion does not point. However, the palm surfaces of the hands are directed outward toward him and, in addition, the hands are placed between the signer and that man.[3] Figure 4.4b illustrates how the semantic pole of ANALYZE$^{\rightarrow y}$ maps onto real space. The verb's semantic pole contains a trajector 'the abstract analyzer' and a landmark 'the entity analyzed'.

Without regard to its directionality, ANALYZE$^{\rightarrow y}$ conveys that one entity analyzes another. The directionality additionally provides mapping instructions. Directing ANALYZE$^{\rightarrow y}$ toward the man opposite the signer is a signal to create a mapping between its landmark and that man, as shown in Figure 4.4b. The landmark in the semantic pole of ANALYZE$^{\rightarrow y}$ is an abstract entity with virtually no specific properties other than being an entity of some sort. Part of understanding the signer's message involves understanding which particular mental space entity corresponds to the landmark in this particular case. The directionality of ANALYZE$^{\rightarrow y}$ above prompts a mapping between the landmark and the addressee. In this example, then, the real-space addressee is the entity mapped onto the landmark.

Making a connection between the trajector and landmark in a verb's semantic pole and other mental space entities is an ongoing process in discourse, regardless of the language used. That is, regardless of whether a language is spoken or signed, the addressee is continually faced with the issue of mapping the trajector and landmark onto other mental space entities. The English phrase *analyze you* conveys similar information, but the mapping between the landmark of *analyze* and the addressee takes place by means of a different logic.

[3] ANALYZE$^{\rightarrow y}$ points by means of its placement and the orientation of the palms. Other verbs point with other parts of the hands (e.g. fingertip, front of fist). The part of the hand that points is a lexical property of the verb itself.

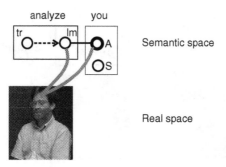

Figure 4.5  Mappings motivated by the semantics of *you* and logic

Figure 4.5 illustrates the semantic pole of the English phrase *analyze you* uttered in the context where the man pictured is the real-space addressee. The verb alone provides no clues as to how to map the landmark. The pronominal object *you*, however, contains the semantic information needed to make a mapping. It profiles the addressee (A) in the domain of a conversation between a speaker (S) and addressee. The bold circle represents the profiled addressee. The presence of a speaker is part of the meaning of *you*, but the speaker is not profiled (Langacker 1987, van Hoek 1988). The verb–object grammatical relationship entails a mapping between the verb's landmark and the entity profiled by the direct object (Langacker 1991). In this case the entity profiled by the object is entity *A*, the addressee in the semantic pole of *you*.

Mapping *A* onto the landmark associates its meaning with the landmark. But even this mapping does not *identify* the addressee. In fact, the linguistic signal does not identify the addressee at all. The identity of the addressee is contextually determined based on who is talking and who is being addressed. In this example, the man shown in the picture is the addressee.

The semantic entity *A*, maps onto the landmark of *analyze* because this is part of the verb–object grammatical construction. *A* maps onto the addressee in real space for semantic reasons since *you* profiles an abstract entity with the characteristic 'addressee' and, in this context, the man in the picture is the addressee. As a result there is a mapping chain from the man in real space to the semantic pole of *you* to the landmark of *analyze*. This indirectly links the man in real space and the landmark of *analyze*. This mapping chain would normally lead to the inference that the landmark should be directly mapped onto the man in real space as illustrated in Figure 4.5. This mapping signifies that the real-space addressee not only corresponds to the entity encoded by the pronoun but also corresponds to the landmark.

In order to understand both the ASL example in Figure 4.4 and the English example in Figure 4.5, the addressee must determine who or what the signer or

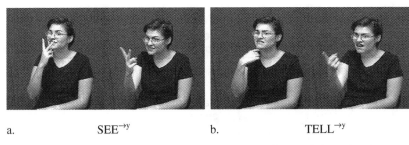

a.                   SEE$^{\rightarrow y}$                   b.                   TELL$^{\rightarrow y}$

Figure 4.6 Verbs directed toward entities to map onto their landmarks

speaker is talking about. This is accomplished through various types of clues. In the ASL example, the clue is directional since ANALYZE$^{\rightarrow y}$ is directed toward the real-space addressee. The directionality prompts the mapping between the verb's landmark and the real-space addressee.

The English example also produces a connection between the landmark of *analyze* and the real-space addressee. This is accomplished through the use of the pronoun *you*, which profiles an entity *A* with the semantic characteristic 'addressee'. This prompts a semantically motivated mapping between *A* and the physically present addressee. Since *A* is already connected to the landmark because of the verb–object grammatical relationship, the landmark can be linked through inference to the physically present addressee.

Since the verb's landmark in Figure 4.5 is mapped onto the profiled entity in the semantic pole of *you*, which is in turn mapped onto the addressee, it might seem unnecessary to perform the direct mapping between the landmark and the man in real space. It turns out to be important because it is not always the case that the landmark and the entity profiled by the direct object will both map onto the same entity outside of the semantic pole of the utterance. Liddell (in press a), for example, describes a case where the directionality of a subject pronoun forces a mapping between it and an entity in real space. The verb's directionality forces a mapping between its trajector and another mental space entity. Since the pronoun's semantic pole and the verb's trajector can map onto different entities, I treat the mappings of the subject and trajector independently and also treat the mappings of the landmark and direct object independently.

With a transitive indicating verb, either there is a mapping between the landmark and some conceptual entity *y* or not. There is no middle ground between these two options. If SEE$^{\rightarrow y}$ (Figure 4.6a) is directed toward a car, that would indicate a mapping between the verb's landmark and the car. If SEE$^{\rightarrow y}$ is not directed toward the car, then there is no such mapping. Suppose there are two cars side by side and SEE$^{\rightarrow y}$ is directed toward one of them. The interpretation is not that the subject sees one car but just missed seeing the other car by a

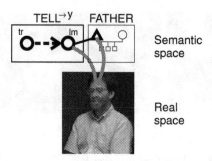

Figure 4.7 Mappings motivated by the directionality of TELL$^{\to y}$ and logic

few feet. There is a seeing relationship with respect to the car SEE$^{\to y}$ is directed toward, and no seeing relationship with the other car. The directionality of SEE$^{\to y}$ prompts a mapping between its landmark and the entity it is directed toward, but does not imply anything at all about any other entity. If SEE$^{\to y}$ is not directed toward the other car, that second car would play no role whatsoever in the meaning expressed by that instance of SEE$^{\to y}$.

The verb TELL$^{\to y}$ is similar (Figure 4.6b). It begins its motion in contact with the chin, then moves outward toward the mental space entity to be mapped onto its landmark. Directing TELL$^{\to y}$ outward toward the addressee identifies the addressee as the real-space entity corresponding to the landmark (i.e. the recipient of the telling). Directing TELL$^{\to y}$ outward toward someone else, identifies that other person as the entity corresponding to the landmark.

(1)    TELL$^{\to y}$ FATHER.
       Tell father.

Let us suppose that in producing (1) the signer directs TELL$^{\to y}$ toward the physically present father shown in Figure 4.7. In (1), TELL$^{\to y}$ has the overt object FATHER and the verb phrase TELL$^{\to y}$ FATHER encodes the meaning 'tell father'. The mapped semantic pole of (1) is shown in Figure 4.7. Directing TELL$^{\to y}$ toward the physically present father is an instruction to create a mapping between the landmark of TELL$^{\to y}$ and that person in real space. The verb–object construction TELL$^{\to y}$ FATHER grammatically encodes a mapping between the entity profiled in the semantic pole of FATHER and the landmark of TELL$^{\to y}$. As a result, the landmark of TELL$^{\to y}$ is mapped onto two distinct entities. The mapping between the landmark and the grammatical object associates the meaning 'father' with the landmark. The mapping between the landmark and the man in real space associates that man with the landmark.

This set of mappings also creates a mapping chain from the man in real space to the landmark to the entity profiled in the semantic pole of FATHER.

As a result, an observer could infer that the physically present person had the property 'father'. This mapping is represented by the connector between the semantic pole of FATHER and the man in real space in Figure 4.7. The mapping in the ASL example shown in Figure 4.7 is similar to mapping in the English example shown in Figure 4.5. In both cases entities at the two ends of a mapping chain are directly linked through inference. In Figure 4.5 inference maps the landmark onto the man in real space. In Figure 4.7 inference maps the semantic pole of the direct object onto the man in real space. In spite of the different motivations for the entire set of mappings in Figures 4.5 and 4.7, the resulting set of mappings are identical. In both cases the landmark and the entity profiled in the semantic pole of the direct object map onto the same person in real space.

There is a great deal of confusion in the sign language literature concerning what pronouns and directional verbs are directed toward. If one accepts the idea that spatial loci can function as pronouns, then a spatial pronoun might conceivably be viewed as functioning as the object of a verb. This may account for the common belief that directional verbs are directed toward their objects. This conception of grammatical object depends on assumptions about spatial loci that I have already shown to be inconsistent with how signers actually sign. However, it is uncontroversial and not dependent on assumptions about spatial loci that the sign FATHER is the object of the verb TELL$^{\rightarrow y}$ in Figure 4.7. Directional verbs are never directed toward *the sign* functioning as the object of a verb. If they were, the verb TELL$^{\rightarrow y}$ would have been directed toward the sign FATHER. After all, the sign FATHER is the object of TELL, not the person the sign is directed toward. Signers do not do this, of course. But if they did, there would then be some basis for claiming that indicating verbs are directed toward their objects.

When a typical transitive indicating verb is directed toward a single entity, that entity will correspond to the verb's landmark. A sampling of verbs of this type includes ABANDON$^{\rightarrow y}$, ABHOR$^{\rightarrow y}$, ADORE$^{\rightarrow y}$, ADVISE$^{\rightarrow y}$, ANALYZE$^{\rightarrow y}$, ANSWER$^{\rightarrow y}$, ARREST$^{\rightarrow y}$, ASK-QUESTION$^{\rightarrow y}$, BAWL-OUT$^{\rightarrow y}$, BEG$^{\rightarrow y}$, BITE$^{\rightarrow y}$, BLAME$^{\rightarrow y}$, BOTHER$^{\rightarrow y}$, BUY$^{\rightarrow y}$, CALL-BY-PHONE$^{\rightarrow y}$, CALL-BY-TTY$^{\rightarrow y}$,[4] CONVINCE$^{\rightarrow y}$, CRITICIZE$^{\rightarrow y}$, DO-BETTER-THAN$^{\rightarrow y}$, DEFEAT$^{\rightarrow y}$, FEED$^{\rightarrow y}$, FLATTER$^{\rightarrow y}$, FLIRT$^{\rightarrow y}$, FORCE$^{\rightarrow y}$, GIVE$^{\rightarrow y}$, GIVE-OWNERSHIP$^{\rightarrow y}$, HATE$^{\rightarrow y}$, HELP$^{\rightarrow y}$, BUTTER-UP$^{\rightarrow y}$, IGNORE$^{\rightarrow y}$, INFORM$^{\rightarrow y}$, INSPECT$^{\rightarrow y}$, LEND$^{\rightarrow y}$, LOOK-AT$^{\rightarrow y}$, MAKE-POINT-IN-ARGUMENT$^{\rightarrow y}$, MOCK$^{\rightarrow y}$, NOTICE$^{\rightarrow y}$, ORDER$^{\rightarrow y}$,

---

[4] The abbreviation TTY stands for teletypewriter. A TTY is a very large, noisy, metallic piece of equipment used to send text messages through phone lines. TTYs have subsequently been replaced by modern, lightweight portable devices, but the name TTY is still commonly used to refer to the newer portable devices.

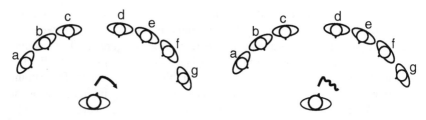

a. ASK-QUESTION[MULTIPLE]ɔd,e,f,g        b. ASK-QUESTION[EXHAUSTIVE]ɔd,e,f,g

Figure 4.8  The shapes of the multiple and exhaustive verb forms

OWE→ʸ, PAY→ʸ, PICK-ON→ʸ, PITY→ʸ, PUT-QUESTION→ʸ, SAY-NO-TO→ʸ, SELL→ʸ, SEND→ʸ, SHOW→ʸ, SPELL-TO→ʸ, TATTLE→ʸ, TEASE→ʸ, TELL→ʸ, and WARN→ʸ.[5]

### Plural objects

ASK-QUESTION[MULTIPLE]ɔy differs from the verbs previously discussed in that it encodes a plural object. Its directionality, however, serves the same purpose as the directionality of a verb with a singular object. The directionality of the sideward movement in ASK-QUESTION[MULTIPLE]ɔy leads to the identification of the entities to map onto its plural landmark. If those entities are physically present, the sideward movement will be directed toward those physically present individuals.

ASK-QUESTION[MULTIPLE]ɔd,e,f,g in Figure 4.8a begins by moving outward toward the individual labeled *d*. The hand then moves along a sideward path from a position between the signer and *d* to a position between the signer and *g*. The sideward sweeping movement clearly identifies *d*, *e*, *f*, and *g*. Had ASK-QUESTION[MULTIPLE]ɔy begun its movement directed at *a* and moved along a path ending with the hand directed at *c*, the movement would have identified persons *a*, *b*, and *c* as the entities to map onto the verb's plural landmark. Changing the directionality of the sign identifies a different group.

ASK-QUESTION[EXHAUSTIVE]ɔd,e,f,g in Figure 4.8b also encodes a plural object. Recall from chapter 2 that the exhaustive form differs from the multiple form by including an oscillating movement as it moves along the sideward path. The oscillating movement is represented in Figure 4.8b by an undulating line. The number of oscillations as the hand moves along its path does not correlate with the number of entities the sign is directed toward. That is, it is the sideward path rather than the number of oscillations that determines the composition of

---

[5] Some of these signs have related forms that are also capable of indicating the entity corresponding to their trajectors. These verbs are discussed later in this chapter.

Figure 4.9  Directing COMPARE[EXHAUSTIVE]ɔy toward objects on a table

the group being identified. The right-to-left movement in Figure 4.8b clearly identifies $d$, $e$, $f$, and $g$.

In Figure 4.8 ASK-QUESTION[MULTIPLE]ɔd,e,f,g and ASK-QUESTION[EXHAUSTIVE]ɔd,e,f,g express different meanings in spite of the fact that they are both directed toward $d$, $e$, $f$, and $g$. The difference in meaning has to do with how the asking is characterized. ASK-QUESTION[MULTIPLE]ɔd,e,f,g characterizes the asking as a single event while ASK-QUESTION[EXHAUSTIVE]ɔd,e,f,g expresses multiple asking events with respect to the group (Klima and Bellugi 1979).

The verb COMPARE (citation form) is a two-handed sign. Each hand uses a B handshape with all the fingers extended and bent over at the joint connecting the fingers to the hand, but with a general upward orientation of the fingertips. One hand moves slightly outward as the forearm rotates so that the palm faces inward, the other hand moves inward as the forearm rotates in the opposite direction. COMPARE is produced with the two hands repeatedly alternating in this way. A related verb COMPARE-DUAL→y,z is restricted to situations involving the comparison of two things. If the two things are physically present, one hand will be directed toward one of them while the other hand is directed toward the other.

The verb COMPARE[EXHAUSTIVE]ɔy is similar to the exhaustive verb forms previously examined in that the hands perform an oscillating movement as the hands move along a path identifying the entities corresponding to the plural landmark. In Figure 4.9 the signer directs COMPARE[EXHAUSTIVE]ɔy along a path identifying a set of videotapes on a table in front of her. She begins the sign with her hands and eye gaze directed toward the right side of the set of videotapes. As the wrists oscillate, the hands move leftward, ending with the hands and eye gaze directed toward the left side of the set of videotapes.

Both the eye gaze and the path movement of the hands identify the videotapes being compared. Figure 4.10 illustrates the mapping resulting from the way COMPARE[EXHAUSTIVE]ɔy is directed in Figure 4.9. COMPARE[EXHAUSTIVE]ɔy encodes a comparison of a collection of entities, represented in Figure 4.10 as

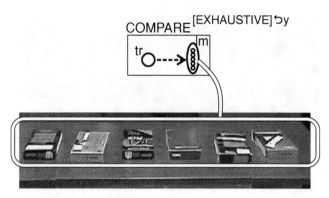

Figure 4.10  Mapping the landmark of COMPARE[EXHAUSTIVE]ɔy onto the set of objects the verb is directed toward

an ellipse containing five things. The intent of the diagram is not to specify a specific number, but rather, to indicate a collection. The signer's eye gaze and the directionality of the movement both indicate entities to be mapped onto the landmark. Both clearly indicate the set of videotapes on the table ahead of the signer and constitute a mapping instruction for constructing meaning.

The result of that mapping is shown in Figure 4.10. The landmark is mapped onto the set of videotapes the hands and eyes are directed toward. Klima and Bellugi (1979) analyze the verb I describe here as COMPARE[EXHAUSTIVE]ɔy as the seriated external grammatical inflection of the verb COMPARE. They treat the horizontal path as a fixed feature of the form signaling a comparison of objects of the same general class (p. 290). In the analysis I am propos-ing, the specific path of the hand is not fixed, but depends on the physical location of the things to be mapped onto the landmark. Thus, in Figure 4.10, the hands move along the horizontal path because the things the hand is directed toward are arranged along a horizontal path. Had the entities been arranged dif-ferently the hands would have moved along a different path.

In Figure 4.11 the signer directs COMPARE[EXHAUSTIVE]ɔy along a diagonal downward path that identifies the four diagonally arranged pictures. She begins with the hands and eye gaze directed toward the picture on the upper left, then the hands produce the oscillating movement as they move diagonally downward to the picture on the lower right. I am suggesting that the signs in Figures 4.9 and 4.11 are both examples of COMPARE[EXHAUSTIVE]ɔy and that they encode the same meaning in both instances. The constructed meaning of the two examples will be different since the hands are directed toward different sets of entities in the two examples. The data here demonstrate that COMPARE[EXHAUSTIVE]ɔy

Figure 4.11 Directing COMPARE[EXHAUSTIVE]ɔy diagonally toward a set of pictures

does not have a fixed horizontal movement, but rather, has the ability to be directed toward the entities arranged in other physical configurations as well.

Klima and Bellugi also describe a formationally similar form that moves vertically downward. They identify it as a seriated internal form of COMPARE. This downward moving form is described as signifying "distribution of action with respect to (some list of) typical components, characteristics, or internal features of objects" (1979:290). Rather than a single list, I suggest that this sign is directed toward two paired lists. I would gloss this sign as COMPARE-DUAL[EXHAUSTIVE]ɔy,z, where $y$ and $z$ represent paired lists. One can see how this works if this sign is produced in the presence of two paired lists. One hand will begin directed toward the top of one list while the other hand is directed toward the top of the other list. Both hands then move vertically downward past the items on each list. Further, the physical placement of the lists influences the placement of the hands in producing the sign. Since each hand is directed toward one of the lists, the hands will be close together in the case of narrowly separated lists and further apart in the case of widely separated lists.

### Transitive verbs with $^{x \rightarrow y}$ forms

The verbs described below are directed in space toward the entities corresponding to both their trajectors and their landmarks. This set of verbs includes ABANDON$^{x \rightarrow y}$, ADVISE$^{x \rightarrow y}$, ARREST$^{x \rightarrow y}$, ASK-QUESTION$^{x \rightarrow y}$, BAWL-OUT$^{x \rightarrow y}$, BITE$^{x \rightarrow y}$, BLAME$^{x \rightarrow y}$, BOTHER$^{x \rightarrow y}$, CRITICIZE$^{x \rightarrow y}$, DEFEAT$^{x \rightarrow y}$, DO-BETTER-THAN$^{x \rightarrow y}$, FLATTER$^{x \rightarrow y}$, FORCE$^{x \rightarrow y}$, FREQUENT$^{x \rightarrow y}$, GIVE$^{x \rightarrow y}$, GIVE-OWNERSHIP$^{x \rightarrow y}$, HATE$^{x \rightarrow y}$, HELP$^{x \rightarrow y}$, INFORM$^{x \rightarrow y}$, LEND$^{x \rightarrow y}$, LOOK-AT$^{x \rightarrow y}$, MAKE-POINT-IN-ARGUMENT$^{x \rightarrow y}$, PICK-ON$^{x \rightarrow y}$, PITY$^{x \rightarrow y}$, PUT-QUESTION$^{x \rightarrow y}$, SAY-NO-TO$^{x \rightarrow y}$, SEND$^{x \rightarrow y}$, SHOW$^{x \rightarrow y}$, STUDY$^{x \rightarrow y}$, and TEASE$^{x \rightarrow y}$.

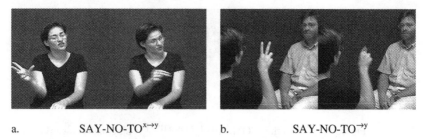

a.              SAY-NO-TO$^{x\to y}$              b.              SAY-NO-TO$^{\to y}$

Figure 4.12  Two related verbs that differ in their indicating properties

SAY-NO-TO$^{x\to y}$ is typical of verbs in this category. Consider the way it is directed in Figure 4.12a. It begins directed toward a person on the right and ends directed toward a person on the left. The mapping instructions are clear. The person on the right maps onto the trajector and the person on the left maps onto the landmark. The resulting mappings would be understood to mean that the person on the right said "no" to the person on the left.

The verb SAY-NO-TO$^{\to y}$ in Figure 4.12b is different. It begins slightly above and ahead of the shoulder then moves outward toward the addressee. Its direction toward the addressee indicates that the addressee maps onto the landmark.

Since Padden (1983) it has been widely accepted that the type of verbs I am describing move in space in order to show grammatical agreement with their subjects, objects, or both. Padden argues that a verb capable of agreeing with its subject and object may optionally omit subject agreement (1988:136). In my analysis, however, the directionality of signs has nothing to do with grammatical agreement. Instead, the directionality of the sign provides mapping instructions telling the addressee which mental space entities to map onto the trajector or landmark in the verb's semantic pole.

The verbs I am describing here as having an $^{x\to y}$ form would be identified in Padden's analysis as verbs showing agreement with both their subjects and objects. In Padden's analysis subject agreement is optional. In the framework I am developing here, this claim would be equivalent to stating that $^{x\to y}$ verbs could optionally be produced as $^{\to y}$ verbs. I will discuss this issue in more depth shortly. But for now, it is important to understand what kind of verb the sign in Figure 4.12b is.

Bahan (1996) claims there is a distinction between first person agreement on a verb and an unmarked form of subject agreement: "So, this suggests that what has previously been identified as the citation form of GIVE found in examples like (14) is not, in fact, devoid of agreement inflection. Rather, this example reflects the unmarked form of subject agreement, which, in ASL morphology, is generally very similar in appearance to first person inflection" (107–108). In this view, the verb in Figure 4.12b could be marking first person subject agreement or could be an unmarked form of subject agreement. In my terms, it could be either SAY-NO-TO$^{x \to y}$ or SAY-NO-TO$^{\to y}$. If the subject were PRO-1 then the starting location ahead of the signer would "agree" with the first person subject PRO-1. This would be understood as support for the verb being SAY-NO-TO$^{x \to y}$. If the subject were not PRO-1, the same verb form would be understood to be SAY-NO-TO$^{\to y}$.

The problem here is that the beginning of the sign in Figure 4.12b does not appear to convey anything about the identity of the element to map onto the trajector. The addressee is still dependent on syntax or other aspects of the pragmatic context to determine who said "no." As a result, I conclude that the sign in Figure 4.12b is SAY-NO-TO$^{\to y}$ since it only identifies the entity to map onto the landmark. Its initial location does not identify anything.

### Lexical verb forms with first person landmarks

The verb SAY-NO-TO-1 is illustrated in Figure 4.13. It is produced with the same handshape changes as SAY-NO-TO$^{x \to y}$ and SAY-NO-TO$^{\to y}$, but the activity takes place just ahead of the nose. In this lexically fixed form the hand does not have the flexibility to move to different locations in space to indicate the entity to map onto the trajector. It is a first person form in that the verb's landmark (i.e. its semantic object) has the property 'current signer'. Since the landmark has that property, it will map onto the signer.

There are many additional verbs with first person landmarks. LOOK-AT-1, for example, is produced just ahead of the nose; INFORM-1, ASK-QUESTION-1, and STUDY-1 move toward the chin/neck; and a large number begin ahead of the sternum, including BAWL-OUT-1, BITE-1, BLAME-1, CRITICIZE-1, DEFEAT-1, DO-BETTER-THAN-1, FORCE-1, GIVE-1, GIVE-OWNERSHIP-1, HATE-1, PICK-ON-1, PITY-1, and TEASE-1.

Normally, verbs with first person landmarks are directed toward a bilaterally central location on the body. For example, GIVE-1 contacts the sternum. TELL-1 contacts the top of the sternum. SAY-NO-TO-1 is directed toward the nose. REMIND-1 is unusual in that it does not contact the body at a central location. Figure 4.14 illustrates both REMIND$^{\to y}$ and REMIND-1. REMIND$^{\to y}$

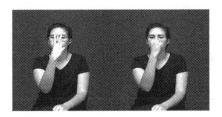

Figure 4.13  SAY-NO-TO-1

a.          REMIND$^{\to y}$          b.          REMIND-1

c.          CONVINCE$^{\to y}$          d.          CONVINCE-1

Figure 4.14 Two pairs of signs with -1 forms not produced on the centerline of the body

(Figure 4.14a) makes a repeated outward movement toward the entity to map onto the landmark while REMIND-1 makes a repeated contact at the shoulder with the fingertips (Figure 4.14b).

CONVINCE$^{\to y}$ is produced as shown in Figure 4.14c. To produce CONVINCE-1 the hands turn over and make contact with both sides of the neck as illustrated in Figure 4.14d. This form is unusual because the palms reorient to face down as each hand makes contact at the side of the neck.

ANALYZE$^{\to y}$ indicates by orienting the palm surface toward the entity to map onto the landmark. For example, in producing ANALYZE$^{\to y}$, the signer directs the hands outward as in Figure 4.15a. The hands begin in a V configuration. The fingers bend as the hands move apart and slightly downward. Each subsequent repetition takes place at a slightly lower level. Figure 4.15a illustrates two repetitions of this movement. ANALYZE-1 is illustrated in Figure 4.15b. The palms are directed inward toward the signer and the hands are located near the signer.

In addition to these typical forms, there is also the unique form ANALYZE-SELF. The hands move down the front of the chest with the radial surface of the hands directed inward as in Figure 4.15c.

## The lexical status of $^{x \to y}$, $^{\to y}$, and -1 verb forms

Given popular assumptions about directional signs, the signs SAY-NO-TO$^{x \to y}$, SAY-NO-TO$^{\to y}$, and SAY-NO-TO-1 would all be considered instances of a

a.                           ANALYZE$^{\to y}$

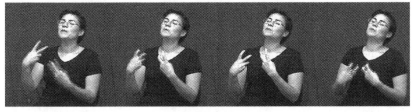

b.                           ANALYZE-1

c.                           ANALYZE-SELF

Figure 4.15 Three closely related, but distinct, verbs

single lexical unit. That is, it is currently assumed that there is a single verb SAY-NO-TO that moves from or toward the locations of spatial "affixes" marking "subject agreement" or "object agreement." The problem with the view that there is a single verb is that not all indicating verbs have all three verb forms. For example, TELL$^{\to y}$ and TELL-1 both exist, but TELL$^{x \to y}$ does not. Similarly, FLIRT$^{\to y}$ exists, but neither FLIRT$^{x \to y}$ nor FLIRT-1 exists. Attempting to account for these facts by means of constraints on what the hands are able to do physically does not work. For example, signs produced in contact with the body have been described as "body-anchored" verbs. It might be possible to argue, for example, that there is no TELL$^{x \to y}$ form because the sign is body-anchored in that TELL begins in contact with the chin. Since its initial location is fixed, its outward movement can only identify the single entity $y$. The problem with this argument is that there is a variant of INFORM$^{x \to y}$ that begins in contact with the forehead. From the forehead, the hand moves to indicate $x$ then moves to indicate $y$. Thus, one cannot use body anchoring as a constraint on directional verbs.

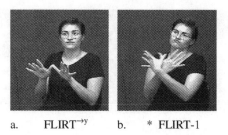

a.     FLIRT$^{\to y}$     b.     * FLIRT-1

Figure 4.16  Comparing FLIRT$^{\to y}$ with the non-existent FLIRT-1

The fact that FLIRT$^{\to y}$ exists but not FLIRT$^{x \to y}$ or FLIRT-1 presents similar problems. The acceptable FLIRT$^{\to y}$ is illustrated in Figure 4.16a.

Although it is physically possible, and not uncomfortable, to turn the hands around so that the tips of the fingers point to the signer, *FLIRT-1 (Figure 4.16b) does not exist for the signers I have consulted.[6] If a signer wanted to express that someone was flirting with her, she could do that syntactically. An example appears in (2), where the citation form FLIRT appears along with its syntactic object, the first person pronoun PRO-1.

(2)     THAT MAN FLIRT PRO-1
        That man was flirting with me.

The verb BAWL-OUT$^{[\text{INTENSIVE}] \to y}$ (Figure 4.17a) is a non-reduplicated verb that moves from ahead of the chest outward toward $y$ then returns to a position ahead of the chest. It has a corresponding first person object form BAWL-OUT-1$^{[\text{INTENSIVE}]}$, illustrated in Figure 4.17b. This is a non-reduplicated intensive form that begins ahead of the torso, moves inward, then returns to its initial configuration. It has roughly the same amount of twisting of the wrist as would be needed to produce the unacceptable *FLIRT-1 (Figure 4.16b).

BAWL-OUT-1$^{[\text{INTENSIVE}]}$, however, is a perfectly acceptable sign even though FLIRT-1 is not. The unacceptability of FLIRT-1 is not due to a physical constraint, but is simply a lexical fact.

Thus, the idea that a single lexical unit underlies all the possible directional uses associated with a particular verb (e.g. INFORM, SAY-NO-TO) is unable to account for the distribution of $^{x \to y}$, $^{\to y}$, and first person object forms that actually occur.

Figure 4.18 schematically illustrates the typical movement possibilities of the $^{x \to y}$ and $^{\to y}$ verb forms.

The $^{x \to y}$ forms begin directed toward $x$, where $x$ is not the signer, and end directed toward $y$. Although the signer could not be entity $x$, the signer could

---

[6] Since orienting the hands inward is not physically difficult, there is no reason that such a sign could not come into existence.

a.                    BAWL-OUT[INTENSIVE]→y

b.                    BAWL-OUT-1[INTENSIVE]

Figure 4.17  The verb BAWL-OUT[INTENSIVE]→y and the closely related form
BAWL-OUT-1[INTENSIVE]

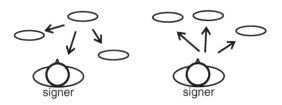

a. x→y movement patterns        b. →y movement patterns

Figure 4.18  Comparing the movement possibilities of x→y verbs and →y verbs

potentially be entity y. The →y forms begin from a non-pointing place on the
signer's body or just ahead of the signer, then move outward toward some entity
y. Starting near the signer does not indicate a mapping between the signer and
the verb's trajector, though there could be such a mapping for independent
reasons (e.g. syntax or context). In addition to these two verb forms, some
of the signs with →y forms also have lexicalized first person landmark forms.
These forms are produced just ahead of the signer. Some signs such as GIVE-1
move to make contact with the signer and others, such as ASK-1, do not.

Figure 4.19 illustrates the semantic poles of the three related verb forms SAY-
NO-TO x→y, SAY-NO-TO→y, and SAY-NO-TO-1. These three verb forms have
already been illustrated in Figures 4.12 and 4.13.

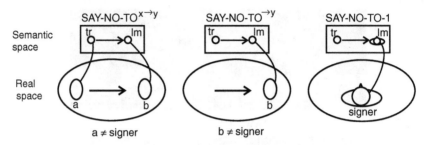

Figure 4.19 Three distinct verbs and their lexical mapping instructions

The semantic poles of SAY-NO-TO$^{x\rightarrow y}$ and SAY-NO-TO$^{\rightarrow y}$ are highly similar. Both contain a trajector carrying out the action of saying "no" to the landmark. They differ, however, in their spatial characteristics as well as in restrictions on their trajectors or landmarks. The beginning location for SAY-NO-TO$^{x\rightarrow y}$ indicates the entity to map onto its trajector and the final location indicates the entity to map onto its landmark. SAY-NO-TO$^{\rightarrow y}$ is similar except that its initial placement does not indicate an entity to map onto the trajector. There is a restriction in the trajector of SAY-NO-TO$^{x\rightarrow y}$ in that it is not first person. That is, it cannot map onto the signer. There is a similar restriction on the landmark of SAY-NO-TO$^{\rightarrow y}$, which is also not first person. That is, it will not map onto the signer. Finally, SAY-NO-TO-1 has a fixed lexical form that encodes action toward the signer.

The three-way analysis above (SAY-NO-TO$^{x\rightarrow y}$, SAY-NO-TO$^{\rightarrow y}$, and SAY-NO-TO-1) can be generalized to many other verbs as well. Not all indicating verbs, however, have all three forms. As described earlier, however, some verbs such as FLIRT or TATTLE have only the $^{\rightarrow y}$ form. Others such as TELL have both the $^{\rightarrow y}$ and -1 forms. I know of no instances of verbs with a -1 form that do not also have the $^{\rightarrow y}$ form. Thus, the existence of a -1 form also implies the existence of the $^{\rightarrow y}$ form. Similarly, the existence of the $^{x\rightarrow y}$ form implies existence of the $^{\rightarrow y}$ form. These two implications suggest that the $^{\rightarrow y}$ form is probably the most basic form. From it the $^{x\rightarrow y}$ form or the -1 form can develop.

### Backward verbs

Padden (1983) identifies a category of verbs including BORROW, COPY, EX-TRACT, INVITE, MOOCH, STEAL, TAKE, and TAKE-ADVANTAGE-OF as *backward verbs*. A backward verb is described as being like any other "agreement verb" except that its movement path begins by showing "object agreement" and ends by showing "subject agreement." In the framework being developed here, the start of the path movement of such a backward verb would identify

a. Backward $^{x \leftarrow y}$ movement patterns    b. Backward $^{\leftarrow y}$ movement patterns

Figure 4.20  Comparing the movement possibilities of $^{x \leftarrow y}$ verbs and $^{\leftarrow y}$ verbs

the entity to map onto the landmark while the end of the movement would identify the entity to map onto the trajector. This is the reverse of verbs like ASK-QUESTION$^{x \rightarrow y}$. I will use the notation $^{x \leftarrow y}$ to show a backward verb that indicates the entity corresponding to the landmark then moves toward the entity corresponding to the trajector. Similarly, the notation $^{\leftarrow y}$ will be used with a backward verb that indicates the entity to map onto its landmark by moving away from it.

It appears that backward verbs only exhibit two of the three possibilities available to indicating verbs. For example, INVITE $^{x \leftarrow y}$ begins its movement directed toward the entity to map onto the landmark, then moves toward the entity to map onto the trajector. The movement possibilities for $^{x \leftarrow y}$ verbs are illustrated in Figure 4.20a. The entity to map onto the landmark can be either the signer or not. The entity to map onto the trajector will be someone other than the signer.

The movement possibilities for $^{\leftarrow y}$ verbs are illustrated in Figure 4.20b. INVITE$^{\leftarrow y}$, for example, begins its movement directed toward the entity to map onto the landmark then moves to a location ahead of the signer. Although each instance of INVITE$^{\leftarrow y}$ moves to a location ahead of the signer, that movement does not indicate that the signer corresponds to the verb's trajector.

The movement patterns available to INVITE$^{x \leftarrow y}$ and INVITE$^{\leftarrow y}$ are typical of the class of backward verbs. I have been unable to identify any backward verbs with a -1 form (i.e. INVITE-1).[7]

### Head rotation and eye gaze

When producing the verb HONOR$^{\cup \rightarrow y}$, the face and eye gaze should be directed toward the entity to map onto the landmark. I symbolize this requirement with the symbol $^{\cup}$. Thus, the notation$^{\cup \rightarrow y}$ symbolizes the requirement for the face

---

[7]  Cole (2000) identifies a form of INVITE that begins very near or in contact with the chest and moves a short distance away. She describes its meaning as 'be invited', noting that it can be used with both first person and non-first person subjects.

a.        HONOR (citation form)    b.           HONOR<sup>ᵕ→ʸ</sup>

c.           HONOR<sup>ᵕ→ʸ</sup>

Figure 4.21 Comparing the citation form HONOR with two instances of HONOR<sup>ᵕ→ʸ</sup>

and eye gaze to be directed toward *y* (ᵕ) and the requirement for the hands to be directed toward *y* (→).

HONOR<sup>ᵕ→ʸ</sup> is a two-handed sign that begins with one H hand at the forehead and the other H hand slightly below and ahead of it. Both hands move outward and down producing an arc-shaped movement, with a downward bow in the arc (Figure 4.21a). The hands do not change shape during the sign.[8]

With the face and eye gaze properly directed, the hands move directly outward from the face toward *y*. In Figure 4.21b the signer directs HONOR<sup>ᵕ→ʸ</sup> upward and to the left toward some entity. In Figure 4.21c she directs HONOR<sup>ᵕ→ʸ</sup> downward and to the left toward a different entity at a lower level.

By focusing on the requirement to direct the face and eyes properly in producing HONOR<sup>ᵕ→ʸ</sup>, I do not mean to imply that the face and eyes do not point when other indicating verbs are used. The distinction here is that for signs such as HONOR<sup>ᵕ→ʸ</sup>, properly directing the face and eye gaze throughout the production of the sign is required. The number of signs in this category is relatively small, but includes RESPECT<sup>ᵕ→ʸ</sup>, FASCINATED-BY<sup>ᵕ→ʸ</sup>, and INTERESTED-IN<sup>ᵕ→ʸ</sup>.

These are not the only signs, however, that identify a mental space entity by rotating and orienting the head. In general, -1 verb forms also have this

---

[8] Brita Bergman observed that in producing the signs in Figure 4.21b–c, the signer has reversed the hand closest to the body. This is a case where ease of articulation provides an easy explanation for the reversal.

capability. Thus, while it is possible to produce SAY-NO-TO-1 with a forward head position that does not point at anything, it is also possible for the signer to direct the face and eyes toward the entity to map onto the verb's trajector. Given this capability, it is possible also to talk about verb forms such as SAY-NO-TO-1$^{\cup x}$. For this sign, the lexical form has a first person landmark that will map onto the signer, while head direction and eye gaze identify element $x$.

### Reciprocal verbs

The verb GIVE$^{x \rightarrow y}$ in Figure 4.22a is one-handed. It begins its motion nearer to entity $x$ and moves toward entity $y$. GIVE$^{[RECIP]x \leftrightarrow y}$ is illustrated in Figure 4.22b. Each hand appears to be producing a meaningful instance of GIVE$^{x \rightarrow y}$. The two instances differ in the way they are directed. One hand indicates that entity $x$ on the right gave something to entity $y$ on the left, while the other hand indicates the reverse.

The symmetry of the hands producing GIVE$^{[RECIP]x \leftrightarrow y}$ raises the issue of whether the signer is performing two signs at once, or whether the reciprocal form is a grammatical unit. If it were possible to find instances of two independent verbs being produced at once, that would provide support for GIVE$^{[RECIP]x \leftrightarrow y}$ being two simultaneous verbs. For example, it is possible to conceive of directing the verb ASK-QUESTION$^{x \rightarrow y}$ from left to right while simultaneously directing the verb SAY-NO-TO$^{x \rightarrow y}$ from right to left. Such simultaneous and referentially opposite verb combinations do not occur in ASL.

If reciprocal verbs are treated as grammatical units, then it is possible for a reciprocal form to have grammatical properties that belong to the unit rather than to any of its parts. INFORM$^{[RECIP]x \leftrightarrow y}$ illustrates this point. INFORM$^{\rightarrow y}$ is a two-handed sign, where both hands perform very similar movements (Figure 4.23a). INFORM$^{\rightarrow y}$ also has the one-handed variant shown in Figure 4.23b. INFORM$^{x \rightarrow y}$ is also a one-handed sign that begins pointing at entity $x$ then moves toward entity $y$. INFORM$^{[RECIP]x \leftrightarrow y}$ in Figure 4.23c

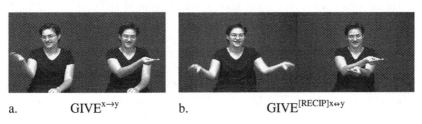

a.            GIVE$^{x \rightarrow y}$            b.            GIVE$^{[RECIP]x \leftrightarrow y}$

Figure 4.22 Comparing the one-handed verb GIVE$^{x \rightarrow y}$ with the corresponding two-handed reciprocal verb GIVE$^{[RECIP]x \rightarrow y}$

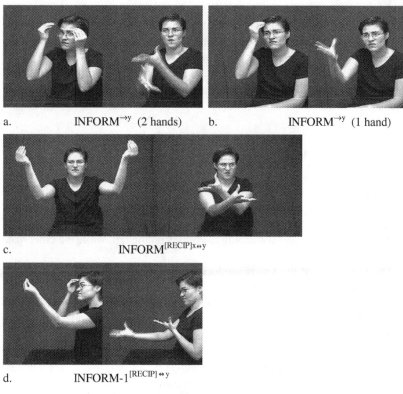

a.          INFORM$^{\to y}$ (2 hands)          b.          INFORM$^{\to y}$ (1 hand)

c.                      INFORM$^{[RECIP]x \leftrightarrow y}$

d.          INFORM-1$^{[RECIP] \leftrightarrow y}$

Figure 4.23 Comparing INFORM$^{\to y}$ with two distinct reciprocal forms

appears to contain two instances of INFORM$^{x \to y}$ directed in opposite directions. Its meaning appears to express the sum of the meanings provided by each hand individually.

So far, no special grammatical properties need to be described. The reciprocal form in Figure 4.23d, however, does require explanation. I analyze it as a lexical first person reciprocal verb, which I gloss as INFORM-1$^{[RECIP] \leftrightarrow y}$. Individually, the two hands do not express opposite meanings. The left hand produces INFORM$^{x \to y}$ while the right hand produces INFORM$^{\to y}$. If understood as a separate but simultaneous sign, the right hand does not indicate that the signer corresponds to the trajector of INFORM$^{\to y}$, since this sign does not indicate the entity to map onto the trajector. INFORM$^{\to y}$ is equivalent in this respect to signs such as TELL$^{\to y}$ and SEE$^{\to y}$ (Figure 4.6).

However, the reciprocal meaning is part of the meaning expressed by INFORM$^{[RECIP] \leftrightarrow y}$. Therefore, it makes sense to attribute the property 'reciprocality' to the lexical verb rather than to the sum of its individual parts.

Figure 4.24 CORRESPOND-WITH-1$^{[RECIP]\leftrightarrow y}$

The two hands begin opposed to one another, then cross paths in the middle and again end up on opposite sides. Conceived of in this way, the two hands are both on the same line or path. They traverse it from opposite directions. Each end of the path points at a conceptual entity to map onto a semantically encoded participant in the reciprocal relationship. Other reciprocal forms produced by doubling hands and reversing the directions include FINGERSPELL-TO$^{[RECIP]x\leftrightarrow y}$, GIVE$^{[RECIP]x\leftrightarrow y}$, HATE$^{[RECIP]x\leftrightarrow y}$, INSULT$^{[RECIP]x\leftrightarrow y}$, PITY$^{[RECIP]x\leftrightarrow y}$, PREACH$^{[RECIP]x\leftrightarrow y}$, SAY-OK-TO$^{[RECIP]x\leftrightarrow y}$, and SAY-YES-TO$^{[RECIP]x\leftrightarrow y}$.

There are other verbs that express reciprocal meanings that do not even have the option of being analyzed as simultaneous verbs since the activity of each hand individually does not constitute a verb. The sign CORRESPOND-WITH-1$^{[RECIP]\leftrightarrow y}$, shown in Figure 4.24, is a verb of this type. If the two hands are examined separately, one appears to be producing an instance of PUT-QUESTION$^{x\rightarrow y}$ while the other produces PUT-QUESTION$^{\rightarrow y}$. However, this verb does not mean 'ask each other questions'. This verb is a lexical unit deriving its meaning from what both hands are doing together rather than from meanings derived from what each hand is doing individually.

Other signs of this type include CLASH-WITH$^{[RECIP]x\leftrightarrow y}$, COMMUNI-CATE-TELEPATHICALLY$^{[RECIP]x\leftrightarrow y}$, and LOCK-HORNS-WITH$^{[RECIP]x\leftrightarrow y}$.

### Intransitive verbs

In general, intransitive ASL verbs are not meaningfully directed in space. However, a small number of ASL verbs can be directed toward the entities to map onto their trajectors. One such verb is BE-ALONE$^{\rightarrow x}$, made with a small, horizontal, circular motion of the vertically oriented index finger.[9] Producing BE-ALONE$^{\rightarrow x}$ in the direction of another person identifies that person as entity $x$. BE-ALONE-1 is produced at the chest so that the ulnar surface of the hand brushes the chest along one arc of its circular motion.

---

[9] In its most reduced form, the motion appears as more of a side-to-side oscillating motion rather than a circular motion.

The verbs ALL-USED-UP$^{\rightarrow x}$, BREAKDOWN$^{\rightarrow x}$, DIE$^{\rightarrow x}$, DISAPPEAR$^{\rightarrow x}$, MISSING/GONE$^{\rightarrow x}$, PASS$^{\rightarrow x}$, and FAIL$^{\rightarrow x}$ can also be produced toward the entities to map onto their trajectors.[10]

### Entities, locations, and directions

The first sign I will describe here has been treated in the literature as a verb that (in my terms) does not identify an entity, but rather shows a path or location (Padden 1983, 1988). The sign is MOVE, which I will gloss as MOVE$^{L1 \rightarrow L2}$. Padden (1988) describes MOVE as a *spatial verb*, which she defines as a verb that does not show agreement with a subject or object, but rather marks "location and position" (p. 28), with a subclass of spatial verbs marking for path and manner of movement.

In order to describe how these verbs work, I will first explore the distinction between entities and locations. We prototypically think of locations with respect to a two-dimensional grid. This sense of location includes addresses, surveys, maps, etc. On a two-dimensional surface such as a map, a location can be conceptualized as a single point. This is what lies behind the concept of an *X* on a map. The intersection of the two lines produces the *X* that "marks a spot" (a location) on the map. But even on a two-dimensional surface, a location can be larger than a single point. Suppose, for example, that someone spills coffee on a map and that the coffee leaves a stain. The location of the stain is much larger than a single point and is actually co-extensive with the stain itself. Thus, in (3), the respondent *B* uses place names on a map to describe the location (extent) of the coffee stain. Such a description of extent is needed because there is no single point that locates the stain.

(3)     A: Where is the coffee stain?
        B: The stain covers most of Utah, Colorado, and Wyoming.

In language about a three-dimensional space, the idea that "X marks the spot" also does not work well. Suppose, for example, that the aim is to describe the location of a tree. It is hard to imagine someone identifying the location of a tree by saying, "right there," and pointing at the place where the trunk meets the ground. One could begin describing the locations of various parts of the tree, as in (4), but such a description would be terribly cumbersome.

(4)     The trunk is about ten feet ahead of me. There is one large branch
        about three feet high extending outward toward me. The tip of
        the branch extends...

---

[10]  The verb DIE$^{\rightarrow x}$ is a one-handed sign while the non-indicating form DIE is two-handed. For the other signs listed here, both the indicating forms and the non-indicating forms are two-handed.

A more typical way to describe the location of the tree is with a locative expression such as "over there" or "right there" accompanied by a pointing gesture. The most natural way to produce such a pointing gesture would be to direct the fingertip somewhere toward the perceived center of the tree.

Just as the location of a coffee stain is co-extensive with the area it covers, the location of a tree is co-extensive with the space it occupies. By pointing toward the space occupied by the tree, the pointing gesture simultaneously points at the tree itself.

Evidence that pointing at an entity can either serve the function of identifying it or locating it is easily found in a vocally produced language like English. In (5), for example, A asks B to identify the person who started an argument. B answers with the clause, *he did*, while simultaneously pointing at someone. The pointing serves the purpose of identifying the individual being talked about.

(5)     A: Who started the argument?
        B: *He* did. (The speaker points at a person while saying *he*.)

As *he* is produced B points at the person who started the argument. The pronoun *he* attributes the characteristics 'single male' to the one who started the argument. The simultaneous pointing gesture identifies the particular male person B is talking about. In (6) A asks B for Sue's location. B responds with the phrase *over there*. As the locative phrase *over there* is produced, B points at Sue. Pointing during the phrase *over there* serves the purpose of identifying Sue's location.

(6)     A: Where is Sue?
        B: Over there. (The speaker simultaneously points at Sue.)

The person speaking points at a person in both (5) and (6). The functions accomplished, however, are different. In (5) B points toward a male while producing *he* with the purpose of identifying the person. In (6) B points toward the location of Sue while producing *over there* with the purpose of showing where Sue is.

While pointing at an entity can serve the function of either identifying or locating the entity, pointing at a location does not always identify an entity. Suppose, for example, A and B are standing in the middle of a large lawn. In (7) A asks B to identify where A should put a box.

(7)     A: Where should I put this box?
        B: Over there. (The speaker simultaneously points at a location on the lawn.)

B responds with the locative phrase *over there* while pointing toward a location on the lawn. Although the gesture is toward the lawn, it is obvious that B does not mean to identify the lawn (all of it) as a suitable location for the box. Rather,

Figure 4.25  MOVE$^{L1 \rightarrow L2}$

the pointing gesture identifies a particular place on the lawn where the box is to be put. In this case *B* mentions a location (over there) and simultaneously points at it with the purpose of identifying it. The two instances of *over there* with simultaneous pointing in (6) and (7) are understood differently because the discourse is about different things. The first instance of *over there* is uttered in response to the request for the location of a person and the gesture points to the location of the person. The second request is about a place to put a box and the gesture identifies a specific place on the lawn rather than the entire lawn.

With this understanding that the location of a physical thing is co-extensive with the space it occupies, we can now examine the behavior of signs like MOVE$^{L1 \rightarrow L2}$. Figure 4.25 illustrates a typical use of MOVE$^{L1 \rightarrow L2}$ in the form of an instruction to move the coffee cup from where it is to another location on the table.

In terms of its semantic pole, MOVE$^{L1 \rightarrow L2}$ is conceptually very similar to the transitive verb *move* in English. It signifies that some entity causes another typically inanimate entity to change its location from one place to another. Spatially, however, MOVE$^{L1 \rightarrow L2}$ is more complex than either *move* in English or previous indicating verbs we have examined because it requires the signer and the addressee to conceptualize the spatial result of the movement. This can be seen from a careful examination of the initial and final directionality of the hand.

In Figure 4.25 there are two coffee cups on the table. MOVE$^{L1 \rightarrow L2}$ begins with the fingertips of the flat O handshape directed toward the coffee cup to be moved. The hand then moves in an arc toward a different location. It is clear that, both initially and finally, the fingertips are not pointing at a location on the surface of the table. That is, in English it is normal to say things like, "the cup is on the table." The prepositional phrase *on the table* treats the surface of the table as the cup's location. In fact, an English speaker could say, "move the cup here," and simultaneously touch the top of the table showing where the cup is to be placed. This is not the way MOVE$^{L1 \rightarrow L2}$ points in Figure 4.25. It begins by pointing at the cup itself and ends by pointing at the intended final location

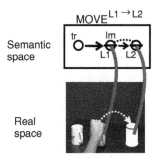

Figure 4.26  Using directionality to map MOVE$^{L1 \rightarrow L2}$

of the cup. This involves conceptualizing the space the cup will occupy in its new location and directing the hand to that space, as if it were there.

In sum, MOVE$^{L1 \rightarrow L2}$ begins pointing at the initial location of the cup and ends pointing at the final location of the cup. The one caveat here is that if the cup is present, there is no physical difference between pointing at the current location of the cup and pointing at the cup itself. Thus, the hand begins by simultaneously pointing at the current location of the cup and at the cup itself. It ends by pointing only at the intended final location for the cup, where there is no cup.

MOVE$^{L1 \rightarrow L2}$ could also begin by pointing at a previous location of the cup and end pointing at its current location. This could happen, for example, if a signer notices that a cup has been moved and comments that someone has moved the cup. In that situation MOVE$^{L1 \rightarrow L2}$ would begin directed at the previous location of the cup and end pointing at the current location of the cup (and at the cup itself). In both this example and the previous one MOVE$^{L1 \rightarrow L2}$ begins by pointing toward the initial location of an entity and ends by pointing at its final location.

Figure 4.26 shows how the semantic pole of MOVE$^{L1 \rightarrow L2}$ maps onto *L1* and *L2*. In the semantic pole of this transitive verb the trajector causes the landmark to change its location from *L1* to *L2*. The landmark is a thing, not a location. The verb encodes the movement of that thing from one location to another. I am using a horizontal bar through the landmark to represent its location. The initial location is labeled *L1* and the final location is labeled *L2*. Since *L1* is co-extensive with the cup at *L1*, directing MOVE$^{L1 \rightarrow L2}$ initially toward *L1* identifies the cup at *L1* as the entity to be moved. In order to direct the hand toward *L2* properly, the signer must conceptualize the cup in the new location and direct the hand as if the cup were there.

The English verb *move* in (8) is also a transitive verb. In this example it is followed immediately by its object *the book*.

(8)     I moved the book from the desk to the floor.

English uses prepositions to identify the initial and final locations of the thing moved. The prepositional phrase *from the desk* identifies the initial location as the desk. The prepositional phrase *to the floor* identifies the floor as the final location. MOVE$^{L1 \rightarrow L2}$ accomplishes the same functions by very different means. Although it is possible to describe the thing moved with an overt direct object, it is often easily omitted. The identity of the thing moved will be apparent because, either initially or finally, the hand will point toward the thing. Recall that pointing at the current location of a thing is indistinguishable from pointing at the thing itself. The hand points at the thing because it points at its initial and final locations. The thing being talked about will be in one of those locations. Thus, MOVE$^{L1 \rightarrow L2}$ is not locative as opposed to transitive, or locative as opposed to being able to identify a thing, it is locative in addition to being transitive and being able to identify the thing being talked about.

Padden (1988) also treats the verb GO-TO as a spatial verb (p. 44). Here I will consider evidence that although GO-TO has been considered a single spatial verb, we are actually dealing with a set of verbs, each with distinct spatial properties. I will first consider the intransitive verbs GO$^{\rightarrow}$ and GO$^{x \rightarrow}$. Both verbs point toward a direction for travel, symbolized by the arrow not followed by any other symbol. Either verb could be used to tell an addressee to go in a particular direction by directing the sign in that direction. They differ in whether or not they also indicate the agent. GO$^{x \rightarrow}$ begins by indicating the agent then moving in the direction of travel while GO$^{\rightarrow}$ begins ahead of the body and moves in the direction of travel. They also differ in the orientation of the hand as the sign is produced. GO$^{x \rightarrow}$ is produced with the index finger oriented horizontally and the radial surface of the hand up throughout the sign while GO$^{\rightarrow}$ begins with the index finger vertical but ends with the finger oriented horizontally and the palm oriented down.

The transitive verb GO$^{\rightarrow y}$ resembles GO$^{\rightarrow}$. The two signs differ in that GO$^{\rightarrow y}$ is directed toward a destination while the path movement of GO$^{\rightarrow}$ corresponds to a direction of travel. Like typical transitive verbs in ASL GO$^{\rightarrow y}$ can be used with or without an overt object. Figure 4.27 illustrates two distinct physical settings in which GO$^{\rightarrow y}$ could be used. For purposes of these two examples we can assume that both participants in the discourse are familiar with the locations of things in their immediate environment. In Figure 4.27a if the addressee had mentioned being in a hurry to get to the store, the signer could now respond with the directive GO$^{\rightarrow y}$, directed toward the store on her left.

In this situation the movement path of GO$^{\rightarrow y}$ leads directly to the store, raising the issue of whether the hand's movement path is showing a path leading to the store (i.e. a direction) or is directed toward the store itself. The physical

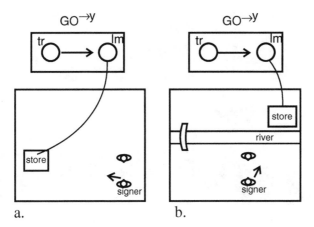

Figure 4.27 Directing the transitive verb GO$^{\rightarrow y}$ toward the entity correspond-ing to its landmark

situation in Figure 4.27b is different. Now there is a river blocking the shortest route to the store. In this situation the normal path to the store involves first moving to the signer's left toward the bridge, crossing the bridge, then coming back toward the store. In this situation, GO$^{\rightarrow y}$ will still be directed toward the actual location of the store. This demonstrates that in producing GO$^{\rightarrow y}$ the hand moves toward the goal, not the initial path to the goal. Directing GO$^{\rightarrow y}$ toward the bridge while producing GO$^{\rightarrow y}$ STORE would be incorrect.[11]

The verb THROW$^{\downarrow L \rightarrow}$ in Figure 4.28a does not identify an entity as a target, but rather, shows the location of the throwing and the initial trajectory of the thrown entity.[12] This can be seen by examining the sign following THROW$^{\downarrow L \rightarrow}$ in Figure 4.28a, which depicts the trajectory of the thrown entity.

The signs illustrated in Figure 4.28b and c are both instances of THROW-AT$^{x \rightarrow y}$ capable of indicating the thrower and the target. Like previously de-scribed $^{x \rightarrow y}$ verbs, both ends of its movement path point to a conceptual entity. The beginning configuration points toward $x$ and the final configuration points toward $y$. In Figure 4.28b the sign begins by pointing toward a person on the

[11] The presence of the direct object STORE in this example provides evidence that we are dealing with the transitive verb GO$^{\rightarrow y}$ rather than the intransitive GO$^{\rightarrow}$.

[12] The notation $^{\downarrow L}$ will be explained in chapter 9 (Depicting verbs). For now I will simply observe that the placement of the verb in this example corresponds to the location at which the throwing took place and the trajectory described by the signer corresponds to the movement of the entity thrown from one place to another. These aspects of the production of the verb *depict* the event. This sign takes us outside of the realm of real space since it does not suggest that the initial location of the throwing was a location a few inches ahead of the signer's sternum. The signer is using a spatial conceptualization that goes beyond real space. She has created a blend with real space. Real-space blends will be introduced in subsequent chapters.

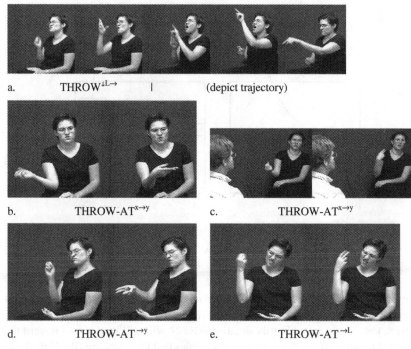

a.        THROW$^{\downarrow L\rightarrow}$        |        (depict trajectory)

b.        THROW-AT$^{x\rightarrow y}$        c.        THROW-AT$^{x\rightarrow y}$

d.        THROW-AT$^{\rightarrow y}$        e.        THROW-AT$^{\rightarrow L}$

Figure 4.28  Four closely related verbs

right and ends pointing toward a person on the left. In Figure 4.28c THROW-AT$^{x\rightarrow y}$ begins directed toward the man opposite the signer then moves toward the signer herself. This identifies him as the thrower and identifies the signer herself as the target of the throwing.

Earlier, I suggested that if an $^{x\rightarrow y}$ verb form exists (e.g. GIVE$^{x\rightarrow y}$), one can also expect that a $^{\rightarrow y}$ form will also exist (e.g. GIVE$^{\rightarrow y}$). Thus, the existence of THROW-AT$^{x\rightarrow y}$ implies the existence of THROW-AT$^{\rightarrow y}$, illustrated in Figure 4.28d. Like many other $^{\rightarrow y}$ forms, it begins ahead of the shoulder then moves toward the entity to map onto its landmark. In this case, it is directed toward an entity ahead of and below the signer. Such an entity could be a wastebasket or even an entity located on the floor. Although the sign moves from the signer outward, it does not identify the signer as the thrower.

The sign THROW$^{\rightarrow L}$ in Figure 4.28e appears to be different from both THROW$^{\downarrow L\rightarrow}$ and THROW-AT$^{x\rightarrow y}$. The directionality of the movement toward the signer's head corresponds to the end of the movement path of the thrown entity. By placing the hand signing THROW$^{\rightarrow L}$ close to the side of the head and also directing it toward the side of the head, the signer identifies the side

a.     SHOOT-GUN-AT$^{x\rightarrow y}$     b.     SHOOT-GUN-AT$^{\rightarrow y}$

c.     SHOOT-GUN$^{\downarrow L\rightarrow}$     d.     SHOOT-GUN$^{\rightarrow L}$

Figure 4.29 Four closely related verbs

of the head as a target. In this case, THROW$^{\rightarrow L}$ conveys the meaning, 'throw at side of head' rather than 'throw at me'.[13]

Thus, instead of a single sign THROW, there appear to be several distinct signs. In addition to the citation form THROW, which is not meaningfully directed, there are four additional signs which are meaningfully directed. The directionality of THROW$^{x\rightarrow y}$ identifies the thrower and the entity serving as the target. The directionality of THROW$^{\rightarrow y}$ is similar except that it only identifies the entity serving as the target. The verb THROW$^{\rightarrow L}$ indicates the end of the path movement of the thing thrown by being directed at the location to map onto the destination in the verb's semantic pole. Thus, instead of identifying the signer as the target of the throwing, it identifies the side of the head as the target. The hand producing THROW$^{\downarrow L\rightarrow}$ is placed initially at a location corresponding to the location of the throwing action. The path movement of the hand also depicts the initial path of the entity thrown.

SHOOT-GUN, SHOOT-GUN-AT$^{x\rightarrow y}$, SHOOT-GUN-AT$^{\rightarrow y}$, SHOOT-GUN$^{\downarrow L\rightarrow}$, and SHOOT-GUN$^{\rightarrow L}$ constitute a parallel set of signs. Four of these verbs are illustrated in Figure 4.29. Figure 4.29a illustrates SHOOT-GUN-AT$^{x\rightarrow y}$, which begins directed toward entity $x$ on the right and moves along a path toward $y$. SHOOT-GUN-AT$^{\rightarrow y}$ begins ahead of the torso then moves toward $y$. The two signs differ only with regard to whether the start of the movement points at the entity to map onto the trajector. While these two verbs

---

[13] One can take the posture of the signer's head as indicating a response to the head being the target of the throwing.

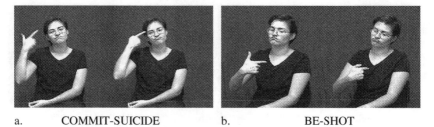

a.    COMMIT-SUICIDE         b.              BE-SHOT

Figure 4.30 Non-directional lexical verbs

have targets (both semantically and physically), the sign SHOOT-GUN$^{\downarrow L\rightarrow}$ in Figure 4.29c has neither. Semantically it encodes shooting a gun from a place and in a direction. Physically, in this instance, the place is slightly above the shoulder and the direction is straight up. SHOOT-GUN$^{\rightarrow L}$ in Figure 4.29d is produced on a path leading to the signer's shoulder. This identifies a body part as the place that was shot.

In addition to the citation form and these four directional verbs, there are two related, non-pointing verbs: COMMIT-SUICIDE and BE-SHOT (Figure 4.30). COMMIT-SUICIDE looks like SHOOT-GUN$^{\rightarrow L}$ directed toward the temple. BE-SHOT looks like SHOOT-GUN$^{\rightarrow L}$ directed toward the sternum. It has a passive semantic structure in that its syntactic subject corresponds to the person shot.[14]

There are a large number of signs related to looking, many of which have previously been treated as the same sign and glossed as LOOK. I will illustrate some of them here, beginning with LOOK-AT$^{x\rightarrow y}$ in Figure 4.31a. It begins with the hand away from the signer pointing at the entity to map onto its trajector. At the same time the fingertips are directed toward the entity to map onto the landmark. The hand then moves toward that entity and stops. LOOK-AT$^{x\rightarrow y}$ can also be directed toward the signer as shown in Figure 4.31b. Recall that for $^{x\rightarrow y}$ verbs and $^{\rightarrow y}$ verbs, if $y$ is a person, the verb will be directed toward a specific part of the body. LOOK-AT$^{x\rightarrow y}$ is directed toward the eyes and nose.

LOOK-AT$^{\rightarrow y}$ is like many other $^{\rightarrow y}$ verbs in that it begins ahead of the torso and then moves toward $y$, the entity to map onto the landmark. An example is illustrated in Figure 4.31c. LOOK$^{\cup\rightarrow}$ (typically glossed as STARE) differs from both LOOK-AT$^{x\rightarrow y}$ and LOOK-AT$^{\rightarrow y}$ in that it is not produced with a path movement. That is, the hand simply holds its position in space with the fingertips pointing in the direction of looking. LOOK$^{\cup\rightarrow}$ has the additional requirement

---

[14] Cole (2000) provides examples of several such nondirectional passive verb forms.

a.          LOOK-AT$^{x \to y}$          b.          LOOK-AT$^{x \to y}$

c.          LOOK-AT$^{\to y}$          d.          LOOK$^{\cup \to}$

Figure 4.31 Three closely related verbs

that the signer assume a looking posture corresponding to the looker. Note that the signer's gaze is aligned with the direction of the fingers and the signer's face is also facing the same direction.[15]

Figure 4.32 illustrates two short sentences. Figure 4.32a illustrates the sentence, PRO-1 LOOK-AT$^{\to y}$ and Figure 4.32b illustrates PRO-1 LOOK$^{\cup \to}$.

There are both semantic and formational differences between the two verbs. Note the obvious path movement of LOOK-AT$^{\to y}$. In contrast, LOOK$^{\cup \to}$ is produced by merely rotating the wrist from the inward configuration of PRO-1 to the configuration seen in Figure 4.32b. Semantically, LOOK-AT$^{\to y}$ encodes making visual contact with entity y. LOOK$^{\cup \to}$ only encodes looking in a direction. As a result, LOOK$^{\cup \to}$ can be used in a situation where the looking does not result in making visual contact with anything. For example, looking toward where a bird is supposed to be in a tree, but failing to see the bird. LOOK-AT$^{\to y}$ could not be used under that circumstance since it signifies making visual contact with some entity y.

The covert directive LOOK$^{\to}$ is used to direct the addressee's attention and gaze toward something of interest. The aim appears to be not to call attention to oneself in directing the addressee's attention.

The forms illustrated in Figure 4.33 serve to illustrate this type of covert directionality. These covert 'look over there' directives include the lip configuration illustrated along with a kind of oscillating up and down tongue movement. These nonmanual features along with directed eye gaze are sufficient to get an

---

[15] This involves creating a surrogate blend, which will be discussed in chapter 5.

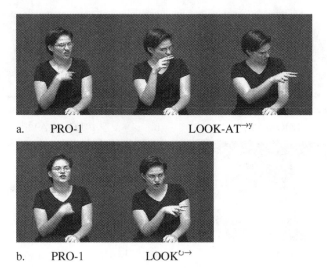

a.    PRO-1                    LOOK-AT$^{\rightarrow y}$

b.    PRO-1          LOOK$^{\cup \rightarrow}$

Figure 4.32 The meaning of LOOK-AT$^{\rightarrow y}$ includes making visual contact with the entity looked at while the meaning of LOOK$^{\cup \rightarrow y}$ does not

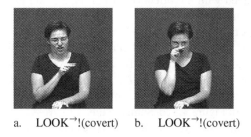

a.    LOOK$^{\rightarrow}$!(covert)    b.    LOOK$^{\rightarrow}$!(covert)

Figure 4.33  Covert instructions to look in specific directions

addressee to look in a particular direction. The forms in Figure 4.33 include these nonmanual features as well as the handshape for LOOK$^{\rightarrow}$ placed at or near the sternum as in Figure 4.33a or on the nose as in Figure 4.33b. I have also seen a covert form LOOK$^{\rightarrow}$ placed at the waist level. Although these signs still include eye direction, part of their covert nature involves not directing the face toward the direction of looking.

Although there are many more 'looking' verbs, I will end this description with just three additional verbs. MANY-LOOK-AT$^{x \rightarrow y}$ in Figure 4.34a is parallel to LOOK-AT$^{x \rightarrow y}$ except that it encodes a plural trajector. In this case, MANY-LOOK-AT$^{x \rightarrow y}$ is being used as a directive for those ahead of the signer to look at her. This is the type of directive a teacher might use with her students.

a.     MANY-LOOK-AT$^{x\rightarrow y}$

b.     LOOK-TOWARD$^{x\rightarrow y}$          c.     MANY-LOOK-TOWARD$^{x\rightarrow y}$

Figure 4.34 Three different verbs of looking

LOOK-TOWARD$^{x\rightarrow y}$ in Figure 4.34b is produced with a wrist rotation rather than a path movement. It also signifies $x$ looking at $y$, but implies that $x$ was not previously looking at $y$. There is a corresponding plural form, MANY-LOOK-TOWARD$^{x\rightarrow y}$, illustrated in Figure 4.34c. Formationally, it differs from LOOK-TOWARD$^{x\rightarrow y}$ in two ways: it is two handed and uses 4 handshapes rather than V handshapes. The placement of the hands indicates $x$ and the final orientation of the fingers indicates $y$.

### Summary of indicating verb types

The directionality of indicating verbs provides instructions for mappings between trajectors, landmarks, locations, and even conceptualized directions. Table 4.1 provides an example of each of the types of indicating verbs discussed in this chapter. If one considers the semantic pole of a verb as providing the mapping medium, then verbs have come into existence that allow mapping onto that medium in a large number of ways. Verbs like SEE$^{\rightarrow y}$ are directed toward $y$, which maps onto its landmark. In producing verbs like HONOR$^{\cup\rightarrow y}$, not only are the hands directed toward $y$, so are the signer's face and eyes. Verbs such as INVITE$^{\leftarrow y}$ are "backward" in that they initially point toward $y$ then move away from it. Verbs like BE-ALONE$^{\rightarrow x}$ are unusual in that they are directed toward the entity to map onto the trajector. Such verbs form a small set among the indicating verbs of ASL.

Verbs such as ASK$^{x\rightarrow y}$ move from being directed toward $x$ to being directed toward $y$. Verbs like BORROW$^{x\leftarrow y}$ also indicate two entities, but do it

Table 4.1 *Verb types discussed in this chapter*

| Sign type | Example sign | Significance of directionality |
|---|---|---|
| Citation form | SEE | None |
| $\to y$ | SEE$^{\to y}$ | The hand is directed toward $y$. |
| $\cup\to y$ | HONOR$^{\cup\to y}$ | The hand is directed toward $y$. The face and eye gaze are directed toward $y$. |
| $\leftarrow y$ | INVITE$^{\leftarrow y}$ | The hand begins directed toward $y$, then moves away from $y$. |
| $\to x$ | BE-ALONE$^{\to x}$ | The hand is directed toward $x$. |
| $x\to y$ | ASK$^{x\to y}$ | The hand is directed toward $x$ then moves toward $y$. |
| $x\leftarrow y$ | BORROW$^{x\leftarrow y}$ | The hand begins directed toward $y$, then moves toward $x$. |
| -1 | SAY-NO-TO-1 | None. |
| $-1^{\cup x}$ | SAY-NO-TO-1$^{\cup x}$ | Face and eye gaze are directed toward $x$. |
| [RECIP]$x\leftrightarrow y$ | INFORM$^{[RECIP]x\leftrightarrow y}$ | Hands are directed in opposite directions between $x$ and $y$. |
| $\to$ | GO$^{\to}$ | The hand points in the direction of the action. |
| $\cup\to$ | LOOK$^{\cup\to}$ | The hand points in the direction of the action. The head and eye gaze also point in the same direction. |
| $L1\to L2$ | MOVE$^{L1\to L2}$ | The hand is directed at the initial then final location of an entity. |
| $\to L$ | THROW$^{\to L}$ | The hand is directed toward location $L$, corresponding to the sign's semantic destination. |
| $\downarrow L\to$ | THROW$^{\downarrow L\to}$ (depicting verb) | Location of the hand corresponds to the location of the action. The movement path corresponds to the initial path of the entity. |

"backward." They begin nearer to $y$ then move toward $x$. SAY-NO-TO-1 has a lexically fixed first person landmark and is produced just ahead of the nose. SAY-NO-TO-1$^{\cup x}$ additionally indicates $x$ through rotating the face and gaze toward $x$. INFORM$^{[RECIP]x\leftrightarrow y}$ is a reciprocal verb in which one hand begins directed toward $x$ and produces a motion toward $y$, while the other hand does the reverse.

The direction of the fingertip in the verb GO$^{\to}$ indicates the direction of the action. LOOK$^{\cup\to}$ is similar except that in addition to the pointing of the fingers, the face and eyes are also directed in the same way. MOVE$^{L1\to L2}$ is unusual in that it is directed at the location of things. If the thing is physically present there is no distinction between directing the sign at a thing's location and directing the sign at the thing itself. In the case of MOVE$^{L1\to L2}$ the sign begins directed at the initial location of the thing and ends directed at its final location. This is true regardless of whether the thing currently occupies the initial or final location. The direction of the hand producing THROW$^{\to L}$ indicates the target location of the thing being thrown.

I have also included the depicting verb THROW$^{\downarrow L \rightarrow}$, because of its similarity to the other verbs of throwing. The initial placement of the hand and the directionality of the movement depicts the location of the throwing action and the initial path of the entity thrown. Depicting verbs are discussed in detail in chapter 9.

In some cases, directional verbs have led to the formation of directionally fixed forms with meanings that differ from the corresponding indicating verbs. Signs of this type include ANALYZE-SELF, BE-SHOT, and COMMIT-SUICIDE. Since the forms of these signs are fixed and describable in phonological terms, they are like words in any spoken language. Their forms are linked to lexically determined meanings, regardless of the iconic or directional nature of their production.

### Phonological representations

It is uncontroversial that, in the production of a typical non-indicating sign, the hand moves from one phonologically describable location to another (see chapter 2). For example, the sign PARENTS begins by making contact with the chin then making contact with the forehead. Non-indicating signs made in space are describable in the same terms. REBEL$_V$, for example, is produced with the hand a short distance ahead of the shoulder. WILL begins in the same location as REBEL$_V$ then moves directly outward from the body. There are a number of proposed systems of phonological representation and each has its own way of placing the hand at spatial locations (*inter alia*, Brentari 1998, Liddell and Johnson 1989, Sandler 1989, Uyechi 1996). The descriptive and analytical problem posed by both indicating verbs and pronouns is the variability of their directionality and placement. One instance of TELL$^{\rightarrow y}$ will be produced differently from the next, depending on the location of the entity corresponding to its landmark. The initial location of the hand at the chin is fixed and easily describable but its final location is not.

In producing TELL$^{\rightarrow y}$ the signer must select a final location for the hand such that the path from the chin to that location will point toward the entity to map onto the landmark. Figure 4.35 provides a concrete physical setting in which John is standing to the right of the signer and Sarah is standing to the left. The signer could direct TELL$^{\rightarrow y}$ as shown by the arrow in Figure 4.35 to indicate a mapping with its landmark and John. In producing the verb the hand will begin in contact with the chin then move along a path toward John. When the hand stops moving outward it will be at a locus in the space ahead of the signer. I have labeled that locus *a*. Directing TELL$^{\rightarrow y}$ toward locus *a* in this physical setting will prompt a mapping with John.

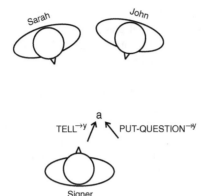

Figure 4.35  Why point *a* is not meaningful

In my description above, I am not claiming that the spatial locus *a* either points at anything by itself or has any independent semantic significance. It is the sign that points toward the entity to map onto the landmark by moving from the chin to *a*. The locus *a* does not by itself point at or signify anything.

Figure 4.35 also illustrates the result of directing PUT-QUESTION$^{\rightarrow y}$ toward locus *a* in the same physical setting. PUT-QUESTION$^{\rightarrow y}$ begins several inches ahead of the shoulder. Thus, it has a different starting point from TELL$^{\rightarrow y}$, which begins in contact with the chin. Directing PUT-QUESTION$^{\rightarrow y}$ from its starting point ahead of the shoulder to locus *a* creates a path movement toward Sarah. This would signal a mapping between the landmark of PUT-QUESTION$^{\rightarrow y}$ and Sarah. Directing TELL$^{\rightarrow y}$ and PUT-QUESTION$^{\rightarrow y}$ toward exactly the same locus ahead of the signer produces two distinct mappings because the two signs have different starting points. TELL$^{\rightarrow y}$ begins at the chin and PUT-QUESTION$^{\rightarrow y}$ begins ahead of the shoulder. The fact that both signs can be directed toward the locus *a* and have entirely different mappings demonstrates the meaningless nature of the locus *a*. It is the direction of the path movement of the sign that points, not the spatial locus where the hand stops its movement.

The concept of a meaningful spatial locus appears to have been motivated, at least in part, by the desire for phonological stability. That is, no matter how difficult it might be to describe a spatial locus, at least there is only one such locus per referent. The idea was that all signs making reference to that referent would be directed toward that single locus. However, describing a spatial locus in terms of some type of phonological or phonetic feature has proven to be extremely difficult and there is currently no satisfactory feature system capable of doing this. The two examples described in Figure 4.35 demonstrate that this is not even the right goal. The locus $a$ in Figure 4.35 is not conceptually linked with either of the physically present individuals ahead of the signer. The concept of a meaningful locus in this situation is an artifact of the search for a part of a sign – its location – that could account for the meaning that results from its directionality.

The final location of the hand is not describable in terms of a fixed set of phonological or phonetic features. The final location of the hand in producing TELL$^{\rightarrow y}$ or PUT-QUESTION$^{\rightarrow y}$ will depend on the locations of the entities these verbs are directed toward and the signer's judgment about making a path that leads from the starting point of the sign toward the entity to map onto its landmark.

### The boundaries of grammar and language

In the analysis of spoken language discourse, it is relatively easy to distinguish between discrete, categorical linguistic units (e.g. words and morphemes) and pointing gestures. They differ both formationally and semantically. Formationally, words and morphemes are composed of abstract phonological parts and encode meanings shared across a community of speakers. Pointing differs along both these parameters. Formationally, speakers can point with their fingers, with a tilt of the head, with a coffee cup, with eye gaze, etc. Further, pointing does not symbolize the entity pointed at – it points at it. Following Peirce's well-known distinction between icon, index, and symbol, the pointing is indexic, not symbolic. That is, uttering the word *book* encodes an instance of an entity of the type 'book'. Pointing toward a book does not do this. Rather, it shows a direction that leads to an entity that happens to be a book. Changing the pointing direction could lead to a different entity.

Linguistics has traditionally focused on issues surrounding encoding and decoding grammatical utterances. But understanding the message being sent by the speaker involves more than encoding and decoding. It also involves the ability of an addressee to construct cross-space mappings equivalent to those of the speaker. Co-occurring deictic gestures provide essential clues in making those cross-space mappings.

Since the 1970s linguists studying ASL have treated a verb's directionality as encoding rather than pointing. This is primarily due to the assumption that the "linguistic" messages consist entirely of encoded information. Since the directionality of signs contributes so clearly to the message, linguists have assumed that a verb's directionality *encodes* meaning. In general, linguists studying sign languages are not inclined to treat a verb's directionality as pointing because pointing is outside the realm of phonological description. If directionality is outside the realm of phonological description then it is not "linguistic."

A few years ago the issue of whether something was "linguistic" or not seemed like an important question to me. It no longer does. The entire issue is based on the idea that structured (grammatical) arrangements of words carry the meaning being expressed and can somehow be abstracted away from their actual use in a specific context. Important theoretical advancements during the 1980s and 1990s have shown that a speaker's meaning is not constrained in this way. This concept is at the very foundation of mental space theory.

> Language, as we know it, is a superficial manifestation of hidden, highly abstract, cognitive constructions. Essential to such constructions is the operation of structure projection between domains. And therefore, essential to the understanding of cognitive construction is the characterization of the domains over which projection takes place. Mental spaces are the domains that discourse builds up to provide a cognitive substrate for reasoning and for interfacing with the world. (Fauconnier 1997:34)

Mental space theory and cognitive grammar demonstrate that grammatical arrangements of words account for only a part of those hidden, highly abstract, cognitive constructions. If the directional aspects of ASL verbs are removed from consideration, important clues needed for making mental space mappings will be removed from the analysis and the appropriate cognitive constructions cannot be made.

In contrast to other theoretical models, cognitive linguistics is quite amenable to considering gesture to be part of a word's structure. For example, consider the following statement from Langacker (1991) in addressing the issue of the pointing that frequently co-occurs with the English word *this*: "in cognitive grammar, this gesture is unproblematically considered an aspect of the demonstrative's form, and its import an aspect of its meaning" (p. 102). Here it is not the nature of the gesture, or its direction that is significant. Speakers can point in lots of ways and in lots of directions. Rather, what is significant here is *the need to gesture*. I have been arguing in this chapter and the previous one that the need to gesture comes from the need to construct cognitive mappings between entities within the semantic pole of a pronoun or verb and entities in real space.

McNeill (1992) provides what appears to be an irrefutable demonstration that language and gesture are inextricably intertwined.[16] He presents considerable, convincing evidence that, "gestures are an integral part of language as much as are words, phrases, and sentences – gesture and language are one system" (p. 2). As part of that demonstration, McNeill describes a set of mismatch experiments in which a videotaped narration is shown to an experimental subject. The videotaped narration was carefully prepared such that there were mismatches between the gestures and the grammatically encoded meanings. In one instance,

---

[16] McNeill credits Kendon (1972, 1980) with discovering the unity between speech and gesture.

the narrator describes Sylvester the cat exiting a drainpipe with the clause, "and he [came out] the pipe." During the words *came out*, the speaker produces an up-and-down bouncing gesture. The lexical choice *came out* expresses exiting the pipe, but does not express the manner of movement. The up-and-down gesture was one that might accompany phrases like, *and he bounced out of the pipe*. At issue was what the person watching the videotaped narration would make of the mismatch. In order to find this out, the experimental subject was asked to retell the narrative. In doing so the subject described Sylvester exiting the drainpipe with both speech and gesture: *and the cat [bounces out] the pipe*. As *bounces out* was produced the subject also performed an up-and-down gesture. This demonstrates that the speaker had performed a conceptual integration of the grammatical and gestural meanings in comprehending the videotaped narration. That integrated message was then expressed both grammatically and gesturally in the retelling.

Directional verbs and pronouns in ASL contribute substantially to this issue. Suppose one wished to maintain a distinction between grammar, narrowly defined in terms of grammatically arranged morphemes/words/signs, and gestural aspects of language use. One would then have to say that there was no grammatical distinction between indicating verbs in ASL and verbs in any spoken language. In that case, the distinction between ASL indicating verbs and verbs in spoken languages would not be a linguistic distinction, but a gestural one.

The ASL data demonstrate that such a position is untenable. Each individual verb has specific gestural characteristics associated with it. Each verb's directional characteristics are potentially distinct from those of any other ASL verb. Some verbs are unable to point, some point toward entities corresponding to their trajectors, some point toward entities corresponding to their landmarks, and some point to both. For those that do point, if they are directed at a person, they are directed at specific parts of the person (e.g. forehead, nose, chin, sternum). These are not general characteristics of gestural "accompaniments" to signing. These are specific, semantically relevant, properties of individual verbs. One cannot know ASL without knowing how to direct each sign capable of being meaningfully directed in space.

Indicating verbs are unique to sign languages. There are no verbs in any spoken languages that have the same or comparable properties. Syntactically or semantically, however, indicating verbs are like verbs found in any spoken language. What makes indicating verbs unique is their *additional* ability and requirement to provide directional instructions for making mental space mappings. This is what verbs in spoken languages are unable to do because of the tongue's inability both to produce words and to point simultaneously at mental space entities.

It is not that speakers of vocally produced languages are unable to provide such clues, but rather, that the tongue is unable to provide such clues when articulating words. It is obvious that in spoken language discourse speakers frequently provide directional clues. These clues generally take the form of pointing co-speech gestures (e.g. "Please sit over there," "I like this one better than that one."). In ASL, however, providing such pointing gestures is a codified property of each individual indicating verb. Knowing the facts about directionality described in this chapter constitutes a central part of knowing ASL.

# 5    Surrogates

We frequently conceive of people and things around us as if they were someone or something else. When we watch a play, for example, we know that the actors are real people playing roles, but in a well-acted play we temporarily conceive of the actors as the characters whose roles they are playing. This can quickly change, however, if an actor can't remember or misspeaks a line. Then we are immediately brought back to the reality of observing actors, as opposed to the reality of the play itself. At the conclusion of the play we also return to our immediate reality and applaud the actors for their performances.

Signers also frequently conceive of areas of the space around them, or even themselves, as if they were something else. For example, consider the signing in Figure 5.1. This stretch of discourse is from a videotaped explanation of how to cook a salmon. The signer is describing slicing open a salmon.

She produces the two instances of the verb SLICE-OPEN$^{\downarrow L1-L2}$ illustrated in Figure 5.1. The downward arrow in the notation $^{\downarrow L1-L2}$ signifies that the hand is produced *at* a location rather than directed toward it. The notation $^{\downarrow L1-L2}$ signifies that the path of the movement begins at *L1* and ends at *L2*. SLICE-OPEN$^{\downarrow L1-L2}$ is produced with a bent B handshape with the thumb extended away from the palm but along the same plane as the palm. In producing the verb in Figure 5.1a, the fingertips begin in contact with the upper chest just below her neck and maintain contact as they move all the way to her lower abdomen. The second instance of SLICE-OPEN$^{\downarrow L1-L2}$ in Figure 5.1b is produced horizontally in the space ahead of her. This time the B handshape passes between the thumb and fingers of her left hand.[1]

Chapters 3 and 4 describe how pronouns and indicating verbs can be directed toward entities in real space. In Figure 5.1, however, if we understand the signs to

Chapter 5 draws upon and expands upon text from the following articles: Spatial representations in discourse: Comparing spoken and signed language, *Lingua* 98:145–167, by Scott K. Liddell (copyright 1996 with permission from Elsevier Science); Gesture in sign language discourse, *Journal of Pragmatics* 30:657–697, by Scott K. Liddell and Melanie Metzger (copyright 1998 with permission from Elsevier Science); Grounded blends, gestures, and conceptual shifts, *Cognitive Linguistics* 9.3:283–314, by Scott K. Liddell.

[1] This type of depicting verb will be described in chapter 9.

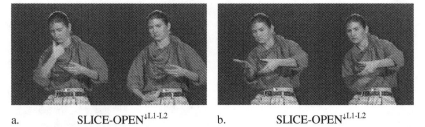

a.          SLICE-OPEN↓L1-L2          b.          SLICE-OPEN↓L1-L2

Figure 5.1  A sequence of two instances of SLICE-OPEN↓L1–L2 mapped onto different blended spaces

be directed toward elements of real space, we will misunderstand the meaning. That is, one does not clean a fish by first slicing oneself open from the neck to the stomach. In addition, one does not clean a fish by passing a blade between the thumb and fingers of an empty hand held out in space. It is apparent, then, that the significance of the hand's movement does not come from its relationship to elements of real space. Some other conceptualizations must be involved. The answer has to do with the way the signer has conceptualized both herself and the space around her.

### Blended mental spaces

Fauconnier and Turner (1996) describe a general cognitive process that they refer to as *blending*. It is a process that operates over two mental spaces as inputs. Structure from each of the two input spaces is projected to a third space, which they refer to as the blend. The blend inherits partial structure from each of the input spaces and also includes structure that belongs only to the blend. They use the following example of a philosopher speaking to a class to illustrate a blend: "I claim that reason is a self-developing capacity. Kant disagrees with me on this point. He says it's innate, but I answer that that's begging the question, to which he counters, in *Critique of Pure Reason*, that only innate ideas have power. But I say to that, what about neuronal group selection? And he gives no answer" (p. 113). In this example, the speaker creates a world in which there is a debate between himself and Kant. In the blend the philosopher and Kant are together, having a debate. Fauconnier and Turner observe that once the blend is established, the speaker operates within that space as an integrated unit. Within the blend, for example, the speaker is able to ask Kant a question about neuronal group selection, for which Kant has no answer.

Fauconnier and Turner (1994, 1996), Turner and Fauconnier (1995), and Fauconnier (1997) show that blending can provide a simple account of superficially complex syntactic phenomena as well as an understanding of metaphor.

They also show that blending is fundamental to understanding the concept of meaning in language use.

Fauconnier and Turner (1996) discuss another example of a blended space using a riddle from Koestler (1964). The riddle involves a Buddhist monk and a mountain. The Buddhist monk begins at dawn and spends the first day walking from the bottom of the mountain to the top, arriving at the top at sunset. He meditates for several days then begins walking down the mountain the following dawn. He arrives at the bottom at sunset. The riddle requires a demonstration that there is a place on the path such that the time of day the monk reaches that place on the trip up the mountain is the same as the time of day that the monk reaches that same place on the way down the mountain.

There is not enough information about pace and distance to calculate mathematically the place on the path asked for in the riddle. There are too many unknowns. Clearly the solution to this problem is not going to be based on mathematical calculations. The solution involves imagining that both journeys take place at once. This requires that the monk be in two places at once. One of the two identical monks starts walking up from the bottom of the mountain while the other starts walking down from the top. Given that there is only a single path, they must meet at some point along the path. They will have reached that point at the same time of day on both the upward and downward journeys.

Fauconnier and Turner argue that conceptualizing a situation in which the single monk becomes two monks, and then meets himself as the two of him walk in opposite directions involves a blending of mental spaces. The two input spaces and the resulting blend are shown in Figure 5.2.

Input space 1 is the mental space in which the monk walks up the mountain from the bottom. The upward journey takes place on a specific day, $d_1$. Input space 2 is the space in which the same monk walks down from the top. This journey takes place on $d_2$. Elements from both input spaces are projected onto a third space, called a blended space. Each of the input spaces includes a mountain. Both instances of the mountain are projected onto the single mountain in the blended space, symbolized by the sloping line in each space. The monk in input space 1 is projected onto the bottom of the mountain in the blend. The monk in input space 2 is projected onto the top of the mountain in the blend. As a result, the blend contains a single mountain with the same monk at the top and at the bottom. The two days of the two different journeys, $d_1$ and $d_2$, merge in the blend, becoming the single day, $d'$. Both monks begin walking at the same time and eventually the monk meets himself at some point on the path.

Note the unusualness of the phrase *the monk meets himself at some point on the path*. Under ordinary circumstances, such a phrase would be highly unusual. Within the blended space, however, the language is very natural. However,

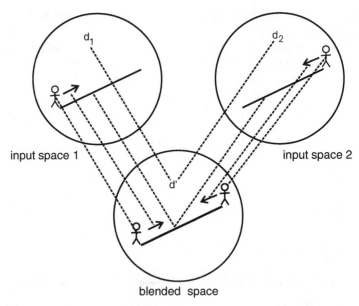

Figure 5.2  A blended space from two input spaces

it is not the grammatical structure that is unusual, but rather, the situation being described. Fauconnier and Turner make the point that once the blend is established, it can then be elaborated. That is, in this blend, not only do the two identical monks appear at two places on the mountain, they then begin to walk. As a result of walking in opposite directions they meet one another. Their eventual meeting is the logical consequence of the impossible situation created by the blend. They describe this as *running the blend*.

In describing the structure of blended spaces, Fauconnier (1997) proposes that there is a generic space that includes the elements the two input spaces have in common. This is the uppermost mental space shown in Figure 5.3. The generic space maps onto each of the input spaces and "reflects some common, usually more abstract, structure and organization shared by the inputs and defines the core cross-space mappings between them" (Fauconnier 1997:149). In addition, there are cross-space mappings, shown by the solid horizontal lines in Figure 5.3. This maps the counterparts in the two input spaces. Note that not all the elements of the two input spaces are counterparts. It is also only a partial mapping since not all the elements from each of the two input spaces need be projected into the blended space. The rectangular space in the blend represents what Fauconnier and Turner call *emergent structure*, which develops by means of three interrelated processes: composition, completion, and elaboration. Composition results from placing elements together that were not

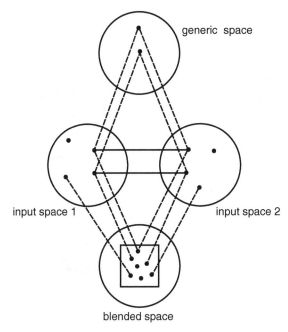

Figure 5.3  The four spaces participating in a blend

together before and allows for new relations between elements that did not exist prior to the blending.

Completion depends on an understanding of cultural models and background knowledge that allows the elements in the blend to become a coherent self-contained structure rather than simply a collection of elements. The blend involving the two monks, for example, becomes a conceptually real setting with a mountain and a path, in which both instances of the monk can walk on the path at the same time. Finally, elaboration allows the completed blend to take on a life of its own. The two monks are able to begin walking and meet each other. This meeting is a consequence of events that happen within the blend itself.

### Real-space blends

#### Creating a map

Consider a situation in which small model ships are placed on a large table. The top of the table is painted blue with two irregular areas on the top of the table painted brown. The model ships are placed in specific positions in blue areas on the top of the table. The resulting map conceptualized on the top of the table

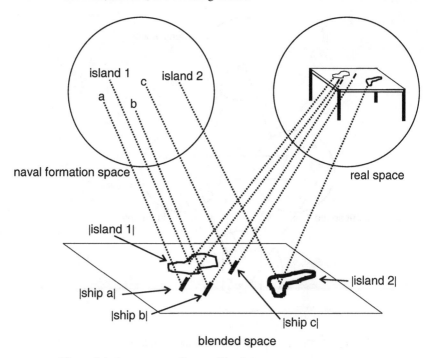

Figure 5.4  A map as a real-space blend

is a blended mental space. The two input spaces and the resulting real-space blend are illustrated in Figure 5.4.[2]

One of the input spaces is the naval formation space containing a conception of the ocean, the islands, and the locations of the ships. The other input space is the top of the table in real space, including the model ships, the areas of blue paint, and the areas of brown paint. The two islands and the surrounding ocean in the naval formation space and the two outlined shapes on the top of the table surrounded by a blue painted surface in real space are counterparts and project into the blend as the two islands and surrounding ocean in the blend. Likewise, the ships in the naval formation space and the model ships in real space are projected into the blend as the ships in the blend. The result is a visible three-dimensional map. Its very nature as a map is an example of emergent structure in this blend, since neither input space by itself constitutes a map. Since elements of the naval formation space are projected onto visible entities in real space,

[2] A generic mental space (Figure 5.3) is conceived of as including what the input spaces have in common. In the grounded blends I analyze in this book, whatever the input spaces have in common must be very abstract. Since the blends are understandable and coherent without the representation of the generic space, this and subsequent diagrams will include only the two input spaces and the blend.

such as the painted parts of the top of the table and the model ships, some elements within the blended space are visible. That is, one can see the locations of the ships with respect to the islands simply by inspecting the blended space.

The two input spaces differ in their groundedness.[3] The naval formation space is not grounded because the islands and the surrounding ocean are not part of the immediate environment of the sailors putting together the map on the top of the table. They understand that they are in a room rather than at the place where the ships are in formation. The tabletop and the models, however, do exist in each of the sailor's real space. Real space is grounded and the sailors understand that the table and the models are physically present and that they can reach out and touch the top of the table or that they can pick up the model ships. The blended space is created from a partial mapping of both input spaces into the blended space. For example, the trees and mountains on the islands have not become part of the blend. Only the general shape of the coastlines of the islands appears in the blend. Thus, only some aspects of the topography of the naval formation space have been projected into the blend. Similarly, only some aspects of real space have been projected into the blend. The top of the table and the model ships are part of the blend, but the sides of the table, its legs, the floor, and the sailors are not.[4]

Blending introduces an additional referential ambiguity since it is possible to use the phrase *that ship* to talk about the wooden model on the table or the ship in the blend. For example, one sailor could point at the model ship on the table in real space (i.e. the wooden object) and make the statement in (1). In doing so the sailor utters the phrase *that ship* while pointing at a piece of wood with a crack in it. The crack exists in the model ship, not in the real ship in the ocean. This is a statement about the model in real space. A sailor could also point to a ship in the blended space and make the statement in (2). In this case the speaker utters *that ship* while pointing at the ship that results from blending a ship in the naval formation space with a small piece of wood. In this case, however, the speaker is not talking about the need to send a message to the captain of the piece of wood. The sailor is making a statement about the need to send a message to the captain of a real ship on the ocean corresponding to the ship in the naval formation blend.

(1)     That ship (points at the piece of wood) has a crack in it.

(2)     We need to send a message to the captain of that ship (points at the blended ship).

---

[3] See chapter 3 for an explanation of a grounded mental space.

[4] Hutchins (2000) describes how blending processes give significance to everyday objects such as watches or calendars. He describes such objects as "material anchors" for conceptual blending. Using the terminology in this book, I would describe a watch or a calendar as a "real-space anchor."

When I talk about the conceptual entity that results from blending the real-space model ship and the mental representation of ship *a* I will enclose the word naming that entity in vertical brackets. Thus, when I talk about |ship a|, I mean the entity that results from blending ship *a* and the real-space model.

In the real-space blend |ship a| becomes another conceptual instance of ship *a*. It is distinct from ship *a* in the naval formation space and also distinct from the corresponding real ship on the ocean. The |ocean|, |ship a|, |ship b|, |ship c|, |island 1|, and |island 2| have the physical characteristics of the entities projected from real space but the conceptual attributes of the entities they have blended with. For example, a sailor could point toward one side of |island 1|and remark that there is no harbor on that side of the island. Similarly, a sailor could point toward a particular location on |ship a| and remark about the type of armament there.

One of the characteristics the blend inherits from real space is that it is grounded. That is, the elements of the blend now have a presence in the immediate environment. In chapter 3 I stated that I would talk about elements of real space as if they existed at their conceptualized locations outside the brain. Thus, when I talk about the real-space model ship on the real-space table, I mean the real-space ship is conceptualized as existing at that location on the conceptualized real-space table.

In contrast to a non-grounded mental representation of the ship hundreds of miles away, |ship a| is a grounded conceptual counterpart of the same ship. This means that there are two immediate realities the sailors can talk about and gesture toward: real space and the real-space blend. These two realities are conceptualized as existing in the same physical space at the same time. As a consequence, there is no physical distinction between pointing toward |ship a| and pointing toward the corresponding piece of wood in real space. This is why the pointing in (1) and (2) would look the same.

### The economy of maps

It is possible for an English speaker to describe the physical relationships between buildings in a neighborhood without an overt spatial representation. For example, an English speaker could use the description in (3) to talk about the physical relationships between a house, an adjacent apartment building, and a street.

(3)     There is a big apartment building on the left side of my house. Both
        buildings face Florida Street.

The addressee would easily be able to understand the meaning of (3). Descriptions which attempt to convey more elaborate locative information such as (4) require more extended description.

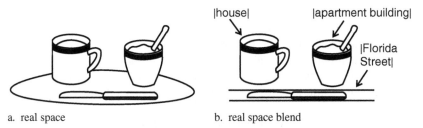

a. real space                              b. real space blend

Figure 5.5  A blend with a cup, sugar bowl, and a knife

(4)      As you are facing the house there is a bicycle about forty feet behind
         the house but off to the right about fifteen feet or so from the right
         rear corner of the house.

It is possible to simplify such descriptions greatly through the use of a real-space
blend. The statements in (5), for example, create a real space blend depicting
the physical relationships between the house, apartment building, and street.

(5)      OK, the coffee cup is my house. The sugar bowl is the apartment
         building next door and the knife is Florida Street.

While uttering (5) the speaker would place the coffee cup at a specific place on
the table, then place the sugar bowl nearby, and finally place the knife in front
of both the coffee cup and the sugar bowl. One such arrangement is illustrated
in Figure 5.5a.

Once the items are placed on the table both the speaker and the addressee
are able to take advantage of the spatial representation – the real-space blend –
each constructs in front of them. Figure 5.5b illustrates the blend created by
the person uttering (5). In contrast to real space, which contains a placemat, a
coffee cup, a sugar bowl, and a knife, the real-space blend contains a |house|,
an |apartment building|, |Florida Street|, and the |land| on which these things
rest. The placemat is missing from the blend since it has not been blended with
any other conceptual entities.

It is now a simple matter to identify the location of the bicycle by uttering
(6) while pointing to a specific |place| behind the |house| and slightly toward
the |apartment building|.

(6)      There is a bicycle right about here.

As was the case with the model ships on the table discussed previously, there
are two grounded mental spaces ahead of the speaker at the same time – real
space and the real-space blend. By pointing to a location within the blend the
speaker simultaneously points at a location on the table in real space. This follows because both real space and the blended space are grounded and occupy

the same physical space. Thus, the phrase *right about here*, accompanied by a gesture toward the top of the table, could potentially be about the table or about the blend. The fact that the speaker is talking about the house and the apartment building, together with the fact that there is no bicycle visible on the top of the table makes the potential ambiguity easy to resolve in this case. The signer is identifying a location within the blend rather than a location in real space.

The efficiency of the combination of spoken language and a simultaneous gesture toward the real-space blend is obvious. When English is used alone, for example, without a real-space blend and without gestures, it requires substantial linguistic effort to describe the location of the bicycle. Thirty-four words were used in (4) while seven words were sufficient in (6) where English was used along with a gesture pointing toward the real-space blend.

The ease with which such spatial representations are created and used belies the cognitive complexity underlying their use. For example, after having created the grounded blend containing the |house| and the |apartment building|, it would be perfectly normal for an English speaker to utter (7) while pointing toward the side of the |house|.

(7)    This side of my house gets direct sunlight in the morning.

Interestingly, (7) has the form of an utterance which would be appropriate if the speaker were standing in front of the house while gesturing toward the side of the house. Instead, the speaker is sitting at a table pointing at the side of a coffee cup. Under ordinary circumstances the phrase *this side of my house* would be completely inappropriate when pointing at a coffee cup, yet its use in (7) is fine, because the speaker is pointing at the |house|. Because of blending with the real-space coffee cup, the |house| has the physical form of a coffee cup but the conceptual attributes of the house. Just as it would be appropriate to gesture toward the real house if the speaker were standing in front of it, it is also appropriate to gesture toward the |house| ahead of the speaker.

Note that the knife in Figure 5.5 is not long enough to extend much beyond the coffee cup or the sugar bowl. It would be a mistake to assume, however, that the length of the knife corresponds to the length of |Florida Street| in the blend. Rather, it would be normal to assume that |Florida Street| continues in both directions past both buildings and that the knife merely blends with a part of it.

We have looked at examples in which the speaker talks about a real-space blend as a coherent conceptual scene. That is, by pointing at the side of the |house| while saying "this side of my house...," the speaker is operating within the coherence and logic of the blend. It is also possible to step back from the blend and comment about the construction of the blend itself.

(8)     You put your house too close to the street. (while moving the coffee
        cup away from the knife)

(9)     You put the cup too close to the knife. (while moving the coffee cup
        away from the knife)

When doing so, it seems possible to use terms appropriate for describing either
the elements of the blend, as in (8), or elements of real space, as in (9). In
producing these two utterances, the speaker is not operating within the logic
of the blend, but is commenting on the structure of the blend itself. In both
cases the speaker is claiming that the blended space is incorrectly constructed
because the coffee cup is too close to the knife.

### Signers as part of blends

A signer can become part of a real-space blend. In the following example a
signer is describing an interaction between the cartoon character Garfield and
his owner Jon.[5] The signer was asked to look through a cartoon then to set it
aside and explain what happened in the cartoon. Just prior to the event I focus
on, Jon tells Garfield that the remote control for the television does not work
because he removed the batteries and that Garfield will have to get out of the
chair in order to change channels on the TV. Garfield's initial response is to
look up at Jon. This is the part of the narrative I will be examining below. After
looking up at Jon, Garfield makes a comment then grabs Jon and holds him out
toward the television – using him as a human remote control, pressing buttons
on the TV with his finger.

The clause I have selected consists of the subject CAT and the verb LOOK-
TOWARD$^{\cup \rightarrow y}$. Prior to this sentence the signer has been describing Garfield
sitting in a chair. Garfield looks away from the television and up at Jon in
response to Jon's comments about the remote control not working. The entities
involved in this action are represented in the event space on the lower left in
Figure 5.6 in their approximate physical relationships to one another as viewed
from above.

Semantic space represents the meanings encoded by these two signs in this
grammatical construction and can be found underneath the images of the signs
CAT and LOOK-TOWARD$^{\cup \rightarrow y}$ in Figure 5.6. The subject–verb relationship
between CAT and LOOK-TOWARD$^{\cup \rightarrow y}$ entails a mapping between the semantic pole of CAT and the verb's trajector. This connection signifies that an
entity of the type 'cat' looked toward something.

The meaning expressed by the signer goes beyond what is encoded by the two
signs. In addition, the signer also creates a partially visible demonstration of

---

[5] Metzger (1995) analyzes this narrative with a focus on constructed dialogue. The narrative was
later analyzed in terms of blended mental spaces in Liddell and Metzger (1998).

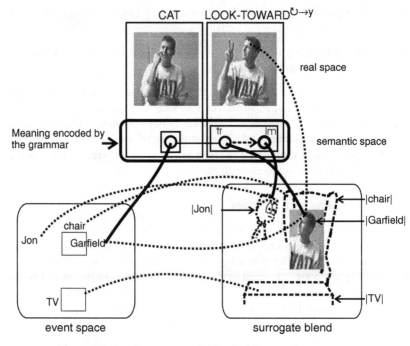

Figure 5.6  Creating a surrogate blend while narrating

the event being described. He does this by blending his own face and torso with that of Garfield. As a result of blending, the signer becomes the visible blended entity |Garfield|, illustrated in Figure 5.6 on the lower right. If the signer's body becomes someone or something else through blending, I describe the resulting blended space as a *surrogate space* and describe the elements within that space as *surrogates*.

The signer provides clear evidence for the existence of the surrogate |Garfield| by looking up and to the right as if he were Garfield looking up and to the right toward Jon. He also provides clear evidence for an invisible surrogate |Jon|, since he directs LOOK-TOWARD$^{\cup \rightarrow y}$ toward |Jon|. Thus, the blend creates a partially visible representation of the event in which Garfield looks up at Jon.

In addition to |Garfield| and |Jon|, Figure 5.6 also includes a |chair| and |TV| in the surrogate blend. Although this particular clause does not provide evidence for the presence of the |chair| and the |TV|, signs in other parts of the narrative are directed toward these other elements of the surrogate blend, thus providing evidence for their existence in the blend. Thus, the blended space in Figure 5.6 is a surrogate space containing the surrogates |Garfield|,

|Jon|, the |television|, and the |chair|, all integrated as part of a conceptual scene.

The semantic space represents the meanings encoded by the individual signs and the subject–verb construction. The surrogate space is also meaningful in that it provides a partially visible instance of the event being described. Understanding the meaning constructed in this context involves mappings that relate the event space, the surrogate blend, and semantic space. Figure 5.6 illustrates how these spaces and the elements within them are related to one another.

Immediately preceding this part of the narrative, the standing Jon had directed a comment to his left toward Garfield. Next, overtly mentioning CAT as the subject of LOOK-TOWARD$^{\cup \to y}$ brings the narrative back to a description of what Garfield did. The addressee is faced with the issue of how to construct the mental space mappings for this clause. During CAT the signer's head and eye gaze are directed forward. At this point the signer has not yet blended with Garfield in the event space to become |Garfield| in the surrogate blend. The surrogate blend only comes into existence during the verb LOOK-TOWARD$^{\cup \to y}$, where the signer provides evidence for the blend by directing the fingertips toward |Jon| in the blend and by turning his head and directing his eye gaze up toward |Jon|. Once the surrogate blend comes into being there are two Garfields in the mental space network. One is the Garfield in the event space and the other is |Garfield| in the surrogate blend. However, at the time CAT is signed, the only available instance of Garfield is the one in the event space. Therefore, Figure 5.6 shows the semantic pole of CAT mapped onto the Garfield in the event space.

Immediately after signing CAT, however, the signer creates the surrogate blend by rotating his face and eye gaze up and to the right. He blends with Garfield to become |Garfield| looking up and to the right toward |Jon|. Recall that if the entity to map onto the landmark of a $^{\to y}$ verb is physically present, the verb will be directed toward that entity. Such verbs function exactly the same way in surrogate spaces. By directing LOOK-TOWARD$^{\cup \to y}$ toward |Jon|, the signer provides an instruction for mapping its landmark onto |Jon|.

The verb LOOK-TOWARD$^{\cup \to y}$ has the grammatical requirement that the signer not only direct the fingertips toward the entity being looked toward, but also gaze in the same direction. This requirement is reflected in the sign's gloss by the symbol $^{\cup}$. This involves creating a surrogate space in which the signer's gaze demonstrates the gaze of the one described as doing the looking. As a result, the verb's trajector always maps onto the surrogate doing the looking. In this case the surrogate doing the looking is |Garfield|. This accounts for the mapping between the trajector and |Garfield|.

Note that the signer is only partially mapped onto |Garfield|. We don't know, for example, what |Garfield|'s arms are doing because the signer's arms are not conceptualized as |Garfield|'s. If they were, then |Garfield| would be understood as signing LOOK-TOWARD$^{\cup \to y}$. But that is not what |Garfield| is doing. |Garfield| is looking up and to the right toward |Jon|, not talking about looking up at Jon. Since the signer's hands are not part of the surrogate space, they are free to be used for narration. Thus, the signer is narrating by producing the verb with his right hand at the same time that he is demonstrating through blending the very action he is narrating about.

The blend inherits its conceptual setting from the event space. Physically, however, the blend is a here-and-now representation of the same event. It inherits its here-and-now nature from real space. Thus, the blended space actually has both a cartoon conceptual setting and a here-and-now physical setting.

There is an important distinction to be made here between the mental conceptualizations of the signer and an addressee. The blend comes into existence *for the signer* prior to the verb LOOK-TOWARD$^{\cup \to y}$. The signer must conceptualize the blended space in which |Jon| is located to the right of the seated |Garfield|. This conceptualization gives the verb something to be directed toward. Based on that conceptualized blend, the signer directs the verb toward |Jon|. Things are different from the perspective of the addressee. The addressee does not know what blend is in the mind of the signer until the signer provides evidence of that blend. That evidence does not emerge until after the sign CAT. During LOOK-TOWARD$^{\cup \to y}$ the signer directs the sign toward |Jon| and also rotates his face and gaze toward |Jon|. The addressee can then make use of the looking action of the signer and the directionality of the verb to create the blend that already exists in the mind of the signer.[6]

Surrogates can exist virtually anywhere. They can be near the signer or at a great distance. They can be above, below, to the side of, or even behind the signer. Surrogate representations are spatially unbounded and make up part of a here-and-now conceptual scene distinct from real space. The use of space in ASL is often characterized as a means of keeping track of referents. This is not the primary function of the blend in Figure 5.6. Its primary function is to provide a real-time partial demonstration of the event being described.[7] Thus, the addressee is able to watch |Garfield| turn and look up at |Jon|. The addressee

---

[6] In producing the mental space diagrams in this book, I attempt to present sufficient mappings and projections to show how blending takes place and how semantic structure maps onto elements of other mental spaces. I do not attempt to represent every possible mental space connection. For example, I have not illustrated the projection of unoccupied space to the right of the signer that blends with Jon in the event space to create |Jon| in the blend. The same applies to projections from real space into the blend in creating the |chair| and the |TV|.

[7] There have been various attempts to analyze eye gaze and movements of the head as morphemic. For example, Shepard-Kegl's (1985) description of a Role Prominence Clitic (later called a Role Prominence Marker) might be thought to apply to the Garfield example. A Role Prominence Marker is realized by a slight shift of the signer's head and/or torso toward a spatial location associated with the subject of the verb. It is proposed as a meaningful, abstract grammatical element which gives role prominence to the subject of the clause. Bahan (1996) describes what

is not able to see everything in the scene because |Jon| is invisible. |Garfield|, however, is visible, and |Garfield|'s actions are directly observable. One can simply observe |Garfield| to see that |Garfield| looks upward and to the right toward |Jon|.

Figure 5.6 presents a static image of the conceptual mappings associated with the meaning encoded by CAT LOOK-TOWARD$^{\cup \to y}$. This is a useful, but incomplete picture. It is useful because this set of mappings provides the key to understanding the interrelationships between these four spaces. It is incomplete because the real-space blend is not static. It is a dynamic, gestural, non-morphemic, here-and-now demonstration of |Garfield| turning and looking up at |Jon|. The demonstration brings the actions associated with the encoded meaning to life.

Surrogate spaces can also occur in the absence of signing. In this Garfield cartoon, the remote control for the TV does not work. Since Garfield does not want to get up out of his chair, he holds Jon out toward the TV to act as a human remote control. In explaining this, the signer creates a blend in which the signer as |Garfield| grabs |Jon|, still to his right, and holds him out in space toward the |TV| ahead of him. The initial signing related to this blend appears in Figure 5.7a. |Garfield|'s facial expression appears to indicate that some effort was involved in holding |Jon|. This facial expression is immediately replaced with an expression showing surprise as illustrated in Figure 5.7b. This change in facial expression provides evidence of a new blend. The signer has created a blend in which he becomes |Jon|, flailing his arms while leaning both his head and body very far forward. His head eventually faces down, as shown in the final image in Figure 5.7b.

In the gesture sequence in Figure 5.7b the signer not only makes flailing movements with his arms, he also makes pressing movements with his index finger, as if pressing buttons on a TV. The third frame in Figure 5.7b shows an instance of this pressing motion by the index finger of the right hand. This gestural sequence does not involve the production of any signs. It is a fully gestural demonstration of |Jon| flailing his arms and pressing buttons.[8] This adds a visual component that enriches the story. The visible action in which we

appears to be the same phenomenon as an abstract marker of subject agreement. In his analysis eye gaze marks object agreement by being directed toward a location in space associated with "phi features," features relevant to syntactic agreement (Chomsky 1981). He does not discuss the semantic contribution of the agreement markers. It is clear, however, that the proposed agreement morphemes do not carry meanings such as looking in a given direction, who is looking, etc. These analyses do not apply well in this case. In the Garfield example the head and eye gaze show what Garfield did. It is not the realization of an abstract syntactic morpheme. See Liddell and Metzger (1998) for a more detailed discussion of these alternative interpretations of head position and eye gaze.

[8] This gesture sequence in which no signs were produced is described in detail in Liddell and Metzger (1998). Additional examples of gestures in the absence of signs can be found in Emmorey (1999).

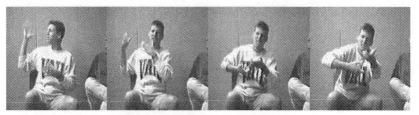

a. |Garfield| grabbing and holding |Jon| toward the |TV|

b. |Jon| flailing and pressing buttons

c. |Garfield| holding |Jon| (alternate view of the events in 'b')

Figure 5.7   A sequence of surrogate spaces

see |Jon| struggling adds considerable interest and humor. There are times when an ASL story is so funny that the members of the audience are laughing so hard that they are crying. Trying to explain the humor to a non-signing passerby is hopeless because a translation does not capture the visual aspects of the story presented in real space blends.

The signer next describes |Garfield| throwing |Jon| back over his shoulder. This sequence begins with a configuration shown in Figure 5.7c. Note that this is essentially the same as the one which ended the first sequence in which |Garfield| held |Jon| out toward the |TV|. This shows that the signer's actions are now to be understood again as the actions of |Garfield| holding |Jon| toward the |TV|.

In describing the events in the Garfield cartoon, the signer provides three sequential views of |Garfield| holding |Jon| out toward the |TV|. Figure 5.7a ends with one view in which the signer blends with Garfield and |Jon| is invisible. All the activity in Figure 5.7b provides a view in which |Jon| is visible but |Garfield| is not. One can directly observe |Jon| flailing his arms and pressing buttons. Figure 5.7c begins with a third sequential representation in which the visible |Garfield| is holding |Jon| toward the TV. The changes in the signer's face, eye gaze, or body posture show which blended space is active. If the addressee is unable to determine which blend is active, the narrative will not make sense. The use of the configuration of the face or body to signal which blended space is active is an important part of understanding ASL narratives.

### Constructed action

The presence and importance of spontaneous gestures of various types during speech is well-known (Ekman and Friesen 1969, Kendon 1972, 1980, Mc-Neill 1992). For example, McNeill (1992) describes iconic gestures, metaphoric gestures, beats, cohesive gestures, and deictic gestures accompanying speech. Iconic gestures are pictorial in that they illustrate concrete actions. The signer's head and eye gaze illustrating |Garfield| looking up at |Jon| in Figure 5.6 is an example of what McNeill would call an iconic gesture. Metaphoric gestures are similar, but they present an image of an abstraction rather than something concrete. A beat gesture involves the hand moving in time with the rhythmic nature of speech.[9] Deictic gestures are pointing gestures.

McNeill (1992) presents (10) as an example in which co-speech gestures are present during an English speaker's description of a recently viewed cartoon. In the cartoon, one of the characters, Tweety Bird, drops a bowling ball down a drainpipe.

(10)     and Tweety Bird runs and gets a bowling ball and drops it down the
         drainpipe

During the two words *it down* the speaker's two hands are configured as if holding and pushing down a large round object. Here the speaker is describing an event using spoken English and also illustrating an aspect of that event through gesture. In descriptions of ASL text, Winston (1991, 1992) and Metzger (1995) use the term *constructed action* to refer to these same types of gestures. The idea behind using the term constructed action is that just as constructed dialogue is not a direct copy of the speech being reported (Tannen 1986, 1989), constructed action is also not a direct copy of a character's actions. It is the narrator's construction of another's actions (Metzger 1995). The actions of |Garfield| in turning and looking at |Jon|, in showing the effort in holding |Jon| out toward the |TV|, and the actions of |Jon| in flailing and pressing buttons are all examples of constructed action.[10]

---

[9] A beat gesture has also been called a baton (Efron 1941, Ekman and Friesen 1969).
[10] See also Metzger (1995) for a discussion of simultaneous constructed action and narration.

Constructed actions are extremely common in spoken language discourse. Example (11) is an easy to imagine, ordinary example of a description elaborated by means of a real-space blend that could occur during speech. In (11), the speaker describes an event in which Frank is searching for his keys. As the words are spoken, the speaker also presses his own hands against his shirt pockets then his pants pockets. Of interest here is the motivation for the speaker to press his palms against his own pockets. This only makes sense as an illustration of the behavior being described in the sentence.

(11)     Frank was looking for his keys. (uttered while pressing the palms against shirt pockets then pants pockets)

Although the spoken words describe Frank as looking for keys, there are many ways to search for keys. One could search by opening drawers, looking under newspapers, and so on. One of the ways to search is to check the pockets of the clothing currently being worn. The gestures which are part of (11) provide a visual illustration of the movement of the hands against the torso. The temporal coordination of the verbal description and the constructed action invites the addressee to interpret the pressing movements of the hands as searching movements. As a result, the message expressed in (11) is much more explicit than the meaning encoded by the words. The addressee understands the meanings encoded by the words and also observes the pressing movements of the hands against the body. By integrating these two sources of meaning, the addressee produces a much richer message than that provided by the words alone.

The pressing movements of the hands are not meant to represent the pressing movement of the speaker's hands against his own clothing. That is, the integrated message is not that I pressed my hands against my pockets while Frank looked for his keys. The message is that he pressed his hands against his pockets as an act of searching for his keys. Thus, in order to understand (11), one must see the speaker's actions as Frank's actions. The mental space entity with the property 'Frank' has been projected onto the current speaker. Thus, during the production of that sentence, there is a partial blending of the speaker and Frank that produces the surrogate |Frank|. The blending is only partial since the words being spoken are not meant to be understood as Frank's words, but rather, as the words of the current speaker.

## Constructed dialogue

Figure 5.8 illustrates a part of an ASL narrative in which one character asks another the question in (12). In doing so, the signer does not merely recite the

|                | q              |
|----------------|----------------|

"KNOW          WHERE          MY          HOME"

Figure 5.8  A surrogate asks a yes–no question

signs of the questioner. He directs his eye gaze toward an imagined addressee and asks the question as if that addressee were really present.[11]

$$\overline{\qquad\qquad\qquad\qquad\text{q}}$$
(12)    KNOW WHERE MY HOME
        Do you know where my home is?

The signer is producing a narrative that includes one person asking another a question. In doing so, the signer blends with that character and asks the question as if he were that character. Not only does he have to imagine that he is that character, he also has to imagine where his addressee is. This is because a normal yes–no question in ASL involves eye contact between the signer and addressee. Since the signer has oriented his face and eye gaze to the left, it is apparent that he has conceived of the addressee as being up and to the left.

The signer becomes a blended instance of character *A* asking a question to a blended instance of character *B*, on his left. Once the identities of the characters in the blend are understood, the signing makes sense. It is simply a normal question from one person to another. In fact, the signer has done such a complete job of becoming a character asking a question that it is not possible to determine from an examination of the signs illustrated in Figure 5.8 whether the question is directed at a real or imagined addressee.

In Figure 5.8, MY is part of the nominal MY HOME. But whose home is being talked about? Since MY encodes possession by the signer, the answer has to be the home owned *by the signer*. The problem is that there are two signers: the real-space signer telling the story and the surrogate signer |A|. It is clear that the signer did not stop telling the story in order to ask someone a question. Since the surrogate signer |A| is asking the question, this makes |A| the relevant signer. Therefore, the house being talked about is the house belonging to |A|.

---

[11] This is a prototypical example of what has been called role-shifting or role-switching in the sign language literature (Mandel 1977, Thompson 1977, Baker and Cokely 1980, Liddell 1980, Padden 1986, 1990, Lillo-Martin and Klima 1990).

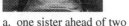
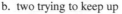

a. one sister ahead of two     b. two trying to keep up     c. one sister ahead of two

Figure 5.9  Three instances of two people behind a single person

Since |A| is the projection of *A* into the surrogate blend, the house being talked about is the one belonging to *A*.

The next example comes from a description of three young sisters aged ten, eight, and six. These children are supposed to walk home from school together but the oldest sister walks faster than the others. In Figure 5.9a the right hand in a 1 handshape is ahead of the left hand in a V handshape. This depicts one sister ahead of the other two. Note that the right hand is directly ahead of the left hand. In Figure 5.9b, the signer's facial expression expresses the effort of the two younger girls trying to keep up with the oldest girl. Again, the lead hand is directly ahead of the other hand. Immediately before creating a surrogate blend in which the eldest sister talks to the other two sisters, the signer places the two hands as shown in Figure 5.9c. The hands only remain in that configuration for approximately 200 milliseconds. Because of the angle of the camera his hands appear to be side by side, but the right hand is still ahead of the left.

The single index finger of the right hand still depicts the older sister ahead of the other two, but now she is depicted ahead of and to the right of the other two sisters. The right–left distinction just introduced allows the signer to make a right–left distinction in describing the interactions of the three sisters in what follows.

In Figure 5.10, the signer represents a brief dialogue between the sisters. It begins with the sign PRO$^{\rightarrow x}$ directed forward and to the right. Directing PRO$^{\rightarrow x}$ this way indicates reference to the sister in the lead, who was depicted in the Figure 5.9c as being forward and to the right of the other two sisters. After a false start, the signer produces LOOK-TOWARD$^{\cup \rightarrow y}$. During LOOK-TOWARD$^{\cup \rightarrow y}$ the signer places his hand ahead of his right shoulder and rotates his hand so that his fingertips are directed toward the left. He also turns his face and gaze to the left. He is explaining that the older sister looked at the two younger sisters and simultaneously demonstrating the looking action of the older sister through his own face and eye gaze. This example is highly similar to the example of |Garfield| looking up at |Jon| (Figure 5.6).

The signer as the |older sister| looks toward the |two sisters| and issues the command HURRY, as shown in the final frame of Figure 5.10a. The signer's

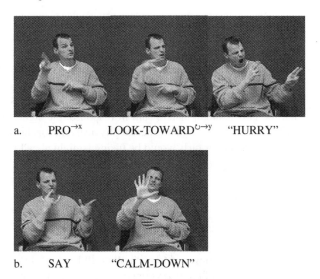

a.     PRO⁻ˣ        LOOK-TOWARD°⁻ʸ      "HURRY"

b.     SAY           "CALM-DOWN"

Figure 5.10  Role-shifting by means of surrogates

face shows that the command is being produced with considerable emotion. In addition, the signer also continues to direct his face and eye gaze to the left toward the other two sisters. The extent of the blended space is different during the verb and the following command. During the verb only the signer's head and face are projected into the blend. During the command HURRY, the blend includes the signer's face, head, torso, and arms.

The actual physical relationship between the sisters was not a right–left relationship. The older sister was directly ahead of, and walking away from, the other two sisters. In order to sign to them, she would need to turn around. Recall that in Figure 5.9, just prior to creating the surrogate blend, the signer placed his index finger representing the older sister slightly to his right and ahead of the two fingers representing the other two sisters. In the preceding descriptions of the girls, the right hand was placed directly ahead of the left. He placed the hand depicting the older sister slightly to the right immediately before describing the older sister turning to look at and give a command to the two younger sisters. He now takes advantage of that rightward physical placement by creating a surrogate blend showing the older sister turning to the left to talk to the other two sisters.[12]

---

[12] It is apparent to me in examining the examples in this book that much of what guides the placement of entities in space is done without conscious awareness. The third placement of the oldest girl both ahead of and to the right of the other two girls is the kind of phenomenon that I have in mind. If correct, it means that physical actions such as the production of language, are only partially under conscious control.

The two younger sisters would not have to rotate their heads or bodies to respond to the older sister. In showing the response of the two sisters (Figure 5.10b), the signer first produces SAY, and simultaneously points to the left with his left index finger. He is taking advantage of the fact that the two sisters were to the left of the signer in the surrogate space during the production of HURRY. Pointing to the left identifies the other two girls as those doing the saying. In presenting what the two younger sisters said in response, the signer does not rotate his body. This is consistent with the actual physical relationships between the girls, since the two younger girls would be facing straight ahead while they responded to the older sister. It is also evident that the response CALM-DOWN is a constructed response because it is not attributed to either of the two sisters individually, but (apparently) to both. That is, in this blended space, the signer's response appears to be the response of both sisters at once.

Figure 5.11 presents a sequence of six blended spaces built from the same two input spaces during the description of the physical relationship between the sisters and ending with what they said to each other. In Figure 5.11a the signer depicts the older sister ahead of the two younger sisters. The older sister blends with the extended index finger on the right hand and the two younger sisters blend with the two extended fingers on the left hand.

In Figure 5.11b the two hands blended with the sisters are gone, but the area of space occupied by the single extended index finger has been blended with the older sister. The signer directs PRO$^{\rightarrow x}$ toward that area of space in order to identify the sister who did the looking. In Figure 5.11c, he partially becomes the |older sister| looking at the two younger sisters. He also continues narrating with the sign LOOK-TOWARD$^{\cup y}$. In Figure 5.11d he fully blends with the older sister and produces the constructed command, "HURRY." In this blend, the |two sisters| are to the left of the |older sister|. In Figure 8.11e, the signer is no longer the |older sister|, but the space to the left still contains the |two sisters|. As narrator the signer points his left hand toward the |two sisters| in order to identify who talks next. In Figure 8.11f the signer becomes the |two sisters| talking to the |older sister|.

During the three seconds needed to produce this sequence of blended spaces, the older sister was represented as the signer's index finger, the space occupied by the signer's index finger, the signer himself (both partially and then more completely), and as a surrogate ahead of the signer. The two younger sisters were represented as the two extended fingers, as surrogates to the left of the signer, and as the signer himself. It was not rehearsed, but arose naturally in producing the description of the activities of the sisters. The ease and rapidity of the conceptualizations underlying this signing is remarkable.

In ASL, blends can also be used to represent someone's thoughts. This is what is happening in Figure 5.12. The signer first mentions BILL. Next she rotates her head, redirects her eye gaze, and changes her facial expression. This

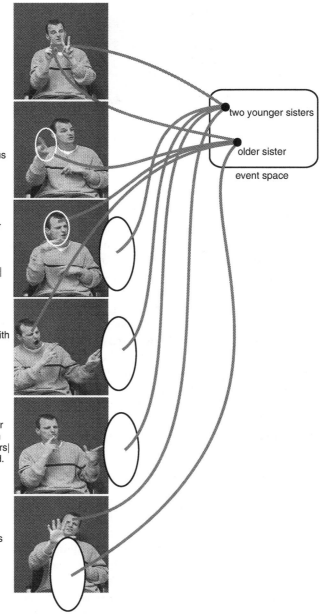

a. The index finger depicts the |older sister| while the two fingers on the left hand depict the two |younger sisters|

b. The signer as narrator directs PRO⁻ˣ to the previous location of the |older sister|

c. The signer's face blends with the older sister to partially become the |older sister|. The |younger sisters| are on his left.

d. The signer completely blends with the |older sister|, telling the |younger sisters| to hurry.

e. Signer as narrator points to the location of the |younger sisters| in the previous blend.

f. The signer as |younger sisters| tells the |older sister| to take it easy.

two younger sisters

older sister

event space

Figure 5.11  A series of rapidly shifting blended spaces

#BILL,            LIKE            JOHN

Figure 5.12  Bill realized with some surprise "(I) like John." (Liddell 1980: 57)

should now be a familiar signal that a blended space is being formed. Next, she signs her construction of what Bill was thinking. Tannen (1986, 1989) uses the term *constructed dialogue* to describe representations of actual or internal speech. The term seems equally applicable to the example in Figure 5.12.

In this example, the signer first mentions Bill, then creates a surrogate blend. Her face becomes part of the blend, by blending with Bill's face. She adopts a surprised facial expression to show Bill's surprise while using signs to represent other aspects of what Bill was thinking.[13] One of the key elements of forming this surrogate representation is directing eye gaze away from the addressee. An analysis that overlooked the change in head orientation, the wide eyes and the change in the direction of the eye gaze, and the dropped jaw, and only looked at the sequence of three signs, might incorrectly conclude that the signer had produced the sentence meaning, 'Bill likes John'. What the signer has actually produced is a construction that would be roughly translated: Bill (realized with some surprise), "I like John." That is, there is no subject–verb relationship between BILL and LIKE, since BILL merely mentions the mental space entity to be mapped onto the signer in the surrogate blend.

## Surrogates in spoken language discourse

### Constructed dialogue

I began this chapter with the observation that in everyday spoken language discourse, we freely conceive of people and things around us as though they were someone or something else. It is so commonplace that we tend not to notice that our conceptions of reality have temporarily changed. To illustrate what I mean, I will compare two instances of the question, *Are you going to eat that?* In (13), a direct question from the speaker to the addressee, there is no

---

[13] In this example, the surprised expression produced by the signer represents Bill's surprise. Engberg-Pedersen (1993) refers to this as the shifted attribution of expressive elements (p. 103).

need to see the speaker and his words as anything other than the speaker and his words.

(13)     Are you going to eat that?
         (The question is spoken with an inquisitive expression on the speaker's face, the speaker's own vocal characteristics, and a pointing gesture directed toward some food.)

This utterance, spoken in a situation in which the addressee has some food, has the following four characteristics: (a) the question calls for a response from the addressee; (b) the speaker's inquisitive facial expression is understood to be an expression of his own feelings; (c) the deictic gesture points at the actual food being spoken about; and (d) the pronoun *you* refers to the addressee.

In (14) the same question has none of these four characteristics. First, it does not call for a response from the addressee. This is because it is understood to be a previously asked question directed to the current speaker by Bill. The speaker is uttering Bill's words, using the present tense, as if Bill were currently uttering the question.

(14)     Bill came up to me and said, "Are you going to eat that?"
         (The question is spoken with an inquisitive expression on the speaker's face, the vocal characteristics of Bill, and a pointing gesture directed toward empty space.)

As in (13), the speaker has an inquisitive expression on his face. The inquisitive facial expression does not belong conceptually to the speaker, but to Bill. Understanding the significance of this facial expression requires the observer to see it as something other than the speaker's expression. Conceptually, it must be seen as Bill's expression, even though physically, it is on the speaker's face. Similarly, even though the current speaker is making a pointing gesture, he is not really pointing at anything physically present. Once again the observer must see the movement of the speaker's arm as something other than simply the movement of the speaker's arm. In this case the movement of the speaker's arm needs to be understood conceptually as Bill's pointing gesture toward some food – even though no food is present.

For the purposes of discussion, let us say that Joan utters (14). It should be evident that Joan creates a surrogate blend similar to the surrogate blends previously described in connection with ASL. Joan first narrates using the words in (15).

(15)     Bill came up to me and said

This bit of narration provides a brief description of the event preceding the constructed dialogue. It also identifies Bill as the person whose speech is about to be represented. In addition, it provides the information that Joan is Bill's addressee. Although there is no surrogate blend during (15), the following constructed dialogue does involve the creation of a surrogate blend. Joan blends with Bill to create the surrogate |Bill| speaking to a surrogate |Joan|.

(16)    Are you going to eat that?

The question in (16) is understood as a question from |Bill| to |Joan| that takes place within the surrogate blend. There is also some |food| in the surrogate blend and |Bill| is pointing at it. The question does not call for a response from Joan's interlocutor because the question is not directed from Joan to the interlocutor. It is directed from |Bill| to |Joan|. The inquisitive facial expression is understood to be a reflection of |Bill|'s feelings rather than Joan's. This follows from the blend since |Bill| is the one asking the question. The deictic gesture is also understood as |Bill|'s gesture toward some food rather than Joan's gesture toward empty space. Finally, the referent of the pronoun *you* is understood to be |Bill|'s addressee |Joan|. All these interpretations follow naturally from the existence of the surrogate blend.

### Conceptual shifts

Pronouns such as *I, me, you,* and *he,* have been called *shifters.* Jespersen (1959) introduced shifters as a class of grammatical units. His claim was that the general meaning of a shifter could not be defined without reference to the message. Jakobson (1971) points out that shifters were thought to be indexic, but not symbolic. He observes that this property of shifters was believed to result from their lack of a single, fixed meaning. He argues that this is incorrect. In his analysis shifters are both symbolic and indexic.[14] Jakobson proposes that pronouns and other grammatical units that express person, mood, tense and what he calls *evidential* information are all shifters.[15] Although the label shifter characterizes the shifting phenomena, it provides no explanation for it.

Consider a situation in which John and Sue are conversing. Sue is disappointed that she hasn't received a raise and John is giving advice.

(17)    John speaks:
    Next Monday you will have worked for your company for three years. If you want a raise you are going to have to ask for it next week. Right now I want you to imagine that this doll is your boss, that it is now next Monday, and that you are in your boss's office. Now I want you to pick up the doll and tell *your boss* that you want a raise.

---

[14] This was the position I adopted in chapter 3, where each individual pronoun encodes a specific meaning (its symbolic nature) and each also mapped onto some mental space entity (its referential nature).

[15] "Evidential" was a tentative label for a verbal category that included a narrated event, a speech event, or a narrated speech event.

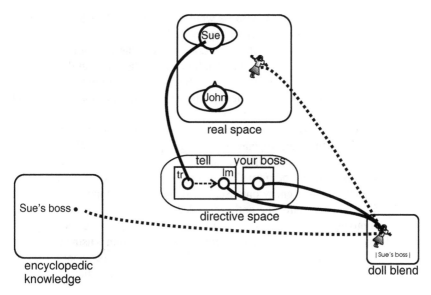

Figure 5.13 Using spoken English with a simple grounded blend

In (17) John asks Sue to imagine a future situation in which Sue is in the same location as her boss and in which she will be asking for a raise. As part of that process John asks Sue to imagine that a doll is her boss. Then he says, "... tell *your boss* that you want a raise."

As a part of making that request John creates a blended space. It is a relatively simple blend in which the doll becomes |Sue's boss|. One of the input spaces is John's encyclopedic, real-world knowledge containing the conceptual element Sue's boss. The other input space is real space, containing the doll. These two elements blend to become |Sue's boss|. The blend he has created is not the same as the space he asks Sue to imagine. He is not recounting or representing an event. By making an association between Sue's boss and the doll, he merely creates the entity, |Sue's boss|. There is no time frame or setting associated with |Sue's boss| other than the here and now. The relevant mental spaces can be found in Figure 5.13.

The blend in Figure 5.13 would seem to be about as simple as a blend gets. A single entity takes on a new property while everything around it remains the same.

The noun phrase *your boss* symbolizes an entity with the property 'your boss'. For mapping purposes, the addressee must determine the proper mapping for this semantic entity. Recall that Sue is being asked to talk to her boss now. In order to do this her boss must be conceived of as physically present. Since John has asked her to conceive of the doll as her boss, the natural mapping for the semantic entity encoded by *your boss* would be onto the blended doll, |Sue's boss|. This is the mapping shown in Figure 5.13.

John is not asking Sue to talk to the doll, because the doll in real space is not her boss. It is just a doll. In the blend, however, the physical doll inherits characteristics of Sue's boss. This entity, |Sue's boss|, only exists within the context of the blend, since it is neither the real-world doll nor Sue's actual boss.

Note that in Figure 5.13 there are two elements with the property 'Sue's boss'. One is in the encyclopedic knowledge space and the other is |Sue's boss|. I have mapped the semantic entity symbolized by *your boss* onto |Sue's boss|. It may not be immediately apparent why I have done this rather than map that semantic entity onto Sue's boss in the encyclopedic knowledge space. That is, potentially the entity encoded by *your boss* could have been mapped onto either |Sue's boss| in the blend or Sue's boss in the encyclopedic knowledge space. It might be possible, for example, that John is using the phrase *your boss* metonymically to refer to |Sue's boss|. The way personal pronouns are used below suggests that the mapping in Figure 5.13 where the phrase *your boss* points directly at |Sue's boss| is the proper one.

If Sue refused to comply with John's request, he might continue with a demonstration of his own by uttering (18).

(18)     Why not just be straightforward. (John picks up the doll and holds it out in front of him while looking at it.) *I* have been working *here* for exactly three years *today*, and *I* think *you* should give *me* a raise (said while making repeated jabbing motions of the index finger toward the doll).

In (18) words commonly regarded as shifters have been underlined. Although all the words in (18) are physically uttered by John in real space, *I* and *me* identify |Sue|, *here* identifies Sue's place of employment, and *today* describes the day normally described as "next Monday." We can begin to make sense of this by examining the real-space blend that John has created.

The two input spaces for the blend are the Sue's boss's office next week space and real space. The blend created from these two input spaces is illustrated in Figure 5.14. It differs substantially from the blend in Figure 5.13. It inherits its conceptual setting and the two relevant characters from the future space for the meeting in Sue's boss's office next week. The blend inherits the here-and-now, physical setting and the two physical elements, John and the doll, from real space. When these combine, we have |Sue| and |Sue's boss| as the two characters in the blend.

Notice that only part of the real John is mapped onto |Sue|. The part talking and gesturing, which includes the head and one hand, is |Sue|. The part of John holding the doll is not. The real Sue is watching (18) as it is being produced

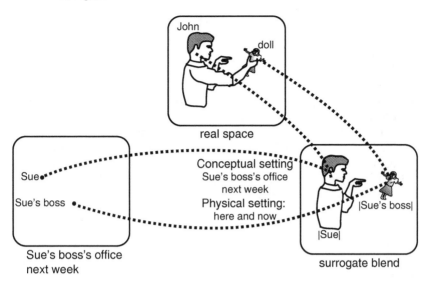

Figure 5.14  Using spoken English with a surrogate blend

and understands that John is providing a demonstration of her counterpart in the blend speaking with and gesturing toward her boss in her boss's office next week. She also understands that she is not supposed to grab her boss around the waist with the other hand. Although the real Sue is physically present in real space, she is not conceptually part of the blend since she does not represent anyone in the imagined office setting. The blended character |Sue| may not talk to the real Sue, point to her, etc. The reason for this would seem to be that in the blended space one blended character is addressing another in another place and time. In the context of that blended mental space, the real Sue plays no role.

When uttering |Sue|'s words to |Sue's boss| John uses the pronoun *you* rather than *she*. We can see, then, that the pronoun *you* is referring to a present entity – the addressee in the blend. If John were using metonymy (mentioning the real boss to refer to |Sue's boss|) he would use the pronoun *she* rather then *you* since *she* would be the appropriate pronoun to refer to either a non-present person or a present non-addressee. For the very same reasons, John's use of the term *your boss* in (18) is also not a case of metonymy. John is also referring directly to |Sue's boss| in the blend.

In English, reference to oneself is normally accomplished with pronouns like *I* and *me*. This is also what occurs in the blend where |Sue| is making reference to herself. *I* appears twice and *me* once to refer to the addresser, |Sue|. Note that *I* and *me* refer to |Sue|, not to the real John or the real Sue. Note also that the conceptual setting of the blend is next week in the office of Sue's boss. Within that context, the word *here* in (18) refers to the conceptual setting of the blend, not the current physical setting in which John and Sue find themselves. The conceptual time frame of the blend is also a date in the future. This can be seen by the description of the length of time |Sue| reports working for the company. That is, completing three years of work will not have been accomplished until the week after (18) is uttered. Thus, even what counts as true and false (what has occurred and what hasn't) is determined by the blend. But inside the blend events happen in that future time's present – the physical here and now provided to the blend by real space. Thus, the tense used in (18) is present, what one would expect in a face-to-face conversation about one person's current desire for a raise. The future date is described as "today" because the following Monday is the current date inside the blend.

The blended space analysis above tells us that John's words (John in real space) are to be understood as |Sue|'s words in the blended space. The same applies to gestures, since John's real-space gestures toward the doll are to be interpreted as |Sue|'s gestures toward |Sue's boss|. Similarly, vocal quality, rate of articulation, facial expression or posture could have been changed or made salient in the blend. Any of these aspects of the production would normally be interpreted as characteristics of |Sue|. Pronouns and other shifters (e.g. *here* and *now*) all have their normal interpretations within the context of the blend. There is no need to assign any shifting properties to any elements of (18).

But shifters are not the only linguistic entities with the dual properties of being symbolic and indexic. The dual properties observed by Jakobson also describe virtually any referential noun phrase. That is, the phrase *Sue's boss* is symbolic in that it describes a boss–employee relationship, with the boss as the entity foregrounded in that relationship. The phrase *Sue's boss* is also indexic. Its referential value also depends on who uses it. If Bill uses the phrase *Sue's boss* it points to the boss in the boss–employee relationship in which the particular Sue he is talking about is the employee. If another speaker is talking about a different Sue, then the phrase points to the boss in that boss–employee relationship.

The phrase *Sue's boss* is both symbolic and indexic and its reference depends on who utters it. Depending on the mental space configurations, the reference of the phrase could "shift" from the current boss to a previous or future boss. Thus, the phrase *Sue's boss* appears to have all the characteristics of a shifter. But if phrases like *Sue's boss* are shifters, then any referential noun phrase could be a shifter.

In the blended spaces examined thus far, the examples of shifters are explained by ordinary usage of lexical items and phrases within the context of the real-space blend. I emphasize here that the conceptual shift evident within the real-space blend is responsible for the way meaning is constructed, rather than the proposed shifting properties of shifters. The speaker creates real-space blends and constructs dialogue and actions appropriate for those blends. This includes referring directly to *conceptually present entities* within the real-space blends using words such as *you, I* and *me*.

### Sequence in the formation of the blend

Notice that the noun phrases *the doll* and *your boss* are not randomly used in John's instructions to Sue. That is, the order in which they are used makes a difference.

(19)     Pick up the doll and tell your boss you want a raise.

(20)     ?? Pick up your boss and tell the doll you want a raise.

The order in (19) is felicitous but the order in (20) is not. Although both sentences are fully grammatical (properly constructed), the content of (20) is inappropriate. This cannot be the result of a syntactic constraint, or even a more general grammatical constraint of some sort. Speakers select words or construct phrases that appropriately describe entities being talked about. In the most natural interpretation of John's request to Sue, he is asking her first to pick up the doll, and then to imagine that the doll is her boss. Conceptually, first there is a doll, then a doll imagined to be Sue's boss. This is why the ordering in (19) is the most felicitous. The first half of the request makes use of real space and the last half makes use of the blend.

There are also two other possibilities that involve using either *your boss* throughout, or *the doll* throughout.

(21)     ? Pick up your boss and tell her (your boss) you want a raise.

This ordering is strange because it asks Sue first to conceive of the doll as her boss in the context of real space where John is present (as in Figure 5.13). It then asks her to pick up |Sue's boss| within that blend, then to switch mental spaces and conceive of the doll as |Sue's boss| in the context of next week in the boss's office. It is not that this order is impossible, just unusual.

(22)     ? Pick up the doll and tell it you want a raise.

The use of *the doll* and *it* in (22) is also strange because it is inconsistent with the previous request to imagine the doll as Sue's boss. The pronoun *it* would be inappropriate to refer to |Sue's boss|.

*Real-space blends and the pronoun* you

The use of the pronoun *you* raises different issues from the use of *I* or *my*. The problem is to be able to point to evidence that the addressee is conceptualized inside the real-space blend. When |Sue| asks |Sue's boss| for a raise in (18), the evidence for the physically present addressee in the form of the blended doll |Sue's boss| is clear. |Sue| is gazing toward and gesturing toward the addressee, |Sue's boss|. Regardless of the real-space blend, if the speaker in the blend is obviously looking toward, pointing at, touching, or otherwise interacting with the addressee, then the speaker has provided evidence other than the word *you* that the addressee is part of the real-space blend. Without such physical clues, we don't know if the speaker has conceptualized the addressee as present in the blend. If the speaker has not conceptualized the addressee in the blend, then why use the pronoun *you*? The answer is that even if the speaker has chosen to represent only the speaker in the blend, part of that activity involves constructing what the speaker says. If the real speaker were talking to an addressee, the speaker would use the pronoun *you*. Therefore, it would be appropriate to use the pronoun *you* in constructing what the speaker in the blend says.

In ASL this issue appears to be simpler to resolve because ASL has several types of signs that can be directed toward the addressee. For example, if PRO$^{\rightarrow x}$ is to refer to the addressee then it will be directed toward the addressee. Thus, the directionality of the sign PRO$^{\rightarrow x}$ tells us where its referent is located in a real-space blend. Specific classes of verbs might also be directed toward the addressee. Similarly, the normal situation would be for the signer also to face the addressee and direct eye gaze toward the addressee. Any one of the activities would provide a basis for placing an addressee inside the real-space blend.

*Gestures without blends*

I have described the use of some gestures that give evidence for real-space blends. It would be wrong to conclude that the use of any gesture provides such evidence. For example, Ekman and Friesen (1969) identify a category of gestures that they call emblems. Such gestures are part of a cultural inventory of symbolic gestures that members of that culture understand. The American 'thumbs up' gesture is an example of an emblem. If an American says (23) while giving the 'thumbs up' gesture, this would not be evidence for a real-space blend.

(23)     I feel good today!

The person speaking English in this example is not imagining anyone else to be present. The speaker is still conceptually himself. Nothing has been blended either in the space around the speaker or within the speaker. The speaker is simply being symbolic in two different ways: symbolic grammatical elements and a symbolic gesture. In addition, the rhythmic gestures that accompany speech, called "beats" in McNeill (1992), do not provide evidence for blended spaces.

### Plays and more

Tannen (1986) reports on extensive work into constructed dialogue in English and Greek. Here is one of her examples, which demonstrates the importance of vocal changes associated with the person whose speech is being constructed.

(24)    He was sending me out to get tools or whatever (imitates father) "Go get this and it looks like this and the other."

This example is part of Tannen's demonstration that the dialogue is constructed rather than recalled. Clearly the real father never said what the |father| in (24) said. Note that in this example the speaker changes vocal quality to imitate the father. I interpret this to mean that the speaker has incorporated some aspects of the father's speech, such as a deep voice or a demanding tone into her own speech. Later, Tannen describes a more elaborate narrative produced by a medical resident as follows: "In telling about the incident, the resident alternatively took on the voices and gestures of himself, other hospital staff, the wounded young man, the other 2 young men, other patients in the emergency room and a policeman who came to investigate" (p. 319). Tannen's description of the importance of voices and gesture applies equally well to the data considered in the blended spaces described above. Further, the blended space analysis applies equally well to Tannen's data. Tannen describes constructed dialogue as an involvement strategy because first, the constructed dialogue has immediacy and the ability to portray action and dialogue as if it were occurring in the telling time and second, the constructed dialogue forces the hearer to participate in the sense making. Both these characteristics can be seen as resulting from the conceptualization of a real-space blend. First, the blend results from combining elements of real space with elements of another space. Real space is immediate, by definition. Thus, the immediacy of the constructed dialogue follows directly from the fact that it involves a blend with real space and another conceptual space. It also appears to portray the action and dialogue as if it were occurring in the telling time because within the blend, *it is occurring in the telling time.* Second, Tannen describes constructed dialogue as drama. That is, it is a performance that others present witness. Clark and Gerrig (1990) provide extensive argumentation supporting the notion that quotations are demonstrations that provide the observer with a direct experience. They observe that many things are easier to demonstrate than to describe (e.g. tying a shoe). In particular, they describe how it is easier to demonstrate – rather than describe – emotion, urgency, indecision, and sarcasm in tone of voice. Similarly, they describe how gestures and facial expression, level of formality, and disfluencies are all easier to demonstrate than describe. The same, of course, applies to foreign accents, slips of the tongue, grammatical errors, etc.

The claim that quotations are demonstrations and that constructed dialogue is drama share the characteristic that others present are witnesses rather than addressees. This follows directly from the blend analysis. The real-space blend sets up a space in which the speaker is physically present but has a blended identity. The immediacy follows directly from the fact that the speaker is physically present. The drama (and demonstration) follows from the fact that, in general, the blend brings with it a new setting (time and place) as well as a new role for the speaker, and potentially other elements present in the new setting (though they may be invisible to the audience).[16]

Staying with Tannen's metaphor of constructed dialogue as a play, acting consists of more than speaking words. The poorest of actors can use the right words without being effective. Even if an actor utters the correct words, the effectiveness of a performance depends on more than words. Vocal characteristics such as pitch, amplitude, voice quality, prosody, pacing, and accent all contribute to the performance.[17] Physical gestures are also important and can include posture, facial expression, gestures of the hands, changes in the direction of the eye gaze, etc. The skill and effectiveness of the performer will be based on the way the words are uttered as well as the gestures used during the performance.

Here I will stretch Tannen's metaphor a bit by comparing some of what we have examined to illustrated narration. That is, one could conceive of the episode where |Garfield| looks up at |Jon| (Figure 5.6) as illustrated narration. The signer narrates and simultaneously illustrates what is being described. The visual illustration takes place within a real-space blend.

For both types of events (illustrated narration or play) there may be continua. The illustrated narration could range from periods of solely visual elements with no narration, to visual elements with narration, to mostly or even entirely narration. Similarly, the play could range from wonderfully acted to a mere recitation of lines. All these cases, with the exception of pure narration, take place within the context of real-space blends. In addition, the person doing the performance could move back and forth between illustrated narration, play, and pure narration in whatever manner serves the needs of the discourse.

---

[16] In fact, the performance of a real play is built on blending (Fauconnier and Turner 1996). The actors are real people in real space, the characters are elements of a separate non-grounded space, and the performance takes place in a grounded, blended space.

[17] Tannen (1986) mentions all these vocal qualities in her discussion of constructed dialogue.

## Conclusions

In the creation of a real-space blend, mental space elements are mapped onto real space. That cognitive act involves conceptualizing things as something other than what they are. Whether created as part of discourse or not, real-space blends create otherwise impossible entities which have physical properties inherited from real-space and conceptual properties inherited from another mental space. When the signer or speaker is projected into the blend, the result is a surrogate blend. Evidence for the existence of surrogate blends in ASL comes from the directionality of pronouns and verbs as well as from a wide variety of gesture types that add interesting and often dramatic or humorous visual information.

While grammatical constructions symbolically describe events, the gestural elements found in surrogate blends constitute demonstrations of events. When the signer is presenting both symbolic language and a surrogate space demonstration simultaneously, the addressee must integrate both types of information in order to understand the intended message fully. This conceptual integration is a complex cognitive operation involving multiple mental spaces.

Surrogate blends are not unique to ASL discourse. They are also frequent in spoken language discourse. While facial gestures and gestures of the hands and body are equally important in surrogate blends created as part of spoken language discourse, so are vocal characteristics such as pitch, loudness, voice quality, aspects of prosody, pacing, and accent.[18] These aspects of surrogate blends also have the potential to add interest, drama, and humor to the discourse.

As an automatic consequence of the existence of surrogate blends, shifters have their ordinary meanings and appropriate reference within the context of the surrogate blend. As a result, there is no need for the category 'shifter' in a grammatical description. Shifters do not shift anything. They have their ordinary meanings within the context of the surrogate blend.

Finally, it should be clear that both signed and vocally produced discourse make extensive use of surrogate blends. In ASL, properly directing pronouns and verbs depends on the existence of such conceptualizations. As a result, real-space blends appear to be more tightly integrated into the grammatical structure. Only a more careful look will reveal the extent to which such conceptualizations are an expected part of spoken language discourse.

---

[18] Any of the items described as "gestural" have the potential to be (parts of) grammatical elements. Control of pitch during the production of a word could easily become a part of the word and some facial gestures could easily become part of signs.

# 6    Directing signs at locations and things

This chapter examines two categories of signs. Signs in the first category are locative signs. These signs have a lexical requirement to be directed toward a location. Signs in the second category are typically produced in non-pointing citation forms. However, it is not difficult to find instances where the signs in this second category are spatially directed. In some cases such signs are directed toward locations and in others they are directed toward things.

The pronouns and verbs examined in previous chapters have the grammatical requirement to point toward entities corresponding to elements in their semantic poles. Given their grammatical requirement to point, the significance of the pointing is lexically fixed. That is, there is no need to wonder how to interpret PRO$^{\rightarrow a}$. The directionality of PRO$^{\rightarrow a}$ identifies $a$ as the pronoun's referent. Similarly, the directionality of TELL$^{\rightarrow a}$ identifies $a$ as the recipient of the information. For the nondirectional signs examined in this chapter, there does not appear to be any such grammatically fixed means of understanding the directionality. This suggests that neither the need to point nor the semantic function of the pointing are part of their grammatical description. To understand the significance of the ways these signs point, signers need to make use of context and the general cognitive ability to make associations.

### Directing locative signs at locations

The sign THERE$^{\rightarrow L}$ is a lexically locative sign used to talk about a location in the signer's environment. That environment could be real space or a blend with real space. In Figure 6.1a THERE$^{\rightarrow L}$ points toward a location in a real-space blend directly ahead of the signer. It has the same handshape as PRO$^{\rightarrow x}$ and a similar short outward trajectory, but the rotation of the forearm is more variable than PRO$^{\rightarrow x}$. In Figure 6.1a, for example, the forearm is rotated so that THERE$^{\rightarrow L}$ has the palm oriented downward. THERE$^{\rightarrow L}$ and PRO$^{\rightarrow x}$ also differ in what they point at. THERE$^{\rightarrow L}$ points at a location and PRO$^{\rightarrow x}$ points toward a thing. If the location is a point on a two-dimensional plane then THERE$^{\rightarrow L}$ can be directed toward that point. If the location is the location of a three-dimensional entity, then by pointing at the location of the three-dimensional

a.     THERE$^{\rightarrow L}$     b.               BEHIND-THERE$^{\rightarrow L}$

Figure 6.1  Signs required to point at locations

entity, THERE$^{\rightarrow L}$ will also point at the entity itself (see chapter 4 for additional discussion of the issue of things and their locations).

THERE$^{\rightarrow L}$ can also be directed toward a past, future, or hypothetical location of a three-dimensional entity. Suppose, for example, a signer is asked where a refrigerator should be placed. In this case, it would be natural to point at the space the refrigerator would occupy if it were present. This would involve conceptualizing the refrigerator in that place and pointing at the refrigerator conceptualized in that place.

In Figure 6.1b the signer is pointing toward a location behind a black plastic tub. Since the location being talked about is nearby, but obstructed from view by an obstacle, the signer uses the locative sign BEHIND-THERE$^{\rightarrow L}$. She moves her hand outward then flexes her wrist so that at the completion of the sign her index finger points through the plastic tub toward a location behind it.

### Directing locative signs along vectors

The signs FAR-THERE$^{\rightarrow}$ and WAY-OVER-THERE$^{\rightarrow}$ point along vectors, but do not point directly at locations. FAR-THERE$^{\rightarrow}$ (Figure 6.2a) is produced with the index finger oriented slightly up from horizontal. The hand makes a sharp, backward movement, opposite to the direction the finger is pointing. In addition, note the nonmanual components of this sign. The signer begins with his head turned to the right and his eyes nearly closed. As the hand moves backward he straightens his head and opens his eyes.

In Figure 6.2a, the signer is describing the distance to a house. Although the house is far away, it is not up in the air. Thus, the finger is not really pointing at the house. However, by translating the slightly elevated vector of the fingertip into a horizontal vector, that vector would lead to the house.

WAY-OVER-THERE$^{\rightarrow}$ (Figure 6.2b) begins with the hand just ahead of the cheek, and with the index finger pointing at an upward angle. The hand moves upward and away from the signer and ends with the index finger nearly horizontal or perhaps pointing slightly down from horizontal. The outward movement is also produced with an oscillating twisting of the forearm and a

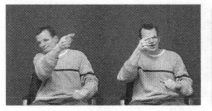

a.          FAR-THERE→          b.          WAY-OVER-THERE→

Figure 6.2  Signs required to point along left-right vectors

nonmanual component consisting of the head configuration shown, narrowed eyes and a repeated lateral tongue flap (Davies 1985). As with FAR-THERE→, the directionality of the sign translates into a horizontal vector leading toward the faraway place even though the finger does not actually point at the place itself.

### Directing non-locative signs at locations

Numerals like ONE, TWO, and THREE are not normally thought of as directional signs. Each has its own lexically fixed place of articulation ahead of the shoulder. There appears to be nothing in the lexical structure of these numerals that requires them to be directed in space. In Figure 6.3, however, the signer is describing where interpreters are to be located on a stage. She first directs TWO outward toward the desired location of two interpreters on the left side of the stage. While keeping the left hand in place, she directs ONE outward toward the right side of the stage. This indicates where a single interpreter is to be located. The same signs could be used to explain that two cars should be located on the left side of the stage and one on the right side. This demonstrates that the signs illustrated in Figure 6.3 are numeral signs rather than depicting verbs (see chapter 9).[1]

If a signer meaningfully directs a sign that does not have a grammatical requirement to be directed, I enclose that sign in square brackets and use a superscript arrow to show that the sign has been directed. For example, in Figure 6.3 the signer directs the nondirectional sign TWO toward a location on the left side of a stage. The gloss [TWO]→left side of stage signifies that the sign in the square brackets has been directed spatially toward the left side of the stage.

---

[1]  The signs in Figure 6.3 are formationally similar to depicting verbs (see chapter 9) produced with small downward (rather than outward) movements followed by holds. If these downward-moving depicting verbs were directed toward the left and right sides of the stage, they would depict two people standing on the left side of the stage and one person standing on the right side. These depicting verbs directed in this way could be used to talk about standing humans, but not sitting humans or nonhuman entities such as cars or dogs.

R:                                    [ONE]→right side of stage
L: [TWO]→left side of stage  --------------------------

Figure 6.3  Directing signs to show the locations of things

[TWO]→left side of stage makes an association between the semantic pole of TWO and the left side of the stage. As part of the discussion of where interpreters should be located, [TWO]→left side of stage identifies the location for two interpreters while [ONE]→right side of stage identifies the location for one interpreter.

There are at least two possible ways of treating signs like [ONE]→L and [TWO]→L. The first is that [ONE]→L and [TWO]→L are lexical signs distinct from ONE and TWO that do, in fact, have the grammatical requirement to be directed toward a location. A second possibility is that [ONE]→L is not a distinct lexical sign, but rather, the signer has chosen to overlay pointing on the production of ONE. This treats [ONE]→L as an instance of the non-locative numeral ONE that the signer chose to direct toward location L.

Producing spoken words while pointing toward locations is not uncommon. In (1), for example, the speaker is describing where two boys and two girls should sit.

(1)     I think they should sit: boy, girl, boy, girl.

As the speaker produces (1) she points to a place as she says *boy*, to the next place as she says *girl*, to the next place as she says *boy*, and to the final place as she says *girl*. This produces a set of associations between the meanings of the words and the locations pointed toward. This is not unlike placing name cards at place settings at a formal dinner for the purpose of showing where guests should sit. Guests find the place with their name and know that they are to sit at that place. The same end could be accomplished less elegantly by taping each person's name on the back of a chair. Guests would still understand that the name on the back of the chair identified the place at the table for each guest to sit. The association is not with the chair, however, but with the location at the table. If the association were merely with the chair, guests would be free to move the chairs to other places, provided that each guest sat in the chair with the appropriate name taped to it.

[SEVEN]⁻ʳⁱᵍʰᵗ ˢⁱᵈᵉ ᵒᶠ |ʲᵉʳˢᵉʸ|    [FIVE]⁻ˡᵉᶠᵗ ˢⁱᵈᵉ ᵒᶠ |ʲᵉʳˢᵉʸ|

Figure 6.4  Directing signs to show the locations of number symbols

There is no need to treat an instance of the English noun *boy* produced while pointing at a chair as a lexical item distinct from *boy* where there is no pointing. Rather, when *boy* is produced while pointing, as in (1), it is up to the addressee to make a conceptual connection between its meaning and the pointing gesture. In the context of discussing where people should sit, it is not difficult to understand that pointing while *boy* is spoken serves to identify a place where a boy should sit.

If the semantic differences between ONE and [ONE]$^{\rightarrow L}$ can similarly be accounted for based on the cognitive ability to associate things and locations, then there is no need to propose the existence of lexical items such as [ONE]$^{\rightarrow L}$ and [TWO]$^{\rightarrow L}$. This is the solution I propose for these signs. If correct, then [ONE]$^{\rightarrow L}$ differs from the English example above involving simultaneous pointing and naming only in the fact that a single hand carries out both functions simultaneously in the ASL example.

Had the issue been where to place one group of eighty-four people and another group of two hundred people, a signer could produce [EIGHTY-FOUR]$^{\rightarrow L}$ toward one location and [TWO-HUNDRED]$^{\rightarrow L}$ toward another. Treating these as instances of pointing overlaid on otherwise nondirectional signs simplifies the grammatical description of ASL since it is not necessary to propose the existence of hundreds of separate directional numerical signs, each paired with a nondirectional counterpart.

Figure 6.4 illustrates another way that numerical signs can be directed. The signer uses her own body to illustrate the placement of the numbers 'seven' and 'five' on a jersey. She produces SEVEN slightly to the right of the midline of her body and FIVE slightly to left of the midline. She directs these two signs in this way to talk about the number '75' on a jersey.

Understanding this example involves conceptualizing the jersey as if the signer herself were wearing it. The hands are directed toward the places on the conceptualized |jersey| where the numbers would appear. The directed numeral sign [SEVEN]$^{\rightarrow \text{right side of } |jersey|}$ associates the semantic pole of SEVEN with the location it is directed toward. Similarly, the directed sign [FIVE]$^{\rightarrow \text{left side of } |jersey|}$ associates the semantic pole of FIVE with the location it is directed toward.

These two numbers placed on the |jersey| in this way would be understood as an instance of the number '75' on the front of the jersey.

There is a semantic difference between talking about the number of interpreters on a stage and the numbers on a jersey. When talking about interpreters the numeral sign corresponds to a quantity. When talking about the numbers on a jersey the numeral sign corresponds to a symbol on the jersey. That is, there are not seven things on the right of the jersey, but rather, the symbol '7' appears at that location. This difference in interpretation can be attributed to the ambiguity of numerals. That is, the numeral TWO can signify either a quantity or a symbol. When confronted with an instance of $[TWO]^{\rightarrow L}$, the addressee has to determine whether the semantic value to associate with the location the sign is directed toward is the symbol '2' or the quantity 'two'. In discussing the placement of interpreters, directing $[TWO]^{\rightarrow L}$ toward the left side of a stage will be easily understood as indicating the placement of two interpreters. In describing what a jersey should look like, directing $[SEVEN]^{\rightarrow L}$ toward the right side of a conceptualized |jersey| would be easily understood as describing the placement of a symbol.

The ability to direct nondirectional signs is not limited to simple numeral signs. A signer could also explain how money was to be laid out on a table by directing $[\{DOLLAR\}\{THREE\}]^{\rightarrow L}$ first toward one location on a table and then toward a second location on the table. This would describe the placement of three dollars at two different locations on the table.

I have illustrated the idea of directing nondirectional signs toward locations by using signs with numerical values. However, the ability to direct signs in this way is not limited to signs with numerical values. In chapter 7, for example, I describe the noun $[COLLEGE]^{\rightarrow L}$, which makes an association between the meaning 'college' and the spatial location it is directed toward. Although $[COLLEGE]^{\rightarrow L}$ is used naturally in creating a blended space, it would never be directed toward a college to identify it as a college.

### Directing numerical signs at entities

In keeping the score of a game we make correspondences between each side in a contest and points on a numerical scale. English has a number of conventional ways of making these correspondences. One involves the use of the possessive ("I *have* three points."). Another involves a simple ordering in which the speaker's position on the scale is mentioned first. Using this convention, the statement "three five" indicates that the value 'three' corresponds to the speaker and that the value 'five' corresponds to the other player. Still another convention involves a potentially unordered naming of values on the scale followed by a phrase mentioning the side with the higher value ("The score was seventeen sixteen in John's favor.").

[FIVE]$^{\rightarrow\text{addressee}}$        [TWO]$^{\rightarrow\text{self}}$

Figure 6.5 (The score is) five to two

In ASL discourse involving scores, the participants are faced with exactly the same task of making associations between players and scores. Figure 6.5 illustrates the use of [FIVE]$^{\rightarrow\text{addressee}}$ and [TWO]$^{\rightarrow\text{self}}$ to indicate a score. The signs in Figure 6.5 would indicate that the addressee has five points and the signer has two. The placement of the hand producing the numeral sign associates the numerical value of the sign with the individual that the hand points toward.

Signs with incorporated numeral handshapes, such as {DOLLAR}{TWO}, can also be directed toward entities. For example, if a signer was standing in front of a group of people, and the conversation was the amount of money each individual owed the signer, the amounts could be indicated by directing the signs indicating the appropriate number of dollars toward each individual. [{DOLLAR}{TWO}]$^{\rightarrow\text{person a}}$ would indicate that that person $a$ owed two dollars. [{DOLLAR}{SIX}]$^{\rightarrow\text{person b}}$ would indicate that that person $b$ owed six dollars, etc. If the topic of conversation was the amount of money each individual had won, then directing the same signs toward the same individuals would indicate how much money each had won.

In the example below, the signer is describing how the student population at the residential school he previously attended had dropped over the years. Through blending he had already located the 1986 graduating class directly ahead of his chest and a previous graduating class slightly ahead of his forehead. In Figure 6.6a the signer is producing the sign SMALL$^{\rightarrow\text{|class of '86|}}$. Directing SMALL$^{\rightarrow\text{x}}$ toward the |class of '86| associates the meaning 'small' with that graduating class. He has not yet identified the year associated with the larger previous graduating class.

Later he identifies the previous graduating class with the sign [EIGHTY-ONE]$^{\rightarrow\text{|previous graduating class|}}$. As shown in Figure 6.6b, he does this by directing EIGHTY-ONE upward toward the |previous graduating class| and also directing his face and eye gaze upward toward that spatial entity. This identifies the previous graduating class as the class of '81. This, however, is not the only possible interpretation of the directed numeral. It could also be interpreted to

Table 6.1 *Types of associations resulting from directing numeral signs at people or things*

| Numeral sign | Directed toward | Conceptual result |
|---|---|---|
| TWO | person | associates person with score |
| TWO | \|first wife\| (spatial entity) | associates two Deaf children with the first wife |
| {DOLLAR}{TWO} | person | associates $2 with the person (amount person will pay, receive, owe, etc.) |
| EIGHTY-ONE | \|graduating class\| (spatial entity) | identifies the class of '81 |
| FORTY-FIVE | \|oldest brother\| (signer's thumb) | identifies the oldest brother's age as forty-five years old |
| TWENTY | \|first half\| | associates twenty minutes with the first half of a basketball game |

a.   SMALL<sup>→|class of '86|</sup>          b. Identifying the class of '81

Figure 6.6  The signer directs signs toward two tokens he has created

mean that at an earlier time there were eighty-one members of his own class of students.[2] Although the signer was identifying the class of '81, the fact that the example can be interpreted in a different way lends support to the idea that when typically nondirectional signs are directed in space, the significance of the directionality is not fixed by the grammar.

Examples to be discussed in later chapters also include associating people with their ages, mothers with the numbers of Deaf children they have, and numbers of minutes with each half of a basketball game. A sampling of various types of associations between numeral signs and the things they are directed toward is listed in Table 6.1.

Directing [TWO]<sup>→x</sup> toward a person can show a person's score when playing a game. In the context of a game, understanding that [TWO]<sup>→x</sup> was being used to associate a score with a player would be straightforward. In another context

---

[2]  MJ Bienvenu, personal communication.

the interpretation could be different. In describing how many children each person present had, directing [TWO]$^{\rightarrow x}$ toward a person would associate two children with that person. Chapter 7 includes an example in which [TWO]$^{\rightarrow x}$ is directed toward a spatial entity (representing a person's first wife) to associate two Deaf children with that wife. Directing [{DOLLAR}{TWO}]$^{\rightarrow x}$ toward a present person associates two dollars with that person. The money could represent the amount of money the person will pay, the amount of money the person has won, the amount of money the person owes, etc. Directing [EIGHTY-ONE]$^{\rightarrow x}$ toward a spatial entity identifies it as the class of '81, but could also be understood as showing how many members there were in the graduating class. Chapter 8 also contains examples of numeral signs directed toward spatial entities. For example, producing [FORTY-FIVE]$^{\rightarrow x}$ in contact with the signer's thumb, used to represent the signer's oldest brother, identifies the age of the oldest brother as forty-five. In another example, the index finger and middle fingers held together represent the first half of a basketball game. Producing [TWENTY]$^{\rightarrow x}$ in contact with those two extended fingers associates a duration of twenty minutes with the first half of a basketball game.

These examples demonstrate the variety of relationships that can exist between the entity the numeral sign is directed toward and its semantic pole. In each case there is an association to be made between the meaning of the directed sign and the entity it is directed toward. The nature of that association, however, is dependent on the conceptual context in which the sign is produced. For this reason I am treating these signs as combinations of pointing and lexically encoded information that result in an association between the meaning encoded by the sign and the entity the sign is directed toward. The addressee determines the significance of the relationship based on the meanings of the signs and the context in which they are used.

### Directing signs to express spatial metaphors

The idea that thoughts and ideas are objects with physical substance located within the head is a common metaphor among English speakers (Lakoff and Johnson 1980). There is evidence for the same metaphor among ASL signers (Taub 2001, Wilcox 2000). This metaphor motivates ASL signs such as IDEAS-ZOOM-BY-HEAD (Figure 6.7a) and IDEA-DEFLECT-OFF-FORE-HEAD-1$^{[\text{HABITUAL}]}$ (Figure 6.7b).

In producing the single movement of IDEAS-ZOOM-BY-HEAD, the two hands change from closed 1 handshapes (index fingers restrained by the thumbs) to 1 handshapes as the hands move past the sides of the head. The index fingers metaphorically depict the paths of the rapidly moving ideas, which pass by the head without entering. Initially, the lips are pressed together with the lower lip slightly rolled inward. As the hands move, the mouth opens to the configuration

a.    IDEAS-ZOOM-BY-HEAD

b.              IDEA-DEFLECT-OFF-FOREHEAD-1[HABITUAL]

Figure 6.7 Lexical signs involving the metaphor 'head as a container of ideas'

shown and the head is thrust forward. These nonmanual components combine to give the impression that the ideas passed by at a rapid rate. A typical use for this sign would be to describe a lecture that was too difficult to comprehend.

In Figure 6.7b the signer has created a narrative in which a friend has been preaching to her that she should start an exercise program. She uses the aspectual form IDEA-DEFLECT-OFF-FOREHEAD-1[HABITUAL] to explain that her friend's preaching has had no effect.[3] It is produced with the repeated movement shown in Figure 6.7b. Metaphorically, the index finger represents the path of the friend's ideas and the palm represents the forehead. Given these mappings, it is apparent that the ideas move toward the forehead but continually deflect off its surface without entering the head. In the context of this metaphor, only ideas that enter the head can have an effect.

Figure 6.8 also depends on the metaphor that the head is a container for ideas. The lecturer is describing characteristics of culture, including the fact that how people think is part of their culture. She is explaining that a person's values, beliefs, and mental processes are located in the brain. She expresses where values, beliefs, and mental processes are located using the five signs in Figure 6.8.

She initially taps the top of her head with her index finger to identify it as the thing she is talking about. The signs VALUE and PROCESS are both normally produced directly ahead of the torso. BELIEF normally begins with the active

---

[3] I am tentatively describing this as habitual aspect because it is clearly composed of repeated individual brushing movements rather than a single oscillating movement.

tap top of head     [VALUE]$^{\rightarrow \text{in head}}$     [BELIEF]$^{\rightarrow \text{in head}}$     [PROCESS]$^{\rightarrow \text{in head}}$ tap top of head+

Figure 6.8  Locating values, beliefs, and processes inside the head

hand in contact with the forehead and the weak hand directly ahead of the torso. The active hand then moves from the forehead to the weak hand. In Figure 6.8, however, she locates values, beliefs, and mental processes in the head by producing [VALUE]$^{\rightarrow \text{in head}}$, [BELIEF]$^{\rightarrow \text{in head}}$, and [PROCESS]$^{\rightarrow \text{in head}}$.[4] She completes this idea by using both index fingers to make repeated pointing taps on the top of her head. Tapping the top of her head at both the beginning and the end of this sequence appears to emphasize that she is talking about the head as a container for concepts and mental processes.

She is not suggesting that her own head is the unique source of values, beliefs, and processes. Rather, she is explaining that all members of a culture carry their cultural knowledge inside their heads. For the purpose of these few signs, through blending, her head has become the head of a surrogate member of a culture. Given the existence of the blend, the signs in Figure 6.8 place values, beliefs, and mental processes inside the head of a member of a culture.

### The front and back of the mind

ASL makes a metaphorical distinction between the significance of ideas at the front and back of the head. Ideas at the front occupy one's attention and are capable of being acted upon. Those at the back may be important, but they do not occupy one's immediate attention and are not acted upon. This metaphor motivates signs such as PUT$^{\rightarrow \text{back of mind}}$, which makes contact with the back of the head behind the ear. This sign signifies, in accordance with the metaphor just described, that the information will be kept in the back of the mind for later use. When it is time to use that information, the sign MOVE$^{\text{back of mind} \rightarrow \text{front of mind}}$ signifies bringing the information to the front of the mind for immediate attention and use. This metaphor differs from a similar metaphor reflected by the English example, "I kept it in the back of my mind," primarily by making an overt front–back distinction. It explicitly treats the front of the mind as

---

[4] The signs VALUE$_N$, BELIEF, and PROCESS$_N$ are highly similar in form, possibly even the same in form, as the signs IMPORTANT, BELIEVE, and PROCESS$_V$. I am tentatively treating VALUE$_N$, BELIEF, and PROCESS$_N$ as distinct nouns.

GIRL             "WELL            FINE"

TRUE        BACK-OF-MIND                "NO++"

Figure 6.9 The girl said, "Well, fine," but really wanted to say, "no."

the location that occupies immediate attention and upon which a person takes action.

In Figure 6.9 the signer describes a situation in which a boy asked his girl-friend for permission to dance with another girl. Although she wanted to say "no," she gave him permission. The signs used to describe her response and her thoughts are shown in Figure 6.9.

The signer first describes the girl's response to the boy with the signs GIRL, "WELL, FINE." The sign GIRL identifies the girl as the person who will blend with the signer to produce a surrogate. What follows is the |girl|'s response to the |boy|. Thus, the signer establishes a surrogate blend in which she becomes the |girl| answering the |boy|, clearly located to her right. Note that the |girl| is looking up at the |boy|. This could be because the signer has conceptualized the |boy| as standing and the |girl| as sitting, or perhaps she has conceptualized the |boy| as very tall. The |girl| gives her answer to the |boy| with a polite smile.

In fact, the girl really wanted to say "no." The signer explains this with the final three signs in Figure 6.9: TRUE BACK-OF-MIND, "NO++." The signer appears to place the desire to turn down the boy's request in the back of her mind because this is the area for thoughts not acted upon.

*Combining metaphors*

Signs expressing alphabetic characters can also be directed toward locations. In Figure 6.10 the signer describes a sweater with the name 'Sam' written across

$[S]^{\rightarrow \text{right side of }|\text{sweater}|}$     $[A]^{\rightarrow \text{center of }|\text{sweater}|}$     $[M]^{\rightarrow \text{left side of }|\text{sweater}|}$

Figure 6.10  Describing a sweater with the name 'Sam' across the front

$[B]^{\rightarrow \text{right side }|\text{girl's forehead}|}$     $[O]^{\rightarrow \text{right center }|\text{girl's forehead}|}$     $[Y]^{\rightarrow \text{center }|\text{girl's forehead}|}$     $[S]^{\rightarrow \text{left center }|\text{girl's forehead}|}$

Figure 6.11  The concept 'boys' occupying the front of the girl's mind

the front. She expresses this by conceptualizing the sweater being worn and pro-ducing the signs $[S]^{\rightarrow \text{right side of }|\text{sweater}|}$ $[A]^{\rightarrow \text{center of }|\text{sweater}|}$ $[M]^{\rightarrow \text{left side of }|\text{sweater}|}$.

This is like the previous example where the signer describes the placement of the symbols '7' and '5' on the front of a jersey. The placement of the three symbols described in Figure 6.10 would spell the name 'Sam' across the front of the sweater.

Placing signs for alphabetic characters also appears in familiar, humorous examples where words are spelled across the forehead. For example, one could describe a person who is always thinking about food by spelling F-O-O-D across the forehead. Similarly, a girl constantly thinking about boys could be described by spelling B-O-Y-S across the forehead, as in (2).

(2)     $\overline{\phantom{DET GIRL TEND}}^{\,t}$
DET GIRL TEND THINK$^{[\text{INCESSANT}]}$ $[B]^{\rightarrow \text{right side }|\text{girl's forehead}|}$
$[O]^{\rightarrow \text{right center }|\text{girl's forehead}|}$ $[Y]^{\rightarrow \text{center }|\text{girl's forehead}|}$
$[S]^{\rightarrow \text{left center }|\text{girl's forehead}|}$

That girl, she is constantly thinking about boys.

The placement of the final four signs in (2) is illustrated in Figure 6.11. They are spaced across the entire front of the |girl's forehead|, and thus locate the concept 'boys' there.

This example takes advantage of not only the spatial metaphor in which the head is a container for ideas, but also the front–back metaphor. The signer is expressing that the concept 'boys' occupies the entire front of the girl's mind. Since this is the location of ideas occupying someone's immediate attention and capable of being acted upon, thinking about boys guides her everyday behavior.

## Summary

Some signs are directed at locations because the requirement to do so is part of their lexical structure. Some otherwise nondirectional signs can be directed at locations for the purpose of making an ad hoc association between the meaning expressed by the sign and the location the sign is directed toward. Numeral signs in general appear to have this ability. When a grammatically nondirectional sign is directed toward a location or thing, the addressee cannot rely on lexical facts about pointing in order to understand the nature of the association between the lexical meaning and the location or thing the sign is directed toward. Instead, the addressee must rely on context and the cognitive ability to make reasonable associations between the meaning expressed by the sign and the location the sign is directed toward.

# 7    Tokens

Signers frequently create blends such that the entire blend exists ahead of the signer and the signer is not a part of the blended space. Tokens are elements of such blended spaces ahead of the signer. Token blends contrast with surrogate blends in two significant ways. Unlike surrogate blends, where the signer is at least partially projected into the blend, the signer does not become part of a token blend. Also in contrast with surrogates, which are virtually unrestricted in where they can be located, tokens are restricted to the space ahead of the signer. Token blends also contrast with depicting blends (see chapter 9) in that token blends are non-topographical. A token merely exists as an isolated entity within a token space, where concepts like near, far, above, and below are not relevant.

### A simple example

The signing in Figure 7.1 takes place as part of a discussion about the way basketball games are divided into time periods (i.e. quarters and halves) and the length of each period. The signer is asking whether college and professional basketball games are played for the same number of minutes.

He begins in Figure 7.1 with the topic $\overline{\text{BASKETBALL}}^{\text{t}}$. The next five signs produce the question asking whether college and professional basketball are the same (in the number of minutes played). The question is marked as a yes–no question by the raised eyebrows and the head position. The extent of the nonmanual signal is indicated by the symbol $q$ over the signs making up the question.

(1)    $\overline{[\text{COLLEGE}]^{\rightarrow \text{ahead of left shoulder}} \, [\#\text{PRO}]^{\rightarrow \text{ahead of right shoulder}}}$,
$\overline{\text{PRO}^{\rightarrow |\text{professional basketball}|} \text{PRO}^{\rightarrow |\text{college basketball}|}}$
$\overline{\text{SAME-DUAL}^{|\text{college basketball}| \leftrightarrow |\text{professional basketball}|}}^{q}$

Are college and professional (basketball) the same (in the number of minutes played)?

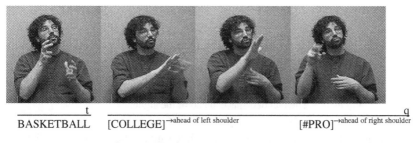

_____t_____   _____q
BASKETBALL   [COLLEGE]<sup>→ahead of left shoulder</sup>                    [#PRO]<sup>→ahead of right shoulder</sup>

_____q
PRO<sup>→|professional basketball|</sup>  PRO<sup>→|college basketball|</sup>  SAME-DUAL<sup>|college basketball|↔|professional basketball|</sup>

Figure 7.1  Are college and professional (basketball) the same?

The signer begins his question by directing the nondirectional noun COLLEGE ahead of his left shoulder: [COLLEGE]<sup>→ahead of left shoulder</sup>. The signer has chosen to direct COLLEGE toward the space ahead of his left shoulder in order to indicate the presence of a token. For the addressee, creating the token involves making an association between the meaning of the sign and the space the sign is directed toward. In this case, it involves making an association between the concept 'college' and the location ahead of his left shoulder.[1] The nature of the resulting token depends on more than the meaning associated with COLLEGE. This sequence begins with the topic BASKETBALL. In that context, [COLLEGE]<sup>→ahead of left shoulder</sup> prompts the creation of the blended entity |college basketball| ahead of the signer's left shoulder. This blended entity is a token.

Prior to signing [COLLEGE]<sup>→ahead of left shoulder</sup>, the signer must have already conceptualized the existence of the token in that place. By directing COLLEGE in this way, he is making aspects of his own conceptualization of space known to the addressee. It is still up to the addressee to create the appropriate token |college basketball|, rather than |college basketball courts| or |basketballs used in college basketball|. This is not unlike a sighted person describing the location of a glass of juice to a blind person. The sighted person has a real-space conceptualization of the location of the glass of juice unknown to the blind person.

---

[1]  See chapter 6 for a full discussion of how some nondirectional signs can be directed in space.

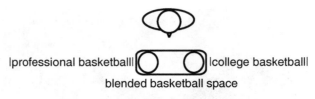

blended basketball space

Figure 7.2  The blended space ahead of the signer

Describing the location of the glass of juice gives the blind person knowledge of its existence at a specific place. Signing [COLLEGE]$^{\rightarrow\,\text{ahead of left shoulder}}$ is similar in that the signer has a spatial conceptualization unknown to the addressee. By directing COLLEGE toward the area of space ahead of the left shoulder, the signer communicates to the addressee that there is a token there and that the token is related to the concept 'college'. Similarly, signing [#PRO]$^{\rightarrow\,\text{ahead of right shoulder}}$ prompts the addressee to create a token blending the concept 'professional basketball' with the space ahead of the signer's right shoulder.

The real-space blend containing the two tokens is illustrated in Figure 7.2. The two tokens are three-dimensional areas of space that have taken on a new significance through blending and bear no physical resemblance to the entities they are blended with. As a result of blending, the space ahead of the signer is conceptualized as containing the two tokens |college basketball| and |professional basketball|. The two tokens in this example are quite abstract. The signer is using |college basketball| as a generic instance of the concept 'college basketball'. By directing signs toward it the signer refers to the concept 'college basketball'. The signer is not talking about any specific instance of college or professional basketball. He is talking about generalities across these two sports. Through blending with real space, he has given these two abstract concepts an immediate here-and-now presence.

In response to seeing [COLLEGE]$^{\rightarrow\,\text{ahead of left shoulder}}$ and [#PRO]$^{\rightarrow\,\text{ahead of right shoulder}}$, the addressee will construct the two tokens |college basketball| and |professional basketball| at the locations indicated by the directionality of the two signs. Now, if the signer directs signs toward those tokens, the significance of that directionality will be apparent to the addressee. This is exactly what happens next. The signer directs the singular non-first person pronoun PRO$^{\rightarrow x}$ first toward one token then the other. By signing PRO$^{\rightarrow\,|\text{professional basketball}|}$ then PRO$^{\rightarrow\,|\text{college basketball}|}$ the signer identifies the referents of the two pronouns as |college basketball| and |professional basketball|. The question ends with the verb SAME-DUAL$^{|\text{college basketball}|\leftrightarrow|\text{professional basketball}|}$. In producing this verb the hand oscillates back and forth between |college basketball| and |professional basketball|.

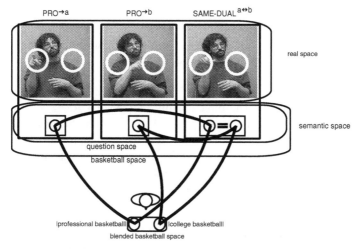

Figure 7.3  Mappings between semantic space and the blended space

The semantic poles of the final three signs of the question map onto the token space as shown in Figure 7.3. Marking BASKETBALL as a topic (Figure 7.1) sets up a basketball space. The question that follows is embedded within that basketball space, as shown in Figure 7.3. Since the written description of the two tokens in this example is lengthy, I use $a$ in place of |professional basketball| and $b$ in place of |college basketball|. The directionality of PRO$^{\rightarrow a}$ is an explicit instruction to map its semantic pole onto |professional basketball|. This mapping is shown in Figure 7.3 by the association line between the semantic pole of PRO$^{\rightarrow a}$ and the token |professional basketball|. Similarly, the directionality of PRO$^{\rightarrow b}$ motivates the mapping between its semantic pole and the token |college basketball|. The verb SAME-DUAL$^{a \leftrightarrow b}$ makes an oscillating movement back and forth between |professional basketball| and |college basketball|. Its directionality motivates the mapping between the two elements of its semantic pole and the two tokens in the blend. With the exception of the initial topic BASKETBALL, every sign in Figure 7.1 is meaningfully directed or placed in space.

Since PRO$^{\rightarrow a}$ and PRO$^{\rightarrow b}$ combine to compose the dual subject of the verb, there is also a syntactically motivated mapping, connecting the semantic representation of each of the pronouns to the two entities in the semantic pole of SAME-DUAL$^{a \leftrightarrow b}$. The constructed meaning represented in Figure 7.3 involves the semantic pole of his utterance and the spaces it is embedded within, real space, the token space ahead of him, and the multiple connections between those spaces.

### Multiple tokens within a blended space

The next example demonstrates how several entities can be simultaneously blended in the space ahead of the signer. The signer is describing a movie club with several categories of movies with the phrase DIFFERENT$^{\text{[MULTIPLE]}}$ ɔ|movie categories| CATEGORY$^{\text{[MULTIPLE]}}$ɔL1–L5 'several different categories'. The directionality of CATEGORY$^{\text{[MULTIPLE]}}$ɔL1–L5 in Figure 7.4 serves to locate the physical extent of the blended set of movie categories. As the hands move from right to left, he produces an oscillating forearm rotation. This is an oscillating movement corresponding to the single forearm rotation that is part of producing the sign CATEGORY$^{\rightarrow \text{L}}$. The oscillating rotation of the forearms as the hand moves from *L1* to *L5* distinguishes CATEGORY$^{\text{[MULTIPLE]}}$ɔL1–L5 from several individual instances of CATEGORY$^{\rightarrow \text{L}}$.

Having established the spatially expansive token |movie categories| extending from ahead of his right shoulder to ahead of his left shoulder, the signer describes individual categories within it. He associates the first category 'old movies' with the space ahead of him on the far right using the first four signs in Figure 7.5. The first sign CATEGORY$^{\rightarrow \text{L1}}$ associates a movie category with the far right of the movie category space. SPECIALIZED$^{\rightarrow}$ |movie category| at L1 indicates that this is a specialized category. The final two nondirectional signs, OLD MOVIE, explain the nature of the specialized category.

Next he signs CATEGORY$^{\rightarrow \text{L2}}$ SPECIALIZED$^{\rightarrow}$ |movie category| at L2 FOREIGN PRO$^{\rightarrow}$ |foreign movies|, where *L2* is just to the right of center. The glosses represent the order in which information is available to the addressee. That is, CATEGORY$^{\rightarrow \text{L2}}$ associates a category with a location *L2*, but without yet providing any details about the category. SPECIALIZED$^{\rightarrow}$ |movie category| at L2 indicates that this is a specialized category. FOREIGN identifies the specialized category as 'foreign movies' and the final pronoun PRO$^{\rightarrow}$ |foreign movies| is

CATEGORY$^{\text{[multiple]}}$ɔL1–L5

Figure 7.4 There are several different categories (of movies) here

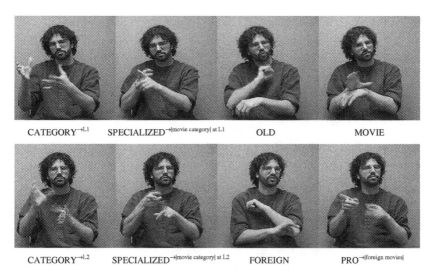

CATEGORY$^{\rightarrow L1}$     SPECIALIZED$^{\rightarrow |movie\ category|\ at\ L1}$          OLD                    MOVIE

CATEGORY$^{\rightarrow L2}$     SPECIALIZED$^{\rightarrow |movie\ category|\ at\ L2}$     FOREIGN          PRO$^{\rightarrow |foreign\ movies|}$

Figure 7.5  They have old movies, foreign movies, . . .

also directed toward that specialized category, now understood to be 'foreign movies'.[2]

Directing CATEGORY$^{\rightarrow L}$ toward two different locations within the blended movie category space locates two distinct movie categories. Using additional instances of CATEGORY$^{\rightarrow L}$ directed toward different parts of the movie category space, he locates art movies slightly to the left of center, commercials further to the left, and animation to the far left.

Producing such a blended space need not be done as a mere recitation of the categories. In fact, the signer makes comments about some of the categories as he introduces them. He describes art movies as strange, and in introducing commercials, he takes some time to describe part of a commercial introduced at a Super Bowl football game. When he has finished locating and introducing each category, he has provided the addressee with sufficient information to produce the blend in Figure 7.6. This blend involves six tokens. The largest is |movie categories|. Contained within this token are the five tokens, |old movies|, |foreign movies|, |art movies|, |commercials|, and |animation|.

He continues with the clause PRO-1 LOOK-OVER$^{\circ|movie\ categories|}$. The beginning and ending configurations of the hand in producing LOOK-OVER$^{\circ|movie\ categories|}$ are illustrated in Figure 7.7. I am treating the verb as

[2] Ending a clause with a pronoun referring back to the entity associated with the trajector of the main verb in the clause (i.e. in this case, SPECIALIZED$^{\rightarrow a}$) is generally used for emphasis (see chapter 2).

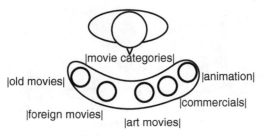

Figure 7.6  The |movie categories| space containing five categories of movies

LOOK-OVER<sup>ɔ|movie categories|</sup>

Figure 7.7  Directing LOOK-OVER<sup>ɔʸ</sup> toward |movie categories|

directed toward |movie categories| – the space as a whole. Treating it as directed at individual categories within that space would appear to force the conclusion that it begins directed at |animation|, then toward |commercials|, |art movies|, and finally |foreign movies|. The movement of the hand does not extend far enough to the right to have been directed toward |old movies|. The fact that the movement is fluid and smooth along with the fact that his eye gaze is not carefully directed at individual categories supports the conclusion that the sign is directed toward the entire set of categories.

He next produces the summary statement shown in Figure 7.8. It begins with the statement LIKE #ALL<sup>ɔ|movie categories|</sup>, where #ALL<sup>ɔ|movie categories|</sup> moves from the right side of the blended category space to the left side just past the midline of the body, without going near either end of the blended category space. This is sufficient to indicate that #ALL<sup>ɔ|movie categories|</sup> is directed toward the category space as a whole. THIS-SET<sup>ɔ|movie categories|</sup> is also directed toward the category space as a whole. It is produced by slightly wiggling the fingers as the hand moves right, up, left, and down in a small, nearly vertical, circular motion.

He concludes that with respect to captioning, foreign movies are best. He does this by first producing the topic CAPTION, narrowing the scope of discourse down to captioned movies.[3] Following the topic CAPTION, the rhetorical

---

[3] In addition to the head back, brows up topic marking identified in Liddell (1977, 1980), Aarons (1994) describes two additional combinations of head configuration and head movement that

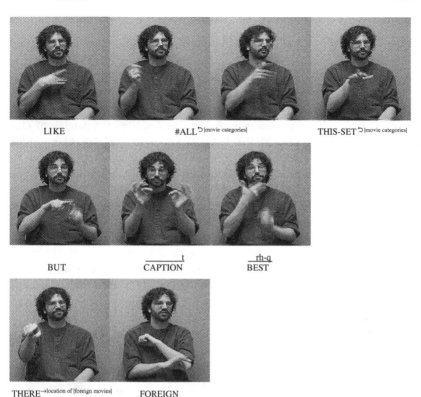

LIKE                    #ALL ᶜ|movie categories|              THIS-SET ᶜ|movie categories|

                                  ___t             _rh-q_

BUT                    CAPTION                BEST

THERE→location of |foreign movies|    FOREIGN

Figure 7.8 I like all of them, but as far as captioning is concerned, the best movies are the foreign ones

question BEST asks which category is best with respect to captioning. Rhetorical questions are marked with a brow raise and frequently a tilting of the head symbolized by *rh-q* (Baker and Cokely 1980). He identifies the best category with respect to captioning with the locative sign THERE→location of |foreign movies|. He adds the sign FOREIGN, apparently as a means of assisting his addressee in case he didn't recall the entity blended at that location.

In this example the signer makes use of an extensive blended space into which specific elements are added. Both the enclosing space and the elements within it can be treated as tokens. Some signs can be directed toward the token space as a whole (e.g. DIFFERENT[MULTIPLE]ᶜ|movie categories|, LOOK-OVERᶜ|movie categories|, #ALLᶜ|movie categories|), toward locations within the space

accompany raised brows and mark topics. The topic marking shown in this example has the brows raised and head forward at the beginning of the sign, making it different from all three previously described topic-marking nonmanual signals.

(CATEGORY$^{\rightarrow L1}$, THERE$^{\rightarrow \text{location of|foreign movies|}}$), or toward individual tokens within the space (e.g. SPECIALIZED$^{\rightarrow \text{|movie category| at L1}}$).

### Changes to tokens

In the following example the signer describes the number of Deaf and hearing students in his class as a graduate student. He describes the number of Deaf students by signing {PRO-MULT-1}{FIVE}$^{\supset x}$ 'five of us' near his chest and very slightly to the right of center, as illustrated in Figure 7.9. This pronoun refers to a group of five people including the signer. When the other four members of a group of five are physically present, {PRO-MULT-1}{FIVE}$^{\supset x}$ is produced near the chest, but its outward arc points toward those other members of the group. Those four and the signer make a total of five. In Figure 7.9 the other members of the group are not present. Rather than directing {PRO-MULT-1}{FIVE}$^{\supset x}$ toward an area of space associated with the other four Deaf students, the signer appears to have created a blend in which all five students (including the signer) form a conceptual group immediately ahead of his chest. The sign {PRO-MULT-1}{FIVE}$^{\supset x}$ appears to be produced right at that location. Evidence for this comes during a repetition of this sign (final photo in Figure 7.9) where the signer directs his gaze at the hand producing

{PRO-MULT-1}{FIVE}$^{\supset\text{|Deaf students|}}$ (fragment)------------------------------------------------------------

PRO$^{\rightarrow b}$                    HEARING            [SEVEN]$^{\rightarrow\text{|hearing students|}}$

[SEVEN]$^{\rightarrow\text{|hearing students|}}$ (fragment)

{PRO-MULT-1}{FIVE}$^{\supset\text{|Deaf students|}}$

Figure 7.9  There were five of us (Deaf students) and seven hearing students

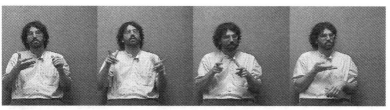

TIME-GO-FORWARD          BECOME-FEWER-SUDDENLY<sup>→|Deaf students|</sup>          {PRO-MULT-1}{FOUR}<sup>ↄ|Deaf students|</sup>

BECOME-FEWER-SUDDENLY<sup>→|Deaf students|</sup>     {PRO-MULT-1}{THREE}<sup>ↄ|Deaf students|</sup>

Figure 7.10  As time went on, the five of us dropped to four, and then three

the sign. The eye gaze provides evidence that the right hand is *at* a significant location (i.e. the location of |Deaf students|).

After initially signing {PRO-MULT-1}{FIVE}<sup>ↄ|Deaf students|</sup> with his right hand, he holds his right hand in place as he directs PRO<sup>→b</sup> toward the unnamed entity *b* in the space to his left. The sign HEARING, identifies entity *b* as |hearing students|. [SEVEN]<sup>→|hearing students|</sup> associates the semantic pole of SEVEN with |hearing students|. In the final frame of Figure 7.9 he repeats {PRO-MULT-1}{FIVE}<sup>ↄ|Deaf students|</sup> while maintaining a fragment of [SEVEN]<sup>→|hearing students|</sup>.[4]

In this stretch of signing, |Deaf students| and |hearing students| are physically separated. The token |Deaf students| is located directly ahead of the signer's chest while |hearing students| is higher and to the left. In addition to the distinct placements of the two tokens, he makes another articulatory distinction between the two groups by describing the Deaf students with the right hand and describing the hearing students with his left.[5]

Having established the two tokens representing the two sets of students, the signer describes how the number of Deaf students in his class decreased. He begins in Figure 7.10 with the sign TIME-GO-FORWARD, produced by

---

[4] Sign fragments are discussed in chapter 8.
[5] Winston (1993) describes examples where either a known or secondary entity is located on the weak hand side while the unknown or primary entity is located on the dominant side. In this signer's description of the change in the number of Deaf students, the discussion focuses on the Deaf students and how their numbers decreased over time. This is compatible with the primary–secondary distinction observed by Winston.

[MY                          CLASS]$^{\rightarrow L}$                    NINETEEN-EIGHTY-SIX
(two horizontal circular movements)

Figure 7.11  My class was the class of 1986 – here

wiggling the fingers of a 5 hand as the hand slowly moves forward. The forward movement of the hand in this lexical sign metaphorically maps time onto space.[6]

In producing the verb BECOME-FEWER-SUDDENLY$^{\rightarrow |Deaf\ students|}$ in the second and third frames of Figure 7.10, the hands begin about shoulder width apart and slightly above |Deaf students|. The signer's head begins tilted back. As the hands move closer together and slightly downward his head also moves downward. The head movement is an integral part of the sign. The directionality of BECOME-FEWER-SUDDENLY$^{\rightarrow |Deaf\ students|}$ changes the nature of the blend by decreasing the number of students within it. The next sign {PRO-MULT-1}{FOUR}$^{\supset |Deaf\ students|}$ specifies the result of becoming fewer in number. One student has left the program. As a result, the token |Deaf students| now has the significance 'four Deaf students'. He then signs BECOME-FEWER-SUDDENLY$^{\rightarrow |Deaf\ students|}$ again, which once more changes the nature of the token by signifying another reduction in the number associated with that token.

{PRO-MULT-1}{THREE}$^{\supset |Deaf\ students|}$ identifies the total number of Deaf students remaining as three. This example illustrates that the nature of a token can change over time. In this brief example, the number of students associated with |Deaf students| decreased from five to four, then from four to three. The location of the token did not change – only its significance changed.

The next example also involves a reduction in number, but this time the reduction takes place over several years. He begins in Figure 7.11 where the signs [MY CLASS]$^{\rightarrow L}$ NINETEEN-EIGHTY-SIX explain that he was a member of the class of 1986. For the sake of economy, the sign NINETEEN-EIGHTY-SIX is represented in Figure 7.11 as a single image, with the hand in the final 6 handshape.

---

[6] In this sign the passage of time is metaphorically mapped onto forward spatial movement. The directionality of the hand is not free. That is, there is no equivalent sign with the fingers wiggling and the hand moving backward toward the signer that signifies moving backward in time. See Taub (2001) and Wilcox (2000) for revealing discussions of not only time metaphors, but a wide range of other metaphorical uses of signs in ASL.

REALLY                            $\overline{\qquad\text{tg}\qquad}$
                                  BECOME-FEWER-OVER-TIME$^{a\rightarrow|\text{class of '86}|}$

SMALL$^{\rightarrow|\text{class of '86}|}$

BECOME-FEWER-IN-STEPS$^{a\rightarrow|\text{class of '86}|}$

Figure 7.12  The graduating classes became smaller. My class was small. They became smaller in steps (year by year).

I am treating the entire phrase MY CLASS as directed toward a location *L* because the signer directs his face and gaze downward toward the location ahead of his abdomen beginning with MY and continuing through CLASS. Thus, [MY CLASS]$^{\rightarrow L}$ associates his graduating class with the space directly ahead of his abdomen, where CLASS is produced. Evidence for the existence of the token |class of '86| ahead of his torso emerges as he begins to direct signs toward this token.

The signer goes on to explain that there were twenty-three members of his graduating class. After a false start, he then states, as shown in Figure 7.12, REALLY BECOME-FEWER-OVER-TIME$^{a\rightarrow|\text{class of '86}|}$ SMALL$^{\rightarrow|\text{class of '86}|}$ BECOME-FEWER-IN-STEPS$^{a\rightarrow|\text{class of '86}|}$.

He uses the verb BECOME-FEWER-OVER-TIME$^{x\rightarrow x'}$, which characterizes the number of entities associated with some set *x* (e.g. graduating classes, the class of '91, the Deaf club, etc.) at time$_1$ as higher in number than the corresponding set *x'* at time$_2$. In Figure 7.12, BECOME-FEWER-OVER-TIME$^{a\rightarrow|\text{class of '86}|}$ begins directed at an unnamed entity *a* ahead of his forehead then moves downward toward the |class of '86 |. This identifies the |class of '86| as the second stage in the change from a larger number of entities to a smaller number. In producing BECOME-FEWER-OVER-TIME $^{a\rightarrow|\text{class of '86}|}$, the hands begin at a higher level, directed toward *a*, and move smoothly down toward |class of '86|. During the downward movement the signer's tongue briefly protrudes with the tip contacting the lower lip, then retracts so that at the

BECOME-FEWER-OVER-TIME<sup>a→|class of '86|</sup>

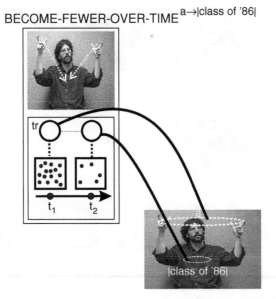

Figure 7.13 Mapping the semantic pole of BECOME-FEWER-OVER-TIME<sup>a→|class of '86|</sup>

conclusion of the sign it is no longer visible. This tongue movement *tg* appears to express that an event simply happened, without fault or without assigning blame or responsibility. That is, the reduction in size just happened that way. There is also a change in head position and head movement, similar to that seen in BECOME-FEWER-SUDDENLY<sup>→|Deaf students|</sup> in Figure 7.10.

SMALL<sup>→|class of '86|</sup> associates the semantic pole of SMALL with the token |class of '86|. BECOME-FEWER-IN-STEPS<sup>a→|class of '86|</sup> is produced like BECOME-FEWER-OVER-TIME<sup>a→|class of '86|</sup> but with brief holds (pauses) along the path between the start and end of the movement. This expresses that the change was incremental rather than continuous. The initial picture illustrating BECOME-FEWER-IN-STEPS<sup>a→|class of '86|</sup> shows the hands in transition prior to the start of the sign. Note that during this transition the signer's gaze is directed upward toward *a*. By the time the sign begins, his gaze has already moved away from *a* and back to the addressee. Thus, the signer signals the importance of *a* prior to the start of the verb.

The verb BECOME-FEWER-OVER-TIME<sup>x→x′</sup> differs from BECOME-FEWER-SUDDENLY<sup>→x</sup> (Figure 7.10) in the speed of the movement, the nonmanual component of the sign, and the number of entities the hands are directed toward. In particular, BECOME-FEWER-OVER-TIME<sup>x→x′</sup> is directed at two entities rather than one. Figure 7.13 diagrams the mapped semantic pole of

[EIGHTY-ONE]$^{\rightarrow a}$                          BIG$^{\rightarrow|class\ of\ '81|}$

BECOME-SMALL-OVER-TIME $^{|class\ of\ '81|\rightarrow|class\ of\ '86|}$

Figure 7.14  The class of '81 was big, then subsequent classes became smaller all the way up to my graduating class

BECOME-FEWER-OVER-TIME$^{a\rightarrow|class\ of\ '86|}$ in Figure 7.12. The sign begins at the location of the as yet unidentified entity $a$ as it existed at $t_1$ then moves to the |class of '86| at time $t_2$. Ending the sign by directing it toward the |class of '86| is a signal to map the entity at $t_2$ in the verb's semantic pole onto the |class of '86|.

The signer entered the school in 1981, graduated in 1986, and is describing the drop of enrollment during that period. By directing [EIGHTY-ONE]$^{\rightarrow a}$ toward $a$ as shown in Figure 7.14, he associates the year 1981 with that entity. This association creates the blended entity |class of '81|. We now know that the drop in enrollment being described occurred between 1981 and 1986.[7]

Spatially, BECOME-FEWER-OVER-TIME$^{x\rightarrow x'}$ is directed at two entities: the entity corresponding to $x$ at $t_1$ and the entity corresponding to $x'$ at $t_2$. The two entities $x$ and $x'$ are instances of the 'same' entity at two different points in time. Seeing the class of '81 and the class of '86 as two different instances of a single entity involves an abstraction. One graduating class differs from every other instance of a graduating class because the set of students making up a graduating class is always different from year to year. But each is also an instance of the abstract entity 'graduating class', which becomes smaller over time. The verb BECOME-FEWER-OVER-TIME$^{x\rightarrow x'}$ treats the two distinct sets of students as instances of the abstraction 'graduating class'. This is how those sets of students can be understood as instances of the same entity.

BIG$^{\rightarrow|class\ of\ '81|}$ associates the semantic pole of BIG with the token |class of '81|, and thereby with the class of '81. Figure 7.14 ends with the verb

---

[7] In this instance, the sign [EIGHTY-ONE]$^{\rightarrow b}$ allows for another possible interpretation (MJ Bienvenu, personal communication). One could also associate eighty-one students with that token, rather than the year 1981.

BECOME-SMALL-OVER-TIME$^{|\text{class of '81}|\rightarrow|\text{class of '86}|}$. This verb is like BE-COME-FEWER-OVER-TIME$^{x\rightarrow x'}$ except that it focuses on size (e.g. big, small) rather than quantity.

He ends the discussion by wondering whether the school will close down and commenting that it has now been combined with the school for the blind. Beginning with the sign BECOME-FEWER-OVER-TIME$^{x\rightarrow x'}$ he directs six successive signs toward the blended space containing the |class of '81| and the |class of '86|. The first sign tells us that the class of 1986 was much smaller than previous classes and that the decline had been going on for some time. The next sign characterizes the class of 1986 as small. The next sign characterizes the reduction as taking place in steps (year by year). The next sign tells us the initial year being described was 1981, and simultaneously associates that year with the upper token. The next sign characterizes the class of 1981 as big. The final directional sign characterizes becoming small as happening over time.

In the examples described in this section the signer makes use of blended spaces in which the significance of the tokens changes over time. In the first example, a group of five becomes a group of four, then finally a group of three. The same blended space is used for the group, regardless of the changes. Later the signer describes changes in the abstract entity 'graduating class'. This involved conceptualizing the initial stage of the entity as a token ahead of the forehead at time $t_1$ and the final stage as a token ahead of the chest at time $t_2$. Directing signs such as BIG toward a token assigns the property 'big' to that token. Interestingly, the signer made use of the token ahead of the forehead twice prior to explaining what it was. Only later did he identify the token ahead of his forehead as the |class of 1981|. Thus, the changes to the tokens in the latter example change from the perspective of the addressee since the nature of the tokens unfolds as the signer provides more and more information about them.

### Unusual token placement

In the following example a left-handed signer is describing the four children of one of his brothers. The excerpt begins with the signer describing the number of children as FOUR. He explains that there were two different wives involved, followed by the signs [FIRST]$^{\rightarrow L1}$ and [SECOND]$^{\rightarrow L2}$. The placement of [FIRST]$^{\rightarrow L1}$ is unusual. In citation form, FIRST would be signed with the hand ahead of the shoulder. The fact that he signs [FIRST]$^{\rightarrow L1}$ near the forehead is a clear signal that he has made a spatial association between the concept 'first' and the brother's first wife. He produces [SECOND]$^{\rightarrow L2}$ ahead of the shoulder as shown in Figure 7.15. Since this is where SECOND is produced in citation form, it raises the question of whether he has produced SECOND or

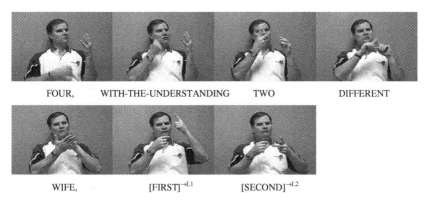

FOUR,        WITH-THE-UNDERSTANDING        TWO                DIFFERENT

WIFE,              [FIRST]$^{\rightarrow L1}$          [SECOND]$^{\rightarrow L2}$

Figure 7.15  (The number of deaf children that the man had was) four. Under-stand that there were two different wives, the first (here) and second (here).

NOW                SECOND                WIFE.            TWO-EACH$^{\rightarrow a,b}$

Figure 7.16  He is currently married to his second wife. Each wife had two children.

[SECOND]$^{\rightarrow L2}$. The fact that the two signs contrast in their spatial placement suggests that the signer has made two different spatial associations. Subsequent signing demonstrates the existence of the two tokens |first wife| and |second wife|.

The most remarkable thing about these two tokens is the lack of immediate attention they receive. That is, given the clear distinction he makes between the placement of [FIRST]$^{\rightarrow L1}$ and [SECOND]$^{\rightarrow L2}$, one might expect that he would immediately begin to take advantage of the two recently created tokens. He does not. Instead, he continues by signing NOW SECOND WIFE, TWO-EACH$^{\rightarrow a,b}$ as an explanation that the man is currently married to his second wife and that each of the wives had two children.[8] This sequence is illustrated in Figure 7.16.

I am treating the sign following NOW as SECOND, rather than as a di-rected form of SECOND since it is produced at its citation form location and

---

[8] The sign NOW is barely discernible in this example. This is due to the informal register being used. NOW is normally a two-handed sign but here it is produced with his dominant left hand only, and without the full movement or palm-up orientation seen in the citation form of the sign.

Table 7.1 *The blends between the creation of the |first wife| and |second wife| tokens and signs directed toward those tokens.*

| Time relative to FIRST, SECOND | Blended entities | Locations of blended entities |
| --- | --- | --- |
| 0:00 | FIRST, SECOND | Near forehead Ahead of shoulder |
| 0:02 | Two wives | Left and right space ahead of signer |
| 0:04 | Children's father | Left space ahead of signer |
| 0:05 | Children's father's brothers | Extended thumb and fingers of right hand |
| 0:10 | Third generation of Deaf children | Extended index finger of right hand |
| 0:12 | Fourth generation of Deaf children | Directly ahead and away from signer |
| 0:13 | Spatial metaphor (history of deafness through different generations) | Space ahead of right shoulder |
| 0:16 | New spatial metaphor (history of | Space directly ahead of signer |
| 0:16 | deafness through different | |
| 0:16 | generations) | |
| 0:19 | [ends turn] | |
| 0:23 | [begins turn] | |
| 0:26 | Signer's two children | Space ahead of signer |
| 0:28 | [ends turn] | |
| 0:31 | [begins turn] | |
| 0:31 | Signer's two children | Index and middle fingers |
| 0:34 | Surrogate signer and youngest child | Self and space ahead of signer on left |
| 0:36 | Signs used by youngest child | Index and middle fingers |
| 0:43 | Surrogate (becomes youngest child signing) | Self |
| 0:44 | Surrogate signer and youngest child | Self and space ahead of signer on left |
| 0:55 | [ends turn] | |
| 0:58 | [begins turn] | |
| 0:58 | Signer's oldest child | Index finger |
| 0:59 | Signer's oldest child | Space to right of signer |
| 1:00 | Two languages | Index and middle finger |
| 1:01 | [ends turn] | |
| 1:04 | [begins turn] | |
| 1:05 | Father of four Deaf children | Middle finger, with thumb and all fingers extended |
| 1:09 | |first wife|, |second wife| | Near forehead Ahead of shoulder |

FOUR          CHILDREN          DEAF          FOUR

[TWO]$^{\rightarrow|first\ wife|}$   [TWO]$^{\rightarrow|second\ wife|}$

Figure 7.17 He has four Deaf children. Two by each wife.

there is no compelling evidence that he is directing it toward the token |second wife|.[9]

He then signs TWO-EACH$^{\rightarrow a,b}$, produced by alternating inward and outward movements of the two hands. This sign makes a left–right spatial distinction between the two wives. It is consistent with a blend placing a token *a* representing one wife well ahead of the signer on the left and a token *b* representing the other on the right. That is, TWO-EACH$^{\rightarrow a,b}$ is not directed at the tokens made evident by |FIRST|$^{\rightarrow L1}$ and |SECOND|$^{\rightarrow L2}$ in Figure 7.15. Signs making use of those two blended entities do not appear until more than a minute later. By that time, the signer has created or reactivated the seventeen additional blended spaces listed in Table 7.1.

For each blend in Table 7.1 I have listed when it occurred relative to the initial |first wife|–|second wife| blend. The sequence of blends will give the reader unfamiliar with sign languages a feel for the continuous nature of spatial blending in ASL signing. The table merely lists the existence of the blends, without going into the details of how many times signs are directed toward entities within the blends.

The signer concludes the sequence of blends in Table 7.1 by returning to a brief discussion of the brother with four children. Without any further discussion of the two wives, the signer repeats that the brother has four Deaf children then signs [TWO]$^{\rightarrow|first\ wife|}$ and [TWO]$^{\rightarrow|second\ wife|}$, as illustrated in Figure 7.17.

The placements of these two signs depend on the blend created more than a minute earlier by the signs in Figure 7.15. Note also that the signer completes four turns as signer and is in his fifth turn when he finally makes use of those

---

[9] Since the second wife has already been associated with the location ahead of the shoulder, he could also be producing [SECOND]$^{\rightarrow|second\ wife|}$. This seems unlikely, however, since the property 'second' has already been associated with the second wife.

two tokens. Directing these signs in this way associates two children with each wife. Out of context, the signs [TWO]$^{→ |first wife|}$ and [TWO]$^{→ |second wife|}$ in Figure 7.17 are incomprehensible. In this context, and given the ability to keep track of a large number of sequentially produced blended spaces, the signs are straightforward and meaningful.

### Distinct spaces

The following sequence occurred during a teleconference about Deaf culture and involves a more complex set of spatial associations. The lecturer outlines three major parts of her teleconference. The first part involves a discussion of theoretical issues surrounding language and culture. While summarizing her plan for this part of the teleconference she keeps her torso rotated toward the left. In describing her plan for the second part of the teleconference she keeps her torso rotated toward the right, as illustrated in Figure 7.18. She is explaining that she is going to make a comparison of Deaf people and hearing people.

With her torso rotated to the right she produces the four signs, [DEAF]$^{→L1}$ [HEARING PEOPLE]$^{→L2}$ COMPARE-DUAL$^{→ |Deaf people|, |hearing people|}$. During [DEAF]$^{→L1}$ she uses her body to point by leaning to the right. During [HEARING PEOPLE]$^{→L2}$ her posture is more erect, and therefore no longer pointing to the right. This difference in posture can be seen by examining the position of her head with respect to the vertical pattern in the background. During [DEAF]$^{→L1}$ her head is further to the right than during [HEARING PEOPLE]$^{→L2}$. This contrasting right–left difference in posture prompts the creation of a real-space blend with |Deaf people| in the space ahead of her on the right and |hearing people| in the space ahead of her on the left. She signals the presence of the two tokens |Deaf people| and |hearing people| by coordinating the production of the signs and her subtle changes in posture. The blend making both those abstractions conceptually present is illustrated in Figure 7.19.

The approximate locations of the two elements of the blend are outlined in the blended space. The rectangular shape enclosing the two blended entities

[DEAF]$^{→L1}$          [HEARING          PEOPLE]$^{→L2}$     COMPARE-DUAL$^{→|Deaf people|,|hearing people|}$

Figure 7.18  Creating and using the tokens |Deaf people| and |hearing people|

|Deaf people|

|hearing people|

blended space

Figure 7.19 COMPARE-DUAL$^{\rightarrow [\text{Deaf people}], [\text{hearing people}]}$

shows the extent of the blended space. In Figure 7.19 she is signing COMPARE-DUAL$^{\rightarrow |\text{Deaf people}|, |\text{hearing people}|}$ by directing one hand toward |Deaf people| and the other toward |hearing people|. This identifies these two abstract entities as the things corresponding to the verb's dual landmark. Note that her eye gaze is also directed at the space conceptualized as containing the two tokens, providing additional evidence that the verb is directed at |Deaf people| and |hearing people|.[10]

She next explains that the comparison of Deaf and hearing people will relate to the discussion of theoretical issues, which in turn, will apply to that comparison. She does this by means of the signs in Figure 7.20. She begins with the sign THAT$^{\rightarrow |\text{comparison}|}$. Although she has not identified any single entity located centrally ahead of her, that is where she directs THAT$^{\rightarrow |\text{comparison}|}$. Doing so reflects a change in the blended space. She has changed the space ahead of her so that while it still contains |Deaf people| and |hearing people|, the space as a whole takes on the significance 'comparison of Deaf and hearing people'. As a result, THAT$^{\rightarrow |\text{comparison}|}$ refers to *the comparison* of Deaf people and hearing people by being directed toward the comparison space.

JOINED-TO$^{|\text{comparison}| \rightarrow |\text{theory}|}$ begins directed at the center of the comparison space then moves to the location previously associated with the theoretical discussion of linguistics and culture. Thus, its directionality indicates that the comparison of Deaf people and hearing people relates to the theoretical discussion.

Next she produces a THEME buoy (see chapter 8) with her left hand. Placing the THEME buoy toward the theory space identifies the theory as a significant theme in the discourse. While maintaining [THEME]$^{\rightarrow |\text{theory}|}$ in place, she signs THEORY with her right hand, overtly labeling the significance of [THEME]$^{\rightarrow |\text{theory}|}$.

She next explains that she will apply the theory to the comparison of Deaf and hearing people. Here, APPLY$^{|\text{theory}| \rightarrow |\text{comparison}|}$ begins directed toward the

---

[10] Except for her directed eye gaze, COMPARE-DUAL$^{\rightarrow |\text{Deaf people}|, |\text{hearing people}|}$ as produced in Figure 7.18 looks like the citation form COMPARE. However, confirmation of the fact that Deaf and hearing people have been associated with these two areas of space comes in the signing which follows.

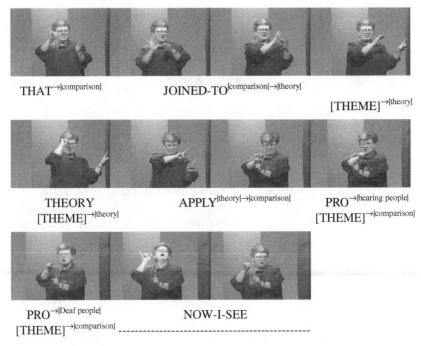

THAT$^{\rightarrow|comparison|}$        JOINED-TO$^{|comparison|\rightarrow|theory|}$

[THEME]$^{\rightarrow|theory|}$

THEORY        APPLY$^{|theory|\rightarrow|comparison|}$        PRO$^{\rightarrow|hearing people|}$
[THEME]$^{\rightarrow|theory|}$            [THEME]$^{\rightarrow|comparison|}$

PRO$^{\rightarrow|Deaf people|}$        NOW-I-SEE
[THEME]$^{\rightarrow|comparison|}$ -----------------------------------------------

Figure 7.20 That comparison relates to the (previous discussion of) theory, which in turn, applies to the comparison of Deaf people and hearing people. At that point it will all become clear

theory space and ends directed toward the comparison space. Once again torso rotation activates the individual spaces. She begins APPLY$^{|theory|\rightarrow|comparison|}$ with her torso rotated to the left toward the theory space and ends with her torso rotated to the right toward the comparison space. The semantic structure, the two blended spaces, and the conceptual mappings involved in this production of APPLY$^{|theory|\rightarrow|comparison|}$ and its two pronominal objects are illustrated in Figure 7.21.

The signer must sequentially activate two distinct blended spaces during the production of a single sign. By rotating her torso to the left, she initially directs APPLY$^{|theory|\rightarrow|comparison|}$ toward the theory space, which is only active while her torso is rotated to the left. Then she rotates to the right, activating the comparison space. Thus, the verb ends directed toward the comparison space. The verb is followed by PRO$^{\rightarrow|hearing people|}$ and PRO$^{\rightarrow|Deaf people|}$. The properly mapped verb and pronouns express the meaning that the theory applies to the comparison of Deaf people and hearing people.

The sign OH-I-SEE is normally used by an addressee as a means of providing feedback to the signer. It shows that the addressee is following and

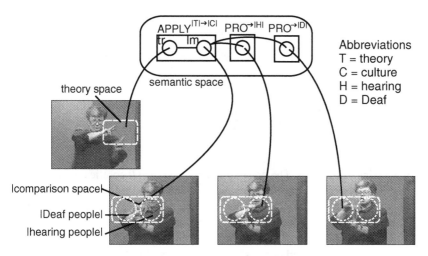

Figure 7.21 Sequentially evoking two blended spaces

understanding the discussion. It is produced with an in and out movement of a Y handshape, similar to the movement of NOW-I-SEE in Figure 7.20, but with much smaller movements directly ahead of the shoulder. OH-I-SEE is also produced without the head movement seen with NOW-I-SEE. NOW-I-SEE would be appropriately used after a period of not understanding the point of what was being signed. It is clear, however, that the lecturer does not intend to say that at that point she will finally understand her own lecture. Rather, the lecturer becomes a surrogate member of the audience. The real members of the audience understand this to mean, 'At this point it will all become clear'.

Note that the lecturer maintains the vertically oriented index finger of her left hand in place after completing the sign APPLY$^{|theory| \to |comparison|}$. This could be an example of meaningless phonological perseveration in that the final weak hand configuration of the verb is maintained during subsequent one-handed signs. There are reasons to treat this as another instance of the THEME buoy, however. First, it has the correct vertically oriented 1 handshape of the THEME buoy. Second, the handshape is placed in the middle of the comparison space. Third, the handshape is maintained with no degradation of either the handshape or its position. Fourth, and perhaps most significantly, it is maintained right in the middle of the signing activity of the following two pronouns. Fifth, it is still maintained as the signer adopts the role of an audience member during the final sign NOW-I-SEE. For these reasons I am treating the weak hand with the vertical index finger as a THEME buoy, signifying the thematic importance of the comparison space.

Conceptually, what the lecturer has done through torso rotation is quite complex. She had previously described the fact that the teleconference would be

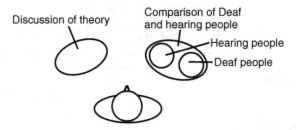

Figure 7.22  Two spaces conceived of as existing at the same time

divided into three parts. The first part is a discussion of theoretical issues. As she describes this part of the teleconference she keeps her torso rotated to the left. She then rotates her torso to the right to discuss the fact that she will compare Deaf and hearing people. Given this context, and given the way the hands move in this example, one could get the impression that there are now two separate conceptual spaces ahead of the signer, as illustrated in Figure 7.22.

Recall that the signer associated Deaf people and hearing people with two locations in the space ahead of her as her torso was rotated to the right. In addition, the comparison of Deaf people and hearing people is associated with the entire space itself. On her left, the signer described the portion of her teleconference devoted to the discussion of theoretical issues related to language and culture. If one simply puts all those pieces together, the result is a conceptualization of space shown in Figure 7.22. If this were the correct conceptualization then it ought to be possible for the signer to direct signs toward these areas of space regardless of her torso orientation. But this is not what she does.

At the conclusion of COMPARE-DUAL$^{\rightarrow|Deaf\ people|,\ |hearing\ people|}$, her torso is leaning to the right and also rotated to the right. During THAT$^{\rightarrow|comparison|}$ her body rotation is more neutral, though her body has moved further to the right. She begins JOINED-TO$^{|comparison|\rightarrow|theory|}$ with her body still facing forward. At the end of JOINED-TO$^{|comparison|\rightarrow|theory|}$ her torso is rotated to the left – the torso orientation used when introducing the discussion of theoretical issues. These differences in torso rotation suggest that rather than a single all-encompassing space, the signer has created two distinct spaces.[11] One is active when she rotates her torso to the left and the other is active when she rotates her torso to the right. The problem here is that she needs to direct the beginning of JOINED-TO$^{|comparison|\rightarrow|theory|}$ toward the comparison space and direct the end of the same verb toward the theory space. In order to direct the verb this way, she signs THAT$^{\rightarrow|comparison|}$ while her body is still rotated to the right. This identifies

---

[11] Winston (1993:173) describes body rotation as pointing with the torso. She also describes a signer "stepping back into" a space to talk about a specific topic. I do not present any examples of moving the body to a different place to activate a new space, but as Winston's data show, such examples do occur.

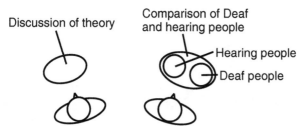

Figure 7.23  Spaces conceived of as existing when the signer faces them

the |comparison| as the entity she is talking about. She directs the beginning of JOINED-TO|comparison|→|theory| toward the location of |comparison|. During the production of the verb she rotates to the left. This activates the theory space, allowing the end of the verb to be directed toward that space. By means of these torso rotations, a single verb can be directed toward two distinct spaces.

In this example, rotating her torso to the left activates the theory space, illustrated on the left in Figure 7.23. Rotating her torso to the right activates the comparison space, illustrated on the right in Figure 7.23. In the rightward rotated position, she leans her body to the right as she signs DEAF then straightens her body as she signs HEARING PEOPLE. This makes a left–right distinction in the space ahead of her rightward rotated torso, thereby indicating the presence of the tokens |Deaf people| and |hearing people|. Once the spatial associations are made, she directs the verb COMPARE-DUAL→|Deaf people|,|hearing people| toward these tokens and subsequently directs pronouns toward them. She is also able to reify the comparison by treating the space containing the two tokens as a comparison space. She provides clear evidence for the reification by directing THAT→|comparison| toward the center of that space.

### Entities and settings

A single area of space may sometimes be associated with more than one thing (van Hoek 1992, 1996; Engberg-Pedersen 1993). In one example from van Hoek (1992), Chicago was associated with the space on the right and New York was associated with the space on the left. When the person being talked about was described as having moved to New York, the signer not only directed signs to the left to talk about New York, but also directed signs to the left to talk about a person who moved to New York. Van Hoek observes that the use of a single spatial location to represent both the person and New York goes beyond simply representing two things in the same spatial location. Rather, the location serves as a conceptual setting. The person is conceived of as existing within that conceptual setting.

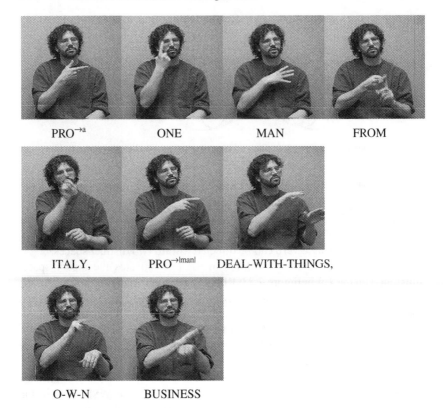

PRO$^{\rightarrow a}$          ONE          MAN          FROM

ITALY,          PRO$^{\rightarrow |man|}$     DEAL-WITH-THINGS,

O-W-N          BUSINESS

Figure 7.24 One man from Italy was occupied doing things – he owned a business.

Engberg-Pedersen (1993) describes similar examples in Danish Sign Language. One signer, for example, directs signs ahead and to the right when talking about her father and also when talking about the factory where her father worked. Engberg-Pedersen describes this as *semantic affinity*, which can include the relation between a person and the place where he or she works, the relation between a person and a place the person frequents, as well as the relation between the possessor and the thing possessed.

The following narrative includes examples similar to those described by van Hoek and Engberg-Pedersen. Early in the narrative the signer introduces the main character of a movie he had recently seen. The character's introduction begins with the sign PRO$^{\rightarrow a}$ directed toward an as yet unidentified entity *a* on the left, as illustrated in Figure 7.24. The immediately following phrase ONE MAN FROM ITALY identifies a man from Italy as the pronoun's referent. The combination of PRO$^{\rightarrow a}$ and immediately naming the referent provides the addressee with sufficient information to create a token to the signer's left at roughly shoulder height. The token is a blend of the space to the left of the signer and the person described – a man from Italy.

The signer next produces the clause PRO$^{\rightarrow|man|}$ DEAL-WITH-THINGS. Understanding the directionality of PRO$^{\rightarrow|man|}$ is straightforward since he has just made an association between that area of space and the man from Italy. He produces DEAL-WITH-THINGS with a small leftward then rightward movement of his two hands as the fingers wiggle. By the time the verb begins, his face is directed to the left, his eyes are narrowed, and his head is tilted back slightly. This posture gives the impression of a person occupied doing something. This suggests that the signer has created a surrogate blend in which he has blended with the man and is occupied doing things.[12] The signer then faces forward again to provide the information needed to understand the surrogate blend: O-W-N BUSINESS 'he owned a business'. So it appears that the man was occupied doing things for his business in Italy. It is interesting to observe that in the token blend and in the hypothesized surrogate blend the relevant settings are on the left. In the token blend, the man from Italy is associated with the space on the left. In the proposed surrogate blend, the signer is also facing left. He will shortly be using the space on the right to create a new token blend involving Turkey.

The proposed surrogate blend would be distinct from the original token blend. That is, in a surrogate blend the signer would partially become that man through blending. In such a surrogate blend, the token |man| would no longer be present to the left. As soon as the signer discontinues the surrogate blend, however, he once again makes use of the token |man| on the left as shown in Figure 7.25. He introduces the man's aunt with the topic POSS$^{\rightarrow|man|}$ AUNT followed by the clause LIVE THERE$^{\rightarrow|Turkey|}$ to right at shoulder height T-U-R-K-E-Y. By immediately identifying the location THERE$^{\rightarrow|Turkey|}$ is directed toward as Turkey, he identifies a token space with the setting Turkey.

The weak hand is simultaneously producing a THEME buoy (see chapter 8), expressing that the aunt is an important theme in the discourse. The aunt is important in the story since she owns a bathhouse in Turkey. When she dies she leaves the bathhouse to the man in Italy.

He talks about the aunt by directing the pronoun PRO$^{\rightarrow|aunt|}$ slightly upward from shoulder height and to the right in the sentence, PRO$^{\rightarrow|aunt|}$ CONTACT ZERO ('There had been no contact with the aunt'). The signs THERE$^{\rightarrow|Turkey|}$ and PRO$^{\rightarrow|aunt|}$ are similar, but not identical. First, the palm is oriented down in the sign THERE$^{\rightarrow|Turkey|}$. PRO$^{\rightarrow|aunt|}$ is oriented with the palm to the side.

---

[12] I am treating DEAL-WITH-THINGS as a nondirectional sign. I have not seen enough examples of this verb to be confident about its structure. It is possible, for example, that it is a directional sign like HONOR$^{\cup\rightarrow x}$ requiring the signer to face and direct the hands toward some entity $x$.

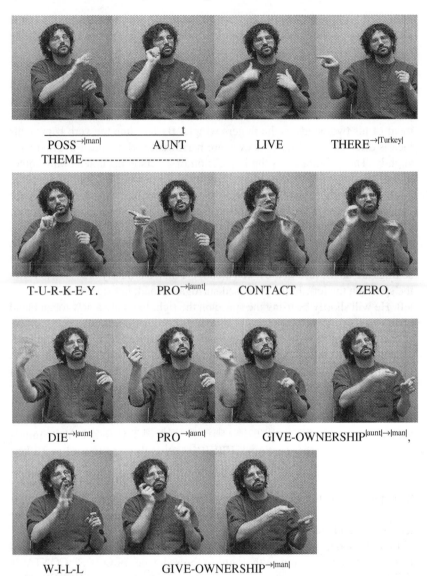

POSS<sup>→|man|</sup>      AUNT       LIVE       THERE<sup>→|Turkey|</sup>
THEME--------------------------

T-U-R-K-E-Y.      PRO<sup>→|aunt|</sup>   CONTACT       ZERO.

DIE<sup>→|aunt|</sup>.      PRO<sup>→|aunt|</sup>   GIVE-OWNERSHIP<sup>|aunt|→|man|</sup>,

W-I-L-L      GIVE-OWNERSHIP<sup>→|man|</sup>

Figure 7.25  His aunt lived in Turkey. There had been no contact with the aunt. She died and left something to him in her will.

There is also a significant directional difference between these two signs. THERE$^{\rightarrow|\text{Turkey}|}$ is directed horizontally while PRO$^{\rightarrow|\text{aunt}|}$ is directed slightly upward. This provides evidence for a vertical distinction within |Turkey|, with the |aunt| at a high level within that space.

There are two important points concerning the blended entities |aunt| and |Turkey| in this example. First, as van Hoek (1992) has observed, spatial settings can be associated with a located referent. Second, recall that in the lecture about Deaf culture, discussed earlier in this chapter, the signer created a space containing two tokens: |Deaf people| and |hearing people|. These two tokens were embedded inside a comparison space. I treat the space to the right of the signer in a similar way by analyzing |Turkey| as the conceptual setting for the blended space and the token |aunt| as an element embedded within that space.

The next sign DIE$^{\rightarrow|\text{aunt}|}$ is also directed high and to the right. The one-handed sign DIE$^{\rightarrow x}$ is interesting in that it is not generally directed toward physically present entities – including dead ones. However, it is common to direct DIE$^{\rightarrow x}$ toward tokens. Since tokens are restricted to the space near the signer, the hand can easily be placed *at* the location of the token rather than merely toward it. This is what the signer does in Figure 7.25 when he places the hand producing DIE$^{\rightarrow|\text{aunt}|}$ high and to the right. By placing the hand at the location of the |aunt|, he indicates that the aunt died. In the following clause PRO$^{\rightarrow|\text{aunt}|}$ GIVE-OWNERSHIP$^{|\text{aunt}|\rightarrow|\text{man}|}$, the pronoun is directed toward the token |aunt| as is the beginning of the verb. The verb begins at that high level on the right and moves diagonally down toward the token |man| on the signer's left. The directionality of GIVE-OWNERSHIP$^{|\text{aunt}|\rightarrow|\text{man}|}$ indicates that the |aunt| gave something to the |man|. He then spells W-I-L-L, then GIVE-OWNERSHIP$^{\rightarrow|\text{man}|}$. This final verb does not begin directed toward the |aunt|, though it does move toward the |man|. Perhaps this is because the signer has just clarified that the man was given something by means of the aunt's will.

After a brief pause he explains that she left the man her bathhouse, which he describes as characteristically Turkish, using the signs in (2).

(2)     BATH HOUSE QUOTE, POSS-CHARACTER$^{\rightarrow|\text{Turkey}|}$ T-U-R-K-I-
        S-H, BATH HOUSE POSS-CHARACTER$^{\rightarrow|\text{Turkey}|}$ FAMOUS,
        POSS-CHARACTER$^{\rightarrow|\text{Turkey}|}$
        A bathhouse, a characteristically Turkish bathhouse; it was a well-
        known type of Turkish bathhouse.

The sign POSS-CHARACTER$^{\rightarrow x}$ associates characteristics with a referent. By first signing BATH HOUSE then POSS-CHARACTER$^{\rightarrow|\text{Turkey}|}$ the signer is expressing that the bathhouse has Turkish characteristics. In other words, it is a characteristically Turkish bathhouse. The three instances of

a.        POSS-CHARACTER<sup>→|Turkey|</sup>    b.        POSS-CHARACTER<sup>→|Turkey|</sup>

c.        POSS-CHARACTER<sup>→|Turkey|</sup>

Figure 7.26 Three instances of POSS-CHARACTER<sup>→|Turkey|</sup> directed at |Turkey|

GO<sup>|man|→|Turkey|</sup>                SELL<sup>→|bathhouse|</sup>

Figure 7.27  He went to Turkey to sell the bathhouse

POSS-CHARACTER<sup>→|Turkey|</sup> appearing in (2) are illustrated in Figure 7.26. Although they become progressively more abbreviated in form, each is directed toward the right at about shoulder level.

A short time later he explains that the man went to Turkey to sell the bathhouse. The sequence GO<sup>|man|→|Turkey|</sup> SELL<sup>→|bathhouse|</sup> occurs as part of that explanation and is illustrated in Figure 7.27.

GO<sup>|man|→|Turkey|</sup> begins directed toward the |man| and ends directed toward |Turkey| – also about shoulder level. This indicates that the man went to Turkey. The next sign, SELL<sup>→|bathhouse|</sup>, is directed toward the lower part of |Turkey|. The signer has made no previous spatial association with the bathhouse in the |Turkey| space. The signer has just described that the man went to Turkey to

Figure 7.28  The two blended spaces

sell something. Logic tells us he must have gone in order to sell the bathhouse. Therefore, the bathhouse must be associated with the lower part of the token |Turkey|.

Based on the signing at this point in the narrative, there is evidence for the two token spaces illustrated in Figure 7.28, with the |man| from Italy on the left and |Turkey| on the right. |Turkey| contains two tokens |aunt| and |bathhouse|, as illustrated in Figure 7.28.

Figure 7.29 offers a sampling of the signs directed toward each of the tokens in Figure 7.28. The signs shown in Figure 7.29a are all directed toward the token |man| and are all consistent with |man| conceptualized as being located to the left of the signer at about shoulder height. The signs in Figure 7.29b are all directed toward the |aunt|, to the right and above shoulder level.

If a sign is directed toward a physically present, inanimate entity, it is generally directed at the center of the entity. If the same principle applies to a token like |Turkey|, signs directed at |Turkey| ought to be directed at the center of the space. The signs in Figure 7.29c show that signs referring to Turkey are all directed to the right at shoulder level. This appears to be a central height between the |aunt| and the |bathhouse|. This supports the idea that |Turkey| encloses these other two tokens. The single sign referring to the bathhouse shown in Figure 7.29d is directed low and to the right.

**Token blends versus surrogate blends**

To this point I have examined two types of real-space blends. Chapter 5 examines surrogate blends and this chapter examines token blends. The primary distinction between the two is whether or not the signer takes on a new role by at least partially becoming part of the blended space. If the signer does take on a new role through blending then the result is a surrogate blend and the signer has become a surrogate. In creating a token blend, the signer remains the signer, but creates a non-topographical blend in the space ahead of the torso.

PRO<sup>→|man|</sup>          POSS<sup>→|man|</sup>     GIVE-OWNERSHIP<sup>|aunt|→|man|</sup> GIVE-OWNERSHIP<sup>→|man|</sup>

a.  Signs directed toward the |man|

PRO<sup>→|aunt|</sup>          PRO<sup>→|aunt|</sup>          DIE<sup>→|aunt|</sup>          GIVE-OWNERSHIP<sup>|aunt|→|man|</sup>

b.  Signs directed toward the |aunt|

THERE<sup>→|Turkey|</sup> POSS-CHARACTER<sup>→|Turkey|</sup>     GO<sup>|man|→|Turkey|</sup>

c.  Signs directed toward |Turkey|

SELL<sup>→|bathhouse|</sup>

d.  The one sign directed toward the |bathhouse|

Figure 7.29  Signs directed toward each of the tokens in the two blended spaces

Because of the nature of a surrogate blend, the signer in a new role may exist conceptually among other surrogates within the setting of the blend. In such a situation it is possible for the signer-as-surrogate to converse with or otherwise interact with another surrogate. Because the signer does not take on a new role as part of creating a token blend, conversing with tokens is impossible. This follows from the nature of the token space. A signer-as-signer does not exist conceptually within a token blend with other tokens. The tokens are conceptually separate, and in cases where the token blend includes a setting, the tokens are conceptually in that setting rather than in the here and now with the signer.[13]

## Summary

Token blends are created by blending an area of space and some conceptual content. Signers can direct signs toward tokens to refer to that conceptual content. In a blend, the number of tokens can range from one to several and can also change during the discourse. Further, the semantic characteristics associated with a token can also change over time. Another characteristic shared by many of the examples in this chapter is that the space containing tokens may have its own value distinct from the individual tokens within that space. For example, the token |movie categories| exists as a distinct conceptual entity, in spite of the fact that it encloses other tokens within the space. A large token space enclosing other tokens was also apparent in the final example, where |Turkey| encloses both a |bathhouse| and the |aunt|. This final blend also demonstrates that describing directionality as merely left or right may be missing potential height differences, since in this example, the |aunt| was located high on the right and the |bathhouse| was low on the right. Even if the enclosing space was not initially created as a place or thing, it can become a thing through reification, as in the example where the space associated with comparing Deaf and hearing people became the token |comparison|.

In another example a signer creates a blended space but does not take advantage of it immediately. After more than a minute, during which seventeen other blends were created, the signer returns to the original blend by signing [TWO]$^{\rightarrow|\text{first wife}|}$ [TWO]$^{\rightarrow|\text{second wife}|}$. This example also demonstrates the striking number of blends that appear in ordinary discourse. During an ordinary discussion of family members, the signer created eighteen blends within just over sixty seconds. Previous discussions of the use of space in ASL have treated it as a handy means of keeping track of referents. This gives the impression that

---

[13] Additional types of signs and blends will be examined in chapters 8 and 9. While I am presenting all these types of spaces as distinct, it is possible that there may be blends that have properties that may place them between the distinct categories I am presenting here.

a signer simply associates an entity with a locus and that all the signer has to do is recall that association in order to manage reference issues. The fact that spaces are changing every few seconds suggests that keeping track of referents is not the primary issue. If that were the primary issue, the spaces ought to remain fairly stable throughout the discourse.

Perhaps one of the most important aspects of dealing with real-space blends is knowing which blend is active at any specific time. One example examined in this chapter demonstrates that the orientation of the torso plays an important role in indicating which blended spaces are active. By rotating her torso to the right or left the lecturer activated either the 'Deaf–hearing comparison' blend or the 'discussion of theory' blend.

The individual signs examined in this chapter are no more complex than signs examined previously. Signs described as directed toward physically present entities or surrogates in previous chapters are directed toward tokens in token blends in this chapter. The directionality functions in exactly the same way since directing a sign toward a token associates the sign's semantic pole with the token it is directed toward.

# 8    Buoys

Signers frequently produce signs with the weak hand that are held in a stationary configuration as the strong hand continues producing signs. Semantically they help guide the discourse by serving as conceptual landmarks as the discourse continues. Since they maintain a physical presence that helps guide the discourse as it proceeds I am calling them *buoys*. Some buoys appear only briefly whereas others may be maintained during a significant stretch of signing.

### List buoys

Signers use list buoys for making associations with from one to five entities. The five list buoys I describe here are produced with handshapes corresponding to those found in the numeral signs ONE, TWO, THREE, FOUR, and FIVE. These five numeral signs are normally produced by the strong hand ahead of the shoulder with the fingertips oriented upward. Although the five list buoys are produced with the same handshapes, their forms differ from these numeral signs in three ways. First, list buoys are normally produced by the weak hand rather than the strong hand. Second, list buoys are typically located ahead of the chest rather than ahead of the shoulder, and third, the fingers are oriented to the side rather than vertically upward. The list buoys need not be completely horizontal, but they do need to be inclined away from complete verticality.

These differences can be seen by comparing the numeral sign TWO (Figure 8.1a) with the TWO-LIST buoy (Figure 8.1b). Their forms, meanings, and functions are all distinct. TWO is a numeral that can be used either as part of a noun phrase to quantify a noun or alone to serve a pronominal function. The TWO-LIST buoy does not function in either of these ways. Since the numeral TWO is produced by the strong hand, it is typically produced then replaced by the following sign. This is a characteristic it has in common with vocally produced words. The TWO-LIST buoy is produced by the weak hand, which gives it the potential to remain in place as other signs continue to be produced by the strong hand.

a.     TWO          b.     TWO-LIST

Figure 8.1 Strong versus weak hand production of TWO and the TWO-LIST buoy

List buoys can be used to make associations with ordered or unordered sets of entities. For ordered sets, if the thumb is extended, it is associated with the first element of the set. If the thumb is not extended, the index finger is associated with the first element in the set. The next item is associated with the next extended finger. I refer to the extended thumb and fingers of these list buoys as *digits*. The associations between entities and digits are generally made by contacting the tip of the appropriate digit and describing the entity to be associated with it. Sometimes the contact precedes the description, sometimes it follows the description, and sometimes it both precedes and follows the description.

If the entities associated with digits can be described briefly, the weak hand may remain in place as each of the entities is described and associated with a digit. During a lengthy description of an individual entity a signer may temporarily drop the list buoy so that two-handed signs can be produced normally. This avoids the awkwardness of an extended one-handed description while the weak hand is occupied maintaining the list buoy.

I use the symbol *D1* to label the first digit of a list buoy. Thus, in Figure 8.1b, the signer's index finger is *D1* and his middle finger is *D2*. In the figure, the signer is pointing at the tip of *D1*.

In Figure 8.2 the THREE-LIST buoy is present as the lecturer describes the three major parts of her teleconference about Deaf culture. The thumb is *D1*, the index finger is *D2*, and the middle finger is *D3*.

The signs in Figure 8.2 occur after a very brief introduction in which the lecturer expresses her hope that the technology of the teleconference will proceed without problems. The sign NOW introduces a major topic shift. Indeed, she is moving from preliminary remarks to the subject matter of the teleconference. She places the THREE-LIST buoy ahead of her chest. She then makes a pointing motion that begins pointing at the tip of *D1* (the thumb) and moves along a straight path to the tip of *D3*. This accomplishes the result of pointing at *D1*, *D2*, and *D3*, in spite of the fact that the straight path movement does not point directly at the tip of *D2*.

NOW          'these three things'        TIME-BREAK$^{\rightarrow D1\downarrow D2}$

THREE-LIST ------------------------------------------------------

TIME-BREAK$^{\rightarrow D2\downarrow D3}$    PRO-1          GOAL          three taps on D1

THREE-LIST --------------------------------          THREE-LIST

Now, there will be breaks between the three parts (of the teleconference). My

goal, with respect to the first part, ...

Figure 8.2  A typical use of a THREE-LIST buoy

I treat the movement of the index finger of the strong hand as a meaningful gesture pointing to the things she will talk about rather than as a fixed lexical item. I have placed an English phrase describing the significance of the gesture in single quotation marks.

Next, she signs TIME-BREAK$^{\rightarrow D1\downarrow D2}$. The notation D1D2 signifies a location between *D1* and *D2*. By directing TIME-BREAK$^{\rightarrow D1\downarrow D2}$ between *D1* and *D2*, she locates a break between *D1* and *D2*. She next signs TIME-BREAK$^{\rightarrow D2\downarrow D3}$, locating a break between *D2* and *D3*. Although she has not yet told us what the three entities associated with *D1–D3* are, in this context, the fact that there are breaks between them suggests that she is about to describe the three main parts of the teleconference.

After identifying where the breaks will be, she signs PRO-1 GOAL 'my goal', then taps the tip of *D1* three times with her index finger.[1] By tapping *D1* after signing PRO-1 GOAL, she is associating her goal with *D1* – her goal with respect to the first of the three parts of this presentation. Earlier I mentioned that a buoy may be dropped in order to produce two-handed signs. The lecturer does that here by dropping the THREE-LIST buoy in order to produce the two-handed sign GOAL. At the conclusion of GOAL, however, she brings the THREE-LIST buoy back as she continues to describe the three main parts of her teleconference.

---

[1] The signer has used PRO-1 rather than POSS-1 (MY) in this possessive construction. It is not yet clear under what circumstances PRO-1 can be used in this way.

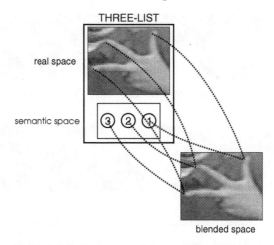

Figure 8.3 Self-blending of the THREE-LIST buoy

She goes on to explain that her goal is to describe aspects of the theory of linguistics and culture. That associates the description of those theories with *D1*. Later, she goes on to associate a comparison of Deaf people and hearing people with *D2*. Finally, she states that she will take questions during the third major part of the teleconference, associating the question–answer session with *D3*.

Prior to describing the three parts of the teleconference, the mere presence of the THREE-LIST buoy involves a blended space. The two input spaces for the blend are the hand in real space and the semantic pole of the THREE-LIST buoy. The 3 hand and the semantic pole of the THREE-LIST buoy are projected into the blended space, as shown in Figure 8.3.

THREE-LIST not only encodes the meaning 'three entities', it also provides a visual representation of those three entities in the form of *D1*, *D2*, and *D3*. In order for *D1* to have the significance 'first of three entities', the physical tip of the thumb must blend with the first of the three conceptual entities in the semantic pole. Similarly, the tip of the index finger blends with the second conceptual entity in the semantic pole, and the tip of the middle finger blends with the third.

As the lecturer makes further associations with *D1–D3*, the complexity of the blend increases. She associates a discussion of the theory of language and culture with *D1*, a comparison of Deaf and hearing people with *D2*, and a question–answer session with *D3*.[2] This blend, illustrated in Figure 8.4, is an

---

[2] A signer can also build an ordered list incrementally, beginning with the two-handed sign FIRST. The weak hand has only the thumb extended while the strong hand with the index finger extended

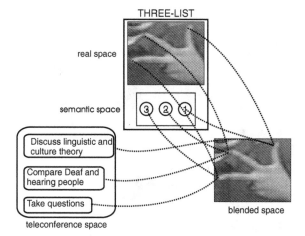

Figure 8.4 Mappings in addition to the self-blending of the THREE-LIST buoy

elaboration of the blend in Figure 8.3. In this case, *D1–D3* additionally blend with the three parts of the teleconference, as illustrated in Figure 8.4.

Figure 8.5 illustrates the set of five list buoys being described here. For each buoy the hands are placed with the fingertips oriented toward the side. The signer in Figure 8.5a, d, and e is left-handed, and thus, produces buoys with his right hand.

There are a number of characteristics that make the signs in Figure 8.5 especially interesting. First, they are unlike words in any vocally produced language in that they are meant to be physically present as other signs or gestures are produced. Second, they are all 'self-blending' signs in that their semantic poles and handshapes automatically blend when they are used. That is, the thumb and fingers are no longer simply what they are in real space (i.e. parts of a hand). They become visible elements of a list. The resulting blend is intended to become more elaborate by associating additional entities with individual digits. This typically occurs by contacting the tip of the digit either immediately before or after the description of the entity. Third, the existence

makes a single horizontal movement, contacting the pad of the thumb. FIRST is normally followed by a description of the first element. SECOND-OF-X is produced by contacting the extended index finger of an L handshape. The L handshape used to be the handshape in the historically older form TWO. This introduces the second item. The third, fourth, and fifth items would be associated with the THREE-LIST, FOUR-LIST, and FIVE-LIST buoys. In each case, the last entity mentioned is associated with the last of the extended fingers. As a result, the baby finger is associated with the fourth element of the FOUR-LIST buoy and also associated with the fifth element of the FIVE-LIST buoy.

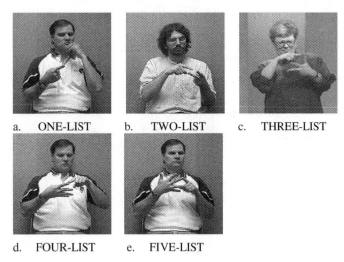

a.    ONE-LIST        b.    TWO-LIST        c.    THREE-LIST

d.    FOUR-LIST        e.    FIVE-LIST

Figure 8.5 Examples of the five list buoys

of these associations allows the signer to refer to those associated conceptual entities either by contacting the appropriate digit or by directing signs
toward it.

### Directing signs toward list buoys

Later in the teleconference the lecturer uses the THREE-LIST buoy again, with
a new set of associations. She associates materialistic, normative, and cognitive aspects of culture with *D1*, *D2*, and *D3*. Using the signs illustrated in
Figure 8.6, she then explains that these three aspects of culture are not independent and have an influence on one another.

After signing NATURAL 'of course', she points at *D1*, already associated with materialistic aspects of culture. Next, she produces the verb
INFLUENCE$^{D1 \rightarrow D2}$ by beginning the verb with the hand near the thumb and
moving toward the tip of the index finger. This indicates that the materialistic aspects of culture have an influence on the normative aspects of cul-
ture. Next, she signs INFLUENCE$^{D2 \rightarrow D3}$, followed by INFLUENCE$^{D3 \rightarrow D2}$
and INFLUENCE$^{D2 \rightarrow D1}$.

An English speaker might say, "The materialistic aspects of culture influence
the normative aspects of culture; the normative aspects of the culture influence
the cognitive aspects of culture; the cognitive aspects of the culture influence the
normative aspects of culture; and so on." Explicitly mentioning some of the influences, then adding "and so on," makes it clear that there are more such
influences. The lecturer accomplishes the same end here by producing four

NATURAL          point to D1               INFLUENCE$^{D1 \to D2}$
          THREE-LIST -------------------------------------------------

INFLUENCE$^{D2 \to D3}$                    INFLUENCE$^{D3 \to D2}$

THREE-LIST ----------------------------------------------------------------------

INFLUENCE$^{D2 \to D1}$
THREE-LIST

Of course these three aspects of culture influence one another.

Figure 8.6 Directing a verb toward elements of a THREE-LIST buoy

rapid instances of the directional verb INFLUENCE$^{x \to y}$. Each instance of
INFLUENCE$^{x \to y}$ is directed differently and shows a different type of influence. The efficiency of the multiple directional uses of INFLUENCE$^{x \to y}$ is
remarkable.[3] An English translation of each instance of that verb would require a full sentence. This is because each individual directed verb involves
considerable conceptual content. Figure 8.7 illustrates the mappings needed to
understand the final verb in Figure 8.6.

[3] She produced four instances of INFLUENCE$^{x \to y}$ in just under two seconds.

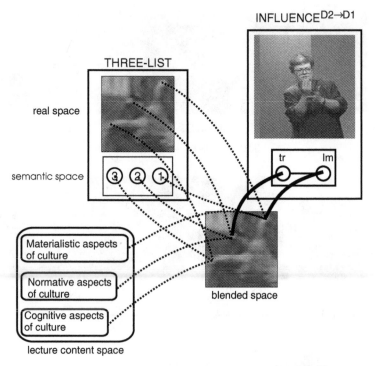

Figure 8.7 Mapping the semantic structure of INFLUENCE$^{D2 \to D1}$ onto the THREE-LIST buoy

Previous discourse has established that *D1* is a blend with materialistic aspects of culture, *D2* with normative aspects of a culture, and *D3* with cognitive aspects of culture. As a result, *D1–D3* already exist as conceptually complex blended elements. INFLUENCE$^{D2 \to D1}$ begins as shown in Figure 8.7, with the base of the strong hand in contact with *D2*. The hand then moves toward *D1*. This associates the trajector of INFLUENCE$^{D2 \to D1}$ with normative aspects of culture and the landmark with materialistic aspects of culture.

The sign INFLUENCE$^{x \to y}$ is an ordinary indicating verb that points at two things. The way it points in Figure 8.7 is no more complex than if it had been directed from an addressee toward the signer. In that case, the directionality would show that the addressee influences the signer. The complexity of the meaning expressed in Figure 8.7 is due to the complexity of the conceptual associations with the THREE-LIST buoy, not because the verb itself is more complex.

The signs in Figure 8.8 are produced by a different signer in the context of a discussion of professional basketball. He is asking whether there are breaks

LIST buoy

TIME-BREAK$^{\rightarrow D1\downarrow D2}$          TIME-BREAK$^{\rightarrow D2\downarrow D3}$ TIME-BREAK$^{\rightarrow D3\downarrow D4}$

FOUR-LIST ------------------------------------------------------------------------------------------

   Are there breaks between each of the four quarters?

   Figure 8.8  Locating breaks by locating the hand with respect to a FOUR-LIST buoy

between each quarter of play. Note that the question is marked by the nonmanual signal for an ASL yes–no question, which tilts the head forward and raises the eyebrows. Within the context of the blend, *D1–D4* are the four quarters of a basketball game.[4] He directs TIME-BREAK$^{\rightarrow L}$ between *D1* and *D2* to ask if there is a break between *D1* and *D2*, the first two quarters of a basketball game. He similarly asks whether there are breaks between each of the other quarters.

   During each instance of TIME-BREAK$^{\rightarrow L}$ the signer is still maintaining the FOUR-LIST buoy ahead of his chest. This buoy is conceptually complex, as illustrated in Figure 8.9.[5] The constructed meaning includes multiple mappings across five different spaces: the semantic pole of the FOUR-LIST buoy, both hands in real space, the professional basketball space, the resulting blend, and the semantic pole of TIME-BREAK$^{\rightarrow L}$. The sign TIME-BREAK$^{\rightarrow L}$ is directed at a place between two elements of the FOUR-LIST buoy. In the context of the question, the signer is asking whether there is a break at that location between *D1* and *D2* – the first and second quarters in professional basketball. The sign TIME-BREAK$^{\rightarrow L}$ is interesting in that its use depends on a spatial metaphor. It uses physical locations to talk about sequences of temporal events. The sign is placed at a physical location between the two entities *D1* and *D2* in order to talk about the "placement" of a break "between" the first and second quarters of a basketball game. It does so by physically placing the hand producing the sign between *D1* and *D2*.

---

[4] The palm-down form of TIME-BREAK$^{\rightarrow L}$ that appears in this example appears to be an allomorph of the palm-up form shown in Figure 8.2. The palm-down form appears to be preferred with horizontal movements.

[5] The notation IS in Figure 8.9 is the abbreviation for the immediate scope of the predication used in Langacker (1999b). The horizontal line through the immediate scope is his symbolization for an imperfective process.

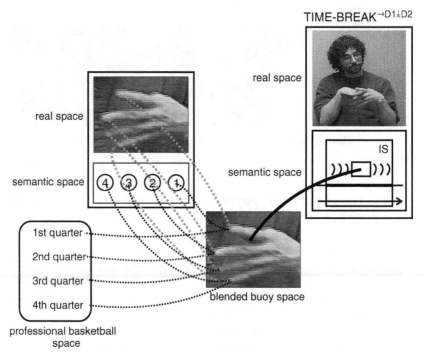

Figure 8.9  The mappings based on the directionality of TIME-BREAK$^{\rightarrow D1 \downarrow D2}$

Illustrating all the projection lines for the self-blending buoys creates diagrams with a large number of projection lines. This can make the diagrams difficult to follow. In order to simplify diagrams involving buoys, I omit the self-blending mappings as I have done in Figure 8.10.

Here, the diagram illustrates only how the four quarters of a basketball game blend with the four extended fingertips. Although subsequent diagrams are simplified in this way, the reader should keep in mind that this is an abbreviated representation since it does not represent the buoy's self-blending nature.

### Manipulating list buoys

In the next example the signer has described the four children of one of his brothers and has associated each one with *D1–D4* of a FOUR-LIST buoy. He has also explained that the first two children come from one marriage and that the remaining two children come from another marriage. Figure 8.11a shows the FOUR-LIST buoy at the conclusion of those descriptions.

TIME-BREAK $^{\rightarrow \text{D1}\updownarrow\text{D2}}$

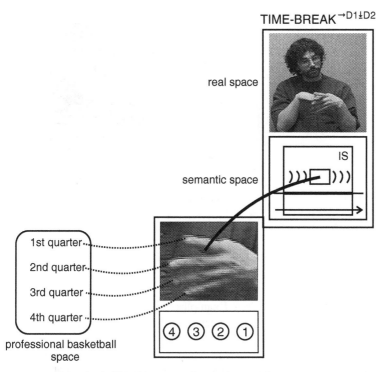

real space

semantic space

1st quarter

2nd quarter

3rd quarter

4th quarter

professional basketball
space

Figure 8.10 Simplifying the diagram by omitting the self-blending mappings
of the FOUR-LIST buoy

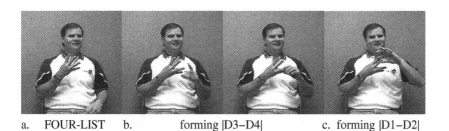

a.   FOUR-LIST   b.            forming |D3–D4|          c. forming |D1–D2|

Figure 8.11 Deforming the FOUR-LIST buoy

The signer then uses his strong hand to deform the buoy. In Figure 8.11b he
squeezes *D3* and *D4* together. Then in Figure 8.11c he squeezes *D1* and *D2*
together. This deformation is a means of showing that the first two children
form a conceptual unit as do the second set of two children. I am calling the
resulting handshape a deformation of the FOUR-LIST buoy because, in general,

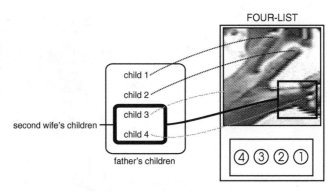

Figure 8.12 Forming the new conceptual unit |D3–D4|

the deformed handshapes appear to be limited only by physical dexterity.[6] The conceptual consequences of squeezing *D3* and *D4* together are illustrated in Figure 8.12. At this point only *D3* and *D4* have been united. *D1* and *D2* are still separate.

By squeezing *D3* and *D4* together, the signer creates |D3–D4|, a new conceptual unit containing both children. Examples of a single conceptual real-space blend containing parts have already been described and illustrated in chapter 7. In one example involving a token blend, the space containing |Deaf people| and |hearing people| was conceptually and spatially reified into a comparison space containing those two entities. Figure 8.12 illustrates a similar conceptual result. The signer does not explain why he joins the fingers together. He has already explained that each of the man's wives had two children. Given that context, it is clear that the children can be understood as consisting of two distinct sets because they have different mothers.

In Figure 8.13 another signer has deformed the FOUR-LIST buoy by uniting *D1* and *D2* and also uniting *D3* and *D4*. Unlike the example in Figure 8.11, he does not use his other hand to produce the deformation. He simply places his fingers in this configuration in order to discuss the two halves of a college basketball game. This occurred in the context of a discussion about the number of minutes in a basketball game and the time differences between high school, college, and professional basketball games. The signer begins with the topic COLLEGE, making it clear that he is now talking about college basketball. Note that the weak hand of COLLEGE, normally a B, is already in the shape of the deformed FOUR-LIST buoy. This is because the signer has already produced

---

[6] I recently watched a native signer talking about five entities. She was attempting to express that the five entities formed two groups. The first group consisted of *D1* and *D2*. The second group consisted of *D3–D5*. She struggled quite a bit trying to form a handshape in which the thumb and index fingers were adjacent and the remaining three fingers were together. The resulting handshape does not occur in any lexical signs of ASL.

_____t
COLLEGE        [TWENTY]$^{\rightarrow|D1-D2|}$    [TWENTY]$^{\rightarrow|D3-D4|}$
FOUR-LIST-------------------------------------------------------------

      grasp |D1–D2|                          grasp |D3–D4|  CONTINUE$^{[\text{HABITUAL}]}$
FOUR-LIST-----------------------------------------------------------

College games have twenty minutes per half, and each half is played continuously.

Figure 8.13  Building additional conceptual units by uniting fingers

the five preceding signs with his strong hand while maintaining the deformed buoy in this position.

As in the previous example, uniting the two pairs of fingers creates two new conceptual entities: |D1–D2| 'first half' and |D3–D4| 'second half'. He next signs [TWENTY]$^{\rightarrow|D1-D2|}$ then [TWENTY]$^{\rightarrow|D3-D4|}$. Producing TWENTY in contact with these two conceptual entities associates the value 'twenty' with each one. Given that he is discussing minutes in a basketball game, these two signs associate twenty minutes with each half.

There is a marked change in facial expression after [TWENTY]$^{\rightarrow|D3-D4|}$. He grasps |D1–D2| then |D3–D4|, identifying these two entities as the entities to associate with the semantic structure of CONTINUE$^{[\text{HABITUAL}]}$. In other words, the signer is stating that the two conceptual entities, |D1–D2| and |D3–D4|, are played continuously (i.e. no breaks between the two parts of each).

### The FOUR-WEEK-LIST buoy

It is common for signers to use what appears to be a variant of the FOUR-LIST buoy to represent four weeks. I use the gloss FOUR-WEEK-LIST to

FOUR-WEEK-LIST

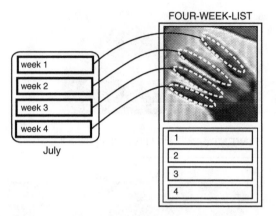

week 1

week 2

week 3

week 4

July

1

2

3

4

Figure 8.14  The entire length of the fingers represents weeks in the FOUR-WEEK-LIST buoy

APPROXIMATELY-THIS-LEVEL

FOUR-WEEK-LIST

Around the final week of the month.

Figure 8.15  Showing an approximate time by the placement of APPROXI-MATELY-THIS-LEVEL

talk about this buoy. Although it looks exactly like the FOUR-LIST buoy, I am treating it as distinct because of the nature of the mappings and the resulting way the strong hand interacts with it. In Figure 8.15, the signer signs #JULY FOUR-WEEK-LIST followed by an up-and-down movement of a bent B hand near *D4*. Signing #JULY prior to the appearance of the FOUR-WEEK-LIST buoy is an instruction to map the weeks of July onto it as illustrated in Figure 8.14. The mappings are different from previous mappings in that the weeks of July are mapped onto the entire length of the extended fingers.

Figure 8.15 captures two frames of the signer moving his active bent B hand up and down twice in the vicinity of *D4*. Given the mappings described in

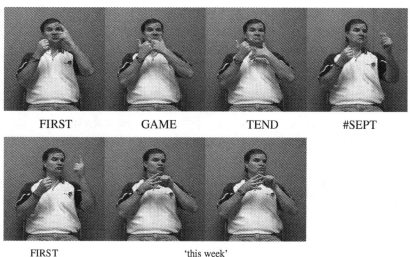

FIRST            GAME            TEND            #SEPT

FIRST                          'this week'
                      FOUR-WEEK-LIST
The first game tends to be during the first week of September.

Figure 8.16  Each entire finger represents a week

Figure 8.14, moving the hand in this way expresses the meaning, 'around the last week of July'.

If the signer's intention is not only to identify a particular week, but to talk about the extent of the week, that is done by contacting the body of the finger. For example, in Figure 8.16 the signer is explaining that the football season tends to start during the first week of September. He does this by signing FIRST GAME TEND #SEPT, FIRST (week), followed by moving the tip of the index finger of his strong hand back and forth along the radial surface of *D1* on the FOUR-WEEK-LIST buoy. This movement is illustrated in Figure 8.16.

The elements of other list buoys are typically identified by contacting the tip of the extended digit. In Figure 8.16, however, the signer moves his fingertip back and forth along the radial surface of *D1* on the FOUR-WEEK-LIST buoy. This motion treats the entire length of the finger, rather than simply the fingertip, as a week. The movement along the body of the finger expresses the meaning '*during* the first week of September' rather than simply 'the first week in September'.

In the following example, another signer also uses the FOUR-WEEK-LIST buoy. She not only makes contact with the fingertips to identify specific weeks, she also utilizes the spaces between the fingers. She begins with the topic OUR PROGRAM MEETING, followed by the explanation that there will be a

OUR            |            PROGRAM

|            MEETING

|            {WILL}-ALTOGETHER            |            FOUR

NOW            SEMESTER

FOUR-WEEK-LIST

Our program will have a total of four program meetings this semester.

Figure 8.17  A description ending with a FOUR-WEEK-LIST buoy

total of four (meetings) during the semester. This explanation is illustrated in Figure 8.17.

The sign {WILL}-ALTOGETHER is produced exactly like ALTOGETHER, except that it begins with the thumb in contact with the cheek. I am treating this contact as a bound future morpheme.[7] I have observed such cheek contact signifying 'future' with only a very small number of verbs: {WILL}-COME (one-handed sign produced with a 1 handshape beginning with fingertip contact with the cheek), {WILL}-DEPART (one-handed sign produced with an outward movement changing from a 5 to an A handshape, beginning with the index finger in contact with the cheek). Graduate students in the linguistics program at Gallaudet University also observed a native signer producing {WILL}-BRING (beginning with the tip of one B hand in contralateral contact with the cheek). These examples could represent the beginning of the development of a prefix or clitic expressing the meaning 'future'. Currently, however, this incipient bound future morpheme appears to be rarely used.

After mentioning that she will have four program meetings, the signer produces what appears to be a FOUR-WEEK-LIST buoy. Note that she produces FOUR with her strong hand and the FOUR-WEEK-LIST buoy with her weak hand. Next, in Figure 8.18, she explains that the meetings will take place every other week by signing the reduplicated {WEEK}{TWO}[EVERY], where each repetition is produced at a lower level than the preceding one. As a result, D1–D4 blend with weeks rather than meetings. For this reason I am treating the buoy as a FOUR-WEEK-LIST buoy rather than a FOUR-LIST buoy. This raises an interesting issue. Normally the FOUR-WEEK-LIST buoy is used to represent a month. In this example, because of the fact that the signer has mentioned that the meetings are two weeks apart, the weeks represented by the FOUR-WEEK-LIST buoy are not adjacent weeks.

In Figure 8.18 she produces {WEEK}{TWO}[EVERY] with five reduplicated movements. It is interesting to note that although the signer has associated four different weeks with four program meetings, she produces five reduplicated movements. This shows that she is not merely producing a movement for each week with a meeting. Rather, {WEEK}{TWO}[EVERY] expresses its meaning through multiple reduplicated movements – not necessarily the same number as the number of meetings. Given the context in which the signer is describing four meetings on alternate weeks, one meeting will be associated with each of the extended fingers, represented on the left side of Figure 8.19.

The mappings between the meetings and the buoy are not blending projections. They are semantic associations between the meetings and the weeks. The extended fingers do not become visual representations of meetings through blending, but rather, remain visual representations of weeks. That is, directing signs toward D1 would identify the week blended with D1, not the meeting that takes place during that week.

---

[7] See Liddell (1996b) for a description of ASL prefixes that attach to numeral signs. Two of these prefixes also involve a single contact that takes on the handshape and orientation of the stem it is prefixed to.

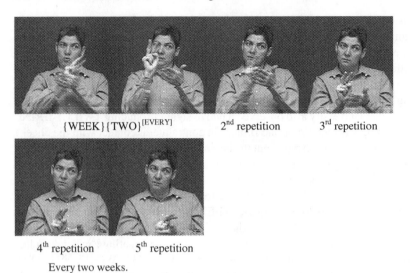

{WEEK}{TWO}[EVERY]          2nd repetition          3rd repetition

4th repetition     5th repetition

Every two weeks.

Figure 8.18 The reduplication of {WEEK}{TWO}[EVERY] at five different levels

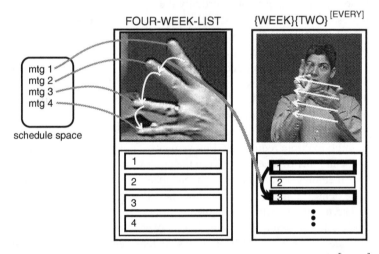

Figure 8.19 Mapping the semantic contribution of {WEEK}{TWO}[EVERY] onto the FOUR-WEEK-LIST buoy

Because of the semantic association between meetings and weeks, each of those weeks has a meeting associated with it. In addition, because of the semantic contribution of {TWO}{WEEK}[EVERY], the meetings are now understood to be two weeks apart. The set of mappings between the semantic structure

'these two weeks'                    CAN                          PRO-1
FOUR-WEEK-LIST-------------------------------------------------------------------------

    I can meet during these two weeks.

Figure 8.20 Pointing at the conceptual weeks between the fingers of the
FOUR-WEEK-LIST buoy

of {TWO}{WEEK}[EVERY] and the FOUR-WEEK-LIST buoy is illustrated on
the right of Figure 8.19. The consequence for the FOUR-WEEK-LIST buoy
blend is that now there are weeks between the extended fingers.

All this description is a prelude to describing possible and impossible times
for scheduling an additional meeting. She states that if the addressee wants to
meet with her, it will have to be during a week when there is no program meeting.
She identifies the weeks when no meeting can be scheduled by sequentially
contacting the tips of *D1* through *D4*. She identifies the available weeks by
pointing to the spaces between each of the extended fingers.

Later, she explains that she is busy during the week between *D1* and *D2*.
She concludes by explaining that she is available for a meeting on either the
week prior to or just after the third program meeting. Figure 8.20 illustrates
how she uses the extended index and middle fingers of her strong hand to point
directly at where those weeks are conceptualized in the blend – on either side
of *D3*.

After using the extended index and middle fingers of her strong hand to
identify the available times, she states CAN, PRO-1 (I can meet during these
weeks).[8] This is possible because she has already explained that the four weeks
*D1–D4* are not consecutive. This leaves a week between each of the extended
fingers.

I am not treating the pointing by the V hand as a lexical unit, but rather, as
a convenient gestural means of pointing at two things at once. A V hand can
similarly indicate both entities associated with a TWO-LIST buoy by tapping
the tips of the two extended fingers of the buoy with the pads of the two fingers

---

[8] The syntax of this example involves the modal CAN followed by the subject pronoun tag (PRO-1),
which adds emphasis to the statement. It is not an example of reversed (verb–subject) constituent
order.

of the V hand. In fact, a signer in another example used a V hand to indicate both entities associated with a TWO-LIST buoy by tapping the inside surfaces of both fingers of the TWO-LIST buoy with the outside surfaces of the two extended fingers of the V hand. In Figure 8.20 the pointing is done by means of inserting the two extended fingers on either side of *D3* on the FOUR-WEEK-LIST buoy, thereby indicating both the week prior to the third meeting and the week after that meeting.

Had the weeks on the FOUR-WEEK-LIST buoy been consecutive, the signing in Figure 8.20 would make no sense. The reason is not grammatical, but conceptual. Had the weeks been consecutive, it would make no sense to point on either side of *D3* since, conceptually, there are no additional weeks between consecutive weeks.

### The THEME buoy

The THEME buoy is different from the previously described list buoys in that its presence signifies that an important discourse theme is being discussed. It takes the form of a raised, typically vertical index finger on the weak hand held in place as the strong hand produces one or more signs.

Figure 8.21 provides an example of the THEME buoy. These signs come after she has explained that in the first part of her teleconference she will analyze several aspects of the theory of language and culture. As she makes this explanation, her torso is rotated slightly to the left and her head and eye gaze are directed to the left. As previously discussed, this creates a blended theory space in front of her leftward-rotated body. She directs the palm surfaces of the hands producing ANALYZE$^{[\text{EXHAUSTIVE}]\,\text{ɔ|multiple entities|}}$ (not illustrated) toward that space as the hands move vertically downward. This indicates that she will analyze multiple things related to language and culture. Next, she produces the signs in Figure 8.21. With her body still rotated to the left, she produces the sign IDENTIFY$^{[\text{EXHAUSTIVE}]\,\text{ɔ|multiple entities|}}$ as a single downward-moving reduplicated sign making three contacts with the palm. The hand oscillates back and forth between contact and non-contact with the palm as it moves downward. The first two frames in Figure 8.21 illustrate the first and third contacts. This verb functions as a single clause without an overt subject or object. It expresses that in the teleconference she will identify multiple things in the process of discussing culture and language theory.

Recall that exhaustive verb forms move along a path directed toward the elements to map onto the verb's semantic pole. She had previously directed ANALYZE$^{[\text{EXHAUSTIVE}]\,\text{ɔ|multiple entities|}}$ toward the same location on the left. Directing IDENTIFY$^{[\text{EXHAUSTIVE}]\,\text{ɔ|multiple entities|}}$ toward the same

IDENTIFY[EXHAUSTIVE]ↄ|multiple entities|.

UNDERSTAND          POSS-CHARACTER[EXHAUSTIVE]ↄ|multiple entities|.
[THEME]→|theory|

(I will) identify several aspects of the theory of language and culture (so that

you will) understand the nature of those things.

Figure 8.21  Keeping a space active by using the THEME buoy

token |multiple entities| within the theory space indicates a mapping between the landmark of IDENTIFY[EXHAUSTIVE]ↄ|multiple entities| and |multiple entities|.

The following clause in Figure 8.21, UNDERSTAND POSS-CHARACTER[EXHAUSTIVE]ↄ|multiple entities|, expresses that the audience will understand the characteristics of those multiple things. The final frame shows the beginning of the downward reduplicated form POSS-CHARACTER[EXHAUSTIVE]ↄ|multiple entities| with the hands doubled and directed toward |multiple entities|. The direction of POSS-CHARACTER[EXHAUSTIVE]ↄ|multiple entities| indicates a mapping between its trajector (the possessor of the characteristics) and |multiple entities|. In other words, she will be describing the characteristics of the multiple entities within the theory space.

As she signs UNDERSTAND, she holds the index finger of her left hand toward the theory space. The raised index finger in Figure 8.21 is producing an instance of the THEME buoy.[9] Here it takes on the significance of the discussion of theory, including the multiple entities that are part of the theory space. Like

---

[9] Boris Fridman first observed the raised index finger serving to represent a significant element of a narrative he and I were examining (see Fridman and Liddell 1998).

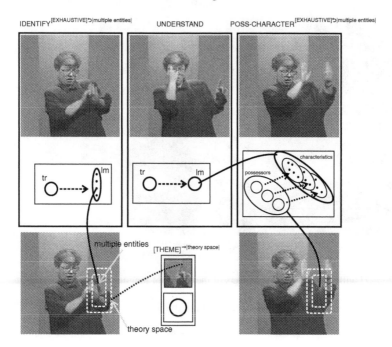

Figure 8.22  Mappings between semantic structure and the |theory| space

all buoys discussed so far, it is self-blending. This means that its form and meaning blend to produce a visible representation of a significant discourse theme. In Figure 8.22 it additionally blends with the theory space to become a visible representation of that space as a significant discourse theme.

I am tentatively treating the THEME buoy as not having a lexical requirement to be directed in space. I am treating the fact that it is directed in this example as an instance of pointing overlaid on the THEME buoy. In chapter 6 I enclose nondirectional signs that have overlaid pointing inside square brackets to indicate that pointing is overlaid on the sign. Thus, if the nondirectional sign TWO were directed at entity $a$, I would transcribe that as [TWO]$^{\rightarrow a}$. Here, where the THEME buoy has been directed toward the |theory| space, I notate that as [THEME]$^{\rightarrow |theory|}$.

By directing the THEME buoy toward the |theory| space, the signer indicates that the discussion of theory is a significant discourse theme. The handshape of the THEME buoy blends with the discourse theme it is directed toward to create a visible representation of the theory space and the multiple entities within it.

I propose in chapter 7 that a signer keeps a blend active by facing the blended space. During UNDERSTAND the lecturer faces away from the space on the left and directs her head and gaze forward toward her audience. Doing so appears to signify that the audience, rather than a lecturer, will understand those aspects of the theory at that point. But in order to face the audience, she must turn away from the theory space on her left. Directing [THEME]$^{\rightarrow |theory|}$ toward the theory space appears to keep the theory space active, even though the signer is not facing that space at that moment.

UNDERSTAND and POSS-CHARACTER$^{[EXHAUSTIVE]\,\circ|multiple\ entities|}$ appear to be in a verb–object relationship since the signer is expressing the meaning 'understand the characteristics of those things'. For that reason I am treating POSS-CHARACTER$^{[EXHAUSTIVE]\,\circ|multiple\ entities|}$ as a nominal encoding multiple characteristics of multiple possessors of those characteristics. The noun's semantic pole includes both multiple possessors and the multiple characteristics of those possessors. The hands producing POSS-CHARACTER$^{[EXHAUSTIVE]\,\circ|multiple\ entities|}$ are directed toward the possessors of the characteristics. The landmark of UNDERSTAND links to the characteristics associated with the possessors.

The next example of a THEME buoy involves code mixing. A high percentage of signers are bilingual in ASL and English. When bilinguals communicate with other bilinguals there are opportunities for code switching and code mixing. In the following example the signer produces a mixture of ASL vocabulary and English sentence structure. Even in this context, the use of the THEME buoy to represent a major discourse theme nevertheless appears. This example is taken from a story in which the narrator describes his experience as a fourth-grader. At the very beginning of the narrative, the signer introduces himself. Shortly thereafter, he explains that his experience as a fourth-grader truly stood out in his mind. This experience is the theme of his approximately six-minute narrative.

In contrast to the previous narrative, the signer does not create the blend by directing the THEME buoy toward a previously established space. Here he places it centrally as he simultaneously signs EXPERIENCE (Figure 8.23). Producing EXPERIENCE and the THEME buoy together signals a blend of their two semantic poles and the extended index finger. In the resulting blend the extended index finger represents the memorable experience.

The sign EXPERIENCE is followed by the sign THAT$_{ENG}$. This sign commonly appears in ASL–English code mixing as a means of representing the English word *that*. It is produced with an active Y hand making contact with the weak hand in a palm-up B configuration. In this case, however, the THEME buoy itself substitutes for the normal B weak hand as a place of articulation for the sign THAT$_{ENG}$. The fact that the THEME buoy remains in place to serve as the base hand for the sign THAT$_{ENG}$ provides additional evidence of its significance.

ONE            EXPERIENCE            THAT$_{ENG}$
                THEME-- ----------------------------------
'One experience that ...'

Figure 8.23  The THEME buoy directly ahead of the signer's chest

PRO-1                THINK^CONTACT[DURATIONAL]
                    THEME
I keep thinking about (that experience).

Figure 8.24  The reappearance of the THEME buoy during the first part of the compound verb THINK^CONTACT[DURATIONAL]

Shortly thereafter, the signer produces the subject–verb sequence shown in Figure 8.24.

During the production of the subject PRO-1, the weak hand with the extended index finger moves up toward the central location the THEME buoy will occupy. At the beginning of the compound verb THINK^CONTACT[DURATIONAL] the THEME buoy is in place, once again signifying his fourth-grade experience.

The THEME buoy appears one more time, approximately five minutes later, at the end of the narrative. Here he is explaining that there were many things that the hard-of-hearing students had in the fourth grade that he enjoyed and misses. That explanation ends with the signs FOURTH G-R-A-D-E, PRO$^{\rightarrow |THEME|}$. As he mentions FOURTH G-R-A-D-E he begins moving his hand into position to produce [THEME]$^{\rightarrow a}$. By the time he produces the sign for the letter *D*, as he is spelling G-R-A-D-E, [THEME]$^{\rightarrow a}$ is fully in place on his left. He then produces PRO$^{\rightarrow |THEME|}$ (the initial sign in Figure 8.25), identifying it as the blended entity associated with those aspects of his fourth-grade experience.

PRO $^{\rightarrow[\text{THEME}]}$.    PRO-1    MISS;    ENJOY

[THEME]$^{\rightarrow a}$ ----------------------------------------------------------------------------

(Produces PRO$^{\rightarrow[\text{THEME}]}$ after mentioning aspects of the fourth grade experience). I miss those things; I enjoyed them.

Figure 8.25 The final instance of the THEME buoy, this time signifying the positive aspects of the fourth grade experience

During the narrative the signer created a token space to his left associated with the school he attended as a fourth-grader and later, another token space on the left associated with his fourth-grade classroom. Placing the THEME buoy on the left is consistent with the placement of those tokens. Now, however, the THEME buoy takes on a slightly different significance. Now he produces [THEME]$^{\rightarrow a}$, with the sign directed toward the left where those token spaces existed, to talk about the positive aspects of his experiences as a fourth-grader.

While keeping [THEME]$^{\rightarrow a}$ in place, he then signs PRO-1 MISS; ENJOY 'I miss those things...I enjoyed them.' The THEME buoy is present throughout this string of signs as shown in Figure 8.25.

ENJOY is the final sign in Figure 8.25 and is normally produced with two hands. It is a semantically transitive sign that typically does not allow an overt object (cf. chapter 2). That is, the thing enjoyed will have been mentioned either as a topic or as a prominent entity in the discourse. The positive aspects of the signer's experiences as a fourth-grader are prominent in the discourse since those positive aspects have blended with the THEME buoy. The signer produces the verb MISS in the presence of the THEME buoy. The significance is that he misses those positive aspects of his fourth-grade experience. He then signs the normally two-handed verb ENJOY with one hand while the other hand maintains the THEME buoy in place. Again, the presence of the THEME buoy makes it clear what he enjoyed.

Five minutes previously he used the THEME buoy when talking about his experience as a fourth-grader. Now, at the end of the narrative, while discussing the positive aspects of that experience, he directs [THEME]$^{\rightarrow a}$ toward the spaces used to talk about the school and the classroom, this time to single out the positive aspects of that fourth-grade experience.

a.         LINGUISTICS              THEORY

b.         IT-IS-TIME                        SPEAK^#OUT

Figure 8.26  Examples of weak hand perseveration

**Fragment buoys**

A typical stretch of discourse consists of both one-handed and two-handed signs. During the production of two-handed signs the movement, placement, handshape, and orientation of the weak hand is significant since it is part of the sign being produced. When a one-handed sign follows a two-handed sign, it is common for the weak hand to maintain its configuration from the preceding two-handed sign as the strong hand produces the following one-handed sign. When this occurs, the weak hand is said to *perseverate* into the succeeding one-handed sign (Liddell and Johnson 1989).

For example, in Figure 8.26a the signer produces the two-handed sign LINGUISTICS followed by the one-handed sign THEORY. After producing LINGUISTICS, the left hand remains in place with the handshape, location, and orientation which ended the sign LINGUISTICS as the other hand produces THEORY. In Figure 8.26b the signer signs IT-IS-TIME SPEAK^#OUT (It is time to speak out). Once again, the weak hand configuration present during the two-handed IT-IS-TIME perseverates into the following sign. Such examples of perseveration involve sign fragments. That is, in Figure 8.26a, after the sign LINGUISTICS is complete, a fragment of the sign remains in view. The fragment does not appear to serve any semantic function. At times, however, a signer may choose to assign semantic significance to a fragment of the preceding sign. Dudis (2000) provides clear examples distinguishing perseveration

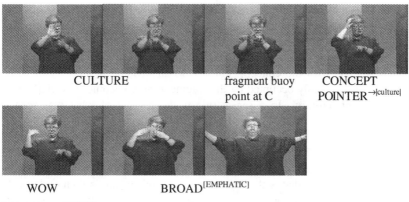

CULTURE                    fragment buoy        CONCEPT
                           point at C           POINTER$^{→|culture|}$

WOW                    BROAD$^{[EMPHATIC]}$
POINTER$^{→|culture|}$

Figure 8.27 Creating a fragment buoy from the C hand that produced
CULTURE

from cases where signers assign meaning to sign fragments. He argues that by
directing attention to the fragment, the signer creates a meaningful blend with
the hand in that configuration.

In Figure 8.27 the lecturer is introducing the concept of culture. She first
signs CULTURE by moving the active C hand in an arc around the stationary
1 hand. At the conclusion of the sign, she twice directs her index finger at
the now stationary C hand. In addition, her eye gaze is also directed at the C
handshape. This accomplishes two things. First, it establishes the concept of
culture as important in the discourse. Second, it produces a blend in which the
C handshape temporarily becomes a buoy signifying 'culture'. I describe such
a buoy as a *fragment buoy*. It differs from the other types of buoys described
previously in that it is created on the fly from a fragment of a just produced
sign.

This particular fragment buoy disappears right after it is created. It is gone
during the production of the very next sign CONCEPT. In spite of its brief
tenure as a fragment buoy, it nevertheless establishes the concept 'culture' as
significant and also creates a blend in which the sign fragment takes on the
significance 'culture'. In this particular example, even though the fragment
buoy disappears, she continues to point toward the right with her left hand even
after the fragment buoy is gone. This reflects a new blend in which culture
is associated with the *space* to the right of the signer, rather than with the
fragment.

Although this particular fragment buoy involves creating a blend with the
active hand, it is probably more typical to create a fragment buoy from the

weak hand. The active hand may have been involved in this case because the hand pointing at the fragment buoy (cf. "the pointer buoy" later in this chapter) is maintained and this is also a weak hand activity.[10]

In this sequence the signer moves from a blend where the visible C hand-shape blends with the concept 'culture' to an invisible spatial blend where the space previously occupied by the fragment buoy becomes associated with the concept 'culture'. In a sense, this is the reverse of what was seen in Figure 8.22. That example began with an invisible spatial blending of a discussion of theory and the space ahead of the signer's leftward-rotated body. By directing THEME toward the left, THEME took on the significance of the space it was directed toward. In Figure 8.27, the signing *begins* with the visible fragment buoy blended with the concept 'culture', which is then replaced by a new blend in which the space containing the buoy takes on the significance 'culture'. Such alternations between visible blends and invisible spatial blends are frequent in ASL discourse.

### The POINTER buoy

The POINTER buoy is also a weak hand configuration maintained while the strong hand produces one or more other signs. The pointing weak hand in Figure 8.27 is an example of a pointer buoy. It continues to point toward |culture| in the spatial blend to the right of the signer as the other hand produces CONCEPT and WOW. The POINTER buoy differs from all the other buoys discussed in this chapter in that the POINTER buoy does not acquire any new significance through blending. Instead, it *points toward* an important element in the discourse.

The sign sequence in Figure 8.28 provides another example of the POINTER buoy. Prior to this sequence the signer was discussing having previously looked through a list of course offerings that did not interest him. This involved a blended space in which he, in the role of a surrogate, looked at a course list conceptualized directly ahead of him. Next, in Figure 8.28, he describes looking at a list of courses two years later. Given the context, it was not necessary to mention course offerings again. Signing GAZE-THROUGH-LIST[ᶜᵖʸ] in this context is sufficient to create a new blend in which he once again becomes a

---

[10] Ahlgren and Bergman (1994) discuss a related, but apparently distinct, phenomenon they describe as producing a *referential cue*. This also frequently involves the weak hand. For example, a signer could be describing a person driving. While holding the weak hand in position, as if holding on to a steering wheel, the other hand can continue signing. By maintaining the weak hand in position the signer provides a referential cue that the actions of the person holding the steering wheel are being constructed. In such a case, the weak hand is not giving special significance to the concept expressed by the verb DRIVE, but rather, provides a referential cue as to the identity of the surrogate whose actions are being constructed.

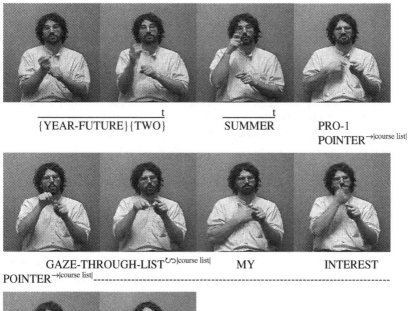

|         t |         t | |
|---|---|---|
| {YEAR-FUTURE}{TWO} | SUMMER | PRO-1<br>POINTER<sup>→|course list|</sup> |

GAZE-THROUGH-LIST<sup>ᴗᴐ|course list|</sup>   MY         INTEREST
POINTER<sup>→|course list|</sup> --------------------------------------------------------------------------------

GAZE-THROUGH-LIST<sup>ᴗᴐ|course list|</sup>
POINTER<sup>→|course list|</sup>

Two summers later I looked through a course list and it had courses I was interested in.

Figure 8.28 Directing a POINTER buoy toward a |course list|

surrogate looking at a course list. The moving index finger of the right hand is directed vertically down the extent of the |course list|.

This sequence begins with two topics. The first is {YEAR-FUTURE}{TWO} 'two years future/later' and the second is SUMMER. I treat these as separate topics because of the slight but significant difference in head position between the two signs. The difference is difficult to see in the still pictures, but there is a perceptible more forward head tilt during SUMMER. These two topics provide the temporal setting for the blended space utilized by the following signs.

These topics are followed by the first person singular pronoun PRO-1. Note that during the production of PRO-1 the left hand has completed its rise to the position it will maintain as the POINTER buoy during the production of the verb and subsequent signs. The index finger actually begins to emerge during the topic SUMMER. The appearance of the POINTER buoy anticipates the blend that serves as the basis for the directionality of the following verb.

The verb's directionality in Figure 8.28 is based on a surrogate |course list| ahead of a surrogate |self two years later|. After signing PRO-1, the POINTER buoy (produced by the weak hand) points at the |course list| during the verb GAZE-THROUGH-LIST<sup>⌣ɔ|course list|</sup>. The path of the strong hand indicates the path of the gazing and, therefore, reflects the vertical nature of the list. This signer's eye gaze moves along the same path as the index finger.

The surrogate |self two years later| begins gazing at the top of the |course list| and his eye gaze moves down the list following the movement of the index finger. Additionally, the surrogate's facial expression shows an interested affect. These characteristics support the conclusion that the spatial representation utilized by the verb is a surrogate space and that, through blending, the signer has become himself in the past at the time of looking, as illustrated in Figure 8.29.

As subject of the verb GAZE-THROUGH-LIST<sup>⌣ɔ|course list|</sup> the pronoun PRO-1 maps its meaning 'current signer' onto the trajector of GAZE-THROUGH-LIST<sup>⌣ɔ|course list|</sup>. This is the horizontal mapping between the semantic pole of PRO-1 and the verb's trajector in Figure 8.29. In addition, because of its semantics, PRO-1 maps onto the 'current signer', who might be the signer in real space or a surrogate signer. During the clause being examined, a surrogate appears during the production of the verb. The one narrating, during both PRO-1 and the following verb, however, is the real-space signer. For this reason I have mapped PRO-1's semantic pole onto the real-space signer. So far, this set of mappings indicates that the current real-space signer corresponds, indirectly through a mapping chain, to the verb's trajector.

We have not yet, however, considered the blended space created by the signer. The current signer and his counterpart in the 'two years later' space being described blend to create the surrogate |self two years later|. Finally, the fingertip of the strong hand and the eye gaze of the surrogate |self two years later| are directed toward the |course list| in the blend. The semantic pole of the verb maps onto the surrogate space as shown by the two solid connectors. The trajector maps onto |self two years later|, the only obvious agent in that space. The directionality of the moving index finger motivates the mapping between the landmark and the |course list|.

The temporal setting of the past event space is also projected into the blend, so that the actions within the surrogate blend take place 'two years later'. But the immediacy of real space is also part of the surrogate blend. Thus, the event that takes place 'two years later' is also taking place in front of the addressee. It is a here-and-now, partial reenactment through blending of the event that took place 'two years later'.

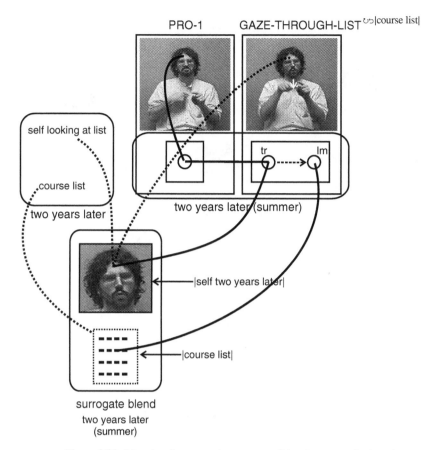

PRO-1            GAZE-THROUGH-LIST<sup>ᵕᵓ|course list|</sup>

self looking at list

.course list

two years later

two years later (summer)

tr        lm

|self two years later|

|course list|

surrogate blend
two years later
(summer)

Figure 8.29 Mapping the semantic structure of the clause onto both real space and the surrogate blend

The POINTER buoy also points at the |course list|. This is followed by the nominal phrase MY INTEREST produced by the strong hand while the weak hand POINTER buoy is still pointing at the |course list|. Here, the POINTER buoy serves an important semantic function by identifying the mental space entity, the |course list|, corresponding to the nominal MY INTEREST. This is followed by a repetition of GAZE-THROUGH-LIST<sup>ᵕᵓ|course list|</sup>, which begins higher than before apparently due to the preceding verb. The POINTER buoy remains in place, pointing at the |course list| during all these signs.

In the next example another signer is describing an imagined trip into Japan's distant past. She is describing some of the cultural differences that Western-ers might encounter. The signs in Figure 8.30 describe the need for the time

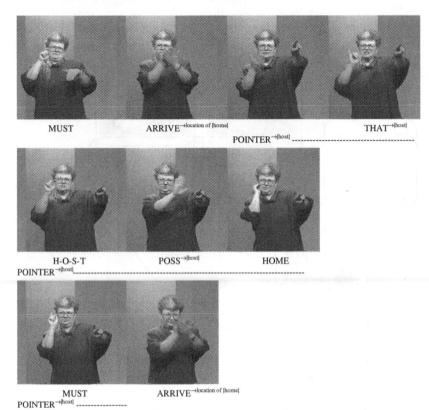

MUST          ARRIVE<sup>→location of |home|</sup>                                    THAT<sup>→|host|</sup>
                        POINTER<sup>→|host|</sup> -------------------------------------------

H-O-S-T          POSS<sup>→|host|</sup>          HOME
POINTER<sup>→|host|</sup>-------------------------------------------------------------------------

MUST          ARRIVE<sup>→location of |home|</sup>
POINTER<sup>→|host|</sup> -----------------
(We) must arrive at the host's home—we must arrive there.

Figure 8.30  An extended use of a POINTER buoy

travelers to arrive at a host's house. She first signs MUST ARRIVE<sup>→L</sup>, where
ARRIVE<sup>→L</sup> is directed toward a location at about shoulder height just to
the left of center. The final instance of ARRIVE<sup>→L</sup> is also directed slightly
to the left of center at about the same height. This sign is directed at a location –
the place the group is supposed to arrive at. Thus, in Figure 8.30, both instances
of ARRIVE<sup>→L</sup> are transcribed as ARRIVE<sup>→location of |home|</sup>. After the first in-
stance of ARRIVE<sup>→location of |home|</sup> the signer directs a pointer to the left with
her left hand. While still pointing to the left she signs THAT<sup>→|host|</sup> H-O-S-T
POSS<sup>→|host|</sup> HOME.

The entity THAT<sup>→|host|</sup> is directed toward is the |host|. This becomes evident
because of the spelling H-O-S-T that immediately follows THAT<sup>→|host|</sup>. Note
that both THAT<sup>→|host|</sup>, the non-first person possessive sign POSS<sup>→|host|</sup>, and
the POINTER buoy are all directed to the left and well ahead of the signer.

BUT              FOOD              DELICIOUS
POINTER$^{\rightarrow|food|}$----------------------
But the food was delicious.

Figure 8.31  A POINTER buoy directed down toward |food|

In addition, both the first and second instances of ARRIVE$^{\rightarrow \text{location of }|home|}$ are directed to the left. But ARRIVE$^{\rightarrow L}$ is directed toward a destination. If one imagines that the host is at home, which is the case in this narrative, then the host and the home are co-located. This allows POSS$^{\rightarrow|host|}$ to be directed to the left toward the |host| and ARRIVE$^{\rightarrow L}$ to be directed toward the left toward the location of the host and his home.

The signer next describes having a meal in the host's home. During the meal the group sits on the floor around a very low table. The signer later describes the food using the clause BUT FOOD DELICIOUS as shown in Figure 8.31. During FOOD DELICIOUS her left hand produces a POINTER buoy at about waist level. It is pointing ahead and slightly downward toward the |food|. In the context of this description, the downward location of |food| makes sense because the meal was described as being eaten while sitting on the floor around a low table.

Since the POINTER buoy has the same handshape as PRO$^{\rightarrow x}$ and since it points similarly to PRO$^{\rightarrow x}$, there may be a temptation to treat it as an instance of PRO$^{\rightarrow x}$. But there are reasons for not treating the POINTER buoy as a pronoun. First, if it were a pronoun, then one would have to say that ASL allows PRO$^{\rightarrow x}$ and other signs to be produced at the same time. If there were evidence that pronouns in general could be produced simultaneously with other signs, that would provide support for a hypothesis that PRO$^{\rightarrow x}$ could be produced simultaneously with other signs. However, I am not aware of any evidence that other pronouns (e.g. PRO-1) are produced and held as other signs are produced. Finally, note that the pointer frequently has a palm-down orientation. This is not the orientation found in PRO$^{\rightarrow x}$.

In Figure 8.32 the signer is describing a possible reaction of the host. She states that he was not impressed and seemed resistant. The index finger of the weak hand extending from a fist is present during the second, third, fifth, and sixth images. I would treat the index finger in the second and third images as a perseveration of the final configuration of BUT, and therefore not assign it any

BUT            NOT            FACE          IMPRESS

SEEM            RESIST$^{\rightarrow a}$
POINTER$^{\rightarrow|\text{host}|}$ ------------------------

But he didn't look impressed. He seemed resistant.

Figure 8.32   Weak hand perseveration followed later by a POINTER buoy

semantic significance. In the final two images, however, the hand is pointing
to the left in a way that could not arise from perseveration. Since the subject is
not expressed by the strong hand, this example could give the impression that
the subject was simply expressed by the weak hand producing PRO$^{\rightarrow x}$. It also
has a palm to the side orientation of the hand, consistent with the orientation
of PRO$^{\rightarrow x}$. However, because of its simultaneity, I am not treating it as an
instance of PRO$^{\rightarrow x}$. It is behaving like the other examples of the POINTER
buoy described earlier, being produced by the weak hand and held in position
as the strong hand produces one-handed signs.

   In the next example the signer is talking about a child. The child notices
something and wants it. This example includes a nonmanual signal similar to
*th*, but without the protruding lip configuration that makes up part of the *th*
adverb (Liddell 1977, 1980). Since it only appears during the two verbs, it
also appears to be functioning as a nonmanual adverb. Since this is the only
example of this nonmanual signal I have encountered, my description is only
impressionistic. It appears to express the lack of control associated with *th*, but
not necessarily the diminished mental capacity frequently associated with it.
That is, *th* is predictably used to describe the way a drunken person walks or
drives a car. In Figure 8.33, the signer seems to be expressing the concept that
it is in the nature of children to be attracted to things and to want them. That

```
         th                              th
NOTICE→a              SOMETHING;    WANT
                     POINTER→a ----------------------
```

(The child) notices something; and wants it.

Figure 8.33  Evidence against considering the POINTER buoy to be a pronoun

is, she seems to be expressing that the child did not plan this out, but rather, is acting (uncontrollably) on impulse.[11]

This example contains the two clauses NOTICE→a SOMETHING and WANT. NOTICE→a has the overt object SOMETHING and an unexpressed subject. The fact that NOTICE→a has its own overt object argues against the POINTER buoy functioning as the object of the verb. The next clause, WANT, has both an unexpressed subject and object. Since the pointer accompanies WANT, and the object of WANT is unexpressed, there could be a temptation to treat the pointer as the object of WANT. However, since the POINTER begins with the previous sign SOMETHING, this virtually eliminates the possibility of POINTER being the object of WANT.

The example in Figure 8.34 demonstrates multiple instances of the POINTER buoy. The signer is talking about looking at photos in a high school yearbook and creates a surrogate blend in which he becomes a surrogate |person| looking at surrogate |photos| in a yearbook. He produces three instances of the sign DISSOLVE as the |person| looks at three photos ahead of him. One of the senses of DISSOLVE relates to concepts such as 'fade away' or 'disappear'. This is the sense he is using here. Since the |person| has lost touch with the people in the yearbook, they have 'faded away'.

The signer's eye gaze makes it evident that the signing is based on a surrogate blend similar to that in Figure 8.29. In that example the signer blends with his counterpart at a previous time looking over a list of courses. The current example involving a yearbook is similar except that he is not recounting a

---

[11] I am tentatively labeling the nonmanual sign *th* since the signer's expression is close to the way I have previously described *th*. Given that I am looking at only a single instance of this expression, I hesitate to give it a new label. It may be a variant of *th* or it may be a separate nonmanual signal.

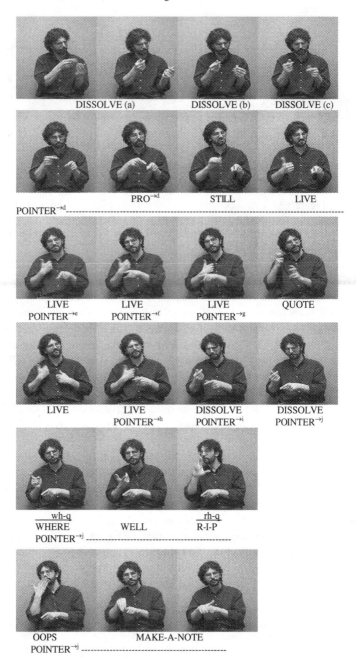

Figure 8.34 Multiple instances of the POINTER buoy directed toward many pictures in a surrogate yearbook

specific instance of looking at a yearbook, but is rather discussing the possible experiences of a hypothetical |person|. A |yearbook| has clearly been projected in front of the |person| in the setting of looking through the yearbook. The |person| looks from |picture| to |picture| in the |yearbook|. As he looks at the first person, $a$, he observes that that person has disappeared. He looks at $b$ and observes that that one has disappeared. The same occurs with $c$. The next one, $d$, is STILL LIVE (i.e. the viewer still has knowledge of that person), and so on.

It is not difficult to imagine an English speaker doing something similar by running his finger from photo to photo making comments about each image. In both the ASL and English examples, the narrator is making comments about people being identified by pointing or gazing at their pictures.

The example in Figure 8.34 presents additional evidence against considering instances of the POINTER buoy as pronouns. The third instance of DISSOLVE is immediately followed by the clause PRO$^{\to d}$ STILL LIVE. Interestingly, PRO$^{\to d}$ and the POINTER buoy are both directed at the same |photo|. In spite of this, their significance is different. The POINTER buoy points at a conceptualized photo while PRO$^{\to d}$ identifies the person in the photo. That is, it is the person, not the photo, that is still alive.[12]

Instances of the POINTER buoy continue throughout fourteen of the remaining sixteen signs. With his left hand slowly moving from left to right producing different instances of the POINTER buoy pointing at different |photos| in the |yearbook|, the signer signs three instances of LIVE, clearly identifying additional |photos| and making the comment that each person is alive. Next, he signs QUOTE LIVE without the POINTER buoy. QUOTE is frequently used to show that a sign is being used in an extended or nonstandard sense. The signer is explaining that he is using the sign LIVE in such an extended sense here. That is, LIVE is used metaphorically to express the idea that he still has knowledge of the person, who is still alive. The surrogate blend with the signer blending with the |person| looking at photos is not active during QUOTE LIVE. This is evident from the change in facial expression and head position (especially during LIVE) as well as the fact that the pointer is not present. Had the pointer been present, it would have provided evidence for the continuation of the surrogate blend since it would still be pointing at the |yearbook|.

The signer reactivates the surrogate blend and continues with the further identification of one 'live' and two missing individuals. The surrogate |person| then asks himself where one particular individual might be. He continues with WELL then the rhetorical question, R-I-P ['Is that person dead?' (resting in peace)]. He ends with the comment OOPS, followed by MAKE-A-NOTE.

---

[12] In this example PRO$^{\to d}$ is directed metonymically toward an image in order to talk about the person corresponding to the image in the photo.

This is quite a long string of signs accompanied by a POINTER buoy. Once the initial POINTER buoy was present, additional instances of the POINTER buoy were present during fourteen of the following sixteen signs. It is even present during the final two-handed sign MAKE-A-NOTE. This verb is normally made against the upward-facing palm of the weak B hand. In this example the POINTER buoy itself serves as the base for the sign MAKE-A-NOTE.

## Summary

List buoys, the THEME buoy, and fragment buoys blend with conceptual entities in the discourse to become visible instances of those entities. List buoys are normally tapped or touched and, at times, they also have signs directed toward them. One signer produces multiple instances of INFLUENCE$^{a\rightarrow b}$ using the blended elements of a THREE-LIST buoy. List buoys can also be manipulated or deformed in order to create conceptual units from entities associated with the buoy. Signers did this to unite two quarters of basketball or to unite two children conceptually with the same mother.

The POINTER buoy points at things. The hand does not become the thing through blending, but rather, directs attention toward it by pointing at it. The POINTER buoy may appear to be similar to PRO$^{\rightarrow x}$, but I have presented evidence that the POINTER buoy is not a pronoun. It is an instance of gestural pointing in order to direct attention toward some entity.

# 9     Depicting verbs

Depicting verbs, like verbs in general, encode meanings related to actions and states. What distinguishes depicting verbs from other verbs is that, in addition to their encoded meanings, these verbs also depict certain aspects of their meanings. This duality, involving both a symbolic lexical verb and depiction, has led to considerable analytical difficulties since these verbs began to be analyzed in the 1970s. Analysts have wanted to see these verbs as entirely symbolic or entirely depictive.

Initially, all verbs capable of being directed in space were called *directional verbs* (Fischer and Gough 1978) or *multidirectional verbs* (Friedman 1976). This large category of verbs included all the types of verbs described in previous chapters as well as depicting verbs. One subcategory of directional signs had characteristics that appeared to distinguish its members from other directional signs. Frishberg (1975) described such signs as being produced with "handshapes in particular orientations to stand for certain semantic features of noun arguments" (p. 715). Frishberg called these oriented handshapes *classifiers* and the signs containing them came to be called *classifier predicates* (Liddell 1977) or *verbs of motion and location* (Supalla 1978). A group of researchers at the University of California at Berkeley used the term *markers* rather than *classifiers*. This terminology appears, for example, in Mandel (1977), DeMatteo (1977), and Friedman (1975, 1977). The terminology was not widely adopted by others.[1] Mandel describes a marker as, "An articulator used in a construct so as to be locatively iconic of an object, so that its behavior and situation in the signing space (whether stationary or moving) represent those of the object" (1977:95).[2]

---

Chapter 9 draws upon and expands upon material from Scott K. Liddell (in press b), *Sources of meaning in ASL classifier predicates*, in *Perspectives on Classifier Constructions in Signed Languages*, ed. Karen Emmorey, Mahwah, NJ: Lawrence Erlbaum Associates.
[1] At the Classifier Workshop held in LaJolla, CA in May 2000, Dan Slobin, also from the University of California at Berkeley, suggested the label *property markers* to describe these handshapes.
[2] The literature on ASL "classifiers" is inconsistent with respect to whether the term *classifier* refers to the handshape only or a combination of handshape and orientation features. In addition, the appropriateness of the label *classifier* has also been called into question by Engberg-Pedersen

a.    VEHICLE-BE-AT$^{\downarrow L1}$    b.    UPRIGHT-PERSON-BE-AT$^{\downarrow L1}$

c. CUP-LIKE-ENTITY-BE-AT$^{\downarrow \text{on |broad surface|}}$
   BROAD-SURFACE $^{\downarrow L1}$

Figure 9.1 Three verbs depicting things at places

### Types of depicting verbs

Depicting verbs can be divided into at least three broad categories. The first consists of verbs signifying the presence of an entity at a place. Verbs in the second category signify the shape and extent of a surface or the extent of a linear arrangement of individual entities. Verbs in the third category signify movements or actions. Each of the verbs in Figure 9.1, for example, signifies the presence of an entity at a location.[3] The signs in this category all share a common formational characteristic in that each is made with a short downward movement followed by a hold. Each also differs from each of the others in handshape and orientation. The verb VEHICLE-BE-AT$^{\downarrow L1}$ in Figure 9.1a is produced with a 3 handshape with the radial surface of the hand up. In this verb, the 3 handshape oriented in this way signifies 'vehicle' and the verb expresses the presence of a vehicle at a place. The symbol $^{\downarrow L1}$ signifies that the hand actually moves to location *L1*. That is, in contrast to a sign such as TELL$^{\rightarrow y}$, where the sign is directed toward *y* (but not placed at *y*), in producing VEHICLE-BE-AT$^{\downarrow L1}$ the hand actually reaches the location *L1*.

The verb UPRIGHT-PERSON-BE-AT$^{\downarrow L1}$ in Figure 9.1b signifies the presence of a standing person at a place. It is also made with a short downward

(1993) and Schembri (in press). I do not use the term *classifier* here, and do not have a replacement term to suggest.

[3] These signs are typical members of a category of verbs identified by Supalla (1978) as derived from a 'contact root'.

movement followed by a hold. It differs formationally from VEHICLE-BE-AT$^{\downarrow L1}$ in both handshape and orientation. UPRIGHT-PERSON-BE-AT$^{\downarrow L1}$ is produced with a 1 handshape with the tip of the index finger oriented up. In this verb, the 1 handshape in this orientation signifies a person in a standing or walking posture.

In Figure 9.1c, the verb CUP-LIKE-ENTITY-BE-AT$^{\downarrow on|broad\ surface|}$-BROAD-SURFACE$^{\downarrow L1}$ expresses the existence of a cup-like entity on a flat surface. In producing the verb in Figure 9.1c, the strong hand produces CUP-LIKE-ENTITY-BE-AT$^{\downarrow on\ |broad\ surface|}$ while the weak hand produces BROAD-SURFACE$^{\downarrow L1}$. Like the verbs in Figure 9.1a and b, CUP-LIKE-ENTITY-BE-AT$^{\downarrow on\ |broad\ surface|}$ is also made with a short downward movement and hold. In this sign, the movement brings the strong hand into contact with the back of the weak hand. The weak hand produces BROAD-SURFACE$^{\downarrow L1}$, which also appears as a component of many other signs. Thus, even though it is produced by two hands, the verb in Figure 9.1c is analyzable as a combination of a one-handed verb that makes contact with BROAD-SURFACE$^{\downarrow L1}$, produced by the weak hand. Under the right discourse conditions, BROAD-SURFACE$^{\downarrow L1}$ can remain in place as other depicting signs are produced. Given its ability to remain in place depicting a broad surface, it is useful to think of it as a *depicting buoy*. We will encounter a number of such depicting buoys later in this chapter.

The signs in Figure 9.2 differ both semantically and formationally from those in Figure 9.1. They express meanings related to the shape and extent of surfaces. The verbs in this class are typically two-handed verbs produced with two identical handshapes. One hand is held stationary while the other moves along a path away from it.

In Figure 9.2a, the verb FLAT-BROAD-SURFACE-EXTEND-TO$^{\downarrow L1-L2}$ describes an extended flat, broad surface. The moving strong hand depicts the extent of the broad surface. This sign appeared as the signer was describing a military requirement for soldiers to make their beds with a very tight, unwrinkled surface.

The verb BUMPY-BROAD-SURFACE-EXTEND-TO$^{\downarrow L1-L2}$ in Figure 9.2b is similar to the verb just described, but differs in two important ways. First, instead of making a smooth movement away from the weak hand, the signer produces an oscillating rotation of the forearm of her active hand as the hand moves outward. Second, her facial expression appears to be a variant of the *th* facial expression indicating lack of control, unawareness, or inattention. The sign in Figure 9.2b might be used to describe a lumpy bed or a poorly made bed.

The verb SMALL-CYLINDRICAL-SURFACE-EXTEND-TO$^{\downarrow L1-L2}$ in Figure 9.2c describes the presence of a pipe-like entity of a particular shape and extent. As in the previous two examples, the weak hand remains in place while

a. FLAT-BROAD-SURFACE-EXTEND-TO$^{\downarrow L1-L2}$

b.                    BUMPY-BROAD-SURFACE-EXTEND-TO$^{\downarrow L1-L2}$

c.  SMALL-CYLINDRICAL-SURFACE-EXTEND-TO$^{\downarrow L1-L2}$

Figure 9.2  Three verbs depicting shapes

the strong hand moves along a path that depicts the extent and shape of the entity being described. The thumb and index finger of each F handshape form a circle, representing a cross-section of the pipe. In this example the left hand remains ahead of the left shoulder while the strong hand moves to the right. After moving to the right a few inches the forearm rotates and the hand moves downward. The change in the direction of the hand's movement depicts a bend in the pipe-like entity being depicted. The nonmanual signal appears to express small size or thinness. Also note the contractions of the muscles around the eyes that lower the brows and make the eyes appear narrowed. This is present in all three of these verbs.

The oriented handshapes in these three examples represent surfaces while the movement of the hand depicts the extent and shape of the surface. Many

a.        VEHICLE-DRIVE-TO$^{\downarrow L1-L2}$

b. UPRIGHT-PERSON-WALK-TO$^{\downarrow L1-L2}$

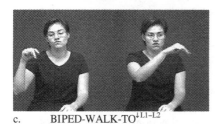

c.        BIPED-WALK-TO$^{\downarrow L1-L2}$

Figure 9.3  Three verbs depicting the movements of entities

verbs depicting extent, however, are produced with oriented handshapes signifying individual entities. In such cases, the verbs depict the extent of the linear
arrangement of many such individual entities. For example, VEHICLE-ROW-
EXTEND-TO$^{\downarrow L1-L2}$ begins with two 3 hands in contact, palm to palm, with the
radial sides of the hands oriented up. The strong hand then moves horizontally
away from the weak hand and ends its movement with a hold. Since each hand
depicts an individual vehicle, the verb depicts a linear arrangement (e.g. a row)
of vehicles rather than a continuous surface.

The signs in Figure 9.3 describe movements along a path. For each of these
signs the hand moves along a path that corresponds to aspects of the movement
of the entity being described.

The verb VEHICLE-DRIVE-TO$^{\downarrow L1-L2}$ in Figure 9.3a expresses the movement of a vehicle driven from one place to another. The hand moves horizontally
from right to left followed by a hold. In addition to signifying a vehicle, the
oriented 3 hand can also be conceptualized *as a vehicle* with a front, back, top,
and bottom. The fingertips correspond to the front of the vehicle and the ulnar

surface of the hand corresponds to its bottom. Thus, in Figure 9.3a the front of the hand-as-vehicle faces in the direction of travel. The fact that it is possible to talk about such correspondences leaves no doubt that more than semantic encoding is taking place when these signs are produced.

In Figure 9.3b the hand producing UPRIGHT-PERSON-WALK-TO$^{\downarrow L1-L2}$ makes a smooth horizontal movement from right to left, followed by a hold. This verb describes the walking movement of a person from one place to another. The vertically oriented 1 handshape is meaningful, signifying a person in a standing or walking posture. The palm-side surface of the finger corresponds to the front of the person. Thus, the vertical 1 handshape also depicts a person in a standing or walking posture, but does so without depicting any particular body parts.

The verb BIPED-WALK-TO$^{\downarrow L1-L2}$ in Figure 9.3c also signifies the walking movement of a person from one location to another. It is produced with a V handshape with the fingertips oriented down. The hand makes a smooth horizontal movement from right to left as the fingers wiggle, followed by a hold during which the fingers do not wiggle. It is easy to see a correspondence between the two extended fingers and the two legs of a walking human. As a human walks, the legs alternate in their movements. In Figure 9.3c, the wiggling of the fingers corresponds to the alternate movements of the legs in walking. This is a very abstract correspondence, however, in that individual movements of the wiggling fingers do not correspond one-to-one with individual movements of the legs of the person whose walking is being described.

The verbs in Figure 9.4 also depict actions. The handshapes in these verbs have come to be called *handling classifiers* or *instrument classifiers* since each sign describes the handling of an entity rather than directly representing the entity itself (Boyes-Braem 1981, McDonald 1982, Supalla 1982, Liddell and Johnson 1987, Schick 1990). In Figure 9.4a, for example, the verb HAND-PICK-UP-FLAT-THIN-ENTITY$^{\downarrow L1-L2}$ begins with a 4 handshape with the thumb opposed. The hand closes to a flat O handshape as it moves upward to a location to the right of the face and ends in a hold. The signer looks continuously at her hand throughout the production of this sign. This verb signifies picking up something thin and flat (e.g. a piece of paper) and looking at it. The visible aspects of what this signer depicts include the hand holding the thin and flat entity and the signer gazing at the entity being held. It should be easy to recognize that the signer has created a surrogate blend in which an |agent| is gazing at a |thin entity| being held by the |agent|'s |hand|. Even though the |thin entity| is invisible to someone observing the signing, it is understood to extend below the |hand| holding it. Similar surrogate blends are created in each of the examples in Figure 9.4.

The verb HAND-PICK-UP-THIN-ENTITY$^{\downarrow L1-L2}$ in Figure 9.4b signifies picking up a thin entity. The index finger and thumb contact one another to

a. HAND-PICK-UP- FLAT-THIN- ENTITY$^{\downarrow L1-L2}$

b. HAND-PICK-UP-THIN-ENTITY$^{\downarrow L1-L2}$

c. HAND-PICK-UP-CUP-LIKE-ENTITY$^{\downarrow L1-L2}$

d. HAND-RELEASE-CUP-LIKE-ENTITY$^{\downarrow L1}$

Figure 9.4  Four verbs depicting the handling of objects

form an F handshape that moves upward to a position ahead of the shoulder where it ends in a hold. In this particular instance, the signer is talking about picking up a dirty diaper. While dirty diapers are not necessarily thin, their corners are. One is to understand that the rest of the |diaper| is below the grasping thumb and index fingers. Her facial expression also appears to reflect an affect related to handling something unpleasant. As before, the signer creates a surrogate blend in which the agent and the agent's hand are visibly depicted. Although not visible to an addressee, the |diaper| extending beneath the |hand| is nevertheless an important part of the blend.

In Figure 9.4c the verb HAND-PICK-UP-CUP-LIKE-ENTITY$^{\downarrow L1-L2}$ signifies the grasping and lifting up of a cup-like entity while gazing at it. The sign begins with a 4 handshape with the fingers slightly bent and the thumb opposed. The hand forms a C handshape and the hand moves upward followed by a hold with the hand to the right and ahead of the signer's face.

The verb HAND-RELEASE-CUP-LIKE-ENTITY$^{\downarrow L1}$ in Figure 9.4d also involves an action by an agent. The agent's action takes place at a single location and, as a result, the signer's hand does not move along a path. In this example, the signer describes releasing a cup-like entity being held. This is expressed in this sign by changing from a C to a 5 handshape. If the action depicted in this sign were carried out where gravity would have an effect on the previously held entity, that entity would fall. The signer's eye gaze in this example is consistent with that result.

Even though the C handshape in this example is identical to the C handshape in Figure 9.1c, its significance is different. The verb in Figure 9.1c has nothing to do with a hand holding a cup-like entity. The C handshape in that example depicts the cup-like entity itself. In Figure 9.4c the C handshape does not depict the cup-like entity, but rather, depicts a hand holding a cup-like entity.

### Analytical assumptions

In the mid-1970s no distinctions had yet been made with respect to the directionality of depicting verbs in contrast to other directional verbs. Liddell (1977) proposes a distinction between the directionality of a transitive verb like BUY, directed toward a locus associated with its object, and a "locative construction," (what I am here calling a depicting verb). The distinction between the two was based on how the directional movement is interpreted. I proposed that with a transitive verb like BUY, the directionality makes an association with a locus, thereby indicating what was bought. Topographical information such as proximity and adjacency are not important in that interpretation. With a "locative construction," such as depicting a cat on a fence, the placement of the hand creates a spatial relationship. Phrasing the distinction in terms of the framework of this book, the directionality of depicting verbs depicts topographical locative information while the directionality of indicating verbs identifies entities.

There have been no attempts to produce a comprehensive list of every possible depicting verb. This is, no doubt, due to the assumption that such an attempt would be misguided. A comparison between creating depicting verbs and creating sentences may help clarify the issue. The grammatical system underlying the production of sentences allows speakers of a language to create novel sentences freely. With such a productive grammatical system, the entire concept of a finite list of possible sentences makes no sense. Since the set of English sentences is unbounded it would be foolhardy to attempt to list every possible sentence. Creating verbs of the type I am describing here has likewise been seen as a productive process with an unbounded number of possible outcomes.

Since treating depicting verbs as listable lexical items was not considered possible, ways were sought to provide a productive means of accounting for all possible signs of this type. In the late 1970s two diametrically opposed views of how to do this emerged. DeMatteo (1977) proposes a type of underlying form in which visual imagery rather than morphemes determines the meaning. Supalla (1978, 1982, 1986) provides an alternate model in which such verbs are composed entirely of morphemes, and in which visual imagery plays no role whatsoever. Liddell (2000b, in press b) examines both approaches in detail. While the visual imagery approach captures important aspects of what depicting verbs express, visual imagery is unable to account for the lexical properties of depicting verbs. That is, certain aspects of the meanings of depicting verbs are lexically fixed. Attempting to account for these lexically fixed aspects of a depicting verb's meaning solely through visual imagery does not lead to a satisfactory result.

On the other hand, the visual imagery described by DeMatteo cannot be ignored since its contribution to the meanings expressed is essential to understanding the significance of depicting verbs. By rejecting visual imagery, Supalla creates the problem of having to propose morphemes to account for all the meanings expressed by depiction. This task appears to be beyond what a morphemic analysis is capable of doing.

Since the intention of this book is to present new analyses rather than criticisms of previous analyses, I will not elaborate here on the problems faced by either the imagery analysis proposed by DeMatteo or the morphemic analysis proposed by Supalla. The reader can find a discussion of those analytical problems in Liddell (in press b).

### Depicting verbs as lexical items

I treat the depicting verbs described in this chapter as being composed of lexically fixed features combined with additional meaningful, gradient aspects of form. Given this analytical approach, the first task in the analysis of a depicting verb is to determine which parts of its production encode the meaning of the lexical verb and which parts are analogical and gradient. I take it as given that in producing depicting verbs the placement of the hands and some aspects of the orientation of the hands must be seen as analogical and gradient. For example, in producing the verb UPRIGHT-PERSON-BE-AT$^{\downarrow L}$ the 1 handshape is oriented vertically and makes a short downward movement followed by a

a.                    UPRIGHT-PERSON-WALK-ALONG$^{\downarrow L1-L2}$

b. UPRIGHT-PERSON-WALK-TO$^{\downarrow L1-L2}$

Figure 9.5 Two similar verbs depicting walking from one place to another

hold. This occurs every time the verb is produced. However, the placement of the hand and the direction the palm faces vary from one instance of the verb to the next. In producing the verb UPRIGHT-PERSON-WALK-TO$^{\downarrow L1-L2}$, the 1 handshape is oriented vertically and makes a straight movement followed by a hold. In addition, the palm is oriented along the path of movement toward L2. The starting and ending locations of the hand are variable, so is the path defined by these two points. Since the orientation of the palm is aligned with the path, the orientation of the palm is also gradient. I am aware of no evidence that would support treating the variable aspects of such signs as part of their lexical representation. Therefore, I will remove location and some aspects of orientation from consideration and will assume that what remains encodes the lexical meaning of a typical depicting verb.

Figure 9.5 illustrates two similar depicting verbs. The verb UPRIGHT-PERSON-WALK-ALONG$^{\downarrow L1-L2}$ in Figure 9.5a is produced with a vertical 1 handshape and a repeated bouncing movement as the hand moves along a path. It is also produced with the nonmanual signal 'mm' (note the lip configuration and head tilt) signifying relaxation and enjoyment. The initial and final locations of the hand are variable elements in this sign. The palm faces along the movement path toward the final location, wherever that happens to be.

The lexically fixed aspects of this verb consist of a vertical 1 handshape, a straight movement with a repeated bouncing movement along a path, and the palm oriented along the direction of movement. These aspects of form encode the meaning, 'person walk along in an unhurried manner'. When this meaningful unit is combined with variable and gradient initial and final locations, as in Figure 9.5a, the result is a verb that encodes the meaning 'person walk along in an unhurried manner' and simultaneously provides a visual depiction of the event.

The verb UPRIGHT-PERSON-WALK-TO$^{\downarrow L1-L2}$ in Figure 9.5b is formationally distinct from UPRIGHT-PERSON-WALK-ALONG$^{\downarrow L1-L2}$ and encodes a different meaning. UPRIGHT-PERSON-WALK-TO$^{\downarrow L1-L2}$ is typically used to describe situations where someone walks with the aim of moving to a specific place. UPRIGHT-PERSON-WALK-ALONG$^{\downarrow L1-L2}$ is not as goal oriented. It seems to put more emphasis on the casual manner of walking than on arriving at a specific place. This difference in meaning is a lexical difference between these two verbs.

Following this same analytical approach with other depicting verbs will identify a vast set of lexical items. At present no one knows how extensive the set is because the set has been considered to be unbounded. It is clear, however, that there are limits on the set of depicting verbs. For example, there is a large set of signs that describe the presence of an entity at a place. Each member of this set shares the formational characteristic of being produced with a downward movement followed by a hold. What distinguishes one such verb from another is the handshape used and its orientation. For example, UPRIGHT-PERSON-BE-AT$^{\downarrow L}$ is produced with a 1 handshape, base of the hand oriented down. AIRPLANE-BE-AT$^{\downarrow L}$ is produced with a handshape with the thumb, index finger, and little finger extended and the palm oriented down. VEHICLE-BE-AT$^{\downarrow L}$ is produced with a 3 handshape with the forearm rotated so that the radial side of the hand is up. ANIMAL-BE-AT$^{\downarrow L}$ is produced with a hooked V handshape (middle joints of both the index and middle fingers are flexed) with the palm oriented down. Additional verbs describe and depict the location of a tree, an immovable object, a cup, a wire-like object, a narrow surface, a wide surface, a seated human, a human standing on two legs, a table, and many other types of entities.

There are many such paradigms and it is not difficult to find gaps within the paradigms. For example, although the depicting verb VEHICLE-BE-AT$^{\downarrow L}$ expresses the presence of a normally oriented car at a location, there is no corresponding verb expressing the presence of a vehicle in any other orientation such as upside down, with the front facing down, etc. There is a verb used to describe a vehicle crashing into something. In producing this verb the 3 handshape changes to a hooked 3 (the middle joints of both the index and middle fingers are flexed). There is no corresponding be-at verb describing a wrecked vehicle at a location using the hooked 3 handshape. Similarly, there are no be-at verbs using the 1 handshape to depict a human in any orientation other than standing. Other verbs can depict a human in other postures, but this is not done with the 1 handshape.

Additionally, just because a meaningful oriented handshape may appear in other depicting verbs does not mean that it will necessarily occur in a be-at verb. For example, although signers generally use a radial-side-up 'baby C' handshape to show the movement of a flying saucer, most of the signers I have consulted are reluctant to produce a corresponding be-at verb depicting the presence of a flying saucer at a place. Some signers, however, will produce FLYING-SAUCER-BE-AT$^{\downarrow L}$. This suggests a difference in the lexicons of those who do use the verb and those who do not. It appears that the verb FLYING-SAUCER-BE-AT$^{\downarrow L}$ is not a widespread, established lexical unit of ASL.

There are other types of gaps as well. For example, the palm faces forward along a path in producing the verb UPRIGHT-PERSON-WALK-TO$^{\downarrow L1-L2}$. There is no corresponding verb UPRIGHT-PERSON-WALK-BACKWARD-TO$^{\downarrow L1-L2}$ in which the back of the hand faces in the direction of movement. Similarly, there is no corresponding verb UPRIGHT-PERSON-WALK-SIDEWAYS-TO$^{\downarrow L1-L2}$ in which the radial or ulnar side of the hand faces in the direction of the hand's movement. Although the verb UPRIGHT-PERSON-WALK-TO$^{\downarrow L1-L2}$ is very common, there is no corresponding verb ANIMAL-WALK-TO$^{\downarrow L1-L2}$ made by moving the hooked V handshape in a smooth movement along a straight path. This is equivalent to noting that although the morphologically complex word *seniority* currently exists as an English noun, the potential English word *juniority* does not. It is a potential, but nonexistent complex word. Such gaps in the be-at paradigm and in other paradigms suggest that these signs are part of a large, semi-productive derivational system.

Since the 1970s I have frequently asked native signers to describe things. I have often been told, "I can't tell you about X because I don't do X." For example, a female signer explained that she could not describe what happens on the football field because she doesn't play football. This response puzzled me for many years because I held the popular view that signers simply assembled the appropriate parts to create one of these verbs. Since a native signer would be intimately familiar with how such parts would combine, the inability to describe an activity one witnesses but does not normally participate in seemed puzzling. I now see this as an issue of technical vocabulary. That is, it is well known that a technical vocabulary develops around specialized activities. Football players develop the technical vocabulary needed to talk about football. Since much of football involves motion, positions, and action, it would be normal for much of that vocabulary to involve depicting verbs. Those who play football learn that vocabulary. A native signer not involved in football would not know that vocabulary – depicting verbs or otherwise.

In addition to gaps in paradigms, phonological and semantic idiosyncrasies are also indicative of a derivational system. Consider, for example, the verb VEHICLE-PASS-BY$^{\downarrow L1}$ in Figure 9.6. It expresses the meaning that a vehicle

Figure 9.6  VEHICLE-PASS-BY$^{\downarrow L1}$

passes by a location. Part of the meaning expressed by this verb is that the vehicle was traveling at a normal or faster rate of speed, and was moving prior to passing by and continued moving after passing by. The form of the sign provides no obvious source of the meaning that the vehicle's movement began prior to passing by and continued afterward.

The verb begins with the fingertips oriented upward. Recall that earlier in describing the verb VEHICLE-BE-AT$^{\downarrow L1}$, I described the fingertips as corresponding to the front of the vehicle and the base of the hand corresponding to the back of the vehicle. If one assumes that the orientation of the hand corresponds to the orientation of the vehicle and applies these correspondences to the sign in Figure 9.6, the wrong meaning would emerge. One would have to say that the vehicle begins its movement past a location with all four wheels facing forward, sliding along on its back bumper. Only later would the car assume a normal orientation with the wheels touching the ground. This is not what the sign means. But derivational systems are well known for including gaps, phonological idiosyncrasies, and semantic idiosyncrasies. If depicting verbs are treated as lexical items within a large derivational system then the kinds of gaps and idiosyncrasies described above are to be expected.

In general, a derivational system consists of sets of lexical items constructed according to schemas evident within that system. This chapter does not focus on the internal structure of depicting verbs. Such an effort would be a study of a different sort than that presented here. A few brief remarks concerning internal structure are nevertheless in order. First, the claim that depicting verbs comprise a large derivational system is neutral with respect to the productivity of the system. However, lexical items within a large derivational system can be expected to show some degree of internal structure. Indeed, without internal structure, there is no basis for even talking about a derivational system.

Beginning with Supalla (1978, 1982), analyses with very large numbers of morphemic affixes have emerged. The numbers of proposed morphemes within any given sign have been sufficiently large that such signs are sometimes referred to as "polysynthetic" (Engberg-Pedersen 1993, Wallin 1996). Supalla's proposal was based on the idea that all meaning must come from morphemes. I suggest an approach in which some meaning comes from identifiable morphemes, some meaning is associated with the full lexical unit itself, and meaning is also constructed by means of mental space mappings motivated by the variable and gradient ways that the hand is located and oriented. Not surprisingly, the number of morphemes identifiable under this set of assumptions is much smaller. In fact, given this set of assumptions, I have been unable to find compelling evidence supporting a polysynthetic analysis of these signs.

My discussion of signs such as UPRIGHT-PERSON-BE-AT$^{\downarrow L}$, AIRPLANE-BE-AT$^{\downarrow L}$, and VEHICLE-BE-AT$^{\downarrow L}$ suggests that the signs could be divided into a verb root {BE-AT}$^{\downarrow L}$ and a morpheme signifying a type of entity. The verb root {BE-AT}$^{\downarrow L}$ appears in a very large number of other depicting verbs. A small sample includes the signs VEHICLE-BE-AT$^{\downarrow L}$, ANIMAL-BE-AT$^{\downarrow L}$, and BIPED-BE-AT$^{\downarrow L}$. In every case, the verb root {BE-AT}$^{\downarrow L}$ takes the form of a small downward movement followed by a hold. The oriented handshapes in these signs could also be analyzed as morphemic. For example, one could identify a morpheme {UPRIGHT-PERSON}$^{\rightarrow}$ in the verb UPRIGHT-PERSON-BE-AT. The arrow in this gloss signifies that the palm can be oriented to depict the direction the person is facing. Thus, instead of the gloss UPRIGHT-PERSON-BE-AT, it would be possible – in this case – to describe this sign with the gloss {UPRIGHT-PERSON}$^{\rightarrow}${BE-AT}$^{\downarrow L}$. The morpheme {UPRIGHT-PERSON}$^{\rightarrow}$ also appears in other depicting verbs, including, UPRIGHT-PERSON-WALK-TO$^{\downarrow L1-L2}$, UPRIGHT-PERSON-WALK-ALONG$^{\downarrow L1-L2}$, UPRIGHT-PERSON-STAGGER$^{\downarrow L1-L2}$, etc. Thus, in the case of UPRIGHT-PERSON-BE-AT$^{\downarrow L}$ I am able to find evidence for two morphemes. This does not mean that all depicting verbs have only two morphemes. One would naturally expect two-handed depicting verbs to be composed of more than two morphemes. It is also possible that a large-scale study of a wide variety of such verbs conducted with the assumptions adopted in this book will find additional morphemic structure within depicting verbs. The nature of the internal structure of depicting verbs will only become apparent after such a study has been undertaken.

I will not attempt to present an English gloss for each morpheme within a depicting verb. If I am correct that depicting verbs make up a large semi-productive derivational system, there are good reasons for not even attempting to produce a gloss for each morpheme. First, a large-scale study will be needed in order to determine the internal structure of depicting verbs. This work has not yet been done. Second, it is possible – even likely – that such a study will uncover signs that are only partially morphemic. The problem is easily illustrated outside the context of a sign language. Consider, for example, how one might write a Spanish gloss for the English word *Tuesday*. Although the meaningful form *day* is an obvious component of *Tuesday* (i.e. it occurs in the English name of every day of the week), there is no obvious meaning for [t$^h$uz] (*Tues*). If *day* were glossed as *dia*, what is to be done with [t$^h$uz] in a

Figure 9.7  VEHICLE-BE-AT$^{\downarrow L1}$

glossing system? Glossing one or more parts of a lexical item that may not be fully composed of morphemes creates insoluble glossing problems.[4] As a result, the gloss *martes* 'Tuesday' is superior to a gloss attempting to include a representation of the morpheme *day*.

### Depicting presence at a place

In Figure 9.7 the signer is producing the depicting verb VEHICLE-BE-AT$^{\downarrow L1}$ to describe the location of a car. The hand begins slightly above the location *L1*, then makes a small downward movement and ends with a hold at *L1*. The short downward movement and hold produced with a 3 handshape with the radial surface of the hand oriented up, are the lexically fixed aspects of the production of VEHICLE-BE-AT$^{\downarrow L}$.

Figure 9.8 illustrates the semantic pole of VEHICLE-BE-AT$^{\downarrow L1}$, which represents the current ongoing, unchanging relationship between a vehicle (the trajector) and the surface it rests upon (the landmark). Langacker (1999b) describes verbs with such semantic characteristics as imperfective verbs and describes the focused temporal component of the semantic pole as the verb's *immediate temporal scope* (p. 223). The gray inner rectangle identifies this verb's immediate temporal scope, which includes the ongoing relationship between the trajector and the landmark. The left-to-right arrow indicates time and the horizontal line passing through the rectangle represents the temporal extent of the process. For this verb, its immediate scope does not include either the start or the end of the profiled process.

Since VEHICLE-BE-AT$^{\downarrow L1}$ is a depicting verb, it not only grammatically encodes its meaning, it also depicts aspects of its meaning. Through blending, the hand becomes a visible instance of the car being described. The way the fingertips are oriented depicts the direction the car is facing and the placement of the hand depicts the car's location. Thus, within the depicted past event space, a |car| is resting on a |surface|.

---

[4] The problems created by the glossing system are not analytical problems. One can satisfactorily proceed with a morphemic analysis of such signs outside the context of glossing. The issue I am raising here has to do with the problems of representing signs by means of English glosses.

VEHICLE-BE-AT$^{\downarrow L1}$

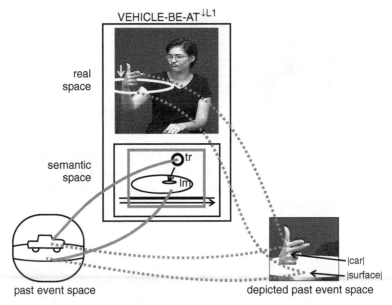

real space

semantic space

past event space                    depicted past event space

Figure 9.8  The constructed meaning of an instance of VEHICLE-BE-AT$^{\downarrow L1}$

Figure 9.8 illustrates how the meaning of this example is constructed, including how blending accomplishes the depiction. First, the vehicle in the past event space being described corresponds to the trajector in the verb's semantic pole. The connector between the two conceptual entities represents this correspondence. Similarly, there is a connector between the landmark and the surface the vehicle is resting upon in the past event space. These are the types of connections one would expect between a non-depicting verb and the event space being described.

In addition to the expected connections between the verb's semantic pole and the event space, the sign also depicts the vehicle at a location. This is accomplished by producing the sign so that the hand ends its movement at a specific location with the fingertips oriented in a specific direction. The blended space that results contains a |car| on a |surface|. Although the |car| is visible, the |surface| is not.

The |car| within the depicted past event space is a blend of the hand in real space and the car in the past event space. In other instances of this verb the hand could blend with a bicycle, a motorcycle, a truck, a bus, etc.[5] One instance of this sign potentially differs from any other instance of this sign in the way

---

[5] The constructed meaning diagrams attempt to illustrate the connections essential to constructing meaning, including the creation of depicting spaces. The diagrams should not be understood to mean that there are no other possible correspondences that could be illustrated.

that the vehicle is depicted. That is, the location at which the hand is placed involves a projection from the past event space onto real space. Similarly, the direction the fingers face also involves a projection from the past event space.[6] In addition, the space around the vehicle in the past event space blends with a plane of space ahead of the signer, identified by the outlined shape around the signer's right hand, to create the |surface| that the |car| is resting on. As a result, the location of the |car| in the depicting blend corresponds to the location of the car in the scene being described.

What makes one instance of this verb potentially different from any other comes from projecting aspects of the space being described into the blend. In the past event space the car is conceptualized as existing at a place facing in some direction. These aspects of the past event space are projected into the depicting space by means of the analogical placement of the hand at a specific place on the |surface| and the analogical directionality of the fingers. The location at which the signer chooses to place the hand becomes the location of the |car| on that |surface| within the depicting blend. Thus, the placement of the hand and the way the fingertips point are not lexically fixed. They are variable, scalar aspects of the production of VEHICLE-BE-AT$^{\downarrow L}$. These two aspects of the verb's production will vary depending on how the signer chooses to depict the location and orientation of the vehicle being described.

The fingertips can be directed in virtually any physically comfortable compass direction. The limits on the direction of the fingertips appear to be physiological rather than grammatical. For example, it is difficult to direct the fingertips of the right hand diagonally backward and to the right because of the physiology of the hand and wrist. But there appear to be no grammatical restrictions on rotating the hand so that the fingertips point in a specific direction.

The signer is looking directly at the |car| in the blend. I interpret this to mean that the depiction is presented from a specific point of view.[7] The signer herself quite literally demonstrates that point of view by gazing at the |car| in the depicting blend. The particular point of view will depend on the specific context in which VEHICLE-BE-AT$^{\downarrow L}$ occurs.

In summary, a depicting verb encodes its meaning just like a verb in any language. VEHICLE-BE-AT$^{\downarrow L}$ is an imperfective verb describing the ongoing physical presence of a vehicle at a place. It is semantically similar to the English *be parked*, which also includes as part of its meaning that a vehicle is stationary at a place. In contrast to the English *be parked*, however, the depicting verb VEHICLE-BE-AT$^{\downarrow L}$ also depicts the scene being described. The hand

[6] Although the orientation of the fingertips is a variable aspect of this sign, the sign can be made with a neutral wrist position that can convey the meaning 'there is a vehicle at a location' rather than 'there is a vehicle at a location facing in a particular direction'.

[7] There have been a number of attempts to treat gaze as a marker of point of view, including Shepard-Kegl (1985), Aarons *et al.* (1992, 1994), and Lillo-Martin (1995).

[FENCE]^{↓L1-L3}                    CAT      ANIMAL-BE-AT^{↓on |fence|}
                                             FENCE-SURFACE^{↓L2}

Figure 9.9  Describing a cat lying on a fence

blends with aspects of the vehicle being described to become a |vehicle| in a depicting space. Thus, what distinguishes a depicting verb from verbs in spoken languages, and from non-depicting verbs in ASL, is its *additional* ability and requirement to depict.

In Figure 9.9 the signer describes a cat lying on a fence. The noun FENCE normally begins with the two hands in contact centrally ahead of the torso. The two hands then move apart in sideways directions, followed by a hold. Although the initial sign in Figure 9.9 looks like the noun FENCE, the two hands move in opposite directions along a *diagonal* path from just ahead of the left shoulder extending outward and away toward the right. Except for its location and the path of the hands, this sign has both the phonological and semantic characteristics of the noun FENCE. Thus, it could be a placed form of the noun (see chapter 6). It could also potentially be a depicting verb that functions in a way similar to the three depicting verbs in Figure 9.2, where one hand remains stationary while the other depicts the shape and extent of the entity or surface being described. ASL does have such a depicting verb capable of depicting a fence within a depicting blend. To produce it the weak hand in a 4 configuration remains stationary while the active hand, also in a 4 configuration, moves away from the weak hand along a path depicting the shape and extent of the fence. Although depicting shapes with two active hands is sometimes possible, it is not as common as leaving one hand in place as the other hand moves.

The evidence below is consistent with the initial sign being a located instance of the noun FENCE.[8] First, the hands begin in contact slightly to the left of center ahead of the body, then move away from one another. The left hand moves back toward the left shoulder and the right moves out and away to the right. The movement of the two hands away from one another after beginning in contact is the type of movement expected of the noun FENCE, but not necessarily expected of a verb depicting a fence.

---

[8] I thank Brita Bergman for her assistance in observing the details of the production of this sign and for her valuable discussions of possible analyses.

a. initial sign in Figure 9.9       b. depicting an uneven surface        c. depicting a flat surface

Figure 9.10  Comparing the facial expression of the initial sign in Figure 9.9
with the facial expressions in verbs depicting surfaces

Second, the lip configurations accompanying this sign are similar to those
that would be part of uttering the initial consonant and vowel of the English
word *fence*. Lip configurations traceable to aspects of spoken English words
have become associated with some ASL signs. Associations between lip configurations and signs is common in some sign languages, including Norwegian
Sign Language, where they were first described (Vogt-Svendsen 1984, 2001).
Vogt-Svendsen calls these lip configurations and movements *word pictures*.
She observes that in Norwegian Sign Language word pictures are much more
likely to be present during the production of a noun or a non-modified verb
than during the production of a modified verb or what I am calling a depicting
verb. My impression with respect to ASL is that the word picture seen with
the first sign in Figure 9.9 is much more likely with the noun FENCE than
with a depicting verb. Thus, in addition to the movement pattern of the two
hands, the accompanying word picture also supports the idea that this is the
noun FENCE.

One additional aspect of the signer's facial expression also supports treating
this sign as the noun FENCE rather than as a depicting verb. Figure 9.10a shows
her facial expression during the production of the initial sign in Figure 9.9. The
pictures in Figure 9.10b and c show her facial expressions as she produces
two verbs depicting surfaces, previously shown in Figure 9.2. Figure 9.10b
shows her facial expression as she begins to produce a verb depicting a broad
uneven surface and Figure 9.10c shows the same signer's facial expression
as she produces the verb depicting a broad smooth surface. The most obvious
global difference between the pictures is the relatively relaxed expression in the
first picture compared with the more obvious contraction of facial muscles in
the other two pictures. Specifically, the second and third images show muscle
contractions around the eyes that lower the brows and narrow the eyes. The
facial expression in Figure 9.10a has neither of these characteristics.

The three lines of evidence discussed above support treating the initial sign
as the placed noun [FENCE]$^{\downarrow L1-L3}$ rather than as a depicting verb. The hands

[FENCE]$^{\downarrow \text{L1–L3}}$

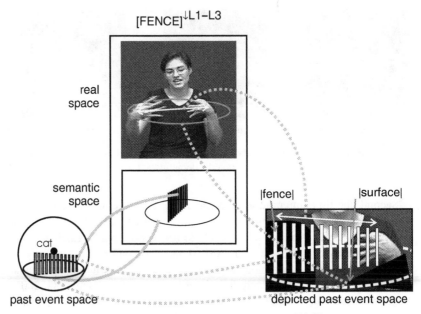

Figure 9.11  The constructed meaning of [FENCE]$^{\downarrow \text{L1}-\text{L3}}$

begin between *L1* and *L3*, then move apart so that the left hand moves backward to *L1* and the right hand moves diagonally ahead and to the right to *L3*. The movement of the hands in producing the placed noun [FENCE]$^{\downarrow \text{L1}-\text{L3}}$ depicts the extent of the fence along the diagonal on which the hands move. Thus, depicting verbs are not the only signs capable of depicting. The placed noun [FENCE]$^{\downarrow \text{L1}-\text{L3}}$ also depicts a |fence| as illustrated in Figure 9.11.

The placed noun [FENCE]$^{\downarrow \text{L1}-\text{L3}}$ is the initial sign in the description of a past event space in which a cat is lying on a fence. Its semantic pole profiles a fence on a surface. The profiled fence corresponds to the fence in the past event space. The surface in the semantic pole corresponds to the surface around the fence in the past event space. These correspondences are shown by the solid connectors between these entities.

The hands producing [FENCE]$^{\downarrow \text{L1}-\text{L3}}$ carry out the normal movements of the sign FENCE, but do so along a path that depicts the location of the |fence| in the depicting blend. The path followed by the hands is a projection into the blend of the location and extent of the fence in the past event space. In contrast to the earlier example in which a 3 hand blends with a car to become a |car|, the hands producing [FENCE]$^{\downarrow \text{L1}-\text{L3}}$ do not themselves blend with the fence in the past event space to become the |fence|. Rather, the vertical extent of the hands

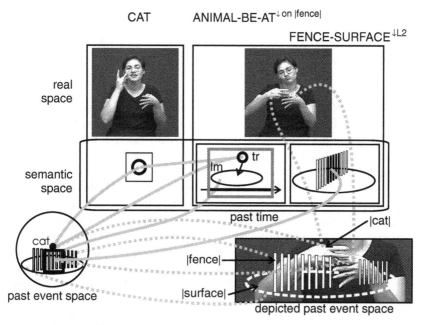

Figure 9.12  The constructed meaning of the clause describing a cat on a fence

and the path on which they move blend with the fence to produce the blended entity |fence|.

In sum, creating the depicted |fence| involves projections from the real-space production of $[FENCE]^{\downarrow L1-L3}$ and the past event space. The path of the signer's hands in real space identifies the line of the fence in the depiction. The past event space projects aspects of its fence and the space on the surface around it into the blend. That is, the signer is depicting a specific fence rather than fences in general. All this conceptual content lies behind the initial sign in Figure 9.9.

Figure 9.12 assumes that the |fence| already exists in the depicted past event space and illustrates how the clause CAT ANIMAL-BE-AT$^{\downarrow on|fence|}$-FENCE-SURFACE$^{\downarrow L2}$ elaborates the depicted past event space. The nondirectional noun CAT, the second sign in Figure 9.9, functions as the subject of ANIMAL-BE-AT$^{\downarrow on\ |fence|}$ and provides semantic information elaborating the verb's trajector. This is the normal syntactic mapping that occurs in an ASL subject–verb construction. Since CAT is the verb's subject, the animal depicted on the fence is a cat.[9]

---

[9] Padden (1988) provides good arguments for treating sequences such as the one being examined here as clauses, and for treating CAT as the subject of the verb.

As CAT is produced, the left hand remains in place at *L1* just ahead of the left shoulder, where it was at the conclusion of the sign [FENCE]$^{\downarrow L1-L3}$. Since it only remains in this position during the single sign CAT it is indeterminate whether it is a meaningless perseveration of a fragment of the preceding sign or a meaningful buoy in which the 4 handshape has blended with the fence.

The verb ANIMAL-BE-AT$^{\downarrow L}$ depicts the location of an animal on a surface.[10] Since the signer is describing a cat in a past event space, there is a connector between the verb's trajector and that cat. Typically the verb's landmark would correspond to a location on the ground in an event space. In this case, however, the landmark corresponds to a surface on the top of the fence in the event space. She moves her left hand from *L1*, just ahead of her left shoulder, to *L2*, a more central part of the depicted |fence|. Now the hand does participate in the blend by producing the depicting buoy FENCE-SURFACE$^{\downarrow L2}$. The depicting buoy makes that part of the |fence| visible. The depicting buoy does not signify the presence of another fence. Rather, it blends with the already conceptualized |fence|. Since the depicting buoy is not a verb expressing the presence of a fence, I gloss it as FENCE-SURFACE$^{\downarrow L2}$ rather than FENCE-SURFACE-BE-AT$^{\downarrow L2}$.[11]

The depicted |cat| involves projections from real space and the past event space. The hand from real space provides the physical substance for the |cat|. Projecting aspects of the cat from the past event space onto the hand makes the blended |cat| a depicted instance of that specific cat.

Since the two hands are simultaneously expressing meanings during the final sign in Figure 9.9, it would be natural to expect that the two were integrated morphologically. That is, it would be natural to assume that FENCE-SURFACE$^{\downarrow L2}$ was part of a two-handed lexical unit. While this is a possibility, it is not the only way to look at this sign. One could also assume that what the two hands are doing is not a single lexical unit. Given this assumption, FENCE-SURFACE$^{\downarrow L2}$ can be understood as conceptually elaborating the depicting blend rather than morphologically elaborating the semantic pole of the verb. That is, in Figure 9.9, ANIMAL-BE-AT$^{\downarrow \text{on |fence|}}$ makes contact with the radial surface of the weak hand, thus depicting the cat on the fence. However, the hand could just as easily have been placed on any surface within the depicting space. It could have been placed on the |ground| right next to the |fence|, on the |ground| near the |fence|,

---

[10] Note that the radial surface of the active hand is facing up. This suggests that wrist rotation may also be variable in the verb ANIMAL-BE-AT$^{\downarrow L}$.

[11] The verb FENCE-SURFACE-BE-AT$^{\downarrow L}$ does not exist in ASL. If it did, it would be produced with a short downward movement followed by a hold. There are instances, however, where there is a potential contrast between a downward-moving be-at verb and a simple hold. One such contrasting pair is the depicting verb UPRIGHT-PERSON-BE-AT$^{\downarrow L}$ and the depicting buoy UPRIGHT-PERSON$^{\downarrow L}$. The former is produced by a downward movement followed by a hold while the latter is produced by a hold only.

ARRIVE$^{\rightarrow L1}$                          [PEOPLE-LINE]$^{\downarrow L1-L2}$

Figure 9.13  The initial description of arriving at the Budget rental car area

or on the |ground| at any of innumerable distances away from the |fence|. Given this range of possible placements of the hand producing the verb, I am tentatively treating FENCE-SURFACE$^{\downarrow L2}$ as morphologically independent from the verb ANIMAL-BE-AT$^{\downarrow L}$. Put in another way, FENCE-SURFACE$^{\downarrow L2}$ elaborates the depicting space into which ANIMAL-BE-AT$^{\downarrow L}$ depicts the presence of a cat on a surface. Placing the active hand on top of the radial surface of the index finger of the weak hand depicts that surface as the |fence|. If this is correct, the weak hand functions to make the blended space more elaborate. In doing so, it provides a possible surface upon which to depict the presence of a cat. The verb ANIMAL-BE-AT$^{\downarrow L}$, produced by the strong hand, might depict a cat on that surface or some other surface within the depicting blend.[12]

## Shifting between a depicting space and a surrogate space

The examples below are taken from a signer's description of his experience renting a car. He first describes calling to reserve a car then arriving at a Budget car rental counter to pick it up. In Figure 9.13 he begins his description of the scene when he arrives at the car rental counter, apparently at an airport. The signs in Figure 9.13 explain that there was a line there when he arrived.

The weak hand of the citation form ARRIVE is normally placed centrally at about the chest level with the elbows bent at roughly a right angle. In Figure 9.13 the weak hand is held very low and is extended outward and slightly to the left. This non-neutral placement is significant. Since he has previously explained that he had a reservation with Budget, it makes sense to assume that he is directing the verb ARRIVE$^{\rightarrow L1}$ toward where the Budget agency at the airport has been

---

[12] It is possible, of course, that the sign depicting an animal on a fence occurs with sufficient frequency that it has become a conventional two-handed lexical unit. Making a determination one way or another would require the examination of large samples of signing in which signers described animals on fences. If such a study revealed consistent idiosyncratic formational or semantic properties, that would constitute evidence supporting the lexical status of the two-handed unit.

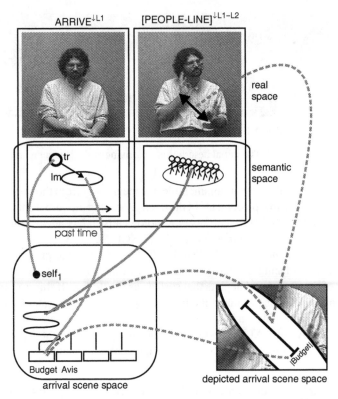

Figure 9.14 The constructed meaning of ARRIVE $^{\rightarrow L1}$ [PEOPLE-LINE]$^{\downarrow L1-L2}$

projected in the blend ahead of him. That is, the directionality of ARRIVE$^{\rightarrow L1}$ suggests that the Budget agency at the airport is projected slightly to the left of center in the space ahead of him.

The placed noun [PEOPLE-LINE]$^{\downarrow L1-L2}$ depicts a line of people extending from the location of ARRIVE$^{\rightarrow L1}$ backward toward the signer. Given that his destination was the Budget agency, the placed noun [PEOPLE-LINE]$^{\downarrow L1-L2}$ is depicting a line in front of the Budget counter.

Figure 9.14 illustrates how meanings are constructed in this example. The arrival scene space the signer is beginning to describe contains the recently arrived counterpart of the signer labeled 'self$_1$', a long snaking line at the Budget counter, and other rental car counters beside the Budget counter. The long line in the arrival scene space is drawn as a long snaking line based on what the signer will explain later. The trajector in the semantic pole of ARRIVE$^{\rightarrow L1}$ maps onto self$_1$, the counterpart of the signer in the arrival scene space. In order to keep figures as simple and readable as possible, they generally only include the relevant mental spaces, mappings between the semantic poles of signs and those spaces, and the projections needed to create the blends. Figure 9.14 does not, for example, include the mapping showing that the current signer is the counterpart of the entity 'self$_1$'.

ARRIVE$^{\rightarrow L1}$ points toward the destination within the depicting space. Since he has already explained that he had a reservation with Budget, it is logical to assume that he has arrived at the area containing the Budget counter. This will prompt the addressee to project the Budget agency into the depicted arrival scene space at that location. Note also that even though the verb ARRIVE$^{\rightarrow L1}$ is directed toward *L1*, this does not place the counterpart of the signer at *L1*. That is, he has arrived at the (general) location of the Budget counter, but is not at the head of the line.

In producing [PEOPLE-LINE]$^{\downarrow L1-L2}$, the two hands begin together then move apart, similar to the production of the placed noun [FENCE]$^{\downarrow L1-L3}$ discussed earlier in this chapter. The right hand moves backward and up toward the right shoulder and the left hand moves forward and down toward a location approximating *L1*, the location he directed ARRIVE$^{\rightarrow L1}$ toward. At the conclusion of the sign, the left hand is much lower than the right. The movement of the hands along a path from *L1* to *L2* depicts the location of a line of people at |Budget|. The depicted |line of people| gets its physical extent from the path of the hands in real space. Since his left hand moves to *L1*, he is depicting a line at the Budget counter.

The depicted |line of people| differs in an interesting way from the depicted |fence| in the preceding example. The depicted |fence| was in a level depicting space. The |line of people| in this example is much lower at the front of the line than at the back. In spite of the fact that one hand is much lower than the other, the signer is nevertheless depicting a line of people on a horizontal surface. Depicting a horizontal surface by means of this inclined space is not limited to this sign. There is, for example, a sign depicting large numbers of people converging at a place. It begins with each hand above its respective shoulder, palm down, and fingertips pointing forward. While the fingers wiggle, the two hands move forward *and down* toward a central location ahead of the signer. The sign does not either signify or imply that the crowds of people traveled downward to the site. Similarly, recall that the depicting verb UPRIGHT-PERSON-WALK-TO$^{\downarrow L1-L2}$ describes the purposeful walking movement of one person from location *L1* to location *L2*. To express that a single person walked from behind the signer to a place ahead of the signer, the hand begins above the shoulder and moves downward toward the appropriate location in the blend ahead of the signer. Signs such as these suggest that depicting a horizontal surface by using a blended surface that inclines upward toward the shoulders is conventional in ASL.

There are physiological reasons why such a convention might develop. For example, because of the structure of the wrist, it would be very difficult to sign [PEOPLE-LINE]$^{\downarrow L1-L2}$ by moving the strong hand horizontally backward toward the body at the trunk level. Thus, it appears that the strong hand moves up toward the shoulder as a result of a convention that may have developed, at least in part, for a physiological reason.

The depicting blend inherits both the past temporal setting of the event as well as the conceptual location of the event from the past event space. In addition, it also inherits its real-space, here-and-now immediacy from real space. As a result, it is an immediate, here-and-now depiction of the past event at another location. Although the signer is not gazing at the elements of this blend, it nevertheless creates the blend from his point of view since it depicts the line from the perspective of someone at the end of the line rather than from the perspective of someone at the beginning of the line, someone viewing the line from the side, someone viewing the line from behind the Budget counter, etc.

Thus far the signer has only described the presence of a line at a place. This places the burden of conceptualizing the blend on the addressee. An addressee familiar with car rental counters at an airport is likely to conceive of |Budget| being located on a floor inside the airport. If rental car counters were typically circular, then an addressee would probably assume a circular shape for the counter. Since rental car counters in an airport are typically located side by side and are not typically circular, this is the type of depicting blend the addressee is likely to conceptualize.

The signs in Figure 9.15 add additional information about the area surrounding the Budget counter. The signer explains that there is an Avis counter to the left by directing THERE$^{\rightarrow L3}$ to the left and signing A-V-I-S with his strong hand.[13] Next he directs WAY-OVER-THERE$^{\rightarrow L4}$ to the far left. Rather than naming the businesses in that far left location, he produces what appears to be a reduced form of DIFFERENT$^{[EXHAUSTIVE] \supset x}$ with only two contacts between the fingers. This is followed by THAT-AREA$^{\supset L4}$, also directed to the far left. This is how he explains that there are a number of different car rental counters in that area.

He then adds the comment, SMALL PEOPLE-LINE, while his face and body are still facing left. I am treating this as a phrase consisting of the nondirectional adjective SMALL and the nondirectional noun PEOPLE-LINE because both signs are produced directly ahead of his body. An additional reason for not considering PEOPLE-LINE to be placed is that it is highly reduced. The two

---

[13] Since he produces THERE$^{\rightarrow L3}$ with his weak hand, it is confusable with POINTER $^{\rightarrow}$. I treat this sign as THERE$^{\rightarrow L3}$ because is has an outward movement component and because he also signs the third and fifth signs in this utterance with his left hand.

A-V-I-S;
THERE<sup>→L3</sup>--------------------   WAY-OVER-THERE<sup>→L4</sup>

DIFFERENT<sup>[EXHAUSTIVE]</sup> כx  ;

THAT-AREA<sup>כL4</sup>

SMALL          PEOPLE-LINE

Figure 9.15 Using a surrogate blend to talk about the area near the Budget counter

hands merely appear to make contact and I am unable to detect any of the expected movement of PEOPLE-LINE that would separate the two hands along a line. Since his face and body are oriented to the left, it is as if he were giving a commentary about the things he encounters on his left. In other words, the lines at the counters to the left were small.

There are significant differences between the signing in Figures 9.13 and 9.15 that result in different types of blends. The key differences can be found in the signer's eye gaze, the angle of his head, and the height of the directional signs. In Figure 9.13 his head and eye gaze, at least initially, are directed slightly downward and the resulting blended space extends from a low level well ahead of his trunk to a higher level ahead of his shoulder. The final frame in Figure 9.13 shows the head and eye gaze at a higher level, apparently beginning a transition to the signing in Figure 9.15.

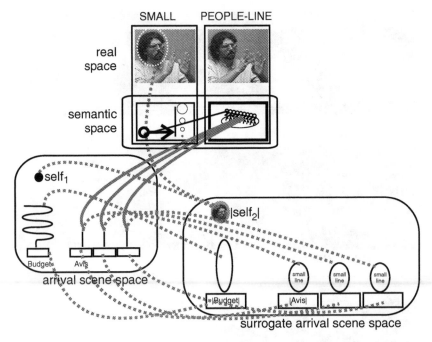

Figure 9.16  Elaborating the surrogate blend with SMALL PEOPLE-LINE

The directional signs in Figure 9.15 are directed and placed at roughly the shoulder level. In addition, in many of the frames in Figure 9.15, the signer's head is tilted back slightly and he appears to be gazing at things well ahead of him. These differences signal the existence of a surrogate blend, which is also topographical, but now *includes* the signer. It is difficult to represent the scale of this blend graphically. The blend cannot be represented as the area immediately in front of the signer as in Figure 9.14 because the signer is signing as if he were there looking at the expansive scene around him. The Budget counter is ahead of him and the other car rental counters spread out to his left.

Figure 9.16 represents the surrogate space and the projections from the other spaces needed to construct it as he signs SMALL PEOPLE-LINE. Creating the surrogate |self$_2$| involves blending his face and head from real space with self$_1$ in the arrival scene space. The surrogate blend is much more expansive than the previous depicting blend and includes the previously mentioned Budget counter as well as the counters to the left of it from the signer's perspective. To understand the scale of the blend properly, one must imagine a full-sized signer in the actual car rental area. As the signer produces THERE$^{\rightarrow L3}$ followed by A-V-I-S, his eye gaze is directed to the left at |Avis| in the large surrogate blend. Similarly, his body posture, eye gaze, and the directional signs

WAY-OVER-THERE$^{\rightarrow L4}$ DIFFERENT$^{[EXHAUSTIVE]\supset x}$ and THAT-AREA$^{\supset L4}$ indicate that there are additional rental car agencies even further to the left.

He signals the existence of the surrogate space by rotating his face and torso to the left and raising the level of his gaze. The signer from real space and the entity 'self$_1$' (his counterpart in the past event space) are projected into the surrogate space to create the surrogate |self$_2$|, who has just arrived at the surrogate arrival space. The signer has already described the presence of a line of people at the Budget counter. He is now describing additional lines at other rental car counters to the left of the Budget counter.

He produces the phrase SMALL PEOPLE-LINE with his face and body rotated to the left. Both signs are produced at a relatively high level, but directly ahead of his rotated torso. This phrase is describing several lines to the left of the Budget counter. The way the phrase SMALL PEOPLE-LINE is signed in Figure 9.16 gives the impression that he is commenting on what he is seeing at the moment. His eye gaze is directed toward the left of the very large blend in Figure 9.16, and he appears to be mentioning simply what is there on the left. This associates the phrase's semantic structure with the space to the left. This association elaborates the surrogate space with surrogate lines at each of the other rental car counters.

It is very common in ASL discourse to alternate between different types of blended spaces. Recall that the signer began the discussion of renting a car by creating a depicting blend with the signs ARRIVE$^{\rightarrow L1}$ [PEOPLE-LINE]$^{\downarrow L1-L2}$. Then he created a surrogate blend with his description of the other rental car counters and the short lines in front of each. Now he returns to the previously developed depicting blend with the signs in Figure 9.17.

With his strong hand, he directs THERE$^{\rightarrow L1}$ low and directly ahead and simultaneously produces POINTER$^{\rightarrow L1}$ with his weak hand. THERE$^{\rightarrow L1}$ is directed toward |Budget| in the depicted arrival scene space illustrated in Figure 9.14. Directing THERE$^{\rightarrow L1}$ in this way along with changing his own body orientation and eye gaze signals the return to the depicting blend. It is possible that the information presented about the other car rental counters, where they were located, and the short lines at those counters in the previous surrogate blend could also potentially expand the depicting blend. The question is moot, however, since he does not direct any additional signs toward these entities.

Next, he identifies the location he has been pointing at by producing a highly abbreviated spelling of Budget, followed by the verb SNAKING-PEOPLE-LINE-EXTEND-TO$^{\downarrow L1-L2}$, illustrated in the final six pictures in Figure 9.17. A comparison of the positions of his two hands at the conclusion of this sign shows that the hands are approximately at the locations $L1$ and $L2$ previously used by the placed noun [PEOPLE-LINE]$^{\downarrow L1-L2}$.

The left hand is placed at $L1$ – the location of |Budget| in the depicted past event space and the front of the |line of people|. His right hand begins at the

THERE$^{\to L1}$           #BUDGET(reduced)          SNAKING-PEOPLE-LINE-EXTEND-TO$^{\downarrow L1-L2}$
POINTER$^{\to L1}$ ----------------------------------------

(continued)

Figure 9.17  There was a long snaking line there (at the Budget counter)

radial surface of the weak hand, moving to the left, back to the right, back to the left, and then back to the right again to a location approximating *L2*.[14] This sign encodes the meaning 'snaking line of people present at a place' and the movements of his strong hand depict the location and extent of the snaking line.

The snaking way the line at the Budget counter is depicted in Figure 9.17 might appear to conflict with the initial description of the line in Figure 9.13, where the two hands produced [PEOPLE-LINE]$^{\downarrow L1-L2}$. In the initial description of the line at the Budget counter, the hands move along a straight path while in Figure 9.17 the strong hand moves from side to side. The two descriptions, however, are not contradictory. The first description only expresses the presence of a line extending away from the Budget counter, without being explicit about the shape of the line. The second description is explicit about the shape of the line, describing a line that snakes back and forth in front of the counter.

In order to understand the noncontradictory nature of these two ways of representing a line, it is important to distinguish between semantic structure and iconicity. The noun PEOPLE-LINE is used to describe a line of people. The line does not need to be straight in order to describe it with this noun. PEOPLE-LINE is iconic in that a line of people is commonly straight. Although this iconicity is built into the lexical structure of PEOPLE-LINE, it does not govern its semantics. That is, in spite of the iconicity of the noun, [PEOPLE-LINE]$^{\downarrow L1-L2}$ merely expresses the presence of a line between *L1*

[14] The signer does not keep his weak hand stationary as his right hand moves back and forth. When his strong hand initially moves left, for example, his weak hand moves slightly right. Later, when his strong hand moves back to the right, the weak hand moves left. There appears to be no semantic import to this movement, which appears simply to aid in maintaining balance.

and *L2*, without being explicit about its shape. Later, SNAKING-PEOPLE-LINE-EXTEND-TO$^{\downarrow L1-L2}$ provides a more explicit description of the shape of the line.

The straight and snaking movements of these two signs are characteristics of the lexical forms of the signs themselves. The placed noun [PEOPLE-LINE]$^{\downarrow L1-L2}$ is the more constrained of the two signs since its flexibility is in its endpoints only. The verb SNAKING-PEOPLE-LINE-EXTEND-TO$^{\downarrow L1-L2}$ also has variable endpoints, but in addition, has variable widths and variable numbers of left to right movements of the hand, depending on how the signer chooses to depict the snaking line. For example, a snaking line that had very long sideways components could be signed with very long sideways movements. A snaking line with comparatively narrow sideways components could be signed with shorter side-to-side movements.

### Depicting shapes

ASL has a large set of signs that encode and depict aspects of shape. The verb SNAKING-PEOPLE-LINE-EXTEND-TO$^{\downarrow L1-L2}$ is a sign of this type since it not only encodes the presence of a snaking line of people at a place, but also depicts aspects of the extent and shape of the line within a depicting blend. Figure 9.18 provides an additional example. The lecturer is explaining that the concept of culture is difficult to define. She states that anthropologists do not agree about what the term *culture* means and that virtually every anthropologist has a distinct way of defining it. She arbitrarily selects 162 as the number of

TEXT-PAGE-EXTEND-TO$^{\downarrow L1-L2}$      TEXT-PAGE- EXTEND-TO $^{\downarrow L3-L4}$

TEXT-PAGE- EXTEND-TO $^{\downarrow L5-L6}$    TEXT-PAGE- EXTEND-TO $^{\downarrow L7-L8}$

TEXT-PAGE- EXTEND-TO $^{\downarrow L9-L10}$

Figure 9.18  pages and pages and pages . . . filled with text distinct existing definitions of culture and explains that if the audience wishes to read about these definitions there will be a lot of reading to do. In describing the amount of reading, the lecturer depicts pages and pages and pages of reading, as shown in Figure 9.18.

The noun PAGE is produced by the thumb extended from a fist making a repeated brushing motion of the pad of the thumb against the upward-facing palm in the direction of the forearm. This noun expresses the meaning 'page', but is not a depicting sign. The lecturer does not use this sign to talk about pages and pages of reading. Instead, she selects the depicting sign TEXT-PAGE-EXTEND-TO$^{\downarrow L-L'}$ shown in Figure 9.18. Her signing depicts extensive numbers of pages filled with text. The weak hand is placed at *L1*, depicting the beginning of the text while the strong hand depicts the extent of the text by producing multiple instances of TEXT-PAGE-EXTEND-TO$^{\downarrow L-L'}$, with each repeated downward movement further to the right than the previous downward movement. Each individual downward movement depicts the vertical extent of the text and the displaced repetitions show its horizontal extent.[15]

She expands this blended space with each downward repetition of the verb. Not only do these repetitions expand the blend on the right, but her weak hand also expands the blend on the left. During the first downward repetition of the verb her left hand begins ahead of her cheek but moves to above her shoulder. During the next repetition, her left hand moves even further to the left. It remains at this extended position during subsequent repetitions of the verb.

There are two distinct ways that signers use repetition to depict multiple entities. To depict a single stack of papers on a table, for example, the weak hand with a palm-up B shape remains stationary at the level of the depicted table surface while the strong hand in a palm-down B shape moves from palm-to-palm contact upward, thus depicting the stack of papers (see BROAD-HORIZONTAL-ENTITY-STACK-EXTEND-TO$^{\downarrow L1-L2}$ below). In depicting multiple stacks of paper, both hands are relocated to depict the next stack of papers. The signing in Figure 9.18 illustrates the other type of depiction. In this sign, the weak hand does not move to the right along with the strong hand. Rather, it serves as a landmark depicting the starting point of all the pages and pages of information.

The sign BUMPY-BROAD-SURFACE-EXTEND-TO$^{\downarrow L1-L2}$ in Figure 9.19 describes and depicts a broad bumpy surface.[16] The weak hand is placed at one end of the depicted surface while the movement of the strong hand depicts the extent of the bumpy surface.

Similar signs depict linear arrangements of individual entities. For example, BROAD-VERTICAL-ENTITY-ROW-EXTEND-TO$^{\downarrow L1-L2}$ could be used

---

[15] This sign is typically used to describe pages filled with writing. It would not be used to describe extensive numbers of blank pages.

[16] This sign was previously illustrated in Figure 9.2b.

BUMPY-BROAD-SURFACE-EXTEND-TO$^{\downarrow L1-L2}$

Figure 9.19 A verb depicting shape and extent

to depict a row of books, videotapes, or other similarly shaped entities. The placement of the weak B hand depicts the beginning of the row while the sideward movement of the strong B hand depicts the horizontal extent of the row. Subsequent repetitions can be produced at progressively lower levels by movements of the strong hand, while the weak hand maintains its original location.

The verb BROAD-HORIZONTAL-ENTITY-STACK-EXTEND-TO$^{\downarrow L1-L2}$ describes and depicts a vertical stack of (typically) papers. Repetitions depicting additional stacks require the weak hand to move to the location of the next stack being depicted. In addition to the difference with respect to how the weak hand behaves in depicting multiple instances of stacks versus rows, these two signs also differ in the way that the two hands line up with respect to one another. In both verbs, the palm of the strong B hand faces and moves away from the palm of the stationary weak B hand. To produce BROAD-VERTICAL-ENTITY-ROW-EXTEND-TO$^{\downarrow L1-L2}$, the stationary weak hand is held with the fingertips pointing up and the palm to the side. The same applies to the active hand. As a result, the hands contact one another symmetrically, fingers against fingers and palm against palm. BROAD-HORIZONTAL-ENTITY-STACK-EXTEND-TO$^{\downarrow L1-L2}$ is similar, but does not require that the two hands contact one another symmetrically. Although the inside surfaces of the two hands still make contact, it is typical for the directions of the extended fingers of the two hands to cross at an angle. Thus, in addition to the semantic difference between stacks and rows, there are two formational differences that support treating these two verbs as distinct from one another. They differ with respect to whether the weak hand remains in place during the depiction to multiple stacks or rows, and with respect to the angles at which the two hands contact one another.

VEHICLE-ROW-EXTEND-TO$^{\downarrow L1-L2}$ is similar to BROAD-VERTICAL-ENTITY-ROW-EXTEND-TO$^{\downarrow L1-L2}$. It is produced with radial side up 3 handshapes and depicts a row of side-by-side vehicles. Multiple repetitions of VEHICLE-ROW-EXTEND-TO$^{\downarrow L-L}$, with each repetition nearer the signer than the previous repetition, depict multiple horizontal rows of vehicles.

The verb VEHICLE-BE-AT$^{[EXHAUSTIVE]\downarrow L1-L2}$ also depicts a line of vehicles, but is produced with rapid up-and-down movements of the active hand as it moves away from the stationary weak hand. Because it is an exhaustive form, VEHICLE-BE-AT$^{[\text{EXHAUSTIVE}]\downarrow\text{L1}-\text{L2}}$ appears to place more emphasis on the number of individual vehicles making up the row.

The verb VEHICLE-LINE-EXTEND-TO$^{\downarrow\text{L1}-\text{L2}}$ also depicts a linear arrangement of vehicles, but depicts them end to end rather than side by side. In this case the weak hand depicts the front of the line of vehicles and the strong hand moves backward, away from the back of the first depicted vehicle, thereby depicting the line of vehicles.

SMALL-CYLINDRICAL-SURFACE-EXTEND-TO$^{\downarrow\text{L1}-\text{L2}}$ depicts a pipe-shaped entity. Both hands are configured in an F handshape. The curved thumb and index finger touch to produce a round shape. This is the part of the handshape that participates in the depicting blend. The round shape depicts a non-moving cross section of a pipe. The strong hand begins its movement aligned with and in contact with the non-moving weak hand. It then moves along a path depicting the shape of the length of the pipe. It could depict a straight pipe, a curved pipe, a pipe with bends in it, etc.

The signs described in this section vary between those that depict a continuous entity (e.g. a flat surface, small round cross-sectional pipe-like surface) and those that depict a linear arrangement of discrete entities (e.g. a row of cars, a shelf of books, a stack of papers). If the oriented handshape signifies a discrete entity (e.g. a vehicle) then the movement of the hand depicts a linear arrangement of discrete entities. If the oriented handshape signifies part of a surface, then the moving handshape depicts the shape of the surface. The sign describing a snaking line of people depicts a continuous line. That is, we understand a line to be continuous if there are no large distances between the individuals that make up the line. The vertical 4 handshape depicts a section (surface) of such a line, just as the palm-down B handshape depicts a part of a flat surface.

Talmy (2000) describes language use that attributes movement to non-moving entities as fictive motion. Consider, for example, the difference between Talmy's examples in (1).

(1)     a. That mountain range lies (longitudinally) between Canada and Mexico.

b. That mountain range goes from Canada to Mexico.

c. That mountain range goes from Mexico to Canada.

Although all three examples describe the same mountain range, (1a) describes its position statically. In (1b) and (1c) the speaker uses a verb of motion (*go*), a starting point and an ending point. Of interest here is whether ASL verbs depicting shapes are also examples of fictive motion. The answer appears to hinge on how the motion is expressed. In Talmy's treatment, fictive motion is expressed through verbs that encode motion (e.g. *go*).

ASL verbs depicting shapes do not make use of verbs of motion. Rather, they introduce motion by means of *a moving hand*. In other words, the motion is depicted rather than encoded. It is possible to look at fictive motion narrowly by requiring that verbs of motion be a part of how fictive motion is defined. The ASL data allow for a broader look at the concept. If fictive motion is broadly defined such that conceptual motion is used to describe non-moving entities, then the ASL data would fall under that broad definition. This is because the moving, depicting hand expresses the shape and extent of the entity being described. Thus, motion is a conceptually important component of the ASL verbs depicting shape and extent. English can use a verb of motion to describe a static line of people, as in *the line went all the way around the corner*. An equivalent ASL sign describes the static line with a moving hand depicting the shape and length of the line.

### Depicting actions

Verbs depicting actions typically depict movement from one place to another. For example, UPRIGHT-PERSON-WALK-ALONG$^{\downarrow L1-L2}$ depicts the walking movement of a person from a starting location *L1* to a final location *L2*. For other movement depicting verbs, however, the starting and ending locations of the hand may not correspond to the origin and destination of the movement. The sign VEHICLE-PASS-BY$^{\downarrow L1-L2}$ (Figure 9.6), for example, depicts only the movement of the vehicle as it passes by. The initial and final locations of the hand are located on a vector that shows the direction of travel of the vehicle, but not the origin of its movement or its destination. It is understood that the movement started prior to passing by and continued afterward.

Figure 9.20 shows an instance of UPRIGHT-PERSON-WALK-ALONG$^{\downarrow L1-L2}$ (also illustrated in Figure 9.25a). It is produced with a vertical 1 handshape that moves along a path while the hand bobs up and down. It describes a person walking along in an unhurried manner and a normal forward orientation.

UPRIGHT-PERSON-WALK-ALONG$^{\downarrow L1-L2}$

Figure 9.20 A verb depicting movement

UPRIGHT-PERSON-WALK-ALONG↓L1–L2

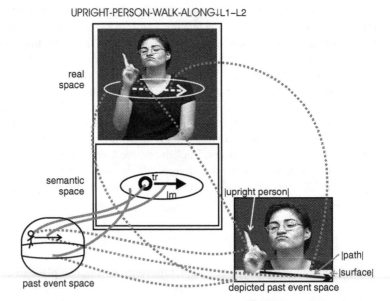

Figure 9.21 The constructed meaning of UPRIGHT-PERSON-WALK-ALONG ↓L1–L2

The depicting blend in this example involves projections parallel to depicting blends seen in previous examples. In Figure 9.21, the depicted |upright person| gets its physical form from the 1 handshape in real space and gets its conceptual attributes from the past event space. The distance and direction of travel blend with the movement path of the hand. The |surface| the |upright person| is depicted as walking on also involves projections from the same two spaces.

UPRIGHT-PERSON-WALK-ALONG↓L1–L2 depicts the movement of the upright person walking along a path. The up-and-down movement of the hand producing UPRIGHT-PERSON-WALK-ALONG↓L1–L2 is part of the lexical form of the sign. It may have some iconic value since a person's head actually does move up and down slightly as a person walks, but it does not appear to contribute symbolically to the meaning of the verb.

### Depicting perceived motion

An additional category of verbs depicts the perceived movement of the environment past a moving object.[17] For example, the depicting verb SURFACE-MOVE-BACKWARD-UNDERNEATH-VEHICLE[habitual]↓L1 illustrated in Figure 9.22 expresses the rapid perceived backward movement of a surface

---

[17] This type of sign was initially investigated in Lucas and Valli (1990).

Figure 9.22    SURFACE-MOVE-BACKWARD-UNDERNEATH-
VEHICLE[HABITUAL]↓L1

Figure 9.23  POLE-PASS-BESIDE-ME

underneath a forward-moving vehicle. The rapidly moving surface underneath
the vehicle is depicted by the rapid back-and-forth oscillation of a palm-down
B handshape underneath a radial side up 3 handshape. The palm-down B handshape signifies a broad flat surface while the radial side up 3 handshape signifies
a vehicle. Since the sign depicts the motion of a non-moving surface through
the movement of the weak hand, this is also an example of fictive motion.

From the point of view of a stationary external observer, the vehicle is moving and the ground is not. From inside the car, however, an observer perceives
a stationary vehicle with the environment passing by. The sign in Figure 9.22
depicts the event from an external perspective, but nevertheless depicts a stationary vehicle and a moving surface. That is, it places the vehicle in the middle
of a 'viewing window' and depicts the relative movement of the surface underneath the vehicle with respect to it. This is similar to the cinematic experience of
seeing a moving vehicle from the perspective of a camera moving alongside the
car at the same speed. Since the camera (viewer) is moving at the same speed
as the vehicle, the vehicle appears stationary while the environment moves
past.

Depicting verbs can also take the point of view of the signer as perceiver. In
Figure 9.23 the signer describes the experience of sitting on a train as it starts
moving. As the train begins to move forward, the signer describes a telephone
pole slowly passing beside her. As the speed of the train gradually increases the
individual telephone poles pass by at faster rates. Finally, the poles are passing

VERTICAL-SURFACE-PASS-IN-FRONT-OF-ME[INCESSANT]          DISAPPEAR-TOWARD[→]

Figure 9.24  A sequence of two verbs depicting a train passing by

by at such a rapid rate that they are no longer individual poles, but appear as a continuous stream of poles passing by.

In Figure 9.23 the signer produces the verb POLE-PASS-BESIDE-ME at a slow speed.[18] She next produces additional instances of the same verb, each more rapid than the preceding one. It is interesting to note that when a train is moving rapidly, the individual poles alongside the moving train appear as a continuous blur of poles rather than as individual poles. The verb VERTICAL-SURFACE-PASS-BESIDE-ME[INCESSANT] captures this perceptual difference.[19] It is produced with a vertical 5 hand, palm to signer, oscillating backward and forward alongside her head.[20] There is also a nonmanual component to this sign. The signer puckers her lips and narrows her eyes as her hand oscillates alongside the head. This verb is produced with a vertical 5 handshape, signifying a faceted surface, to capture the rapidly moving blurry "surface" of poles passing by the moving train.

The verb VERTICAL-SURFACE-PASS-IN-FRONT-OF-ME[INCESSANT], the initial sign in Figure 9.24 also expresses the presence of a rapidly moving "surface" passing by the signer, but in this case the signer is describing a train passing directly in front of a stationary observer. It is produced like VERTICAL-SURFACE-PASS-BESIDE-ME[INCESSANT], but directly ahead of the face with a side-to-side oscillating movement. Like rapidly moving poles as viewed from a moving train, a rapidly moving train when viewed from a vantage point near the train also appears as a blurry surface. This sign, as produced by the right hand, describes a train moving from right to left from the

---

[18] The gloss for POLE-PASS-BESIDE-ME does not specify variable starting and ending points because the starting and ending points appear to be lexically fixed.

[19] Klima and Bellugi (1979) describe the incessant aspect as produced by "short tense iterated movement" (p. 292). The verb VERTICAL-SURFACE-PASS-BESIDE-ME[INCESSANT] is produced with a rapid forward and backward oscillating movement. I suspect that the movements Klima and Bellugi describe as short, tense, and iterated are the same as what I am describing as oscillating movements.

[20] I did not include the direction of the movement of the vertical surface (i.e. backward) in the gloss for this sign. One reason for this is to try to minimize the length of the gloss. Another reason is that there is no contrasting sign with forward movement.

Figure 9.25 SIXTEEN

viewer's perspective. It appears that signers would use the left hand to describe a rightward-moving train.

The oscillating movement depicts the rapidly moving surface of the train passing in front of a viewer. This verb is typically followed by the directional sign I am glossing here as DISAPPEAR-TOWARD$^\rightarrow$, since it expresses the disappearance of an entity in a specific direction. It begins with a 5 handshape and ends with an A handshape. The way the hand changes from a 5 to an A contributes to the meaning 'disappear'. That is, there is more than one way to change handshapes. The change can take place in a physiologically direct way or in a less than direct way. For example, the sign SIXTEEN in Figure 9.25, begins with an A handshape that changes to a 6. The handshape change is direct in that all the fingers open at the same time and the thumb makes contact with the little finger. The sign FEW also typically opens from an A to a 6, but the fingers open in sequence. First the index finger is extended, then the middle finger, etc. This type of handshape change is called *progressive handshape change* (Johnson and Liddell, in preparation). The verb DISAPPEAR-TOWARD$^\rightarrow$ is also produced with progressive handshape change. The little finger begins to close first, followed by the ring finger, the middle finger, the index finger, and finally, the thumb.

Progressive handshape change appears in other signs involving disappearance. For example, Figure 9.26 shows a common string of verbs depicting the motion of a person walking away from the signer, becoming small because of the distance, and finally disappearing from view. Progressive handshape change is an important component of the final sign in this series, which also expresses a disappearance from view.

The first verb, UPRIGHT-PERSON-WALK-ALONG$^{\downarrow L1-L2}$ depicts a person moving along a path from near the signer at *L1* to a more distant location at *L2*. This is immediately followed by the depicting verb ENTITY-MOVE-AWAY-SHRINKING$^{\downarrow L2-L3}$, which depicts the person becoming (perceptually) smaller in size as the distance from the signer increases. The progressively smaller distance between the thumb and the tip of the index finger depicts the change in size. Finally, the index finger and thumb make contact. Since there is no space between them, the person is depicted as no longer having a vertical dimension. In

UPRIGHT-PERSON-WALK-ALONG[⁺L1–L2]     ENTITY-MOVE-AWAY-SHRINKING[⁺L2–L3]

ENTITY-DISAPPEAR-FROM-VIEW[⁺L3]

Figure 9.26 Depicting a person walking away then disappearing because of the distance

Figure 9.27 DISSOLVE

spite of this, the signer adds an additional component signifying disappearance. The flat handshape, created when the pad of the index finger makes contact with the pad of the thumb, next changes to an A through progressive handshape change. This final change to an A handshape through progressive handshape change signifies the ultimate disappearance of the entity. The handshape change is progressive because the thumb slides along the index finger as it moves to its final position on the radial surface of the hand in producing the A handshape.

Interestingly, the sign DISSOLVE (Figure 9.27) is also produced by changing from a stacked O finger configuration (Johnson and Liddell, in preparation), with the thumb in contact with the little finger, to an A handshape through progressive handshape change.

The sign DISAPPEAR-TOWARD[→] (Figure 9.24) begins with the 5 handshape of VERTICAL-SURFACE-PASS-IN-FRONT-OF-ME[INCESSANT] then, during the course of the movement to the left, changes to an A handshape by means of progressive handshape change. What all these signs expressing disappearance have in common is a change from an initial handshape to an A handshape through progressive handshape change. It is not difficult, therefore, to associate a change to an A handshape through progressive handshape change with disappearance. Figure 9.26 ends with the sign I have glossed as ENTITY-DISAPPEAR-FROM-VIEW$^{\downarrow L3}$. Even though the sign describing a train disappearing to the left (Figure 9.24) and the sign DISSOLVE both share the concept 'disappear from view' and are both produced with a progressive handshape change to an A handshape, they are not easily divided into morphemic components. However, regardless of whether the change to an A handshape by means of progressive handshape change is best viewed as a morpheme or just suggestive of the meaning 'disappear', it is a significant component of all these signs in that they share the meaning 'disappear from view' and the change to an A handshape through progressive handshape change.

### Depiction and metaphor

In the example below, the lecturer is emphasizing the inseparability of language and culture. She begins a metaphorical description of the inseparability of the two with the non-depicting signs in (2). She personifies culture and language by treating them as marriage partners.

(2)     NOW, CULTURE LANGUAGE DIVORCE CAN'T.
        QUOTE, MARRY FOR LIFE
        Culture and language cannot be divorced. They are, so to speak,
        "married for life."

The signs QUOTE, MARRY FOR LIFE invite us to understand the inseparability of culture and language as a lifelong bond. One of the normal uses of the sign QUOTE is to identify nonstandard ASL usage. MARRY FOR LIFE is nonstandard in two ways. First, it is a sign-for-spoken-word representation of the English phrase *married for life*. Second, it is nonstandard because the partners in the marriage are culture and language.

She continues the metaphor using depicting signs. The verb DIVORCE, the second sign in Figure 9.28, can easily be seen as iconic. It is produced with two D handshapes that begin together then separate. Its iconicity comes from separating the two D handshapes that began together. That is, in a divorce, the marriage partners separate, and in producing DIVORCE the two hands separate. Although D handshapes do not appear in existing depicting verbs, the similarity of the D and 1 handshapes allows the separation of the two hands to be viewed iconically as the separation of two humans. I am not suggesting that the iconicity is responsible for the meaning of the sign. Iconicity aside, the

SUPPOSE                DIVORCE

DIVORCED-ENTITY-FALL$^{\downarrow L1-L2}$        DIVORCED-ENTITY-BOUNCE$^{\downarrow L2}$
DIVORCED-ENTITY$^{\downarrow L3}$ -----------------------------------------------------------------

DIE$^{\rightarrow a}$
DIVORCED-ENTITY$^{\downarrow L3}$

DIVORCED-ENTITY$^{\downarrow L2}$ ----------------------------------------------------------------
DIVORCED-ENTITY-FALL$^{\downarrow L3-L4}$                    DIE$^{\rightarrow b}$

Figure 9.28  A metaphoric depiction of the divorce and death of language and culture

sign means 'divorce'. However, in the context of a sign meaning 'divorce', the separating handshapes could be interpreted iconically. It is this *potential* that the signer exploits next.[21]

In Figure 9.28, the signer blends personified language and culture with the two hands producing DIVORCE. One of the hands blends with culture and the other blends with language. She does not make this clear until she produces the novel verb DIVORCED-ENTITY-FALL$^{\downarrow L1-L2}$. This sign depicts one of the divorced entities falling downward and striking a surface. The impact is great enough that the entity bounces once before finally coming to rest. She next signs DIE$^{\rightarrow a}$, where *a* is the divorced entity at *L2*.

The verb DIVORCED-ENTITY-FALL$^{\downarrow L1-L2}$ is a novel verb. It is patterned after existing verbs, but differs from existing verbs in the handshape used and the significance of that handshape. Previously illustrated depicting verbs, such as UPRIGHT-PERSON-WALK-ALONG$^{\downarrow L1-L2}$, use a vertical 1 handshape that depicts an upright human. In describing a person falling, a signer would typically use the verb FALL$^{L1\rightarrow L2}$ since there is no depicting verb produced with a 1 handshape depicting a person falling. The verb is also novel because it uses a handshape not seen in other depicting verbs. She produces DIVORCED-ENTITY-FALL$^{\downarrow L1-L2}$ with a D handshape. While both the D and the 1 handshapes are produced with only the index finger fully extended, they differ in the configuration of the remaining fingers and thumb. In a 1 handshape the thumb and remaining fingers form a fist. In a D handshape the tip of the thumb contacts the tip of the middle finger. The remaining two fingers can either be aligned with the middle finger or may be completely closed. In the novel verb DIVORCED-ENTITY-FALL$^{\downarrow L1-L2}$ she uses a D handshape to depict one of the divorced entities falling upon a hard surface. It lands with such impact that it dies. She describes its death with the sign DIE$^{\rightarrow a}$, produced at the location of the impact.

She next depicts the falling of the other entity and its death. During the fall of the second entity, the now dead first entity is once again depicted on the signer's right hand with a D handshape. That is, after signing DIE$^{\rightarrow a}$ she replaces the B handshape used to produce DIE$^{\rightarrow a}$ with a D handshape, depicting the now dead entity at *L2*. Thus, in addition to creating the novel depicting verb DIVORCED-ENTITY-FALL$^{\downarrow L1-L2}$, she also creates a novel depicting buoy DIVORCED-ENTITY$^{\downarrow L2}$.

In a prototypical ideal marriage, marriage partners support one another. Standing together gives the two partners power. If one falters, becomes ill, and so on, the other is there to provide support. If the partners divorce, they

---

[21] Some ASL lexical items also possess the potential for creative metaphoric exploitation. Okrent (1997), for example, examines a case in which a signer takes advantage of the metaphoric iconicity of OPPRESS to create the novel sign REMOVE-OPPRESSION.

no longer have that support. In the physical world, if physical objects are not properly supported they fall down and can be damaged. This is what is depicted in this example. Once separated, the divorced entities 'language' and 'culture' are not able to support themselves and they fall to their deaths. It is particularly interesting to note that the entities did not trip and fall, but rather, went from supported to not supported, then fell.[22]

### Simultaneous blends

The following example is taken from a description of encountering a presidential motorcade in Washington, DC. The signer begins by explaining that he does not remember the exact intersection at which the event took place, but that he was walking along when he came to an intersection. At the intersection he had to wait because a long string of police vehicles was passing by directly ahead of him. The four signs in Figure 9.29 depict the signer walking and encountering the motorcade.

The clause PRO-1 BIPED-WALK-TO$^{\downarrow L1-L2}$ describes and depicts his walking on that day. By starting and ending the movement where he does, he depicts the direction in which he was traveling as well as the location where he encountered the motorcade. He begins the verb BIPED-WALK-TO$^{\downarrow L1-L2}$ just ahead of his sternum. His hand moves outward, creating the mappings illustrated in Figure 9.30.

Since PRO-1 is the subject of BIPED-WALK-TO$^{\downarrow L1-L2}$, the semantic pole of PRO-1 will map onto the verb's trajector. Since PRO-1 encodes the meaning 'current signer', its semantic pole will also map onto the signer in real space.

The depicting blend depicts the signer walking from one location to another. It is created by projections from real space and the past event space being described. As in previous examples, the depicted entity |self$_1$| receives its physical substance from the hand in real space and its location and its orientation from the past event space.

Similarly, the path traveled by the hand and the path in the past event space blend to create the |travel path| in the depicting blend. In addition, the location of the past event space and the space ahead of the signer blend to produce a location in |Washington, DC|.

The next clause consists of the subject POLICE and the verb VEHICLE-PASS-BY$^{[HABITUAL]\downarrow L2}$. The subject–verb construction associates the semantic pole of POLICE with the trajector of VEHICLE-PASS-BY$^{[HABITUAL]\downarrow L2}$. This could mean that police officers were in the vehicles passing by or even that the vehicles themselves were police vehicles. Either meaning is plausible here.

---

[22] The falling of the unsupported entities is reminiscent of cartoon characters who walk or run off a cliff, look down to realize they are no longer supported, and only then fall.

PRO-1                    BIPED-WALK-TO$^{\downarrow\text{L1}-\text{L2}}$.              POLICE

VEHICLE-PASS-BY$^{[\text{HABITUAL}]\downarrow\text{L2}}$----------------------------------------------------------

------------------------------------------

Figure 9.29 A description and depiction of walking along and encountering
a presidential motorcade

Even though the hand moves from a starting location to an ending location in
producing VEHICLE-PASS-BY$^{[\text{HABITUAL}]\downarrow\text{L2}}$, the significant location for this
sign is L2 – the location the hand passes. The sign is produced by beginning
on one side of L2 and then moving past L2. This is the reason only a single
location is identified for this sign.[23]

The reduplicated verb differs from the singular form both in number and per-
fectivity. The singular form describes a single vehicle moving past the signer.
Even though the movement of the vehicle begins prior to passing by and continues afterward, the movement past the 'viewing window' is understood as

---

[23] There are also many nondirectional signs in ASL produced by moving past a single location.
For example, FALSE begins on one side of the nose and moves past it to the other side. To
produce FIRED, the active palm-up B hand begins on one side of the upward-facing radial side
of the fist and makes contact as it moves to the opposite side.

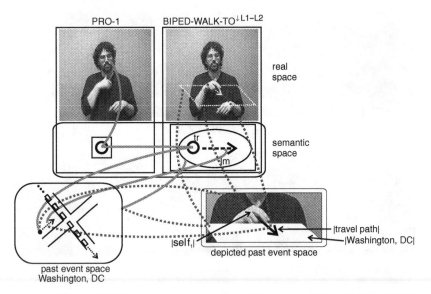

Figure 9.30  The constructed meaning of the clauses PRO-1 BIPED-WALK-TO$^{\downarrow L1-L2}$

completed. Thus, the non-reduplicated verb is perfective. The reduplicated verb expresses multiple vehicles passing by. It does not express either a beginning or an end of the procession of vehicles passing by, which makes it imperfective.

The verb VEHICLE-PASS-BY$^{[\text{HABITUAL}]\downarrow L2}$ makes use of the depicted past event space previously created by the verb BIPED-WALK-TO$^{\downarrow L1-L2}$. It does so because the left hand moves past the location $L2$ – the location of the right hand at the conclusion of BIPED-WALK-TO$^{\downarrow L1-L2}$. Each instance of a depicted vehicle is understood to be passing in front of the depicted location of the signer.

Figure 9.31 illustrates the constructed meaning of VEHICLE-PASS-BY$^{[\text{HABITUAL}]\downarrow L2}$, which includes the mappings between the verb's semantic pole and the past event space as well as the elaboration of the depicted past event space and the creation of a surrogate past event space. I represent the signer in the depicted past event space as |self$_1$|. Since the signer produces the habitual form of the verb with three left-to-right movements, he depicts three vehicles moving from left to right past $L2$, the location of |self$_1$|. Although the verb depicts only three vehicles passing by $L2$, the verb signifies multiple vehicles passing by.

The clue that VEHICLE-PASS-BY$^{[\text{HABITUAL}]\downarrow L2}$ involves the creation of another blended space in addition to the depicting space comes from the signer's facial expression and eye gaze. There is a subtle but significant change in

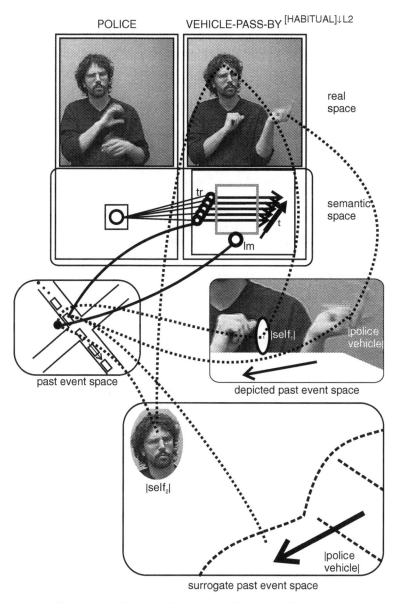

Figure 9.31 Constructed meaning with multiple blends

both facial expression and eye gaze as he produces POLICE VEHICLE-PASS-BY[HABITUAL]↓L2. His eye gaze is raised as if he were looking at something ahead of him and his eyebrows are lowered, creating the impression of someone looking at something unexpected or puzzling. The signer has created a surrogate blend in which a surrogate |self₂| is watching police cars go by.

What is new in this example is that in addition to the depicted past event space, the signer also creates a simultaneous surrogate space. In that space a surrogate |self₂| is watching one surrogate |police vehicle| after another pass by. The surrogate |self₂| is a blending of the signer's head (and potentially more of his body) with his counterpart in the past event space. The scale of the surrogate blend is very different from the scale of the depicting blend. In the depicting blend the vehicle is the size of the hand and the depicted movement of the vehicle is the size of the movement of the hand from left to right. In the surrogate blend the scale is essentially life-size, in that surrogate |self₂| is watching one normal-sized |police vehicle| after another pass by from left to right.

The conceptualizations underlying the two-sign clause POLICE VEHICLE-PASS-BY[HABITUAL]↓L2 turn out to be quite complex. Obviously the signer is present in real space. In addition, there are three counterparts to the signer in three different mental spaces. One is in the past event space being described. In addition, there is a blended instance of the signer in the depicting blend and another blended instance of the signer in the surrogate blend. Understanding what is being expressed depends on the meanings encoded by the two-sign clause, the conceptualizations expressed in the depicting blend, the conceptualizations expressed in the surrogate blend, knowledge of the previous context, and all the mappings between elements of these various mental spaces.

### Simultaneous blends and transitions

It is common for signers to present multiple perspectives during the description of some event. In the previous description of a presidential motorcade, for example, the signer used a depicting blend (depicting walking along) followed by simultaneous depicting and surrogate blends. In the next example, the signer begins with a surrogate blend, then a depicting blend, then a depicting blend with a simultaneous limited surrogate blend. Of particular interest in this example is the final seamless transition from the limited surrogate blend in which only the signer's head is projected into the blend, to a surrogate blend in which the signer's head, torso, and arms are projected into the blend.

This example is taken from a description of a coach with a hot temper. After a particular game the coach called for an immediate team meeting. The signer begins with a surrogate representation of the coach calling for a meeting.

TEAM            MEETING            NOW!

Figure 9.32  A surrogate coach calling for a team meeting

In Figure 9.32 the signer calls for a team meeting as if he were the coach at that time and place. The signs TEAM and MEETING are normally produced at the level of the chest. Here the signer has raised those signs to the level of his face. The overall raised height of the signing is consistent with a coach talking with members of his team and raising his hands so that everyone can see. Although the expression on his face is obscured during the first two signs, the fact that the coach was serious can be seen by examining the signer's facial expression during the sign NOW. The sign NOW is normally produced with a downward-movement of the hands. This emphatic form of NOW moves upward rather than downward.[24] All these factors taken together support the conclusion that the signer has created a surrogate blend in which he has blended with the coach in the past event space to become the |coach| uttering the command for a team meeting.

The sign NOW illustrates an interesting semantic issue. The sign NOW expresses the time of the speech event. But in this example, NOW is not referring to the time of the narration. Rather, it refers to the past time in which the coach called for a meeting. The proper semantic interpretation of NOW follows directly from the surrogate space analysis. Specifically, the physical setting of the blended space is the playing field and the temporal setting is the time just after the completion of the baseball game. All that needs to be said about NOW is that it refers to the time of *that speech event* – just after the conclusion of the game.

Next, the signer produces signs describing the team's activities ahead of his right shoulder. This creates a blended space that locates the team ahead of the right shoulder. After that, he produces the signs in Figure 9.33 describing the team moving (presumably) to their locker room and sitting down. He describes the coach pacing in front of the team and telling his players they are idiots. This is all done using a string of verbs without overt subjects:

---

[24] Although the movement is upward, it does not constitute a reversal of the motion of the sign. NOW is normally made with the back of the hands leading the movement. Even in the upward-moving form, the backs of the hands lead in the direction of the movement.

GROUP-GO-TO$^{\downarrow L1-L2}$          LONG-PEOPLE-LINE-SIT$^{\downarrow L2}$

UPRIGHT-PERSON-PACE-BACK-AND-FORTH$^{\downarrow facing\ |team|}$
PEOPLE-GROUP$^{\downarrow L2}$----------------------------------------------

PRO-PL$^{\circlearrowleft|team|}$

IDIOT

Figure 9.33 Describing the team (presumably) moving to the locker room and sitting down, and an angry coach pacing in front of the team and calling the players idiots

GROUP-GO-TO$^{\downarrow L1-L2}$, LONG-PEOPLE-LINE-SIT$^{\downarrow L2}$, and UPRIGHT-PERSON-PACE-BACK-AND-FORTH$^{\downarrow facing\ |team|}$-PEOPLE-GROUP$^{\downarrow L2}$. Since no subjects are mentioned during these signs, understanding what is being expressed depends on both previous context and sign placement.

The signer uses the verb GROUP-GO-TO$^{\downarrow L1-L2}$ to describe the team moving from the playing field to the location of the meeting with the coach. It begins ahead of the right shoulder and moves to directly ahead of his chest. By moving the hands from ahead of his shoulder to ahead of his chest, the signer is depicting the movement of the team from one location to another. Although the team's starting place and ending place are unspecified, background knowledge, and the fact that the next verb describes the team sitting down in a row, suggests that the team has moved from the playing field to the locker room.

The next verb, LONG-PEOPLE-LINE-SIT$^{\downarrow L2}$, is also produced without an overt subject. The identity of those sitting is transparent since the verb is articulated at $L2$, the final location of GROUP-GO-TO$^{\downarrow L1-L2}$. Its placement and meaning (i.e. a group rather than an individual) indicate that those who sat down side by side were the members of the team.

Figure 9.34 represents the constructed meaning for the verb LONG-PEOPLE-LINE-SIT$^{\downarrow L2}$. The verb depicts the team sitting down side by side in a line. The |team| is a blend of the extended fingers of the two hands and the team in the past event space. Although the set of eight extended fingers depicts the entire team, this does not mean that the team consists of eight members. That is, the individual fingers do not correspond one-to-one with individual team members in the past event space. There are not enough extended fingers for such a correspondence.

The verb LONG-PEOPLE-LINE-SIT$^{\downarrow L2}$ describes what the team members did and that activity is simultaneously depicted in the depicting blend. In addition to the blend involving the hands, there is an additional surrogate blend in which the signer's face demonstrates the mood of the team. The signer's facial expression during the production of LONG-PEOPLE-LINE-SIT$^{\downarrow L2}$ gives us an additional view of the players sitting on the bench. It appears that the purpose of the surrogate blend is to show the mood of the team rather than one individual whose mood might differ from the other team members. Since the signer has not singled out any team members, Figure 9.34 represents the surrogate as a |team member| representing the affect of the entire team.

During the verb LONG-PEOPLE-LINE-SIT$^{\downarrow L2}$, the signer provides two different views of the players on the team. The depicting blend provides a visual image of the team as a whole seated side by side. The surrogate blend provides a close-up view of the emotional state of the team as expressed by the surrogate's facial expression, which gives the impression of a player resigned to enduring what is about to happen. These simultaneous blends make it apparent that the players sat down side by side feeling resigned to enduring what was about to happen.

Next, the signer describes the coach pacing back and forth in front of the team. Figure 9.35 diagrams the constructed meaning for this verb. During this part of the explanation the left hand shows the seated players by means of

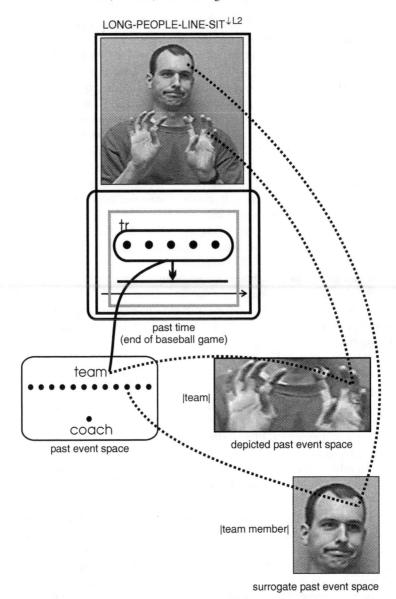

LONG-PEOPLE-LINE-SIT$^{\downarrow L2}$

tr

past time
(end of baseball game)

team

|team|

coach

past event space

|team|

depicted past event space

|team member|

surrogate past event space

Figure 9.34 Meaning construction as the team sits down

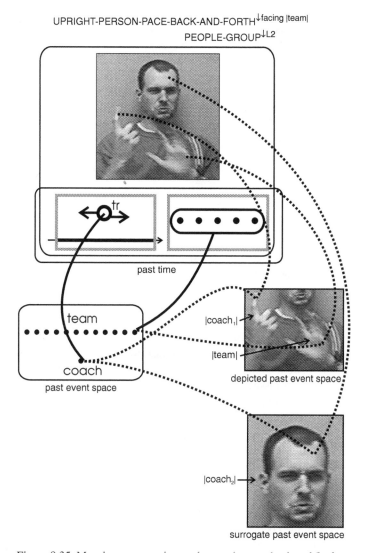

Figure 9.35  Meaning construction as the coach paces back and forth

the depicting buoy PEOPLE-GROUP$^{\downarrow L2}$. Note that PEOPLE-GROUP$^{\downarrow L2}$ is not a fragment of the previous verb LONG-PEOPLE-LINE-SIT$^{\downarrow L2}$. The handshape of PEOPLE-GROUP$^{\downarrow L2}$ is a lax 5 handshape while the final handshapes of LONG-PEOPLE-LINE-SIT$^{\downarrow L2}$ are lax hooked 4 handshapes. That is, the handshape of the depicting buoy PEOPLE-GROUP$^{\downarrow L2}$ is an entirely different handshape than the handshapes in LONG-PEOPLE-LINE-SIT$^{\downarrow L2}$.

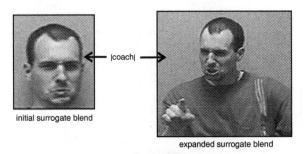

Figure 9.36 The surrogate coach in two distinct surrogate spaces

While the weak hand produces PEOPLE-GROUP$^{\downarrow L2}$, the active hand produces the verb UPRIGHT-PERSON-PACE-BACK-AND-FORTH$^{\downarrow facing \ |team|}$ and depicts the back-and-forth movement of the coach in front of the team. As the active hand moves back and forth, the index finger oscillates between a straight and hooked configuration.

The projections into the depicted past event space follow the pattern seen in previous depicting blends. |coach$_1$| is depicted by the moving index finger and the team is depicted by the depicting buoy PEOPLE-GROUP$^{\downarrow L2}$. There is also a surrogate past event space in this example reflecting the angry face of the coach. Since the signer does not explicitly link the angry expression with the coach, the addressee must deduce the nature of the surrogate blend. In this case it is not difficult.

In a previous surrogate blend (Figure 9.32) a serious |coach| calls for an immediate team meeting. Later we see resigned team members sitting on a bench. In addition, we have been given no reason to assume that the mood of the team has changed. The logic of this situation leads to the conclusion that the coach is angry. By producing this verb in this way, the signer expresses the semantic content of the verb, depicts the coach in the form of a moving index finger, depicts the team with the other hand, and demonstrates the facial expression of the coach in a surrogate past event space.

At this point, we know that the coach is pacing angrily in front of his players, but we do not know what the coach is saying. We find out immediately, however, when the |coach| addresses the team by calling the members of the team idiots.

Figure 9.36 shows two facial expressions produced by the signer in two distinct surrogate blends. The first shows the |coach|'s expression while pacing back and forth in front of his team. In this surrogate blend, only the |coach|'s face is visible. The second shows not only the |coach|'s face, but also the

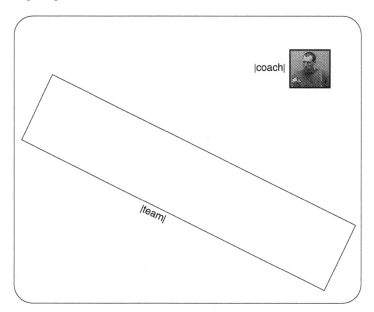

Figure 9.37  The full expanse of the surrogate blend

|coach|'s arms producing signs, telling his team members they are idiots.[25] The
transition from seeing only the |coach|'s face to seeing the |coach| signing does
not take place by dropping one blend and replacing it with another. Rather, the
first surrogate blend simply expands to include (at least) the upper part of the
|coach| signing to the |team|. The signer accomplishes this by allowing more
of his own body to blend with the |coach|. Once his own arms are blended as
part of the |coach|, the signs he produces are the |coach|'s signs addressing the
team. In the continuous signing the signer maintains the |coach|'s expression
in a dynamic way. That is, the expression is not an unchanging mask. However,
even the discontinuous still images in Figure 9.36 make it evident that the same
individual's facial expression is being represented.

Figure 9.36 does not fully represent the extent of the surrogate blend. The
coach tells his players that they are idiots by means of the clause PRO-PL⊃|team|
IDIOT. But PRO-PL⊃|team| is a pronoun that must be directed toward its

---

[25] Lentz (1986) describes degrees of role-shifting. That is, in some circumstances a signer will
show only the facial mannerisms of the character whose role has been adopted. If only the
face is involved, the role-shifting is minimal. If the signer is expressing what a person said,
the role-shifting is maximal. That is, in maximal role-shifting, more of the signer's body is
involved. Although I have been characterizing the phenomena in terms of surrogates rather than
role-shifting, I am nevertheless talking about the same phenomena identified in Lentz (1986).

referents, if they are present. I suggest that in this surrogate blend the players are conceptually present in the blend and PRO-PL$^{⊃|\text{team}|}$ is directed toward them.

If this is correct, the surrogate blend, as represented in Figure 9.37, is quite large. The only visible element of that blended space is the |coach|. But the |coach| is addressing a full |team| of baseball players seated in front of him. I have tried to capture that by showing a |coach| inside a space large enough to contain a |team| of players. This surrogate blend is quite similar to the blend in Figure 9.16, where a different signer was describing the area surrounding the Budget car rental desk.

## Conclusion

Depicting verbs, like verbs in any language, symbolize meanings having to do with actions and states. They differ from other verbs in that the signer is required to depict the action or state simultaneously. This is accomplished by creating a depicting blend by means of projections from real space and the event space being discussed. Depicting blends are conceptually distinct from the types of blends discussed in previous chapters. Token blends provide a means of spatially representing entities without placing them in a topographical setting and without giving them a clear spatial form. In depicting blends, entities are also projected into a blended space, but become part of a topographical representation. Some of the instances of signing involving depicting blends also involve the creation of simultaneous surrogate blends, resulting in two visible representations of aspects of the event being described.

# 10    Five brothers

This chapter examines the signing of a left-handed Deaf native signer describing his immediate and extended family to another Deaf native signer. The two are alone in a room with the camera positioned behind and to the left of the addressee and directed toward the signer. There were no hearing people present during the taping. Although the signer is the one describing his family, the addressee also occasionally takes brief conversational turns. The entire description of his family has a duration of just under two minutes. The signing is casual and, at times, quite rapid. For example, the signer produces the seven signs in (1) in just under two seconds, for a rate of 3.5 signs/second. By comparison, Klima and Bellugi (1979:184) measured the mean number of signs per second of three signers, excluding pauses. For two of the signers the result was 2.3 signs/second. For the third the result was 2.5 signs/second.

(1)    #ALL-OF-US BOY, #ALL-OF-US DEAF, {PRO-MULT-1}{FIVE}, PARENTS DEAF
       We're all boys, all Deaf – all five of us. Our parents are Deaf.

The signer produces the seven signs above within two seconds by eliminating repetition, reducing the distance the hand travels in articulating signs, and reducing the distance the hand has to travel from the end of one sign to the beginning of the next. Figure 10.1 illustrates how this string of signs was produced. Unreduced, #ALL-OF-US would travel ahead of and across the chest. Both instances of this sign in Figure 10.1 make barely discernible rightward movements. Unreduced, BOY is produced with two repetitions of a B handshape closing to a flat O handshape at the forehead. In Figure 10.1 the signer makes a single closing movement with his fingertips located beside and just slightly ahead of his chin. BOY occurs between two instances of #ALL-OF-US, both made ahead of the signer and slightly to his left. By producing BOY at essentially the same location he eliminates the transitional movement to the forehead and back.

Unreduced, DEAF is produced with a contact near the cheekbone and another contact at the side of the chin. It is well known that these two contacts can occur in either order. The instance of DEAF following #ALL-OF-US makes an initial

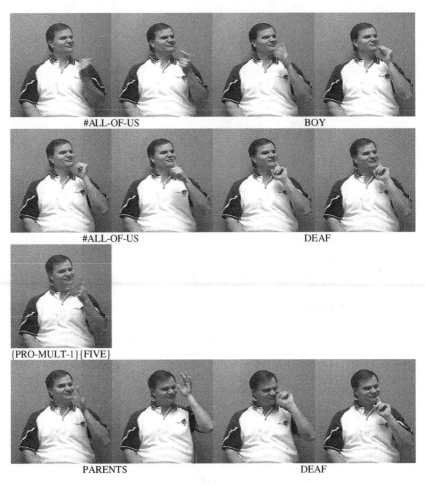

Figure 10.1 We're all boys, all Deaf – all five of us. Our parents are Deaf.

contact low on the side of the chin and a second contact just noticeably in the direction of the cheek, but still below the corner of the mouth. Producing DEAF with the low contact first reduces the distance the hand has to travel between the end of #ALL-OF-US and the beginning of DEAF. Making the second contact very close to the first reduces the distance the hand has to travel in producing DEAF and also reduces the downward distance the hand has to travel to begin the sign {PRO-MULT-1}{FIVE} 'the five of us'. A similar effect can be seen in PARENTS DEAF. The signer produces PARENTS with the lexically specified initial contact at the chin, but does not follow that with a contact at the forehead. Instead, he produces the second contact at the side of his eyebrow. Displacing the final contact of PARENTS puts the hand closer to the beginning contact of DEAF. He then produces DEAF with an initial contact high on the cheek and the final contact on the side of the chin.

By eliminating the repeated movement of BOY, shortening lexical movements, shortening transitional movements by producing signs in locations closer to locations of previous or following signs, and changing the order of the contacts in DEAF, the signer was able to produce this sequence of signs at the rate of 3.5 signs/second.[1]

Since it illustrates most of the types of blends discussed in this book, I selected the signer's description of his immediate and extended family as a means of demonstrating how the analytical approach developed in previous chapters can be applied to continuous discourse. In carrying out his description, he creates multiple token blends, uses several types of buoys including fragment buoys, creates depicting blends, and uses space in expressing metaphors. His description also demonstrates that in ordinary ASL discourse, spatial blends are continually produced, modified, or replaced. Contrary to the widely held view, it is not the norm for spatial representations to appear at the beginning of the narrative as a handy means of keeping track of referents and then to remain unchanged. The signer's description of his family provides several examples of a single individual or entity appearing in multiple blends.[2] In each case, the placement in the new blend serves a different conceptual purpose than the already existing placement.

### Five brothers together

I begin the analysis after the signer briefly mentions his parents and their ages. Next he begins describing his brothers. As he does so, he associates each with one of the extended fingers of a FIVE-LIST buoy. He describes the oldest first, beginning with the signs in (2).

(2)     PRO-1 BROTHER $\{AGE_0\}$-FORTY-FIVE

OLDER, tap D1+++, [$\{AGE_0\}$-FORTY-FIVE]$^{\rightarrow D1}$
FIVE-LIST-------------------------------------------------
My brother is forty-five years old. He is the oldest. He is forty-five.

[1] The idea that signs preceding or following DEAF can influence the order of the two contacts in the production of DEAF is described in Liddell and Johnson (1989). Lucas (1995) proposes that, based on computer-generated statistics, syntax and grammatical categories are the strongest factors influencing the order of the two contacts. She claims the upward-moving variant is more likely to be an adjective while the downward-moving variant is more likely to be a noun or predicate. Preceding and following signs are described as having only a statistically modest effect. Although the example with two instances of DEAF discussed in the text has no statistical significance, it does illustrate two uses of the same sign by the same signer within two seconds of one another in the same syntactic context. One moves up and the other moves down. Clearly, preceding and following signs are the significant factor in these examples.
[2] Representing a single individual in multiple locations was first observed in Van Hoek (1988).

$[\{AGE_0\}\text{-FORTY-FIVE}]^{\to D1}$
FIVE -LIST

Figure 10.2  The oldest brother is 45 years old

First, he describes the age of his oldest brother with the sign $\{AGE_0\}$-FORTY-FIVE. The prefix $\{AGE_0\}$- is produced in this example by contacting the chin with the index finger of the initial 4 handshape of FORTY-FIVE. He completes the sign by producing the numeral FORTY-FIVE in its normal position ahead of the body.[3] The sign OLDER identifies this brother as the oldest one. As he begins to sign OLDER, the FIVE-LIST buoy begins to appear and is in place at the completion of OLDER. Next he taps $D1$ with the index finger of his left hand four times. This makes an association between the older brother and the thumb of the FIVE-LIST buoy, creating the blended entity |first brother|. Next he signs $[\{AGE_0\}$-FORTY-FIVE$]^{\to D1}$. In this and subsequent glosses of signs directed toward the FIVE-LIST buoy, I will use the symbols $D1$ through $D5$ to show how signs are directed. That is, I gloss the just-mentioned sign as $[\{AGE_0\}$-FORTY-FIVE$]^{\to D1}$ rather than $[\{AGE_0\}$-FORTY-FIVE$]^{\to |first\ brother|}$. This serves to shorten the glossed representations and, hopefully, to make the descriptions easier to follow.[4]

Producing $[\{AGE_0\}$-FORTY-FIVE$]^{\to D1}$ associates that age with $D1$. Although the prefix $\{AGE_0\}$- is nondirectional, he produces FORTY-FIVE with the base of the hand in contact with $D1$, as shown in Figure 10.2.[5]

There is some redundancy here since he has already explained that the oldest brother is forty-five years old. It follows, then, that $D1$ already has the

---

[3] The prefix $\{AGE_0\}$- has no inherent handshape. It is produced with the initial handshape of the numeral stem it attaches to. Since the numeral stem is FORTY-FIVE, $\{AGE_0\}$ is produced by contacting the chin with the initial 4 handshape of FORTY-FIVE.

[4] Some indicating verbs directed toward the signer actually make contact with the signer's body. For example, GIVE$^{a \to signer}$ begins directed toward $a$ and ends contacting the signer's chest. Similarly, numerals directed toward $D1$–$D5$ normally make contact with the extended digits. I also notate these signs using the arrow$^{\to}$, indicating that the numeral is directed toward the extended digit.

[5] The sign $\{AGE_0\}$-FORTY-FIVE requires the hand to move to two locations. The first is a contact at the chin and the second is the location at which FORTY-FIVE is produced. I am treating the entire sign as being directed toward $D1$ even though the beginning of the sign is clearly not directed toward $D1$. This is similar to how I treat signs like TELL$^{\to x}$, where the sign also begins without pointing, but ends pointing at $x$.

characteristic 'forty-five years old' associated with it.[6] Next, after a false start, he produces the signs in (3). He appears to be reflecting about the age of the oldest brother.

(3)     PAST MONTH, PAST MONTH {AGE$_0$}-FORTY-FIVE, PAST MONTH {AGE$_0$}-FORTY-FIVE
        ... last month, last month (he was) forty-five years old, last month (he was) forty-five years old.

The final sign in this description of his brother having just turned forty-five is the sign {AGE$_0$}-FORTY-FIVE, after which he produces the description in (4), without the presence of the FIVE-LIST buoy.

(4)     BROTHER FORTY-FOUR+++, FORTY-THREE+, {WILL}-B-E FORTY-FOUR NEAR.
        (The next) brother is forty-four; forty-three; he will be forty-four soon.

In (4) he mentions a brother who is forty-three, about to turn forty-four. He does this by signing BROTHER followed by several repetitions of FORTY-FOUR. He thinks it over and then signs FORTY-THREE, adding that the brother will soon be forty-four.[7] This explanation immediately follows (3), which describes the oldest brother as forty-five years old.

The description in (4) might seem directly to contradict the description in (3). This is not the case, however, since (4) is not about the oldest brother. There are two clues supporting this conclusion. First, there has been only a single instance of the sign BROTHER prior to (4). After initially mentioning the oldest brother, the sign BROTHER was not used again to refer to the oldest brother. Instead, the signer made an association between that brother and *D1*. He tapped on the thumb then produced [{AGE$_0$}-FORTY-FIVE]$^{\rightarrow D1}$, making an association between 'age forty-five' and *D1*. To use the sign BROTHER now without pointing in some way to the thumb is consistent with talking about another brother. Second, and perhaps more significantly, he changes his eye

---

[6] There are additional examples of repeated information occurring later in this description. Such repetitions are not unusual and it is likely that they serve more than one function. At least one possible function is that repetitions maintain the signer's turn as signer while allowing him to consider what he will be describing next.

[7] This clause contains an intrusion from English in the form of the spelled B-E. The signer attaches the bound future morpheme {WILL}- to the spelled B-E, producing {WILL}-B-E. In previous examples discussed in the text, {WILL}- is produced when the extended fingertip of the initial handshape of the root contacts the side of the cheek. In this example, as his hand is coming back to his face, it is his thumb that appears to contact the side of the chin. I am unable to determine from the single video frame with the thumb approximating contact whether the thumb actually makes contact. Next, his bent 5 handshape closes to form a handshape approximating an E handshape.

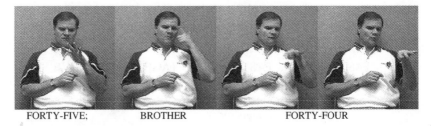

| FORTY-FIVE; | BROTHER | FORTY-FOUR |

Figure 10.3  ... forty-five. A brother is forty-four

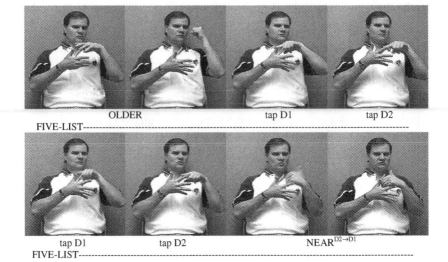

| | OLDER | tap D1 | tap D2 |
FIVE-LIST----------------------------------------------------------------------------------------------

| tap D1 | tap D2 | NEAR$^{D2 \to D1}$ | |
FIVE-LIST----------------------------------------------------------------------------------------------

Figure 10.4  The oldest two are close (in age)

gaze, his posture, and the placement of his hand. The first picture in Figure 10.3 shows the position of his head while completing FORTY-FIVE, the final sign prior to (4). During that sign his face and gaze are directed down and slightly to the right.

Between the end of that sign and the beginning of BROTHER, he changes the orientation of his face and gaze so that both are more nearly centralized. During FORTY-FOUR his face and gaze are oriented to the left. This is another indication that another brother is being talked about. The placement of FORTY-FOUR is also well to the left of the previously signed FORTY-FIVE. So at this point he has described the two oldest brothers. One is forty-five and the other is forty-three, about to turn forty-four. He explains that the two oldest brothers are close in age, using the signs in Figure 10.4.

He signs OLDER followed by tapping $D1$ and $D2$ in sequence twice to indicate that he is talking about the two oldest brothers. Next, $\text{NEAR}^{D2 \to D1}$ moves from $D2$ to $D1$, expressing the closeness in age of the two brothers blended with $D2$ and $D1$. $\text{NEAR}^{x \to y}$ is normally produced by placing the weak hand toward $y$. The active hand begins at a location indicating $x$ and moves so that the back of the fingers of the active hand make contact with the palm of the stationary weak hand. In Figure 10.4, however, the two important entities are $D1$ and $D2$. The signer produces a one-handed form of $\text{NEAR}^{x \to y}$ by moving the active hand from $D2$ to $D1$. He concludes the description of the second brother with the sign $[\{\text{AGE}_0\}\text{-FORTY-THREE+}]^{\to D2}$, making an overt association between 'age forty-three' and $D2$.

The rest of the brothers are briefly mentioned or described by the signs in Figure 10.5. He identifies the third oldest brother by touching $D3$ then signing FORTY-TWO. He identifies himself and his age, thirty-eight, without pointing at $D4$. Logic and the assumption that each brother is being listed in order of birth would nevertheless lead to an association between the signer and $D4$.

Then he signs LAST 'final' to describe the last of the five brothers. LAST is normally produced by moving the I handshape of the strong hand past a non-moving I handshape on the weak hand so that there is a brushing contact between the two extended fingers. Because he maintains the FIVE-LIST buoy, LAST is not produced in its normal form. In Figure 10.5, he moves the extended I handshape on his strong hand past $D5$ on the FIVE-LIST buoy. The two fingers do not appear to make contact as the active hand moves past $D5$. Using $D5$ as the location for LAST simultaneously expresses the meaning 'final' and associates that meaning with $D5$. The entire sequence associating the fifth brother with $D5$ is shown by the final three signs in Figure 10.5: LAST, BABY, $\{\text{AGE}_0\}$-THIRTY-TWO. After completing the signs in Figure 10.5 the signer drops his hands and ends his turn.

As a result of the preceding descriptions, each brother is associated in the order of birth with $D1$ through $D5$ on the FIVE-LIST buoy. Thus, when the FIVE-LIST buoy is present, it has the significance shown in Figure 10.6.

His interlocutor says something off camera, to which the signer responds THAT'S-ALL-OF-THEM, shown in Figure 10.7. This sign expresses that the five brothers constitute the entire set of brothers.

There are at least two possible analyses for THAT'S-ALL-OF-THEM. It is possible that the signer moves his active B hand past $D1$–$D5$, thereby pointing gesturally toward the five brothers in the blend. The alternative I will adopt is that THAT'S-ALL-OF-THEM is a conventional sign that probably had its roots in moving the hand past $D1$–$D5$. Note that in producing THAT'S-ALL-OF-THEM both hands move. The right hand begins just below the sternum

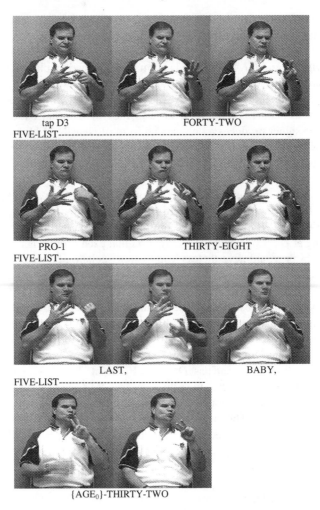

tap D3                          FORTY-TWO
FIVE-LIST-----------------------------------------------------------------

PRO-1                          THIRTY-EIGHT
FIVE-LIST-----------------------------------------------------------------

LAST,                          BABY,
FIVE-LIST------------------------------------------

{AGE$_0$}-THIRTY-TWO

Figure 10.5  The third brother is 42. I am 38. The last one, the baby, is 32
years old.

while the left hand begins above it. The right hand moves up while the left hand
moves down. If the same movement were possible with a FOUR-LIST buoy or
a THREE-LIST buoy, that would support the gestural pointing analysis. Signers
I have consulted, however, reject such signs. This suggests that THAT'S-ALL-
OF-THEM is a conventional lexical sign.[8]

[8] I initially understood this sign to mean 'that is all five' since the active B hand moves past the
FIVE-LIST buoy. However, I later saw a related verb with a slower more deliberate movement
describing the playing of all the innings of a baseball game. This verb, which I would gloss

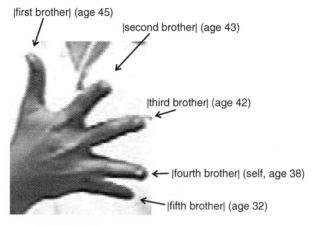

|first brother| (age 45)

|second brother| (age 43)

|third brother| (age 42)

← |fourth brother| (self, age 38)

|fifth brother| (age 32)

FIVE-LIST buoy

Figure 10.6 The significance of the FIVE-LIST buoy after each brother has been described

THAT'S-ALL-OF-THEM

Figure 10.7 That's all of them

Treating THAT'S-ALL-OF-THEM as a lexical item does not deny that the moving B hand still moves past *D1* through *D5*. That is, one can still understand that *D1–D5* maintain their significance in this case. Treating it as a lexical item simply recognizes that the movement of the B hand past the 5 hand is now a codified part of the structure of the sign itself.

**The brothers close in age**

In Figure 10.8 the signer identifies the first four brothers as a group by moving the index finger of his active hand along a straight line from the tip of *D1* to

as PROCEED-THROUGH-ALL-OF-THEM, was also produced by moving the B hand past a FIVE-LIST buoy. This leads me to treat THAT'S-ALL-OF-THEM as not being specifically about five things, but more generally, some number of things five or greater.

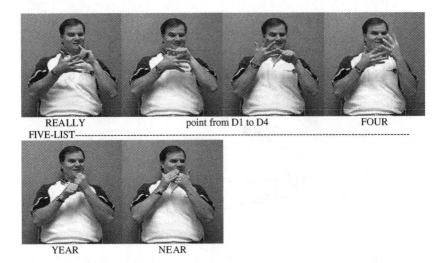

REALLY          point from D1 to D4          FOUR
FIVE-LIST----------------------------------------------------------------------------------

YEAR          NEAR

Figure 10.8  Really, these four oldest brothers are all within four years of each
other

near the tip of *D4*. By moving in a straight line, his index finger does not move
directly past the tips of *D2* and *D3*. That is, the straight-line path identifies the
four brothers associated with *D1–D4* by beginning at the tip of *D1*, moving
past the body of the index and middle fingers, and ending near the tip of *D4*.
Moving in straight lines like this is the conventional way of identifying such
groups of entities on a list buoy.

He singles out the brothers associated with *D1–D4* in order to comment about
the closeness of their ages.[9] The signs FOUR YEAR NEAR express that the
four brothers were born within a four-year period.

Briefly thereafter he states that each was born within two years of the preceding brother. He identifies the four brothers again with OLDER FOUR,
then points again from *D1* to *D4*, as shown in Figure 10.9. He then
signs TWO YEAR NEAR, points from *D1* through *D4* again, then signs
NEAR$^{[\text{MULTIPLE}]\flat|\text{brothers }1-4|}$. In order to produce this sign he had to solve
an articulatory problem. Since NEAR$^{[\text{MULTIPLE}]\flat x}$ is a two-handed sign, he
is not able to maintain the FIVE-LIST buoy and simultaneously produce the
two-handed NEAR$^{[\text{MULTIPLE}]\flat D1-D4}$.

He solves this by creating a spatial blend in approximately the same space
previously occupied by the FIVE-LIST buoy. The straight-line movement of
his index finger from *D1* to *D4* described above identifies the four brothers to

[9] It turns out that here and later the signer appears to have misidentified the correct group of
brothers. That is, his descriptions are all correct and consistent if he limits the description to the
first three brothers rather than the first four brothers.

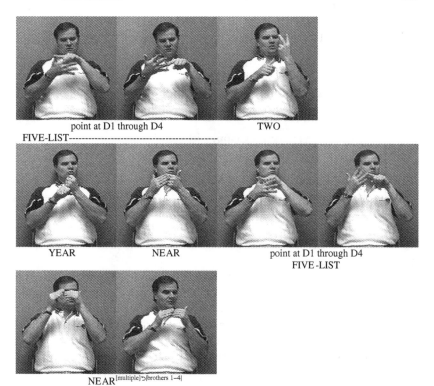

Figure 10.9  Each of the brothers is within two years of the next brother

associate with that spatial blend. He then moves his hands along a downward path indicating the four brothers.

The notation $^{ɔ|\text{brothers }1–4|}$ signifies that the movement of the hands identifies the spatial entity |brothers 1–4| by moving along a path directed toward its extent. In this case, the hands begin above where *D1* would have been if the FIVE-LIST buoy were still present, then move diagonally downward past where *D4* would have been to a location ahead of his chin. This lack of spatial precision is not significant, however, since he has already identified the correct set of four brothers with the signs OLDER FOUR and by pointing from *D1* through *D4*.

Figure 10.9 illustrates both the nondirection NEAR as well as NEAR$^{[\text{MULTIPLE}]ɔ|\text{brothers }1–4|}$. NEAR is produced with the active hand approaching and contacting the stationary weak hand directly ahead of the chest. He produces NEAR$^{[\text{MULTIPLE}]ɔ|\text{brothers }1–4|}$ by moving the two hands downward along a path indicating the entities close to one another. The active hand is situated just beneath the weak hand as both move downward along the same path. At the conclusion of the sign the two hands maintain a brief hold in contact with one another. This sign expresses that each successive brother is within two years of the preceding brother.

### The distant fifth brother

In (5), the signer mentions that his parents had expected him to be the last child.

(5)     PARENTS THINK LAST PRO-1+++
        My parents thought I would be the last.

Then, in Figure 10.10, he provides more details about the birth of the fifth brother. The facial expression accompanying CARELESS suggests 'unexpected' or 'unplanned'. CARELESS is produced with a downward movement followed by an upward rebound and a brief hold. He produces the non-manual signal *tg* 'accidental', suggesting that there is no fault involved. It was an unplanned pregnancy.

He next directs PRO$^{\rightarrow x}$ far ahead to his left without first identifying what the pronoun is directed toward. It is up to the addressee to work this out. Directing PRO$^{\rightarrow x}$ to the left as the subject of BORN after mentioning that his parents thought he (the fourth boy) would be the last leads to the conclusion that PRO$^{\rightarrow x}$ is directed toward a blended instance of the fifth brother. Since it is a blended entity distinct from the association with *D5*, I label it as |baby brother| rather than |fifth brother|. But why create a new blend for the fifth brother? Had the signer wanted to make reference to the youngest brother it would have been a simple matter to touch *D5* on the FIVE-LIST buoy. The signer has something else in mind. He places a blended instance of his baby brother at the location on the left then uses the locative sign FAR-FROM-ME$^{\rightarrow L}$ to identify the location of his brother's birth. At the same time, his weak right hand moves inward to a position slightly to the right and ahead of his chin. The two hands form a vector that extends backward over his right shoulder. This vector provides the key to understanding what he is doing. The vector that begins over the shoulder of the weak hand and extends forward diagonally and down is commonly used in order to map time onto space. Since the two hands producing FAR-FROM-ME$^{\rightarrow L}$ are aligned on this vector, the signer is talking about the location *in time* of the baby brother's birth. I have labeled this location in time as |baby brother's birth in time|. Since PRO$^{\rightarrow \text{|baby brother|}}$ is directed at a higher level than FAR-FROM-ME$^{\rightarrow \text{|baby brother's birth in time|}}$, |baby brother| is located above |baby brother's birth in time|.

The sign FAR-FROM-ME$^{\rightarrow \text{|baby brother's birth in time|}}$ expresses the meaning 'far from me' and is simultaneously directed well ahead of the signer and to the left, toward |baby brother's birth in time|. This introduces distance into the conceptualization of the blend, resulting in a depicting blend with |baby brother|

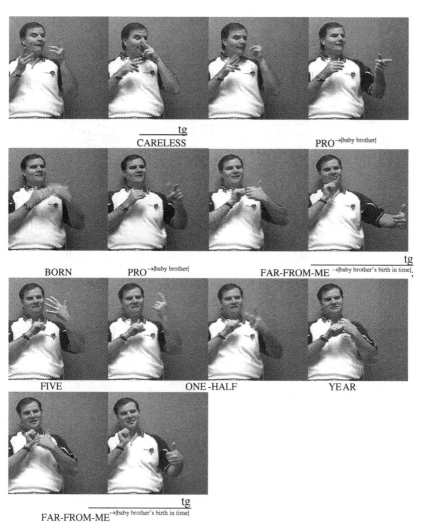

Figure 10.10  Oops. He happened to be born with a five and a half year gap between him and me.

located at a far distance from the signer, above the location in time at which he was born.

The signer next explains the nature of the depicted distance between him and the fifth brother by signing FIVE ONE-HALF YEAR FAR-FROM-ME<sup>→ |baby brother's birth in time|</sup> 'five and a half years away from me'. This explicitly maps time onto the distance between the signer and the fifth brother. Through blending, the *distance* between them is a *time of five and a half years*. Now it is

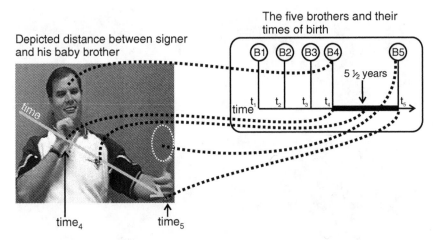

Figure 10.11 The conceptual blend separating the fourth and fifth brothers

clear that the signer locates |baby brother| far ahead of him on his left in order to talk metaphorically about the differences in their ages.

Figure 10.11 illustrates the projections needed to create the depicting blend. Recall that time has been conceptualized as moving forward and diagonally across the body beginning behind the right shoulder. The signer has mapped the time of his own birth ($t_4$) onto the space directly ahead of him. He has also mapped the time of his baby brother's birth ($t_5$) onto the space indicated by his strong left hand. In addition, recall that this explanation begins with PRO$^{\rightarrow |baby\ brother|}$ directed to the left, but higher than the position of his left hand in Figure 10.11. Thus, he has also mapped the baby brother onto the space near the location of his birth in time.

In addition, the signer himself corresponds to *B4* in the space containing the five brothers and their times of birth. This is shown in the diagram as a projection of *B4* onto the signer. That is, for the purposes of this depiction, the signer is the fourth of five brothers. This is a characteristic he already has, of course, but the projection from *B4* to the signer adds him to the depicting blend. In other words, the signer himself becomes a part of the metaphoric depiction. As a result of the blending, the signer is near the location in time of his own birth and |baby brother| is near the location in time of his birth. This is the basis for depicting the signer and his baby brother as being far apart. It is evident that the signer had this metaphorical blend in mind as he began the sequence in Figure 10.10 since PRO$^{\rightarrow |baby\ brother|}$ appears before the nature of the blend is made apparent.[10]

---

[10] Using this physical path to blend with time is conventional in ASL. There are other conventional ways of mapping time onto space in ASL. The physical paths frequently used for mapping time have been called "time lines" (Frishberg and Gough 1973, Friedman 1975, Frishberg 1979).

In the second production of FAR-FROM-ME$^{\rightarrow|\text{baby brother}|}$ his strong hand does not extend out as far as it does in the first production. This appears to be a kind of reduction in form based on the idea that this is a repetition of previously expressed information. That is, the addressee will not need either to create or modify the existing blended space based on this second production. All that is needed is to recognize that this is a repetition based on the existing blended space and that the signer exerts less effort during the second production.

The signer continues talking about the youngest brother with the signs in (6). He is explaining that now, in spite of the five-and-a-half-year gap, his younger brother is 'neat', and everyone gets along fine. But he is still directing both PRO$^{\rightarrow|\text{baby brother}|}$ and DET$^{\rightarrow|\text{baby brother}|}$ in (6) toward |baby brother|, five and a half years away from him.

(6)     PRO$^{\rightarrow|\text{baby brother}|}$ NOW, WELL, FINE. DET$^{\rightarrow|\text{baby brother}|}$ BROTHER NEAT.

As for him now, well, everything is fine. That brother is neat (cool). Several researchers have proposed that ASL uses a determiner produced by a pointing motion of the index finger (Hoffmeister 1977, Wilbur 1979, Zimmer and Patschke 1990, MacLaughlin 1997). Zimmer and Patschke describe this determiner as homophonous with the pronoun I gloss as PRO$^{\rightarrow x}$. This means that PRO$^{\rightarrow x}$ and DET$^{\rightarrow x}$ are distinguishable only through their grammatical context. DET$^{\rightarrow x}$ appears as part of a noun phrase while PRO$^{\rightarrow x}$ appears alone as a pronoun. Deciding whether a sign is DET$^{\rightarrow x}$ or PRO$^{\rightarrow x}$ by looking at grammatical context is not always straightforward. In this example, it depends on the ability to distinguish between a noun phrase beginning with DET$^{\rightarrow x}$ (e.g. DET$^{\rightarrow|\text{baby brother}|}$ BROTHER 'the brother') and a pronoun followed by an appositive (e.g. PRO$^{\rightarrow|\text{baby brother}|}$, BROTHER... 'he, my brother,...'). In (6) I cannot find evidence for a break between the pointing sign and BROTHER, so I treat the sign as DET$^{\rightarrow|\text{baby brother}|}$.

### Together again

In Figure 10.12 he uses the pronoun {PRO-MULT-1}{FIVE} 'the five of us' to explain that the age difference has not been an issue. This sign is making a social statement, signifying that the five brothers constitute a social group.

At this point the signer ends another turn and his interlocutor apparently asks whether all members of the family are Deaf. The signer responds with the signs in Figure 10.13. The signs #ALL DEAF FAMILY #ALL-OF-US describe the entire family as being Deaf.

---

The particular vector used in the text from over the weak shoulder diagonally across the body is similar to a path identified by Engberg-Pedersen from Danish Sign Language that she calls the "anaphoric time line."

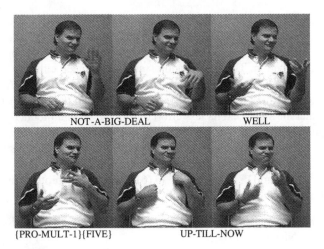

NOT-A-BIG-DEAL                    WELL

{PRO-MULT-1}{FIVE}            UP-TILL-NOW

Figure 10.12 (The age difference) is not a big deal. It has been the five of us all along.

#ALL                              DEAF

FAMILY;                          #ALL-OF-US

Figure 10.13 The family is entirely Deaf. All of us.

There are both spatial and semantic differences between #ALL and #ALL-OF-US. The nondirectional sign #ALL in Figure 10.13 moves along a very short path directly outward from the shoulder. In contrast, #ALL-OF-US begins ahead of the signer's left shoulder and ends almost directly ahead of his chest. It is functioning as a first person plural inclusive pronoun. He continues describing his family in (7). All the signs in (7) after {PRO-MULT-1}{FIVE} are illustrated at the beginning of this chapter in Figure 10.1.

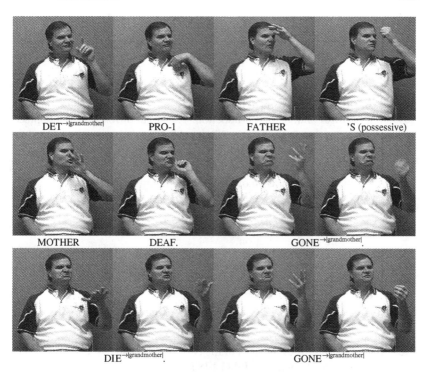

Figure 10.14  My father's mother was Deaf. She is gone. She died; she's gone.

(7)     {PRO-MULT-1}{FIVE}, #ALL-OF-US BOY, #ALL-OF-US DEAF,
        {PRO-MULT-1}{FIVE}, PARENTS DEAF
        We're all boys, all Deaf – all five of us. Our parents are Deaf.

Next he begins to describe other Deaf relatives, beginning with his grandmother.

### The first generation

He begins in Figure 10.14 with a very abbreviated outward moving sign that could be either PRO$^{\rightarrow}$|grandmother| or DET$^{\rightarrow}$|grandmother|. Since the sign in question precedes the noun phrase PRO-1 FATHER 'S MOTHER, and since I can detect no evidence for a break between it and PRO-1, I treat it as an instance of DET$^{\rightarrow}$|grandmother| directed high and to the left toward |grandmother|.[11]

---

[11] The sign 'S is made with an S handshape and a twisting motion of the forearm that orients the palm toward the signer. It originated as part of a sign system for representing English on the hands. This originally non-ASL sign has made some inroads toward being accepted as an ASL sign.

Since DET$^{\rightarrow}$|grandmother| is directional, we should expect the token |grandmother| to be located high and to the left. The signer provides additional evidence the grandmother is blended with that space because the following three verbs are directional. GONE$^{\rightarrow}$|grandmother| begins high and to the left then ends by moving down a short distance. DIE$^{\rightarrow}$|grandmother| is produced where GONE$^{\rightarrow}$|grandmother| ends, then GONE$^{\rightarrow}$|grandmother| is repeated, this time just slightly lower than its first production. The slight differences in the placement of these three verbs are not significant. All three verbs must be understood as mapping onto the token |grandmother|. Having described his grandmother and his parents as Deaf, he then (after a false start) states in (8) that he is a member of the third generation of Deaf family members.

(8)     PRO-1 THIRD GENERATION, PRO-1 THIRD GENERATION.
        I am (in) the third generation (of Deaf family members). I am (in)
        the third generation.

Having described himself as a member of the third Deaf generation, he next talks about his children.

### His own children

Next the signer describes the ages of his two children and associates each with one of the extended fingers of a TWO-LIST buoy. He associates the oldest with *D1* and the youngest with *D2*. Then he describes them both as 'hearing', using the signs in Figure 10.15. First he signs HEARING, then simultaneously taps *D1* and *D2* with the backs of the two extended fingers of his strong hand in a V shape. I interpret his facial expression as that of a proud father.

It is not clear whether this tap should be treated as a sign or as a convenient gesture that points to both fingers at once. At present there are no clear criteria to help distinguish between these two possibilities. My description 'tap *D1* & *D2*' in Figure 10.15 describes what he does without treating the movement of his active hand as an established sign.

He then signs HEARING again, then taps *D1* and *D2* individually. Next, he briefly talks about each of his two children's mothers, then goes on to talk about his nieces and nephews.

### Deaf children in the fourth generation

The signer's initial description of his nieces and nephews is shown in Figure 10.16. He begins with the sign PRO-PL$^{\circ}$|nephews−nieces|, produced with his weak (right) hand, before mentioning who he is talking about. PRO-PL$^{\circ}$|nephews−nieces| begins centrally, moves in an arc out to the right, forward, and back to the left at

HEARING          tap D1 & D2 with a V handshape
TWO-LIST---------------------------------------------

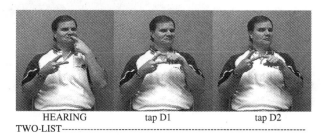

HEARING                     tap D1                         tap D2
TWO-LIST---------------------------------------------------------------------------

Figure 10.15  Both of them are hearing

about the neck level. This is directed toward a set of multiple unidentified entities conceptualized as spread out directly in front of him. He immediately identifies that blended space as |nephews-nieces| with the signs PRO-1 NEPHEW NIECE 'my nephews and nieces'. Next he signs THIS-SET$^{\supset|\text{nephews}-\text{nieces}|}$ ALTOGETHER [TEN]$^{\rightarrow|\text{nephews}-\text{nieces}|}$, scratches his nose with the same hand, then repeats [TEN]$^{\rightarrow|\text{nephews}-\text{nieces}|}$. Both instances of [TEN]$^{\rightarrow|\text{nephews}-\text{nieces}|}$ are produced by his weak hand. Figure 10.16 only shows the second instance.

TEN is normally produced just ahead of the shoulder. Here he produces [TEN]$^{\rightarrow|\text{nephews}-\text{nieces}|}$ almost directly ahead of his torso and slightly more distant from his body than TEN would normally be produced. Recall that he directs the initial sign in this sequence, PRO-PL$^{\supset|\text{nephews}-\text{nieces}|}$, toward a token ahead of him extending horizontally from side to side, roughly the width of his shoulders at about the level of his neck. In describing the total number of nephews and nieces he directs [TEN]$^{\rightarrow|\text{nephews}-\text{nieces}|}$ with his weak hand toward the center of |nephews-nieces|, associating the meaning 'ten' with it as the number of nephews and nieces. He leaves the hand in place as a TEN-fragment buoy. This allows him to continue the description with his strong hand, where he explains that four of the ten are Deaf. He does so by signing FOUR DEAF, FOUR. The TEN-fragment buoy just to the right of center serves as a reminder of the number of nieces and nephews as he describes the number of Deaf nieces and nephews.

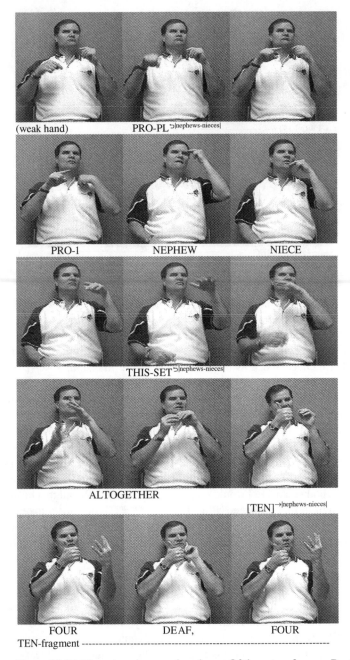

Figure 10.16 I have ten nieces and nephews. Of those ten, four are Deaf.

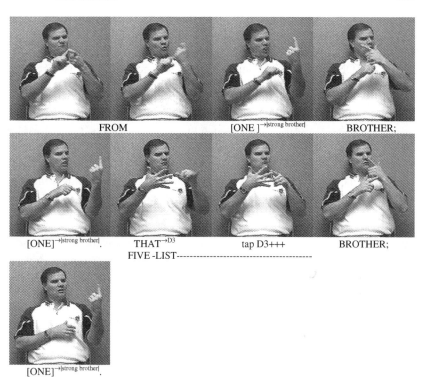

FROM                    [ONE ]<sup>→|strong brother|</sup>              BROTHER;

[ONE]<sup>→|strong brother|</sup>.        THAT<sup>→D3</sup>                    tap D3+++                BROTHER;
                       FIVE -LIST------------------------------------------

[ONE]<sup>→|strong brother|</sup>.

Figure 10.17 From this one brother, just this one – the third brother; just this one.

### The strong and the weak

Although there are five Deaf brothers who constitute the third generation of Deaf family members, only one of them has Deaf children, as described by the signs in Figure 10.17. The brother being described is the third brother, initially associated with *D3* on the FIVE-LIST buoy. Earlier, the fifth brother was blended with the space to the left and ahead of the signer in order to depict the temporal distance between him and the signer. Now the third brother is being singled out and associated with a different location on the left. He is being singled out because he is the only one of the five Deaf brothers with Deaf children.

In Figure 10.17 the third brother is simultaneously associated with two distinct places. The first appears with the signs [ONE]<sup>→ |strong brother|</sup> BROTHER, where [ONE]<sup>→ |strong brother|</sup> is placed to the left at about chin level as the signer gazes in that direction. Again, I am using the signer's knowledge to label blended elements. Later the signer will identify this token as the third brother.

This one brother is described as strong because of his ability to produce Deaf children.

The signer emphasizes that there is only one brother with Deaf children by repeating [ONE]$^{\rightarrow}$|strong brother| in the same place and gazing in that direction. Next he identifies that brother with the sign THAT$^{\rightarrow D3}$ followed by four taps on *D3*, then BROTHER. By bringing back the FIVE-LIST buoy and tapping *D3*, he reactivates the previous blend in which *D1–D5* were associated with each brother in the order of their birth. In that blend *D3* is associated with the third brother.

He produces THAT$^{\rightarrow D3}$ by directing a Y handshape toward *D3*. Since the Y handshape is much wider than a pointing index finger, it does not point with enough precision for a viewer to distinguish between entities very close to one another, such as *D1* through *D5*. That is, it would be difficult to direct the flat palm surface of the Y handshape in a way that singled out *D3* as opposed to *D4*. All that can be seen on the video is that THAT$^{\rightarrow D3}$ moves toward the FIVE-LIST buoy. The transcription in Figure 10.17 showing the sign directed toward *D3* is based on context since it is not possible to determine precisely which finger the sign is directed toward. However, the signer makes it clear that he is talking about the brother associated with *D3* since he follows THAT$^{\rightarrow D3}$ by tapping *D3* with his index finger. Since directing THAT$^{\rightarrow x}$ toward *D3* would produce a sign that looks like what the signer actually did, I treat what he did as THAT$^{\rightarrow D3}$. Figure 10.17 ends with a repetition of [ONE]$^{\rightarrow}$|strong brother|, emphasizing again that only one of the five brothers had Deaf children. This third repetition of [ONE]$^{\rightarrow}$|strong brother| is placed in the same location as the two previous instances.

He explains that this brother has four Deaf children. Figure 10.18 shows that he does this by signing PRO$^{\rightarrow}$|strong brother| FOUR! DEAF, FOUR! The signs I gloss as FOUR! are produced with an inward movement and a slight bending of the wrist that moves the fingers inward toward the signer. The inward movement is followed by a hold. FOUR! is more emphatic than the neutral form FOUR, produced with a hold, but no inward movement.

PRO$^{\rightarrow}$|strong brother|, the first sign in Figure 10.18, is directed at the token |strong brother|. The fact that it points well beyond the location of the hand producing [ONE]$^{\rightarrow}$|strong brother| (Figure 10.17) provides evidence that |strong brother| is located beyond the hand producing [ONE]$^{\rightarrow}$|strong brother|. This provides support for treating [ONE]$^{\rightarrow}$|strong brother| as directed toward |strong brother| rather than produced at its location.

He next explains that the four Deaf children came from two different wives. There are no new tokens in (9).

(9)     FOUR-fragment-------------------------------- DIFFERENT WIFE
          UNDERSTAND PRO$^{\rightarrow}$|strong brother| TWO
        Understand that he had two different wives.

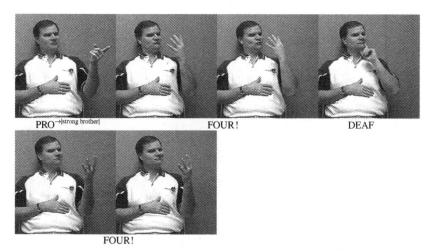

PRO$^{\rightarrow|\text{strong brother}|}$                         FOUR!                              DEAF

FOUR!

Figure 10.18 He has four Deaf (children), four!

Figure 10.19 contains the explanation that each wife had two Deaf children. The signs [FIRST]$^{\rightarrow\text{L1}}$ and [SECOND]$^{\rightarrow\text{L2}}$ will prompt the creation of the token |first wife| in the space ahead of the side of the forehead and the token |second wife| ahead of his shoulder beneath |first wife|. The difference in placement is an unambiguous signal to create tokens at those two locations.[12]

The phrase NOW SECOND WIFE explains that his brother is still married to his second wife. Next the signer explains that each of the two wives had two Deaf children. He does this with the verb EACH-HAVE-TWO$^{\rightarrow x,y}$. To produce this verb the two hands make alternating oscillating in and out movements such that while one hand is out the other hand is in. One might expect that since he has just created the tokens |first wife| and |second wife|, he would direct EACH-HAVE-TWO$^{\rightarrow x,y}$ toward those two tokens. However, in Figure 10.19, the right hand is directed high and to the right. Recall that both |first wife| and |second wife| are on the left. Thus, the right hand is not directed toward either of those tokens. In addition, the left hand appears to move too far away from the body to be directed toward |second wife|. As a result, he appears to have created the two new tokens *a* and *b* (also representing each of the two wives) and directs EACH-HAVE-TWO$^{\rightarrow x,y}$ toward those two tokens.

In this example, lexical choice appears to interact with spatial construction. To produce EACH-HAVE-TWO$^{\rightarrow x,y}$ properly, one hand cannot be directly above the other. This appears to be a lexical restriction on the use of EACH-HAVE-

[12] It is possible that time plays a role in the vertical difference between |first wife| and |second wife|. That is, in addition to representing time as moving forward, time is often represented as moving vertically downward. One example of this appears in chapter 7 and an additional example occurs later in this chapter.

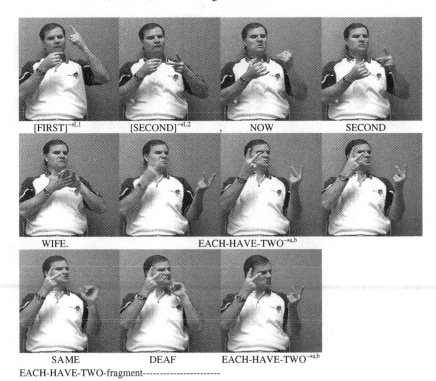

SAME          DEAF          EACH-HAVE-TWO$^{\rightarrow a,b}$
EACH-HAVE-TWO-fragment----------------------

Figure 10.19 Here are his first and second (wives), now (he is married to) his second wife – two kids each. They were all Deaf. Two kids with each wife.

TWO$^{\rightarrow x,y}$. This rules out directing this verb toward the tokens |first wife| and |second wife| because one is above the other. As a result, by selecting the verb EACH-HAVE-TWO$^{\rightarrow x,y}$ it appears that he is forced to ignore the just created tokens |first wife| and |second wife| and to create the token *a* ahead of him on his left and the token *b* ahead of him high on his right. These are the tokens he directs the verb EACH-HAVE-TWO$^{\rightarrow x,y}$ toward.[13]

The one brother with four Deaf children is now described as strong by PRO$^{\rightarrow}$|strong brother| STRONG, the first clause in Figure 10.20. Thus, after describing the two wives and creating new spatial associations with the wives,

---

[13] Some of my students in a seminar discussing a draft of this book noticed the height difference between the two hands producing EACH-HAVE-TWO$^{\rightarrow a,b}$. In the ensuing discussion they suggested the interesting hypothesis that the height difference between |first wife| and |second wife| may have influenced the signer in placing one of the tokens *higher on the right*. This seems like a reasonable hypothesis, and it raises interesting questions about the degree to which language users are consciously aware of certain aspects of language production.

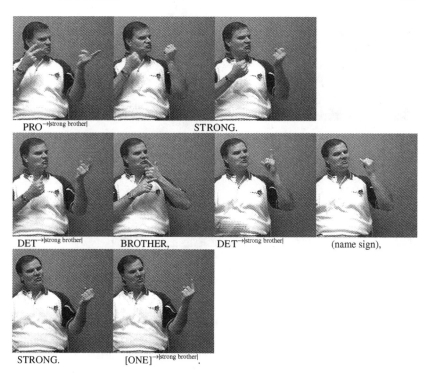

Figure 10.20 He is strong. My brother (name); He is strong. Just this one.

he returns to the previous blend containing the token |strong brother|. He now names the third brother by means of the two phrases that begin (10).

(10)    DET→|strong brother|  BROTHER,  DET→|strong brother|  (name   sign),
        STRONG. [ONE]→|strong brother|.
        This brother, (name), is strong. Just this one.

Figure 10.20 begins with a clear example of PRO→|strong brother| and later, two apparent instances of DET→|strong brother|. It is interesting to note that at least in this example, there are formational differences between DET→|strong brother| and PRO→|strong brother|. He directs the fingertip of PRO→|strong brother| toward |strong brother|. In contrast, he directs the first instance of DET→|strong brother| to the left, but with the finger bent so that the tip points up. The second instance of DET→|strong brother| is also on the left, but with the straight finger oriented straight up. What we see in these two instances of DET→|strong brother| is that the hand – but not the fingertip – is directed to the left toward the token |strong brother|. He ends this description by repeating that this brother is strong and that he is the one brother of the five who is strong in this respect.

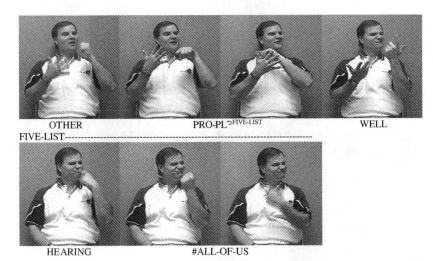

Figure 10.21 The rest of the five, well, (we had) hearing (children). All of us.

He next explains that the other four brothers have hearing children. He refers to the four brothers in two different ways. In Figure 10.21 he begins the description of the four brothers with the signs OTHER PRO-PL$^{\supset\text{FIVE-LIST}}$. As he signs OTHER, he raises the FIVE-LIST buoy into place. PRO-PL$^{\supset\text{FIVE-LIST}}$ then begins well below the FIVE-LIST buoy and moves in an upward arc past it.

Although the index finger moves past all five fingers of the FIVE-LIST buoy in producing PRO-PL$^{\supset\text{FIVE-LIST}}$, the signer is not talking about all five brothers. He is describing only the four brothers with hearing children. The sign OTHER semantically restricts the reference of PRO-PL$^{\supset\text{FIVE-LIST}}$ to the other four brothers.

The interjection WELL separates OTHER PRO-PL$^{\supset\text{FIVE-LIST}}$ from HEARING. Without the interjection it would look like a subject verb construction meaning, 'The other four brothers were hearing'. Because of the interjection, HEARING can be understood as a comment about their children.

#ALL-OF-US, the final sign in Figure 10.21, moves from left to right in front of the signer's chest and means 'all members of a group including the signer'. At issue here is the membership of the group. The signs OTHER PRO-PL$^{\supset\text{FIVE-LIST}}$ identify the most recently mentioned group including the signer as the four brothers with hearing children. Therefore, the reference of #ALL-OF-US is restricted to only the four brothers with hearing children.

Next he wonders, without answering his own question, whether the inability to produce Deaf offspring is a sign of weakness.

(11) MEAN SHOW WEAK, WELL (q)
Does that demonstrate that we are weak?

When hearing parents first learn that their child is deaf, this is generally a time of shock, confusion, and emotional turmoil. But within the Deaf community this is not the case. Within a family using ASL as the primary language of communication, a baby's inability to hear is not an impediment to language acquisition, normal family interaction, normal social development, and normal cognitive development. The Deaf child acquires American Sign Language on a timetable that parallels the acquisition of a spoken language by a hearing child (Newport and Meier 1985). By any social or cognitive measure, a Deaf child growing up in an ASL signing environment is a completely normal child. In this respect, Deaf children within ASL signing families are like hearing children with hearing parents who acquire a minority language as their first language. Unlike hearing children speaking a minority language, however, Deaf children face the additional burden of attempting to acquire the majority language without being able to hear it. The fact that being Deaf is not viewed negatively by the man describing his extended family explains why he is wondering about the weakness of the four brothers with hearing children.

## Still alive

The signer now begins discussing the ability to produce Deaf children across generations within his family. He begins by placing the THEME buoy ahead of his right shoulder. At the same time he places a 4 hand beside the THEME buoy and moves it diagonally forward and down, ending ahead and slightly to the right of his chin (Figure 10.22).

In order to understand what this novel sign is expressing, the addressee must understand the significance of both the THEME buoy and its location as well as the significance of the moving 4 hand and the path it traverses. Out

4 hand moves [THEME]↓|third generation| — WEAK. (tg)

Figure 10.22 These four genetic lines from the third generation are weak

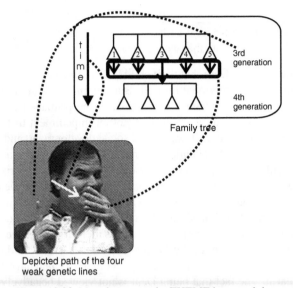

Depicted path of the four
weak genetic lines

Figure 10.23  Mappings onto the THEME buoy and the moving 4 hand

of context, this sign is not interpretable because he is producing something novel in terms of both what the hands are doing and where they are located. He has just previously described the brother with Deaf children as strong and has also wondered whether the inability to produce Deaf children was a sign of weakness. Immediately following this sign, he describes something weak. He produces WEAK with the nonmanual signal *tg*, expressing a meaning that approximates 'happens to be weak'. It follows that the sign preceding WEAK is depicting the weak genetic lines of those four brothers. If so, those genetic lines move in time forward from the third generation. Since the THEME buoy appears to be the starting point of the four genetic lines characterized as weak, it has the significance 'third generation'.

The placement of two hands producing the initial sign in Figure 10.22 is consistent with the existence of a depicting space in which the THEME buoy has the significance 'third generation' and the weak genetic lines move forward in time from there. The path over his right shoulder moving forward diagonally across his body and down appears to be the same physical path used to depict the temporal distance between the signer and the fifth brother illustrated in Figure 10.11. In that case, time also moves forward and down across the body, beginning above the weak hand shoulder.

The blend created by the signer in producing the signs in Figure 10.22 is illustrated in Figure 10.23. The THEME buoy has the significance 'third generation' and is placed in the depicting blend near the location in time of the third

[FOURTH]<sup>→|fourth generation|</sup>                        STILL

LIVE

Figure 10.24 The fourth generation is still alive

generation. I hypothesize that the fingers of the 4 hand depict the four weak genetic lines. This is what the signer describes as weak.[14] He maps the four weak genetic lines onto the four extended fingers of his left hand, and maps time onto the space traversed by the left hand.

It is interesting to note that the hearing children of the four Deaf brothers would not be considered to be members of the fourth generation since the signer is specifically talking about generations of Deaf family members. Thus, we should not expect the four weak genetic lines to lead to the fourth generation in the depicting space. However, in Figure 10.24, he does remark that there is a fourth generation of Deaf family members with the signs [FOURTH]<sup>→ |fourth generation|</sup> STILL LIVE.

The sign [FOURTH]<sup>→ |fourth generation|</sup> is produced further away from the body than the preceding sign WEAK. This places the hand well ahead of the normal space in which the nondirectional sign FOURTH would normally be produced – making it appear to be pointing at something. Based on its meaning and the context, I am assuming that it is directed toward the |fourth generation|.[15]

---

[14] This is only a hypothesis since the signer produces no instances of two or three weak genetic lines to compare this example against. If two weak genetic lines were represented by a moving V handshape and three weak lines by a moving 3 handshape, that would be fully consistent with the hypothesis guiding the analysis here. This is not, however, the kind of thing that can easily be addressed through elicitation techniques since the moving 4 hand is a spontaneous, highly creative production not involving a lexical sign.

[15] The highly reduced signs STILL LIVE are two-handed signs. The left hand is at roughly the same location as it was when producing [FOURTH]<sup>→ |fourth generation|</sup>. However, since both hands are not directed toward |fourth generation| I am not treating these two signs as directional.

|four weak genetic lines|

|third generation|

|fourth generation|

Figure 10.25  Directing FOURTH toward |fourth generation|

The THEME buoy in Figure 10.22 only remains in place while the 4 hand moves past it. While present, it gives physical substance to the third generation through blending. Given the assumption that he is building a blended space that he can continue to use, removing the hand does not remove the significance of the location it occupied. That is, even after the hand is removed, the third generation will still be associated with that location. Time travels diagonally forward and down in this depicting space so the fourth generation should be associated with a location further ahead of the signer. I am assuming that [FOURTH]$^{\rightarrow\,|\text{fourth generation}|}$ is pointing toward the token |fourth generation| in the depicting space. If this is correct, [FOURTH]$^{\rightarrow\,|\text{fourth generation}|}$ provides evidence to the addressee to extend the depicting space by blending the fourth generation with the space ahead of the hand producing [FOURTH]$^{\rightarrow\,|\text{fourth generation}|}$.

Figure 10.25 illustrates the depicting blend at this point, with |third generation| at a location just ahead of his shoulder and |fourth generation| at a location ahead of his left hand in Figure 10.25. The depicted |four weak genetic lines| move forward in time, but end only part way to |fourth generation|. Since FOURTH$^{\rightarrow\,|\text{fourth generation}|}$ is produced well ahead of where the moving 4 hand stopped in depicting the four weak genetic lines, and since |fourth generation| will be located ahead of where FOURTH$^{\rightarrow\,|\text{fourth generation}|}$ is produced, there is a gap between the end of |four weak genetic lines| and |fourth generation|.

The signs in Figure 10.26 provide evidence for the start of a continuous path in the depicting space from |third generation| to |fourth generation|. Of the five potential fathers of Deaf children in the third generation, only one had Deaf children. The signer depicts that drop from five potential to one actual father of Deaf children by signing [FIVE]$^{\downarrow\,|\text{time 1}|}$ with the nonmanual grammatical marker $t$, signaling a topic, followed by [ONE]$^{\downarrow\,|\text{time 2}|}$, signed with the nonmanual adverb $th$ indicating lack of control and negativity. By placing FIVE at the location associated with the start of the forward movement of the four weak genetic lines in the previous depicting space, he makes an association between the placed hand and the five potential fathers of Deaf children at that time. Then he moves the hand diagonally downward to produce [ONE]$^{\downarrow\,|\text{time 2}|}$.

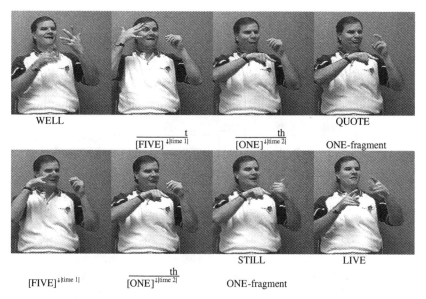

WELL                                          QUOTE

$\overline{[FIVE]}^{\downarrow|time\ 1|}$ (t)     $\overline{[ONE]}^{\downarrow|time\ 2|}$ (th)     ONE-fragment

STILL          LIVE

[FIVE]$^{\downarrow|time\ 1|}$     $\overline{[ONE]}^{\downarrow|time\ 2|}$ (th)     ONE-fragment

Figure 10.26 The five potential genetic lines capable of producing Deaf children resulted in one father of Deaf children. So (the continuation of Deaf family members) is still alive.

This sequence of signs on this downward path depicts the reduction from five potential fathers of Deaf children at time$_1$ to one actual father of Deaf children at time$_2$. He follows these two signs with QUOTE, then repeats them again. QUOTE is often used to mark either a novel construction or the novel use of a sign. It is similar to what an English speaker might do by adding "so to speak" at the end of a novel description. That certainly applies in this case since [FIVE]$^{\downarrow|time\ 1|}$ and [ONE]$^{\downarrow|time\ 2|}$ are being used to depict potential and actual fathers of Deaf children.

The orientation of the hands in producing these two signs is significant. He is talking about genetic lines with the potential to produce Deaf children. Orienting [FIVE]$^{\downarrow|time\ 1|}$ with the fingers directed to the side and slightly forward (rather than upward) and orienting [ONE]$^{\downarrow|time\ 2|}$ with the index finger directed forward adds to the directional depiction of the genetic lines moving forward in time within this blended space.

The conceptual mappings underlying [FIVE]$^{\downarrow|time\ 1|}$ and [ONE]$^{\downarrow|time\ 2|}$ are illustrated in Figure 10.27. The hand producing [FIVE]$^{\downarrow|time\ 1|}$ and the five genetic lines of the third generation blend to create |five potential Deaf lines|. Of these five, only one line produces Deaf offspring. The blended entity |one actual Deaf line| is created by blending the hand producing [ONE]$^{\downarrow|time\ 2|}$ and the single line producing Deaf children in the family tree into the depicting

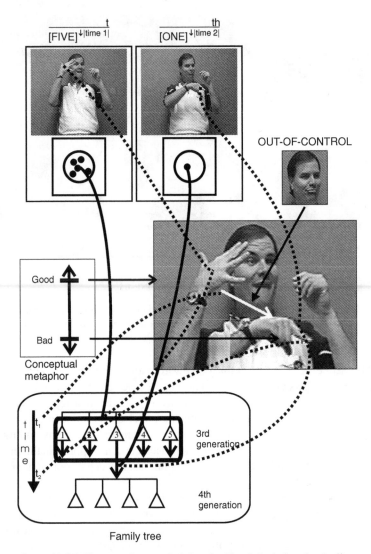

Figure 10.27 The mappings underlying the blend depicting the decline to a single genetic line producing Deaf children

space. The blended entity takes the form of the visible 1 hand. The nonmanual signals accompanying the two signs also contribute to the meaning being expressed. [FIVE]$^{\downarrow|\text{time 1}|}$ is produced with the nonmanual markings for a topic. [ONE]$^{\downarrow|\text{time 2}|}$ is produced with the nonmanual signal *th* signifying lack of control. Thus, the nonmanual signal *th* characterizes the reduction in number from

SPREAD↓|time 2|–|future|                                    AGAIN
ONE-fragment------------------------------------------

Figure 10.28  Future generations of Deaf family members will spring from that one successful line

five to one as negative. In Figure 10.27 I have labeled it with one of its central (negative) meanings, 'out of control'.

In this depicting space, time in the family tree space maps onto the vector beginning above the signer's shoulder and moving diagonally across his body. The 5 hand is placed at time |t₁| in the blend and the 1 hand is placed at |t₂|. The path from |t₁| to |t₂| is both forward and downward, thereby incorporating two different spatial metaphors. The forward direction incorporates 'future is forward' while the downward direction incorporates 'good is up, bad is down'.[16] Since previous downward paths involving time mappings have not been treated as involving the 'good is up, bad is down' metaphor, it may not be immediately apparent why this downward path makes use of this metaphor. It will become apparent shortly since he overtly contrasts this downward path with a subsequent positive upward path.

By creating a forward-downward path, the signer simultaneously incorporates both metaphors. Thus, not only does he overtly describe the change as negative by using the *th* nonmanual signal, he also depicts it as negative by changing the level at which the two signs are produced, consistent with the 'good is up, bad is down' metaphor.

Next he signs STILL LIVE. He leaves the weak hand that produced [ONE]↓|time 2| in place as a fragment buoy while signing STILL with his dominant hand. Leaving the fragment buoy in place signals the continued significance of the depicting space. He produces LIVE with both hands. Thus in spite of the negative, uncontrollable drop from five potential genetic lines to one line with Deaf offspring the presence of that one line means that the existence of Deaf family members from generation to generation is still "alive." He describes one possible future of this line with the signs SPREAD↓|time 2|–|future| AGAIN, as shown in Figure 10.28.

---

[16] See Lakoff and Johnson (1980) for an extensive discussion of metaphors common to English speakers. Wilcox (2000) and Taub (2001) discuss the 'good is up' and many other conceptual metaphors used in ASL.

Five potential genetic lines capable of producing Deaf children

One genetic line that produced Deaf children

Increase in genetic lines capable of producing Deaf family members in the future

Figure 10.29 The depicted spread of future generations of Deaf family members

The position of the ONE fragment buoy at the beginning of SPREAD$^{\downarrow|\text{time 2}|-|\text{future}|}$ is higher than the location of [ONE]$^{\downarrow|\text{time 2}|}$. This appears to be due to the two intervening signs STILL LIVE. Both signs are produced with upward movements. During STILL the ONE fragment buoy is slightly higher than its original position. During LIVE that hand is higher still (since it is one of the hands producing LIVE). As a result when he signs SPREAD$^{\downarrow|\text{time 2}|-|\text{future}|}$, with the back of his dominant hand against the tip of the ONE buoy, the ONE buoy is out of position – it is too high. Note that by the time the verb is completed the ONE buoy has returned to a position consistent with the blend illustrated in Figure 10.27.

SPREAD$^{\downarrow|\text{time 2}|-|\text{future}|}$ further elaborates that blend, as illustrated in Figure 10.29. Since the sign begins at the tip of the finger depicting the one successful line, the spreading is conceptualized as beginning there. The spreading is depicted as moving forward and upward. This depicts future generations of Deaf family members spreading out on that upward positive plane. The width of the spreading corresponds to an increase in numbers of future Deaf family members.

In order to focus on the result rather than the blending process that created it, Figure 10.29 presents only a labeled depicting space without mappings. Having already described the blending projections up to this point, the projections that created this depicting blend should be clear. The signer has created a very complex depiction that begins by depicting five potential fathers of Deaf children at a time $t_1$. Four of those lines are depicted as moving forward in time, but not leading to more Deaf family members. He described them as weak. Figure 10.29 depicts the "drop" from five potential to one actual father of Deaf children, followed by the possible later increase of Deaf family members, depicted as an upward spreading. The forward and upward directional movement takes advantage of two different metaphors. The forward direction takes advantage of 'future is forward' and the upward direction takes advantage of 'good is up, bad is down'. As a result, he is depicting the future increase in the number of Deaf individuals in the family as a positive thing.

gestures-------------------------------------------------------------------------------------

----------------------------- SPREAD$^{\downarrow|\text{time 2}|-|\text{future}|'}$

WHO-KNOWS

Figure 10.30 The number of Deaf family members went from big to small like this. It could spread again from there. Who knows?

The verb SPREAD$^{\downarrow L-L'}$ is produced with an initial flat O handshape that changes to a 5 handshape as the hand moves toward $L'$. As a result, the signs depicting the fall and rise of Deaf family members begin and end with a 5 hand-shape. The initial 5 handshape has the significance 'five'. The final handshape is simply the lexically specified final handshape of the sign SPREAD$^{\downarrow L-L'}$, and does not signify 'five'.

In this example, the single verb SPREAD$^{\downarrow|\text{time 2}|-|\text{future}|}$ takes advantage of the depicting blend created by [FIVE]$^{\downarrow|\text{time 1}|}$ and [ONE]$^{\downarrow|\text{time 2}|}$, contributes its own semantic content, invokes two different spatial metaphors, and further develops the blend by depicting the increased number of Deaf family members through a broadening of the space. That is quite a lot for a single word.

He next produces a gestural depiction of the same family tree. As shown in Figure 10.30, two 4 hands begin at a high level, depicting a generation across a relatively broad space. The two hands come together at a single point as the hands move downward, then spread out again as they move down and out depicting another broad conceptualized space. Even though this set of move-ments involves no lexical signs, it nevertheless depicts a change from broad to very narrow to broad again. Assuming that he is producing a different depiction of the same variations in numbers of Deaf family members producing Deaf children, the broad upper space corresponds to the third generation of Deaf individuals in his family, the narrow central space corresponds to the single Deaf brother with Deaf children, and the broad lower space corresponds to the Deaf members of future generations. In this depiction, time moves downward since future time is below past time.[17] He also maps larger numbers onto wider space, equating width with numerical value.

The non-sign gestures described above create the new depicting space. Next, the hands producing SPREAD$^{\downarrow |\text{time } 2|' - |\text{future}|'}$ begin at the narrow part of the depiction corresponding to time$_2$, then move downward, depicting the increase in number of Deaf family members in the future by the spreading out of both the hands and fingers. It appears not to matter that SPREAD$^{\downarrow |\text{time } 2|' - |\text{future}|'}$ is produced with respect to a depicting blend created by purely gestural means. Figure 10.30 ends with the comment WHO-KNOWS. He follows this with one final comment, BUT STILL LIVE 'But it is still alive'.

### Skipping a generation

After his interlocutor takes a turn, the signer responds with the comment about his own children with the signs in Figure 10.31. After signing POSS-1 CHIL-DREN 'my children', he points along a side-to-side horizontal line in a new depicting space ahead of him at about the level of the center of his torso with the sign RIGHT-ALONG-HERE$^{\downarrow |\text{my children}|}$. By moving his finger along a line from right to left then part way back, he creates an association between his children and the depicted line.

The line lies at a certain point along the forward movement of time. After a false start, he produces the depicting buoy THIN-CYLINDER$^{\downarrow |\text{my children}|}$ to depict his children along that line visibly. His strong B hand moves in an arc that begins before the location of the buoy, passes over it, then comes back down on the far side of it.[18]

Understanding what he is expressing depends on several metaphors. First, the genetic ability to produce Deaf children is treated as an entity that moves through time. We can see that it is a thing since it is associated with the B handshape that moves forward in space (time). Apparently, within the spatial metaphor created here, contact with this moving entity produces Deaf children.

---

[17] This downward movement of time is built into the lexical structure of verbs like BECOME-FEWER-OVER-TIME$^{x \to y}$, which begins at the level of the forehead and ends in front of the trunk (see chapter 7).

[18] He places his index finger at a higher level than the line previously traced by his finger. The false start between the original depiction of the line and placing THIN-CYLINDER$^{\downarrow |\text{my children}|}$ may have something to do with the higher placement.

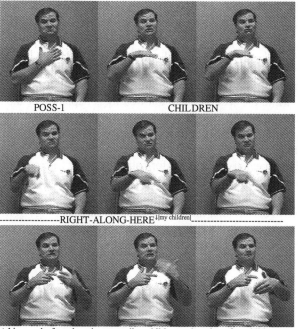

'skip over': from location preceding children to location after children

Figure 10.31  My children are here. (The genetic trait) skipped over them (like this).

His children are not Deaf because the entity made no contact with them. Instead, it moved above and past the buoy giving physical substance to |my children|.

## Summary

The signing examined in this chapter illustrates several common themes of ASL discourse. The signer describes his grandmother, his parents, his four brothers and himself, two wives of one of the brothers, his own two children and their mothers, ten nieces and nephews, and four Deaf nieces and nephews. Of these twenty-four individuals, twenty-one were part of at least one token blend. Some were part of multiple blends. In addition, he also created depicting blends to talk about the four weak genetic lines, one strong genetic line, the movement of those genetic lines through time, as well as the movement through time of the ability to produce Deaf children.

The fact that some entities were represented in more than one blend illustrates that new blends serve new purposes. The fifth brother was separated spatially from the rest to place him five and a half years distant from the signer himself. Later, the third brother was separated spatially from the others in order to be able to distinguish the strength of his genetic line from the weakness of the other four genetic lines. The signer's own children were associated with a TWO-LIST buoy in the order of their birth then later depicted along a line in time. The original blend of his two children with the TWO-LIST buoy provided an ordered list while the second blend allowed for a depiction of the reason his children were not Deaf.

Finally, this narrative demonstrates one theme present throughout the book. The meanings understood by an addressee go far beyond what is lexically encoded. Grammatically encoded information together with pointing and gestural information of various types prompt an addressee to construct both non-grounded mental spaces and real space blends of various types. These spaces are all related to one another through projections and mappings from one space to another. The grammatical, the gradient, and the gestural are so tightly inter-twined in ASL that it is the exception, rather than the rule, when an utterance lacks a gradient or gestural component.

# 11   Grammar, gesture, and meaning

An examination of the grammar of ASL reveals the types of lexical items and grammatical constructions one would expect to find in any vocally produced language. Morphological complexity can be found in its extensive inventory of compound signs, in aspectual and other grammatical forms marked through feature insertion into frames, reduplication, or both, in signs with numeral incorporation, in depicting verbs, and to a small extent in signs with an attached prefix or suffix. Like words in any language, ASL signs are conventionalized form-meaning pairings capable of combining with other such signs as parts of grammatical constructions.

Some signs have not only the properties one would expect of a word in a vocally produced language, but also additional properties such as the need to be directed toward some entity, the need to be placed within a space, the need for the signer to direct the face and eye gaze toward some entity during the production of the sign, or the need to perform constructed actions within a surrogate blend. ASL pronouns, for example, have all the properties one would expect of pronouns in a spoken language, and they also have the additional grammatical requirement to be directed toward their referents. Knowing the grammar of ASL includes knowing that pronouns must be properly directed toward referents in real space or in real-space blends.

Since pronouns encode meanings, they are part of the symbolic inventory of ASL. The need to direct a pronoun such as $PRO^{\rightarrow x}$ is also part of its lexical structure. A pronoun's direction, however, does not depend on a set of symbolic locations or directions, but rather, depends on the locations of things in real space or in real-space blends. Instead of selecting from a grammatically defined list of possible directions, the signer must select a direction that leads to the pronoun's referent, either in real space or in a real-space blend. In this sense, the directionality of the finger during any particular instance of $PRO^{\rightarrow x}$ is gradient. This places the specific direction outside the set of ASL's symbolic resources since it does not encode – it points. For pronouns in general, the *need to point* is part of grammatical knowledge but the specific direction of pointing is not.

Any specific instance of PRO$^{\rightarrow x}$ will be a combination of the lexically fixed features encoding the symbolic pronoun and a nonsymbolic pointing direction selected for the specific context in which it is being used. Using Peirce's well-known distinction between icon, index, and symbol, any specific instance of PRO$^{\rightarrow x}$ will be both symbolic and indexic. The grammatical purpose of the indexic component of the sign is to assist in meaning construction since it leads toward the entity to map onto the sign's semantic pole.

Like pronouns, indicating verbs encode lexical meanings and also have grammatical requirements to be spatially directed. The transitive verb GIVE$^{x\rightarrow y}$, for example, has lexically fixed features. It is produced with a flat O handshape, a palm-up orientation of the hand, and an arc-shaped movement. The hand begins with a hold with the fingertips directed toward the entity corresponding to its trajector. It then moves up, then down in an arc-shaped movement ending with the fingertips directed toward the entity corresponding to the verb's landmark. As with pronouns, the actual placement of the hand during the initial or final hold is gradient and will depend on the locations of the entities it is directed toward. Because the flat O handshape looks like a hand capable of holding something, it can easily be seen as an iconic sign.[1] Thus, instances of GIVE$^{x\rightarrow y}$ are iconic, symbolic, and indexic.

Gradience is perhaps even more obvious in depicting verbs. In addition to encoding lexical meanings, these verbs also have the grammatical requirement to be placed within depicting spaces. For example, in producing VEHICLE-BE-AT$^{\downarrow L}$ the signer places the hand at a specific location within a depicting space – the depicted location of the vehicle. The location itself is not a symbolic element of the grammar. Rather, it is one of innumerable locations the signer could select based on its ability to depict the vehicle's location appropriately.

Other aspects of the language signal are more clearly gestural. For example, the verb LOOK-TOWARD$^{\cup\rightarrow x}$ not only requires the fingertips to point by means of the gradient direction of the fingertips, it also requires the signer to create a surrogate space in which the signer demonstrates the act of looking by becoming, through blending, the entity doing the looking. Carrying out this looking activity is a demonstration of the looking activity encoded by the verb. It is not a demonstration of a decontextualized act of looking, but rather the specific instance of looking by the specific individual being described. Producing LOOK-TOWARD$^{\cup\rightarrow x}$ in this way combines its lexically encoded meaning, gradient orientation of the fingers toward the entity to map onto the verb's landmark, and a gestural enactment of the actions of the head, face, and eyes in the instance of looking being described. Expressing the conventional linguistic form, directing the verb, and enacting the looking action

---

[1]  See Taub (2001) and Wilcox (2000) for in-depth discussions of issues surrounding iconicity and metaphor in ASL.

are all equally part of the verb's production and all contribute to meaning construction.

I have been describing the ASL language signal as consisting of combinations of signs, grammatical constructions, gradience in the signal produced by the primary articulators as signs are being produced, and gestural activities independent of the primary articulators. If one replaces "signs" with "words" in the description above, it applies equally well to spoken language discourse. As speakers articulate vocally produced words, they also control meaningful gradient aspects of the spoken language signal that include pitch, loudness, vocal quality, rhythm, tempo, and duration. The term *prosody* refers to pitch, loudness, tempo, and rhythm (Crystal 1991:283). The term *intonation* can be used to refer to "the distinctive patterns of PITCH or melody" (Crystal 1991:182), or more broadly, also to include pitch range, loudness, rhythmicality, and tempo (Crystal 1969:195).

Speakers also produce gestures of the hands and arms as they speak (Duncan 1996; Haviland 2000; Kendon 1980, 1988, 2000; Kita 1993, 2000; LeBaron and Streeck 2000; McNeill 1985, 1992, 2000; Özyürek 2000). In fact, Duncan (in press) notes that "The culture has not been found whose hearing members do not spontaneously produce meaningful manual, bodily, and facial movements when speaking with one another."

Kendon (1972, 1980) was the first to argue for the conceptual unity of speech and gesture. He uses the term *gesticulation* to mean the movements of the hands and arms that accompany speech and states (1988:131) that, "gesticulation is so closely integrated with speech that it must be considered an integral part of the act of utterance." In his landmark book on co-speech gestures McNeill (1992) writes, "gestures are an integral part of language as much as are words, phrases, and sentences – gestures and language are one system." McNeill clearly makes the case that speech and gesture are both temporally and conceptually integrated in expressing a meaning that goes beyond either one individually.[2] He proposes that speech expresses the conventional, grammatical, sequential rule-governed part of the message while gesture expresses the imagistic, instantaneous, and holistic part (1992:2).[3]

---

[2] Okrent (2002) argues for a modality-free definition of gesture. In her proposal, gesture patterns meaning onto form in a gradient way, is not conventionalized, and expresses the imagistic side of thought. Such a modality-independent definition of gesture would allow the concept of gesture to be applied equally to both spoken and signed languages. This definition also treats meaningful, imagistic, gradient aspects of the spoken language signal as vocally produced gestures.

[3] Armstrong *et al.* (1995:46), following Studdert-Kennedy, define a gesture as, "a *functional* unit, an equivalence class of coordinated movements that achieve some end." Under this much broader definition the formational distinction between language and gesture disappears since coughing, swallowing, signing the ASL sign CAT, speaking the English word *cat*, and pointing at a picture would all be gestures. Regardless of how one defines a gesture, there is still an important distinction between symbolic elements of a grammar and demonstrations, depictions, pointing, etc.

Specialists in intonation have also made convincing cases for the meaningfulness and significance of intonation (*inter alia* Bolinger 1961, 1972, 1986, 1989; Cruttenden 1986; Ladd 1978, 1980, 1990, 1996; Liberman 1979; Pierrehumbert 1980). In spite of these demonstrations, the normal approach to the analysis of a morphological or syntactic construction is to proceed without regard to intonation.

Bolinger describes intonation as the "Cinderella of the communication complex ... only one of several stepsisters who at one time or other have slept beside the hearth" (1986:3). Bolinger has selected an apt metaphor. Cinderella lives in the same house with the other sisters, does valuable and necessary work the others do not do, is not given any respect, and is not treated as a member of the family. If one were to think of a sentence as a family portrait, in the overwhelming majority of modern linguistic work, Cinderella is not called when it is time to take that portrait.

McNeill observes that "We tend to consider 'linguistic' what we can write down, and 'nonlinguistic' everything else; but this division is a cultural artifact, an arbitrary limitation derived from historical evolution" (1985:351). We have a difficult time writing down gradient signals. In tone languages such as Chinese or Thai, a discrete number of tones distinguish words which are otherwise identical in terms of their consonant and vowel structure. Such tones can be labeled and written down as part of an analysis since their forms are conventional and their numbers are limited. For these languages tone is considered linguistic. Intonation, on the other hand, does not come in such easily identifiable packages and is not easily written down. Even though intonation distinguishes one utterance from another, it is not generally considered linguistic.

Once it became clear to me that the ASL language signal integrated lexical, gradient, and gestural components, I began looking for English examples where intonation was not "overlaid" on the "core" grammatical signal, but rather, was a central component of the structure itself. I was led to analyzing the construction below when I heard someone say, "That was cold!" in a way that could only mean 'cold hearted'. The sentence could not be understood to have anything to do with temperature. This semantic restriction on "cold" had to be due to the construction itself. Suprasegmentals including pitch and vocal quality are a central component of the construction itself and the construction does not exist without them (Liddell 2000c). I will briefly summarize the properties of that construction below.

Example (1) illustrates a typical use of this construction along with the differences in tone needed to produce it. It begins at an unmarked pitch level, the pitch rises for the subject, rises further during the copula, drops sharply for the beginning of the adjective then rises at the end of the adjective.[4]

---

[4] In these examples I am adopting Bolinger's convention of writing words at different levels to represent differences in pitch.

```
              was
          that
(1)    Well              pid
          stú
```

The construction often begins with the interjection *well*, though it is not required. When *well* is present, it is prototypically followed by the pronoun *that*, the copula, and a bare adjective. The pitch contour makes up a central part of this construction. In addition, the final adjective is also produced with other suprasegmental modifications. In its most complete form, this construction also involves a tense glottis during the adjective and a glottal stop with a buildup of subglottal pressure prior to the release of the glottal stop. In (1), for example, the stressed initial syllable of *stupid* would be produced with a tense glottis. The glottal stop appears between the [s] and [t], followed by a release with the production of the [t].

This construction prototypically provides a negative evaluation of someone's actions. There are also semantic restrictions on both the subject and the adjective. Since the construction provides a negative evaluation of an action, the subject must refer to an action. As a result, the sentence, *Well that was stupid!*, is acceptable where *that* refers to an action, but unacceptable if *that* refers to something else. Subjects other than *that* are also possible, but their acceptability depends on how well they focus on an action. For example, gerunds work much better as subjects than that-clauses. To my ear (2) sounds bizarre while (3) seems fine. The that-clause in (2) appears to focus on the fact of coming while the gerund in (3) seems to focus more on the action.

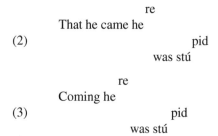

```
                    re
        That he came he
(2)                              pid
                  was stú
```

```
              re
      Coming he
(3)                    pid
          was stú
```

The final adjective also has interesting restrictions. Adjectives with either negative or positive connotations can appear in this construction. When a positive adjective appears in this construction, as in (4), the sentence still expresses a negative evaluation.

```
              was
          That
(4)                      rt
          smá
```

The combination of a positive adjective and a negative evaluation expresses sarcasm. This is not simply a pragmatic interpretation based on the juxtaposition of a negative event and a positive-sounding adjective. That is, let us assume that (4) appears in a context where a blunder has just occurred. Given that the positive-sounding "smart" appears right after a blunder, it might be the juxtaposition of the blunder and the positive-sounding statement that leads to a sarcastic interpretation. If that were so, then in the same context, (5) would also be understood as sarcastic.

```
              smá
      That        a
(5)           was     rt
```

However, even in the context of a recent blunder, (5) would not be understood as sarcastic. Rather, (5) would be understood as an emphatic assertion that someone's recent action was smart. The listener who witnessed an apparent blunder, then heard (5), would be put into a position of having to reconcile an apparent blunder and a clear statement contradicting the occurrence of a blunder.

In addition, while both positive and negative adjectives can appear in the construction, more neutral adjectives such as *adequate* produce a comical result since the adjective is not suitable for either a negative evaluation or a sarcastic comment.

There is an additional restriction on the final adjective. It strongly tends to appear in unmodified form. Adverbs such as *very/extremely/tremendously* do not work in this construction. Thus, (6) is unacceptable, while the same words in the same order are completely acceptable in (7).

```
              was
      That
(6)                       rt
              very smá

              vé
      That
(7)           was    r

                  y smart
```

For present tense forms, where a clitic form of the copula is available, it is required. Thus, in this construction, *Well that is stupid!*, is quite odd compared to the normal sounding: *Well that's stupid!*

It appears that the negative evaluation works best when the subject, rather than the verb, encodes the action. This explains the unacceptability of (8). I am unable to think of any context where (8) could be felicitous.

(8)
```
        ed
  He act
                ly
  stúpid
```

Suppose I see something that is outlandishly green, I can provide a negative evaluation of its (outlandish) greenness using the same construction.

(9)
```
            was
        thát
  Well              en
        ʔgré
```

In my production of (9), the adjective *green* begins with an initial glottal stop with considerable subglottal pressure. Releasing the subglottal pressure as the [g] is produced makes the word *green* be perceived as heavily stressed. With the interjection *well* present, I can still get the negative reading even without the glottal stop. However, without the interjection, as in (10), I can only get the negative reading with the glottal stop preceding *green*.

(10)
```
            was
        Thát
                en
        ʔgré
```

Using the adjective *green* in this construction is not a prototypical use of this construction because the construction prototypically provides a negative evaluation of someone's actions. It is interesting to note that not just any color can be used in this construction. It is hard to imagine, for example, using *red* or *blue* in this construction.

The existence of this construction explains why "cold" in the statement, "That was cold," could be understood only as describing a cold-hearted action. The construction is used to describe an action negatively. In describing the action the only applicable sense of "cold" is 'cold-hearted'.

The syntactic and semantic restrictions associated with this construction demonstrate that this is not a case of an intonation contour being overlaid on a sentence, thereby adding a particular interpretation to it. If that were true, the intonation pattern ought to be independent of the syntax. Rather, the suprasegmentals are a central aspect of this construction, which does not exist without the proper suprasegmental features. In this construction, suprasegmentals and grammar cannot be separated. The tight integration of suprasegmental features into this grammatical construction is just like the integration of gradient directions and locations into the ASL language signal.

Those who study intonation and gesture have provided overwhelming evidence that both intonation and gesture contribute to the meanings expressed by speakers of vocally produced languages. Intonation is integrated into the vocal signal itself. Gestures are timed to co-occur with specific parts of the vocal signal (Duncan in press; McNeill 1992, 2000; McNeill and Duncan 2000). In spite of these demonstrations, gradience and modality have kept intonation and gesture outside of the mainstream of linguistic analysis. This choice is not available in the analysis of ASL. Ignoring gestures and gradient aspects of the signal produced by the hands leaves out too much.

The knowledge that sign languages are real human languages allows us to take a broader look at the concept 'language'. The aspects of ASL examined in this book reveal that the ASL language signal consists of more than conventional linguistic forms. It also includes gradient aspects of the signal (typically directional aspects or placement), and gestures of various types. All of these coordinated and integrated activities constitute the language signal and contribute to expressing the conceptual structure underlying the utterance. There is no evidence that signers give more significance to grammatically encoded meanings than they give to other meaningful aspects of the signal. On the contrary, it is the entire message that is of interest. The gradient and gestural aspects of the signal are not peripheral or paralinguistic. They are required to be present and central to the meanings being expressed. In the case of ASL, restricting the analysis of language to symbolic units and their grammatical organization is hopelessly inadequate. This places ASL at odds with the predominant views of what constitutes language.

It is possible, of course, that ASL in particular, and signed languages more generally, are organized differently than vocally produced languages. If correct, then sign languages simply include more varied kinds of semiotic elements in the language signal than vocally produced languages. This is a highly unlikely result since the human brain with all its conceptualizing power creates and drives both signed and spoken languages. It is much more likely that spoken and signed languages both make use of multiple types of semiotic elements in the language signal, but that our understanding of what constitutes language has been much too narrow.

# Appendix 1 Notational conventions: identifying signs

| | |
|---|---|
| CAT | A single uppercase English word identifies a single ASL sign. Using the gloss CAT to identify a sign does not mean that the sign has the same morphological, syntactic, or semantic characteristics as the English word *cat*. |
| OH-I-SEE | Uppercase English words separated by hyphens also represent a single sign. |
| BOY^SAME | The symbol^indicates that two signs have been combined into a single compound sign. |
| B-U-D-G-E-T | Hyphens between uppercase letters indicate a sequence of alphabetic character signs used to spell a word. |
| #WHAT | A word beginning with the symbol # indicates a lexical sign whose origin is ultimately traceable to a sequence of alphabetic character signs. |
| PRO-1 | The notation -*1* indicates a first person form. In this case, the sign is the first person singular pronoun. |
| {TWO}{O'CLOCK} | A sign composed of the two bound morphemes {TWO} and {O'CLOCK}. |
| {$AGE_0$}-FOUR | A sign composed of the prefix {$AGE_0$}-combined with the root FOUR. |
| WAIT$^{[DURATIONAL]}$ | A sign derived from WAIT. The label in the square brackets identifies the grammatical process underlying the sign being represented. |
| $\overline{\text{SIGN}_1 \ldots \text{SIGN}_n}^{\text{t}}$ | The sequence of signs from $\text{SIGN}_1$ to $\text{SIGN}_n$ is accompanied by the nonmanual signal *t*. |

'this week'                           A gesture that, in the context of its use, has
                                      the significance 'this week'.

$SIGN_1 \ldots SIGN_n$                The top line represents the signing of the
THEME----------                       strong hand while the bottom line
                                      represents the signing of the weak hand.
                                      Here, the weak hand maintains the THEME
                                      buoy in place during the sign sequence
                                      $SIGN_1 \ldots SIGN_n$.

# Appendix 2 Notational conventions: direction and placement

PRO$^{\rightarrow x}$

$^{\rightarrow x}$ indicates that the sign is directed toward entity $x$. Entity $x$ will be either an element of real space or a real-space blend (see Chapter 3).

|Garfield|

Enclosing a word in vertical brackets identifies an entity in a real-space blend (see Chapter 5).

PRO-$^{\rightarrow |aunt|}$

$^{\rightarrow |aunt|}$ indicates that the sign is directed toward the blended entity |aunt|.

PRO-PL$^{\supset a,b,c}$

$^{\supset a,b,c}$ indicates that the hand moves along a path, such that the extent of the path points toward entities $a$, $b$, and $c$.

SAY-NO-TO-1$^{\cup x}$

$^{\cup x}$ indicates that the head and eyes are directed toward entity $x$.

HONOR$^{\cup \rightarrow y}$

$^{\cup \rightarrow y}$ indicates that face and eyes ($^{\cup}$) as well as the hands ($^{\rightarrow}$) are directed toward $y$.

GIVE$^{x \rightarrow y}$

$^{x \rightarrow y}$ indicates that the sign begins nearer to and/or directed toward $x$, then moves toward $y$.

MOVE$^{L1 \rightarrow L2}$

$^{L1 \rightarrow L2}$ indicates that the hand begins directed toward $L1$ and ends directed toward $L2$.

TIME-BREAK$^{\rightarrow D2 \downarrow D3}$

$^{D2 \downarrow D3}$ identifies a location between $D2$ and $D3$. Thus, this sign is directed toward a location between $D2$ and $D3$.

INVITE$^{\leftarrow y}$

$^{\leftarrow y}$ indicates that the verb begins directed toward $y$ then moves away from $y$.

BORROW$^{x \leftarrow y}$

$^{x \leftarrow y}$ indicates that the sign begins nearer to and/or directed toward $y$, then moves toward $x$.

INFORM$^{[\text{RECIP}]x\leftrightarrow y}$    $x\leftrightarrow y$ indicates that the hands move in opposite directions between $x$ and $y$. In this sign, each hand produces only a single movement. In producing a one-handed sign such as SAME-DUAL$^{x\leftrightarrow y}$, the hand moves back and forth between $x$ and $y$.

GO$^{\rightarrow}$    $\rightarrow$ The sign points in the direction of the action.

THROW$^{\rightarrow L}$    $\rightarrow L$ The sign is directed toward location $L$.

[COLLEGE]$^{\rightarrow L}$    [ ]$^{\rightarrow L}$ The nondirectional sign enclosed in the square brackets is directed toward location $L$.

[FIVE]$^{\rightarrow \text{addressee}}$    [ ]$^{\rightarrow \text{addressee}}$ The nondirectional sign enclosed in the square brackets is directed toward the addressee.

[PEOPLE-LINE]$^{\downarrow L1-L2}$    [ ]$^{\downarrow L1-L2}$ The nondirectional sign enclosed in the square brackets is produced between $L1$ and $L2$.

VEHICLE-BE-AT$^{\downarrow L1}$    $\downarrow L1$ The sign is produced at $L1$.

VEHICLE-DRIVE-TO$^{\downarrow L1-L2}$    $\downarrow L1-L2$ The movement of the sign begins at $L1$ and ends at $L2$.

ANIMAL-BE-AT$^{\downarrow \text{on |fence|}}$    $\downarrow \text{on |fence|}$ The strong hand places the sign at a location on the blended entity |fence|.

FENCE-SURFACE$^{\downarrow L2}$    $\downarrow L2$ The depicting buoy is produced at $L2$.

# Appendix 3  Main types of spaces discussed

| Type of space | Description | Grounded |
| --- | --- | --- |
| semantic space | The semantic pole of a linguistic expression. | no |
| event space, knowledge space, situation space, etc. | Aspects of such spaces are encoded into linguistic expressions. However, such spaces are distinct from the semantic pole of a linguistic expression. | no |
| real space | A person's here-and-now conceptualization of the immediate environment based on sensory input. | yes |
| surrogate space | A real-space blend in which the signer blends at least partially with some other entity or character. Entities within a surrogate space are *surrogates*. | yes |
| token space | A non-topographical real-space blend separate from the signer. Entities within a token space are *tokens*. | yes |
| buoy (space) | A real-space blend with the hand producing a list buoy, a fragment buoy, or the THEME buoy. | yes |
| depicting space | A topographical real-space blend separate from the signer. (Note: Depicting buoys are part of depicting spaces. This distinguishes them from other types of buoys.) | yes |

# References

Aarons, Debra. 1994. Aspects of the syntax of American Sign Language. Ph.D. dissertation, Boston University.

Aarons, Debra, Benjamin Bahan, Judy Kegl, and Carol Neidle. 1992. Clausal structure and a tier for grammatical marking in American Sign Language. *Nordic Journal of Linguistics* 15:103–142.

1994. Subjects and agreement in American Sign Language. In Inger Ahlgren, Brita Bergman, and Mary Brennan (eds.), *Perspectives on Sign Language Structure: Papers from the Fifth International Symposium on Sign Language Research,* vol. I. University of Durham, England: The Deaf Studies Research Unit, 13–28.

Ahlgren, Inger and Brita Bergman. 1994. Reference in narratives. In Inger Ahlgren, Brita Bergman, and Mary Brennan (eds.), *Perspectives on Sign Language Structure: Papers from the Fifth International Symposium on Sign Language Research*, vol. I. University of Durham, England: The Deaf Studies Research Unit, 29–36.

Armstrong, David, William C. Stokoe, and Sherman Wilcox. 1995. *Gesture and the Nature of Language.* Cambridge: Cambridge University Press.

Bahan, Benjamin J. 1996. Non-manual realization of agreement in American Sign Language. Ph.D. dissertation, Boston University.

Baker, Charlotte and Dennis Cokely. 1980. *American Sign Language: A Teacher's Resource Text on Grammar and Culture.* Silver Spring, MD: T. J. Publishers.

Baker, Charlotte and Carol Padden. 1978. Focusing on the nonmanual components of American Sign Language. In Patricia Siple (ed.), *Understanding Language through Sign Language Research.* New York: Academic Press, 59–90.

Battison, Robbin. 1974. Phonological deletion in American Sign Language. *Sign Language Studies* 5:1–19.

Bergman, Brita and Östen Dahl (eds.). 1994. Ideophones in sign language? The place of reduplication in the tense-aspect system of Swedish Sign Language. In Carl, Bache, Hans Basbøll, and Carl-Erik Lindberg (eds.), *Tense, Aspect and Action.* New York: Mouton de Gruyter, 397–422.

Bolinger, Dwight. 1961. Contrastive accent and contrastive stress. *Language* 37:83–96.

Bolinger, Dwight. 1972. Accent is predictable (if you're a mind reader). *Language* 48:633–644.

Bolinger, Dwight. 1975. *Aspects of Language* (2nd edition), New York: Harcourt, Brace, Jovanovich.

Bolinger, Dwight. 1986. *Intonation and its Parts.* Palo Alto, CA: Stanford University Press.

Bolinger, Dwight. 1989. *Intonation and its Uses*. Palo Alto, CA: Stanford University Press.

Boyes-Braem, Penny. 1981. Features of the handshape in American Sign Language. Ph.D. dissertation, University of California, Berkeley.

Brentari, Diane. 1998. *A Prosodic Model of Sign Language Phonology*. Cambridge, MA: MIT Press.

Bybee, Joan. 1985. *Morphology: A Study of the Relation between Meaning and Form*. Amsterdam: John Benjamins.

Chinchor, Nancy. 1981. Numeral incorporation in American Sign Language. Ph.D. dissertation, Brown University.

Chomsky, Noam. 1981. *Lectures on Government and Binding*. Dordrecht: Foris.

Clark, Herbert and Richard Gerrig. 1990. Quotations as demonstrations. *Language* 66.4:764–805.

Cole, Debra. 2000. Course paper. Department of Linguistics and Interpretation, Gallaudet University.

Coulter, Geoffrey. 1979. American Sign Language typology. Ph.D. dissertation, University of California at San Diego.

Cruttenden, Alan. 1986. *Intonation*. Cambridge: Cambridge University Press.

Crystal, David. 1969. *Prosodic Systems and Intonation in English*. Cambridge: Cambridge University Press.

1991. A Dictionary of Linguistics and Phonetics (3rd edition). London: Basil Blackwell.

Davies, Shawna. 1985. The tongue is quicker than the eye: Non-manual behaviors in ASL. In William C. Stokoe and V. Volterra (eds.), *SLR '83: Proceedings of the Third International Symposium on Sign Language Research*. Silver Spring, MD: Linstok Press, 185–193.

DeMatteo, Asa. 1977. Visual imagery and visual analogues in American Sign Language. In Lynn Friedman (ed.), *On the Other Hand: New Perspectives on American Sign Language*. New York: Academic Press, 109–136.

Dudis, Paul. 2000. Tokens as abstract visible blended elements. Paper presented at conference, Conceptual Structures in Discourse and Language 5, University of California, Santa Barbara, May 11–14, 2000.

Duncan, Susan. 1996. Grammatical form and "thinking for speaking" in Chinese and English: An analysis based on speech-accompanying gestures. Ph.D. dissertation, University of Chicago.

Duncan, Susan. In press. "Gesture in language: Issues for sign language research. In Karen Emmorey (ed.), *Perspectives on Classifier Constructions in Signed Languages*. Mahwah, NJ: Lawrence Erlbaum Associates.

Edge, Vicki Lee and Leora Herrmann. 1977. Verbs and the determination of subject in American Sign Language. In Lynn Friedman (ed.), *On the Other Hand: New Perspectives on American Sign Language*. New York: Academic Press, 137–179.

Efron, David. 1941. *Gesture and Environment*. Morningside heights, NY: King's Crown Press.

Ekman, Paul and W. F. Friesen. 1969. The repertoire of nonverbal behavioral categories: Origins, usage, and coding. *Semiotica* 1:49–98.

Emmorey, Karen. 1999. Do signers gesture? In L. Messing and R. Campbell (eds.), *Gesture, Speech, and Sign*. New York: Oxford University Press, 133–159.

Engberg-Pedersen, Elisabeth. 1993. *Space in Danish Sign Language: the Semantics and Morphosyntax of the Use of Space in a Visual Language.* Hamburg: Signum Press.

Fauconnier, Gilles. 1985. *Mental Spaces.* Cambridge, MA: MIT Press. Reprinted 1994, Cambridge: Cambridge University Press.

1997. *Mappings in Thought and Language.* Cambridge: Cambridge University Press.

Fauconnier, Gilles and Mark Turner. 1994. Conceptual projection and middle spaces. *UCSD Cognitive Science Technical Report.*

1996. Blending as a central process of grammar. In Adele Goldberg (ed.), *Conceptual Structure, Discourse and Language.* Stanford, CA: CSLI Publications, 113–130.

Fillmore, Charles. 1982. Frame semantics. In Linguistic Society of Korea (ed.), *Linguistics in the Morning Calm.* Seoul: Hanshin, 113–137.

1985. Frames and the semantics of understanding. *Quaderni di semantica* 6.2:222–253.

Fischer, Susan. 1973. Two processes of reduplication in American Sign Language. *Foundations of Language* 9:469–480.

1975. Influences on word order change in ASL. In Charles N. Li (ed.), *Word Order and Word Order Change.* Austin, TX: University of Texas Press, 1–25.

Fischer, Susan and Bonnie Gough. 1978. Verbs in American Sign Language. *Sign Language Studies* 18:17–48.

Fischer, Susan and Wynne Janis. 1990. Verb sandwiches in American Sign Language. In S. Prillwitz and T. Vollhaber (eds.), *Current Trends in European Sign Language Research.* Hamburg: Signum Press, 279–293.

Fridman, Boris. 1994. The collective plural inflection of ASL: Pragmatics and grammar. Paper presented at Georgetown University Roundtable on Language and Linguistics: ASL Pragmatics. March, 1994.

Fridman, Boris and Scott Liddell. 1998. Sequencing mental spaces in an ASL narrative. In Jean P. Koenig (ed.), *Discourse and Cognition: Bridging the Gap.* Center for the Study of Language and Information, Leland Stanford Junior University, 255–268.

Friedman, Lynn. 1975. Space, time, and person reference in American Sign Language. *Language* 51:940–961.

1976. The manifestation of subject, object, and topic in the American Sign Language. In Charles N. Li (ed.), *Subject and Topic.* New York: Academic Press, 125–148.

1977. Formational properties of American Sign Language. In Lynn Friedman (ed.), *On the Other Hand: New Perspectives on American Sign Language.* New York: Academic Press, 13–56.

Frishberg, Nancy. 1975. Arbitrariness and iconicity: Historical change in American Sign Language. *Language* 51:676–710.

1979. Historical change: From iconic to arbitrary (chapter 3). In Edward S. Klima and Ursula Bellugi (eds.), *The Signs of Language.* Cambridge: Harvard University Press.

Frishberg, Nancy and Bonnie Gough. 1973. Morphology in American Sign Language. Ms., The Salk Institute, La Jolla, CA.

Gee, James and Judy Kegl. 1982. Semantic perspicuity and the locative hypothesis: Implications for acquisition. *Journal of Education* 164.2:185–209.

Haas, Mary. 1945. *Spoken Thai.* New York: Holt.

Haviland, John. 2000. Pointing, gesture spaces, and mental maps. In David McNeill (ed.), *Language and Gesture*. Cambridge: Cambridge University Press, 13–46.

Hoffmeister, Robert. 1977. The influential point. In William C. Stokoe, (ed.), *Proceedings of the National Symposium on Sign Language Research and Teaching*. Silver Spring, MD: National Association of the Deaf, 177–191.

Hutchins, Edwin. 2000. Material anchors for conceptual blends. Ms., Distributed cognition and HCI Laboratory, University of California, San Diego.

Jakobson, Roman. 1971. *Selected Writings*. Vol. II, *Word and Language*. The Hague: Mouton.

Janis, Wynne. 1995. A crosslinguistic perspective on ASL verb agreement. In Karen Emmorey and Judy Reilly (eds.), Language, Gesture, and Space. Hillsdale, NJ: Lawrence Erlbaum Associates, 195–223.

Jespersen, Otto. 1959. *Language; Its Nature, Development, and Origin*. London: Allen and Unwin.

Johnson, Robert E. and Scott K. Liddell. In preparation. *Phonology in American Sign Language*.

Kendon, Adam. 1972. Some relationships between body motion and speech. In A. Siegman and B. Pope (eds.), *Studies in Diadic Communication*. New York: Pergamon Press, 177–210.

1980. Gesticulation and speech: Two aspects of the process of utterance. In M. R. Key (ed.), *The Relation between Verbal and Nonverbal Communication*. The Hague: Mouton, 207–227.

1988. How gestures can become like words. In F. Poyatos (ed.), Crosscultural Perspectives in Nonverbal Communication. Toronto: Hogrefe, 131–141.

2000. Language and gesture: Unity or duality? In David McNeill (ed.), *Language and Gesture*. Cambridge: Cambridge University Press, 47–63.

Kita, Sotaro. 1993. Language and thought interface: A study of spontaneous gestures and Japanese mimetics. Ph.D. dissertation, University of Chicago.

2000. How representational gestures help speaking. In David McNeill (ed.), *Language and Gesture*. Cambridge: Cambridge University Press, 162–185.

Klima, Edward S. and Ursula Bellugi. 1979. *The Signs of Language*, with Robbin Battison, Penny Boyes Braem, Susan Fischer, Nancy Frishberg, H. Lane, Ella M. Lentz, Don Newkirk, E. L. Newport, C. C. Pedersen, and Patricia Siple. Cambridge, MA: Harvard University Press.

Koestler, Arthur. 1964. *The Act of Creation*. New York: McMillan.

Lacy, Richard. 1974. Putting some of the syntax back into semantics. Ms., The Salk Institute, La Jolla, CA.

Ladd, D. Robert. 1978. Stylized intonation. *Language* 54:517–540.

1980. *The Structure of Intonational Meaning*. Bloomington: Indiana University Press.

1990. Intonation: emotion vs. grammar. Review of Bolinger 1989. *Language* 66:806–816.

1996. *Intonational Phonology*. Cambridge: Cambridge University Press.

Lakoff, George and Mark Johnson. 1980. *Metaphors We Live By*. Chicago and London: University of Chicago Press.

Langacker, Ronald W. 1987. *Foundations of Cognitive Grammar*. Vol. I, *Theoretical Prerequisites*. Stanford, CA: Stanford University Press.

1991. *Foundations of Cognitive Grammar*. Vol. II, *Descriptive Application*. Stanford, CA: Stanford University Press.

1999a. Discourse in cognitive grammar. Paper presented at the International Cognitive Linguistics Association, Stockholm, Sweden, July, 1999.

1999b. *Grammar and Conceptualization*. The Hague: Mouton de Gruyter.

LeBaron, Curtis and Jürgen Streeck. 2000. Gestures, knowledge, and the world. In David McNeill (ed.), *Language and Gesture*. Cambridge: Cambridge University Press, 118–138.

Lentz, Ella M. 1986. Teaching role-shifting. In Carol Padden (ed.), *Proceedings of the Fourth National Symposium on Sign Language Research and Teaching*. Silver Spring, MD: National Association of the Deaf, 58–69.

Liberman, Mark. 1979. *The Intonational System of English*. New York: Garland, Publishing.

Liddell, Scott K. 1977. An investigation into the syntactic structure of American Sign Language. Ph.D. dissertation, University of California, San Diego.

1978. Non-manual signals and relative clauses in American Sign Language. In *Proceedings of the First National Symposium on Sign Language Research and Teaching*. Silver Spring, MD: National Association of the Deaf, 193–228.

1980. *American Sign Language Syntax*. The Hague: Mouton.

1982. THINK and BELIEVE: Sequentiality in American Sign Language Signs. Paper presented at Linguistic Society of America, University of Maryland, Summer Session.

1984a. THINK and BELIEVE: Sequentiality in American Sign Language signs, *Language* 60.2:372–399.

1984b. Unrealized-inceptive aspect in American Sign Language: Feature insertion in syllabic frames. In J. Drogo, V. Mishra, and D. Teston (eds.), *Papers from the 20th Regional Meeting of the Chicago Linguistic Society*. Chicago: University of Chicago Press, 257–270.

1990. Four functions of a locus: Reexamining the structure of space in ASL. In Ceil Lucas (ed.), *Sign Language Research: Theoretical Issues*. Washington, DC: Gallaudet University Press, 176–198.

1994. Tokens and surrogates. In Inger Ahlgren, Brita Bergman, and Mary Brennan (eds.), *Perspectives on Sign Language Structure. Papers from the Fifth International Symposium on Sign Language Research*, vol. I. University of Durham, England: The Deaf Studies Research Unit, 105–119.

1995. Real, surrogate, and token space: Grammatical consequences in ASL. In Karen Emmorey and Judy Reilly (eds.), Language, Gesture, and Space. Hillsdale, NJ: Lawrence Erlbaum Associates, 19–41.

1996a. Spatial representations in discourse: comparing spoken and signed language. *Lingua* 98:145–167.

1996b. Numeral incorporating roots and non-incorporating prefixes in American Sign Language. *Sign Language Studies* 92:201–226.

1998. Grounded blends, gestures, and conceptual shifts. *Cognitive Linguistics* 9.3:283–314.

2000a. Indicating verbs and pronouns: Pointing away from agreement. In H. Lane and Karen Emmorey (eds.), *The Signs of Language Revisited: An Anthology to Honor Ursula Bellugi and Edward Klima*. Mahwah, NJ: LEA publishers, 303–320.

2000b. Sources of meaning in ASL classifier predicates. Paper presented at the workshop Classifier Constructions in Sign Languages, La Jolla, CA, April 2000.

2000c. Suprasegmentals at the core of an English construction. Paper presented at conference, Conceptual Structures in Discourse and Language 5, University of California, Santa Barbara, May 11–14, 2000.

In press a. Grammar and gesture in American Sign Language: Implications for constructing meaning. In Alyssa Wulf and Andrew Simpson (eds.), *Proceedings of the 27th Annual Meeting of the Berkeley Linguistics Society*. Berkeley, CA: Berkeley Linguistics Society.

In press b. Sources of meaning in ASL classifier predicates. In Karen Emmorey (ed.), *Perspectives on Classifier Constructions in Signed Languages*. Mahwah, NJ: Lawrence Erlbaum Associates.

Liddell, Scott K. and Robert E. Johnson. 1986. American Sign Language compound formation processes, lexicalization, and phonological remnants. *Natural Language and Linguistic Theory* 4.4:445–513.

1987. An analysis of spatial locative predicates in American Sign Language. Paper presented at the Fourth International Symposium on Sign Language Research, July 15–19, 1987.

1989. American Sign Language: The phonological base, *Sign Language Studies* 64:195–277.

Liddell, Scott K. and Melanie Metzger. 1998. Gesture in sign language discourse. *Journal of Pragmatics* 30:657–697.

Lillo-Martin, Diane. 1995. The point of view predicate in American Sign Language. In Karen Emmorey and Judy Reilly (eds.), *Language, Gesture, and Space*. Hillsdale, NJ: Lawrence Erlbaum Associates, 155–170.

Lillo-Martin, Diane and Edward S. Klima. 1990. Pointing out differences: ASL pronouns in syntactic theory. In Susan Fischer and Patricia Siple (eds.), *Theoretical Issues in Sign Language Research*. Chicago and London: University of Chicago Press, 191–210.

Locke, John. 1975. *An Essay Concerning Human Understanding* (edited with an introduction, critical apparatus and glossary by Peter H. Nidditch). Oxford: Clarendon Press.

Lucas, Ceil. 1995. Sociolinguistic variation in ASL: The case of DEAF. In Ceil Lucas (ed.), *Sociolinguistics in Deaf Communities*. Washington, DC: Gallaudet University Press, 3–25.

Lucas, Ceil and Clayton Valli. 1990. Predicates of perceived motion in ASL. In Susan Fischer and Patricia Siple (eds.), *Theoretical Issues in Sign Language Research*. Vol. 1, *Linguistics*. Chicago and London: The University of Chicago Press, 153–166.

MacLaughlin, Dawn. 1997. The structure of determiner phrases: Evidence from American Sign Language. Ph.D. dissertation, Boston University.

Maher, Jane. 1996. *Seeing Language in Sign: The Work of William C. Stokoe*. Washington, DC: Gallaudet University Press.

Mandel, Mark. 1977. Iconic devices in American Sign Language. In Lynn Friedman (ed.), *On the Other Hand: New Perspectives on American Sign Language*. New York: Academic Press, 57–107.

McDonald, Betsy. 1982. Aspects of the American Sign Language predicate system. Ph.D. dissertation, University of Buffalo, New York.

McNeill, David. 1985. So you think gestures are nonverbal? *Psychological Review* 92:350–371.

1992. *Hand and Mind, What Gestures Reveal about the Mind.* Chicago: University of Chicago Press.

2000. Catchments and contexts: Non-modular factors in speech and gesture production. In David McNeill (ed.), *Language and Gesture.* Cambridge: Cambridge University Press, 312–328.

McNeill, David and Susan Duncan. 2000. Growth points in thinking for speaking. In David McNeill (ed.), *Language and Gesture.* Cambridge: Cambridge University Press, 141–161.

Meier, Richard, P. 1990. Person deixis in American Sign Language. In Susan Fischer and Patricia Siple (eds.), *Theoretical Issues in Sign Language Research.* Vol. I, *Linguistics.* Chicago: University of Chicago Press, 175–190.

Meir, Irit. 1998. Thematic structure and verb agreement in Israeli Sign Language. Ph.D. dissertation, Hebrew University of Jerusalem.

Metzger, Melanie. 1995. Constructed dialogue and constructed action in American Sign Language. In Ceil Lucas (ed.), *Sociolinguistics in Deaf Communities.* Washington, DC: Gallaudet University Press, 255–271.

Neidle, Carol, Dawn MacLaughlin, Judy Kegl, Ben Bahan, and Debra Aarons. 1995. Overt realization of syntactic features in American Sign Language. Paper presented at Syntax seminar, University of Trondheim, Norway, May 1995.

Newkirk, Don. 1980. Rhythmic features of inflections in American Sign Language. Ms., The Salk Institute, La Jolla, CA.

1981. On the temporal segmentation of movement in American Sign Language. Ms., The Salk Institute, La Jolla, CA.

Newport, E. L. and Richard P. Meier. 1985. The acquisition of American Sign Language. In D. Slobin (ed.), *The Cross-Linguistic Study of Language Acquisition.* Vol. II, *The Data.* Hillsdale, NJ: Lawrence Erlbaum Associates, 881–938.

Ninio, Jacques. 2001. *The Science of Illusions*, trans. Franklin Philip. Ithaca and London: Cornell University Press.

Okrent, Arika. 1997. The productive use of conceptual metaphor in ASL: How form and meaning can be connected without the bond of convention. Paper presented at Gallaudet Communication Forum. Washington, DC: Department of American Sign Language, Linguistics and Interpretation.

2002. A modality-free notion of gesture and how it can help us with the morpheme vs. gesture question in sign language linguistics (or at least give us some criteria to work with). In Richard P. Meier, K. Cormier, and D. Quinto-Pozos (eds.), *Modality and Structure in Signed and Spoken Languages.* Cambridge: Cambridge University Press.

Özyürek, Asli. 2000. The influence of addressee location on spatial language and representational gestures of direction. In David McNeill (ed.), *Language and Gesture.* Cambridge: Cambridge University Press, 64–83.

Padden, Carol. 1983. Interaction of morphology and syntax in American Sign Language. Ph.D. dissertation, University of California, San Diego.

1986. Verbs and role-shifting in ASL. In Carol Padden (ed.), *Proceedings of the Fourth National Symposium on Sign Language Research and Teaching.* Silver Spring, MD: National Association of the Deaf, 44–57.

1988. *Interaction of Morphology and Syntax in American Sign Language*. New York: Garland Publishing.

1990. The relation between space and grammar in ASL verb morphology. In Ceil Lucas (ed.), *Sign Language Research: Theoretical Issues*. Washington, DC: Gallaudet University Press, 118–132.

Pierrehumbert, Janet. 1980. The phonology and phonetics of English intonation. Ph.D. dissertation, Massachusetts Institute of Technology. Published 1988, Indiana University Linguistics Club.

Sandler, Wendy. 1989. *Phonological Representation of the Sign: Linearity and non-linearity in American Sign Language*. Publications in Language Sciences 32. Providence, RI: Foris.

Schembri, Adam. In press. Rethinking "classifiers" in signed languages. In Karen Emmorey (ed.), *Perspectives on Classifier Constructions in Signed Languages*. Mahwah, NJ: Lawrence Erlbaum Associates.

Schick, Brenda. 1990. Classifier predicates in American Sign Language. *International Journal of Sign Linguistics* 1.1:15–40.

Schubiger, Maria. No date. *The Role of Intonation in Spoken English*. Boston, MA: Expression Company.

Shepard-Kegl, Judy. 1985. Locative relations in American Sign Language: Word formation, syntax, and discourse. Ph.D. dissertation, Massachusetts Institute of Technology.

Stokoe, William C. 1960. *Sign Language Structure: An Outline of the Visual Communication System of the American Deaf*. Studies in Linguistics Occasional Papers, no. 8. Buffalo, NY: Department of Anthropology and Linguistics, University of Buffalo.

Stokoe, William C., Dorothy Casterline, and Carl Croneberg. 1965. *The Dictionary of American Sign Language on Linguistic Principles*. Washington, DC: Gallaudet College Press. Revised 1978, Silver Spring, MD: Linstok Press.

Supalla, Ted. 1978. Morphology of verbs of motion and location. In F. Caccamise and D. Hicks (eds.), *Proceedings of the Second National Symposium on Sign Language Research and Teaching*. Silver Spring, MD: National Association of the Deaf, 27–45.

1982. Structure and acquisition of verbs of motion and location in American Sign Language. Ph.D. dissertation, University of California, San Diego.

1986. The classifier system in American Sign Language. In C. Craig (ed.), *Noun Classes and Categorization: Typological Studies in Language, 7*. Philadelphia: John Benjamins, 181–214.

Supalla, Ted and Elissa Newport. 1978. How many seats in a chair? The derivation of nouns and verbs in American Sign Language. In Patricia Siple (ed.), *Understanding Language through Sign Language Research*. New York: Academic Press, 91–132.

Talmy, Leonard. 2000. *Toward a Cognitive Semantics*. Vol. I, *Concept Structuring Systems*. Cambridge, MA and London: MIT Press.

Tannen, Deborah. 1986. Introducing constructed dialogue in Greek and American conversational and literacy narratives. In Florian Coulmas (ed.), *Reported Speech Across Languages*. The Hague: Mouton, 311–332.

1989. *Talking Voices: Repetition, Dialogue, and Imagery in Conversational Discourse*. Cambridge: Cambridge University Press.

Taub, Sarah F. 2001. *Language from the Body: Iconicity and Metaphor in American Sign Language.* Cambridge: Cambridge University Press.

Thompson, Henry. 1977. The lack of subordination in American Sign Language. In Lynn Friedman (ed.), *On the Other Hand: New Perspectives on American Sign Language.* New York: Academic Press, 181–195.

Turner, Mark. 1991. *Reading Minds.* Princeton, NJ: Princeton University Press.

Turner, Mark and Gilles Fauconnier. 1995. Conceptual integration and formal expression. *Journal of Metaphor and Symbolic Activity* 10.3:183–204.

Uyechi, Linda. 1996. *The Geometry of Visual Phonology.* Stanford, CA: CSLI Publications.

Van Hoek, Karen. 1988. Mental space and sign space. Paper presented at the Annual Meeting of the Linguistic Society of America, December 29, 1988, New Orleans, Louisiana.

1992. Conceptual spaces and pronominal reference in American Sign Language. *Nordic Journal of Linguistics,* 15:183–199.

1996. Conceptual locations for reference in American Sign Language. In Gilles Fauconnier and E. Sweetser (eds.), *Spaces, Worlds, and Grammar.* Chicago: University of Chicago Press, 334–350.

Vogt-Svendsen, Marit. 1984. Word-Pictures in Norwegian Sign Language (NSL) – a preliminary analysis. *University of Trondheim Working Papers in Linguistics 2,* Trondheim: Universitetet i Trondheim, Lingvistisk Institutt, 112–141.

2001. A comparison of mouth gestures and mouthings in Norwegian Sign Language (NSL). In Penny Boyes Braem and Rachel Sutton-Spence (eds.), *The Hands are the Head of the Mouth, The Mouth as Articulator in Sign Language.* Hamburg: Signum Press, 9–40.

Wallin, Lars. 1996. *Polysynthetic signs in Swedish Sign Language,* trans. Don Miller. Edsbruk: Akademitryck AB. (Ph.D. dissertation, University of Stockholm, 1994.)

Wescott, Roger W. 1971. Linguistic iconism. *Language* 47:416–428.

Wilbur, Ronnie. 1979. *American Sign Language and Sign Systems.* Baltimore, MD: University Park Press.

1987. *American Sign Language, Linguistic and Applied Dimensions* (2nd edition). Boston, MA: College Hill Press.

Wilcox, Phyllis P. 2000. *Metaphor in American Sign Language.* Washington, DC: Gallaudet University Press.

Winston, Elizabeth. 1991. Spatial referencing and cohesion in an American Sign Language text. *Sign Language Studies* 73:397–410.

1992. Space and involvement in an American Sign Language lecture. In J. Plant-Moeller (ed.), *Expanding Horizons: Proceedings of the Twelfth National Convention of the Registry of Interpreters for the Deaf.* Silver Spring, MD: Registry of Interpreters for the Deaf, 93–105.

1993. Spatial mapping in comparative discourse frames in an American Sign Language lecture. Ph.D. dissertation, Georgetown University, Washington, DC.

Wulf, Alyssa and Andrew Simpson (eds.). In press. *Proceedings of the 27th Annual Meeting of the Berkeley Linguistics Society.* Berkeley. CA: Berkeley Linguistics Society.

Zimmer, June and Cynthia Patschke. 1990. A class of determiners in ASL. In Ceil Lucas (ed.), *Sign Language Research: Theoretical Issues.* Washington, DC: Gallaudet University Press, 201–210.

# General index

Aarons, Debra 55, 56, 59, 196, 277
affixes in ASL 34–37
Ahlgren, Inger 250
Armstrong, David 357
ASL morphology 14–52
aspect marking 14, 37–42, 44
aspectual frame 37, 40, 46, 355

backward verbs 116–117
Bahan, Benjamin 74, 110, 154
Baker, Charlotte 24, 34, 159
Battison, Robbin 6
Bellugi, Ursula 11, 14, 44, 46, 47, 48, 49, 50, 51, 74, 107, 108, 109, 298, 317
Bergman, Brita xi, 52, 118, 250, 278
Bienvenu, MJ 68, 183, 203
blended mental spaces (introduced) 142–157
body-anchored verbs 113
Bolinger, Dwight x, 70, 358
Boyes-Braem, Penny 266
Brentari, Diane 12, 74, 135
buoys 223–260, 319
Bybee, Joan 50

Casterline, Dorothy 4
chereme 7
Chinchor, Nancy 14
Chomsky, Noam 155
citation form 97–99
Clark, Herbert 173
classifier 261
classifier predicates (see depicting verbs) 261
clitic 72, 73, 239, 360
cognitive grammar (introduced) 87, 99
Cokely, Dennis 34, 159
Cole, Debra 117, 130
compound sign 11, 14, 15–17, 34
constructed action 157
constructed dialogue 158–166, 173, 174
constructed meaning 80, 81, 93, 95, 355
Coulter, Geoffrey 56
Croneberg, Carl 4

Cruttenden, Alan 358
Crystal, David x, 357

Dahl, Östen 52
Davies, Shawna 178
deixis 73
DeMatteo, Asa 261, 269
depicting verbs 127, 261–316, 355, 356
determiner (DET$^{→x}$) 331
digits (*D1–D5* defined) 224
Dudis, Paul 248
Duncan, Susan 357, 362

Edge, Vicki 74
Efron, David 157
Ekman, Paul 157, 172
Emmorey, Karen 155
Engberg-Pedersen, Elisabeth 74, 164, 213, 214, 261, 273, 331
exhaustive verb forms 47
eyegaze xi, 24, 25, 78, 107, 108, 117–119, 174, 209, 250, 252, 257, 268, 277, 287, 288, 289, 306, 321, 322

Fauconnier, Gilles xi, 80, 81, 95, 138, 142, 143, 144, 174
fictive motion 294, 297
Fillmore, Charles 80
Fischer, Susan 14, 37, 44, 53, 56, 64, 72, 261
FOUR-WEEK-LIST buoy 235–242
fragment buoys 248–250, 319, 350
frame (in a morphological analysis, see aspectual frame)
frame (idealized cognitive model) 80
Fridman, Boris 49, 243
Friedman, Lynn 6, 52, 53, 72, 113, 261, 330
Friesen, Wallace 157, 172
Frishberg, Nancy 14, 261, 330

Gallaudet College (now Gallaudet University) 2, 3, 4
Gee, James 74

CPSIA information can be obtained
at www.ICGtesting.com
Printed in the USA
LVHW081004281122
734156LV00030B/681

9 780521 016506